D1175267

PSYCHOLOGY
OF
RELIGION

PHILOSOPHY AND RELIGION INFORMATION GUIDE SERIES

Series Editor: Harvey Arnold, Bibliographer

Also in this series:

INTRODUCTION TO RESEARCH IN PHILOSOPHY—*Edited by Paul G. Kuntz**

OCCULTISM AND MYSTICISM—*Edited by Robert Galbreath**

RELIGION, CULTURE, AND MEDICINE—*Edited by Glen W. Davidson**

SACRED SCRIPTURES AND TRADITIONS—*Edited by Harry M. Buck**

*in preparation

The above series is part of the
GALE INFORMATION GUIDE LIBRARY

The Library consists of a number of separate Series of guides covering major areas in the social sciences, humanities, and current affairs.

General Editor: Paul Wasserman, Professor and former Dean, School of Library and Information Services, University of Maryland

PSYCHOLOGY

OF

RELIGION

A GUIDE TO INFORMATION SOURCES

*Volume 1 in the Philosophy and Religion
Information Guide Series*

Donald Capps

*Associate Professor of Religious Studies
University of North Carolina at Charlotte*

Lewis Rambo

*Assistant Professor of Psychology
Trinity College*

Paul Ransohoff

University of California, Berkeley

Gale Research Company
Book Tower, Detroit, Michigan 48226

**Library of Congress
Cataloging in Publication Data**

Capps, Donald.
   Psychology of religion.

   (Philosophy and religion information guide series;
v. 1) (Gale information guide library)
   Includes index.
     1. Psychology, Religious–Bibliography. 2. Religion–
Bibliography. 3. Mythology–Bibliography. I. Rambo,
Lewis, joint author. II. Ransohoff, Paul, joint author.
III. Title.
Z7204.R4C36   016.200'1'9   73-17530
ISBN 0-8103-1356-1

VITAE

Donald Capps is an associate professor of religious studies at the University of North Carolina in Charlotte. He is coeditor of THE RELIGIOUS PERSONALITY (Belmont, Calif.: Wadsworth Press, 1970) and THE BIOGRAPHICAL PROCESS (Utrecht: Mouton Press, 1975). He is author of articles published in JOURNAL FOR THE SCIENTIFIC STUDY OF RELIGION, JOURNAL FOR THE HISTORY OF BEHAVIORAL SCIENCES, and SOCIAL RESEARCH.

Lewis Rambo is an assistant professor of psychology at Trinity College, Deerfield, Illinois. He received his M.Div. degree from Yale University and his Ph.D. from the University of Chicago. In addition to numerous book reviews which have been published in the JOURNAL OF RELIGION, CHRISTIAN CENTURY, RELIGIOUS EDUCATION, and CHRISTIANITY TODAY, he is currently completing a project on William James' normative vision of human nature, and doing research on the theoretical foundations of the psychology of religion.

Paul Ransohoff is a graduate of Harvard College and a doctoral candidate at the University of Chicago in Religion and Psychological Studies. He is currently studying at the University of California in Berkeley in a special program in parapsychiatry. He has published in the INTERNATIONAL YEARBOOK FOR THE SOCIOLOGY OF KNOWLEDGE AND RELIGION.

CONTENTS

Contents

INTRODUCTION

The biographer Leon Edel has written of his work: "I found my personal reward in the imagination of form and structure...for after all that is the only imagination a biographer can be allowed." The bibliographer is in a similar situation. How he organizes the materials at hand is the most frustrating but at the same time most rewarding aspect of this work. And, given the fact that the proliferation of materials in any given area of study in recent years makes it almost foolhardy for the bibliographer to stake his sense of personal satisfaction on the claim to completeness, organization takes on added importance today.

After giving due consideration to other possible ways of organizing our materials, we concluded that we could best communicate the almost disconcerting diversity of the psychology of religion by casting it in terms of the dimensions of religion to which the discipline has addressed itself. We have organized the bibliography according to six dimensions of religion: the mythological, ritual, experiential, dispositional, social, and directional. We shall not take time here to define these terms in detail. However, the following brief summary will provide the user of this bibliography some notion of the working definitions by which our research and judgments were guided. The mythological dimension includes both the study of mythical consciousness and specific types of religious myths. The ritual dimension includes both the problem of the ritualization of everyday life and specific religious rituals. The experiential dimension deals with personal religion as exemplified by experiences, moods, emotions, and aspirations having religious salience. The dispositional dimension concerns the formal systems of meaning which dispose men to cognize, perceive, and value their lives and the world in consistent ways. The social dimension encompasses the larger social context of which religious organizations are part but whose religious aspect is not exhausted by such organizations. The directional dimension serves as foil to the dispositional dimension, with the dispositional capturing the element of arranging and structuring systems of meaning, and the directional centering on the process of individual and group realization of these systems.

Within each dimension, we have made from four to eight subdimensions. And, in virtually every larger dimension, there were one or two subdimensions whose entries bordered very closely on one or two subdimensions in another dimension. Entries in these almost overlapping subdimensions gave us the most difficulty in terms of accurate placement. But rather than apologize for any errors in judgment this may have entailed, it seems more important to observe that religion is a cultural phenomenon of great fluidity and complexity and we should not be surprised, therefore, if psychological studies of religion reflect this fluidity and do not lend themselves to easy compartmentalization. Of course, we do accept responsibility for errors of placement which are due to our failure in certain cases to penetrate beyond the title of a book or article to ascertain whether, in fact, the work is actually about what its title purports it to be. It was nearly impossible for us to track down physically every entry in this fashion, and especially in subdimensions E:4 through E:6 we relied to a large extent on synopses provided by PSYCHOLOGICAL ABSTRACTS. The same is true in the case of subdimension F:4, where we acknowledge a particular debt for entries published prior to 1965 to the earlier work of Robert J. Menges and James E. Dittes in their annotated bibliography, PSYCHOLOGICAL STUDIES OF CLERGYMEN: ABSTRACTS OF RESEARCH. And, finally, it should be noted that, like other fields of study, certain areas in the psychology of religion have greater coherence and lend themselves more easily to the bibliographer's structuring proclivities than others. If certain subdimensions seem less well defined than others, this may well be due to the nature of the subject and not to any serious failure on the part of the bibliographer.

Turning from the matter of organization to the selection process itself, we were guided by certain initially agreed upon norms. First, we decided to limit our search to materials published from 1950 to the present. In some instances, we have included individual entries which predate 1950 if these items were highly influential on more recent trends. The earlier writings of Anton T. Boisen in section G:5 are a case in point. Freud's writings on religion, found in various places throughout the bibliography, are another. Then, in addition to these individual entries, we have included a whole subsection A:3 which comprises what has come to be known as "classical" or "Jamesian" psychology of religion. We considered the arguments in favor of locating individual items in classical psychology of religion in their appropriate subdimension (e.g., articles on conversion in section D:2), but we eventually decided that there was greater merit in treating classical psychology of religion as a discrete entity. We did not follow the same reasoning with regard to the works of Freud. In this case, we felt it far more difficult to distinguish "classical" from "contemporary" Freudian psychology of religion.

In addition to limiting ourselves, with the aforementioned exceptions, to material published from 1950 to 1974, we were also influenced by the fact that in 1961 W.W. Meissner published his excellent ANNOTATED BIBLIOGRAPHY IN RELIGION AND PSYCHOLOGY. While we saw our task as something other than simply updating Meissner's work, we nonetheless agreed that we should be especially concerned to cover the period from 1960 to 1974. In general, we focused on those 1950s materials which in our judgment have proven most seminal in the psychology of religion of the past decade. Hence, our work does not supplant Meissner's. Indeed, we are quick to acknowledge that his is more complete for the period from 1950 to 1959.

Concerning limitations other than those of time periods covered, we should also point out that this bibliography does not include unpublished materials of any kind, including doctoral dissertations. Also, foreign language materials are limited to items which we considered either worthy of the extra effort expended in securing a copy of the item or of other educational value (e.g., the fact that the user is made aware that the psychological study of a certain topic is not limited to the United States). These particular limitations were in keeping with the publisher's concerns regarding the general accessibility of the materials to the typical user of this volume.

A final observation with regard to the problem of limitations. We experienced great difficulties in determining what items to exclude from our social dimension. Given the nature of this particular dimension, we found ourselves continually plagued by the problem of overlap with the sociology of religion. The fact that a volume in the sociology of religion is not planned for this series made this problem even more acute. Eventually, we regretfully decided to draw a rather firm line between the two disciplines and retained as our subdimensions in this section only those which clearly represented well-defined areas of research in the psychology of religion. We were slightly more liberal in admitting into the volume important psychological works whose relevance to the psychology of religion as such is not clearly stated or even within the author's conscious intention, but has or can be inferred by researchers in the field. Subdimension A:5 on existential, humanistic, and phenomenological psychology is perhaps best illustrative of this somewhat more liberal approach in this instance. However, here, as in the case of sociology of religion materials, we omitted large numbers of entries which at one point in the process were under serious consideration.

Turning from the matter of limitations to annotations, our interest in capturing the rich diversity of published work in the psychology of religion militated against annotation of every item in the volume. Again, by prearrangement, we agreed to annotate books (other than those listed in the classical psychology of religion subsection) and those articles which were either deserving of special mention or whose titles failed in our judgment to communicate adequately their contents. Due to the physical difficulties in locating copies of every book, we were forced to settle for something less than completeness in the annotation of books. But, in many of these cases, we tried at least to identify the author's general point of view or otherwise "place" the book in a more general way.

We have discussed matters of structure and content. A final brief comment concerning our goals. Obviously, bibliographers hope that their work will prove useful in the very concrete sense of alerting users to the existence of books and articles of which they were previously unaware. A bibliography must perform this concrete and clearly recognizable function. But, in addition, it is only fair to say that much of the industry and sheer perseverence which goes into a project of this sort can be attributed to the bibliographers' desire to discover whether or not their discipline admits of any real order and coherence, and to play some role in assuring that what coherence it does manifest will be duly and appropriately recognized. If we have "imagined" a form and structure, it is in the best of psychological traditions to say that, unlike delusions, such imaginations are modest extrapolations from the reality on which they are based.

Finally, we want to acknowledge our debt to Robert I. Menges and James E.

Introduction

Dittes whose general format we have employed here. Karen Capps assisted in the preparation of the indexes and the University of North Carolina at Charlotte provided material assistance in the preparation of the manuscript. Michaeline Nowinski of Gale Research made many valuable suggestions for the improvement of the manuscript. Our special thanks to Harvey Arnold who, as general editor of the Gale Information Guide Series in Religion and Philosophy, encouraged our work and served as a personal example of professional dedication and unflagging good spirits.

Section A

GENERAL WORKS IN PSYCHOLOGY OF RELIGION

Section A

GENERAL WORKS IN PSYCHOLOGY OF RELIGION

A:1   BIBLIOGRAPHIES

Berkowitz, Morris I., and Johnson, J. Edmund. SOCIAL SCIENTIFIC STUDIES OF RELIGION: A BIBLIOGRAPHY. Pittsburgh: University of Pittsburgh Press, 1967. xvii, 258 p.

> Listing of 6000 works on religion by anthropologists, sociologists, psychologists, and religious workers. Organized according to definitions, descriptions, and history of religions; religion and social institutions; and social change and behavior.

Borchardt, D.H. HOW TO FIND OUT IN PHILOSOPHY AND PSYCHOLOGY. New York: Pergamon Press, 1968. 97 p.

> A bibliography of bibliographies with greater emphasis on philosophy than psychology.

Cronbach, A. "The Psychology of Religion: A Bibliographical Survey." PSYCHOLOGICAL BULLETIN 25 (1928): 701-19.

Dittes, James E. "Research on Clergymen: Factors Influencing Decisions for Religious Service and Effectiveness in the Vocation." RELIGIOUS EDUCATION (research supplement) 57, no. 4 (1962): 141-65.

Godin, Andre, et al. "Religious and Pastoral Psychology: Recent Publications, 1967-1970." LUMEN VITAE 26 (1971): 519-44.

Hiltner, Seward. "A Selected Bibliography on Christian Faith and Health." PASTORAL PSYCHOLOGY 12 (January 1962): 27-38.

Kiell, Norman. PSYCHOANALYSIS, PSYCHOLOGY AND LITERATURE: A BIBLIOGRAPHY. Madison: University of Wisconsin Press, 1963. 225 p.

> A bibliography of psychologically oriented writings about literature, with literature broadly construed to include fairy tales, folklore,

and religious myth.

_____. PSYCHIATRY AND PSYCHOLOGY IN THE VISUAL ARTS AND AES-
THETICS: A BIBLIOGRAPHY. Madison: University of Wisconsin Press, 1965.
xiv, 250 p.

Includes large number of entries of use to the psychologist of religion.

Lesh, Terry V. "Zen and Psychotherapy: A Partially Annotated Bibliography."
JOURNAL OF HUMANISTIC PSYCHOLOGY 10 (Spring 1970): 75-83.

Little, Lawrence C. RESEARCH IN PERSONALITY, CHARACTER AND RELI-
GIOUS EDUCATION: BIBLIOGRAPHY OF AMERICAN DOCTORAL DISSERTA-
TIONS, 1885 TO 1959. Pittsburgh: University of Pittsburgh Press, 1962.
215 p.

Contains listing of over 6300 doctoral dissertations and forty-four
page topical index. No annotations.

Meissner, W[illiam] W. ANNOTATED BIBLIOGRAPHY IN RELIGION AND
PSYCHOLOGY. New York: The Academy of Religion and Mental Health,
1961. 235 p.

Approximately 2900 entries, annotated on the basis of PSYCHOLOG-
ICAL ABSTRACTS, organized with the aim of being useful to both
researchers and practitioners of religion.

Menges, Robert J., and Dittes, James E. PSYCHOLOGICAL STUDIES OF
CLERGYMEN: ABSTRACTS OF RESEARCH. New York: Thomas Nelson and
Sons, 1965. 202 p.

Contains abstracts of more than 700 books, articles, and dissertations on clergymen.

National Clearinghouse for Mental Health Information. BIBLIOGRAPHY ON
RELIGION AND MENTAL HEALTH: 1960-1964. Public Health Service Publication no. 1599. U.S. Public Health Service, Washington, D.C.: U.S. Government Printing Office, 1967. 106 p.

Psychologists in Harvard University. THE HARVARD LIST OF BOOKS IN PSY-
CHOLOGY. 4th ed. Cambridge: Harvard University Press, 1971. 108 p.

Includes a brief section of good, general works in the psychology
of religion.

Van Dyke, Paul II, and Pierce-Jones, John. "The Psychology of Religion of
Middle and Late Adolescence: A Review of Empirical Research, 1950-1960."
RELIGIOUS EDUCATION 58 (1963): 529-37.

Zaretsky, Irving I. BIBLIOGRAPHY ON SPIRIT POSSESSION AND SPIRIT
MEDIUMSHIP. Berkeley: Department of Anthropology, University of California,

1966. xvi, 106 p.

A:2 THE RELATION OF PSYCHOLOGY TO RELIGION
(Includes Psychology of Religion Textbooks)

Akerberg, Hans. "The Significance of William James's Psychology of Religion Today." STUDIA THEOLOGICA 26 (1962): 141-58.

Allport, Gordon W. THE INDIVIDUAL AND HIS RELIGION, A PSYCHOLOG-ICAL INTERPRETATION. New York: Macmillan, 1950. xi, 147 p.

> An essentially Jamesian approach to psychology of religion. Con-siders the origins and development of religion in the individual, with emphasis on religion as an expression of intentionality. Also listed in section G:3.

Angers, William P. "Clarifications toward the Rapprochement between Religion and Psychology." JOURNAL OF INDIVIDUAL PSYCHOLOGY 16 (1960): 73-76.

Becker, Ernest. THE BIRTH AND DEATH OF MEANING. 2nd ed. New York: The Free Press, 1971. 228 p.

> An introduction to the diverse findings of sociology, anthropology, and psychology on the nature of man. Religion is considered of central importance in the unification of these sciences.

Becker, Russell J. "Links between Psychology and Religion." AMERICAN PSY-CHOLOGIST 13 (1958): 566-68.

Beit-Hallahmi, Benjamin. "Psychology of Religion 1880-1930: The Rise and Fall of a Psychological Movement." JOURNAL OF THE HISTORY OF THE BE-HAVIORAL SCIENCES 10 (January 1974): 84-90.

Brown, L.B., ed. PSYCHOLOGY AND RELIGION: SELECTED READINGS. Baltimore: Penguin Education Series, 1973. 400 p.

> A collection of thirty previously published studies in the psychology of religion by contemporary psychologists, organized around such topics as dimensionality and orientation to religion, religion as so-cial attitude, measurement, experimental studies, and pathological states.

Capps, Donald. "Contemporary Psychology of Religion: The Task of Theoreti-cal Reconstruction." SOCIAL RESEARCH 41, no. 2 (1974): 362-83.

Capps, Donald, and Capps, Walter H., eds THE RELIGIOUS PERSONALITY. Belmont, Calif.: Wadsworth Publishing Co., 1970. 381 p.

> A collection of readings from autobiographies of religious figures organized according to self-concepts. Includes resigned, chastized,

fraternal, and aesthetic types.

Clark, Walter Houston. "How Do Social Scientists Define Religion?" JOURNAL OF SOCIAL PSYCHOLOGY 47 (1958): 143–47.

_____. THE PSYCHOLOGY OF RELIGION: AN INTRODUCTION TO RELIGIOUS EXPERIENCE AND BEHAVIOR. New York: Macmillan, 1958. xii, 485 p.

> Topics include developmental aspects of religion, conversion, faith, mysticism, prayer, and mental health. Contains large bibliography and section of study aids for teachers.

Collins, Gary R. "Psychology on a New Foundation: A Proposal for the Future." JOURNAL OF PSYCHOLOGY AND THEOLOGY 1 (1973): 19–27.

Crane, A.R. "Psychology and Religion." AUSTRALIA JOURNAL OF PSYCHOLOGY 11 (June 1959): 130–34.

Dittes, James E. "Psychology of Religion." In THE HANDBOOK OF SOCIAL PSYCHOLOGY, vol. 5, 2nd ed., pp. 602–59. Edited by G. Lindzey and E. Aronson. Boston: Addision-Wesley, 1969.

> A comprehensive survey of the field of psychology of religion, with thematic analysis of current research.. Includes an extensive bibliography.

_____. "Beyond William James." In BEYOND THE CLASSICS? ESSAYS IN THE SCIENTIFIC STUDY OF RELIGION, pp. 291–354. Edited by Charles Y. Glock and Phillip E. Hammond. New York: Harper & Row, Publishers, 1973.

> Acknowledging that James does not offer specific categories for contemporary psychology of religion, the author nonetheless contends that the spirit of James' approach should continue to inspire present research.

Drakeford, John W. PSYCHOLOGY IN SEARCH OF A SOUL. Nashville: Broadman Press, 1964. 301 p.

> Probes the religious background of the development of psychology and attempts to show its compatibility with evangelical theology.

Godin, Andre. "Studies in Religious Psychology." LUMEN VITAE 16, no. 2 (1961): 187–388.

> Entire issue devoted to topic.

_____. "The Psychology of Religion." Translated by George G. Christian. INSIGHT: QUARTERLY REVIEW OF RELIGION AND MENTAL HEALTH 5, no. 4 (1967): 1–6.

Gregory, W.E. "The Psychology of Religion: Some Suggested Areas of Research to Psychology." JOURNAL OF ABNORMAL AND SOCIAL PSYCHOLOGY 47 (1952): 256-58.

Guilhot, Jean. METHODE ET VOCATION DE LA PSYCHOLOGIE RELIGIEUSE. Paris: Les Editions Sociales Francaises, 1967. 152 p.

Havens, Joseph. "The Participant's vs. the Observer's Frame of Reference in the Psychological Study of Religion." JOURNAL FOR THE SCIENTIFIC STUDY OF RELIGION 1 (1961-62): 79-87.

_____. PSYCHOLOGY AND RELIGION; A CONTEMPORARY DIALOGUE. Princeton, N.J.: Van Nostrand, 1968. vii, 151 p.

> Edited transcripts of and commentaries on discussions among psychologists, psychotherapists, and theologians on such topics as God, symbols, religious knowledge, anxiety, and ethics. Discussants include David Bakan, W.H. Clark, James Dittes, Paul Pruyser, William Rogers, Richard Rubenstein, and others.

Herr, Vincent V. RELIGIOUS PSYCHOLOGY. Staten Island, N.Y.: Alba House, 1964. 277 p.

> An introduction to the psychology of religion. Major emphasis on religious development and conversion. Also discusses research methodology.

Hillman, James. INSEARCH: PSYCHOLOGY AND RELIGION. New York: Charles Scribner's Sons, 1967. 126 p.

> A Jungian approach to religious experience and life. Emphasizes dream interpretation. Also listed in section G:3.

Hiltner, Seward. "The Psychological Understanding of Religion." CROZIER QUARTERLY 24 (1947): 3-36.

James, William. THE VARIETIES OF RELIGIOUS EXPERIENCE: A STUDY IN HUMAN NATURE. New York: The New American Library Mentor Books, 1958. xviii, 406 p. Paperbound.

> See annotation in section A:3.

Johnson, Paul E. PSYCHOLOGY OF RELIGION. New York and Nashville: Abingdon-Cokesbury, 1945. 288 p.

> Argues for a dynamic and interpersonal approach; discusses religious experience, conversion, prayer, belief, community, and faith-healing.

_____. PERSONALITY AND RELIGION. New York: Abingdon Press, 1957. 297 p.

_____. "Psychology of Religion in America." ARCHIV FUR RELIGION-PSYCHOLOGIE 7 (1962): 42-53.

A concise summary of basic approaches to psychology of religion in America: experimental, educational, clinical, and pastoral.

Loukes, Harold. THE CASTLE AND THE FIELD: AN ESSAY IN THE PSYCHOLOGY OF RELIGION. London: George Allen and Unwin, 1959. 80 p.

Neale, Robert E. IN PRAISE OF PLAY: TOWARDS A PSYCHOLOGY OF RELIGION. New York: Harper & Row, Publishers, 1969. 187 p.

Draws on depth psychology (Freud, Erikson) and history of religions (Otto, Eliade). Distinguishes magic, work, partial play, and full (religious) play as different kinds of responses to the sacred.

Oates, Wayne E [dward]. WHAT PSYCHOLOGY SAYS ABOUT RELIGION. New York: Association Press, 1958. 128 p.

_____. THE PSYCHOLOGY OF RELIGION. Waco, Tex.: Word Books, 1973. 291 p.

A phenomenological and developmental perspective. Topics include development, conversion, magic, mysticism, dreams, ritual, forgiveness, conscience, ecstasy, and faith.

Ostow, Mortimer, and Scharfstein, Ben-Ami. THE NEED TO BELIEVE: THE PSYCHOLOGY OF RELIGION. New York: International Universities Press, 1954. 162 p.

A Freudian approach which emphasizes religious ideation.

Pepinsky, Harold B., and Borow, Henry. "Research Frontier." JOURNAL OF COUNSELING PSYCHOLOGY 8, no. 4 (1961): 363-67.

Emphasizes research on religion.

Poll, Wilhelm. RELIGIONSPSYCHOLOGIE: FORMEN DER RELIGIOSEN KENNTNISNAHME. Munich: Kosel Verlag, 1965. 523 p.

A major study in theories and methods of psychology of religion. Two major chapters distinguish a priori and a posteriori methods in the psychology of religion, and are followed by theoretical discussion of such topics as religious thought, feeling, and symbolization.

Pruyser, Paul W. "Some Trends in the Psychology of Religion." JOURNAL OF RELIGION 40 (1960): 113-29.

_____. "Anton T. Boisen and the Psychology of Religion." JOURNAL OF PASTORAL CARE 21 (December 1967): 209-19.

_____. A DYNAMIC PSYCHOLOGY OF RELIGION. New York: Harper & Row, Publishers, 1968. 367 p.

> Employs a clinically informed ego psychology in developing a general psychology of religion. Centers on the religious aspects of thought and emotional processes, linguistic functions, motor activity, and relatedness to self, objects, and other persons.

_____. "A Psychological View of Religion in the 1970s." BULLETIN OF THE MENNINGER CLINIC 35 (1971): 77-97. Also published in PASTORAL PSY - CHOLOGY 23 (January 1972): 21-39.

Ross, Dorothy. G. STANLEY HALL: THE PSYCHOLOGIST AS PROPHET. Chicago: University of Chicago Press, 1972. xix, 482 p.

> An intellectual biography of a founder of American psychology of religion.

Ross, W.G. "Religion and Psychology." COLLEGE OF THE BIBLE QUARTERLY 42 (April 1965): 7-15.

Sadler, William A., Jr., ed. PERSONALITY AND RELIGION: THE ROLE OF RELIGION IN PERSONALITY DEVELOPMENT. New York: Harper & Row, Publishers, 1970. 245 p.

> A collection of readings on personal world-view and crises, with a few general essays on the scientific study of religion. Includes selections from Freud, Jung, Fromm, McClelland, Bakan, Allport, Weber, and others.

Sharma, Ram N. "Naturalistic Psychology of Religion: Validity and Reliability." PSYCHOLOGICAL RESEARCHES 2, nos. 1-2 (1967): 66-71.

Shepherd, William C. "Religion and the Social Sciences: Conflict or Conciliation?" JOURNAL FOR THE SCIENTIFIC STUDY OF RELIGION 11 (September 1972): 230-39.

> Some attention to psychology of religion.

Silverman, Hirsch Lazaar. "Philosophy, Psychology and Religion: Relationships and Intra-Relationships." RELIGIOUS EDUCATION 57 (1962): 185-88.

_____. "Psychology and Religion." CATHOLIC PSYCHOLOGICAL RECORD 6, no. 2 (1967): 111-15.

Smart, Ninian. THE SCIENCE OF RELIGION AND THE SOCIOLOGY OF KNOWLEDGE: SOME METHODOLOGICAL QUESTIONS. Princeton, N.J.:

Princeton University Press, 1973. 164 p.

> A consideration of religious studies in relation to philosophy and social sciences. Distinguishes the scientific study of religion from theology, criticizes Peter Berger's projectionist theory, and, in a section which takes up Freud's and Reik's views on religions, discusses the question of compatibility of intra- and extra-religious explanations.

Smith, H. Sheldon. "George Albert Coe, Revaluer of Values." RELIGION IN LIFE 22 (1952-53): 46-57.

> Essay on a pioneer in American psychology of religion.

Spilka, Bernard. "Images of Man and Dimensions of Personal Religion: Values for an Empirical Psychology of Religion." REVIEW OF RELIGIOUS RESEARCH 11 (Spring 1970): 171-82.

Spinks, G. Stephen. PSYCHOLOGY AND RELIGION: AN INTRODUCTION TO CONTEMPORARY VIEWS. Boston: Beacon Press, 1963. xv, 221 p.

> A sketch of the history of the psychology of religion, a summary of the views of Freud and Jung, and discussions of religious experiences, prayer, and worship.

Strommen, Merton P., ed. RESEARCH ON RELIGIOUS DEVELOPMENT: A COMPREHENSIVE HANDBOOK. New York: Hawthorn Books, 1971. 904 p.

> A massive volume which surveys pertinent research in the field of religious development ranging from religious education to personality development and old age. More than half of the twenty-six authors are psychologists. Includes extensive bibliographies and summaries of previous research.

Strout, Cushing. "William James and the Twice-Born Sick Soul." DAEDALUS 97 (Summer 1968): 1062-82.

> A psychobiographical study of James by an historian of American intellectual history.

_____. "The Pluralistic Identity of William James: A Psycho-Historical Reading of THE VARIETIES OF RELIGIOUS EXPERIENCE." AMERICAN QUARTERLY 23 (May 1971): 135-52.

Strunk, Orlo, Jr. "Present Status of the Psychology of Religion." JOURNAL OF BIBLE AND RELIGION 25 (October 1957): 287-92.

_____. "A Redefinition of the Psychology of Religion." PSYCHOLOGICAL REPORTS 3 (1957): 138.

_____. "The Psychology of Religion: An Historical and Contemporary Survey." PSYCHOLOGICAL NEWSLETTER 9 (1958): 181-99.

_____. RELIGION: A PSYCHOLOGICAL INTERPRETATION. New York: Abingdon Press, 1962. 128 p.

Uses the personality theories of Combs, Snygg, and Allport in a phenomenological interpretation of religion viewed as a characteristic of the basic human need to maintain and enhance the perceived self.

_____. "Humanistic Religious Psychology: A New Chapter in the Psychology of Religion." JOURNAL OF PASTORAL CARE 24 (1970): 90-97.

_____, ed. THE PSYCHOLOGY OF RELIGION: HISTORICAL AND INTERPRETIVE READINGS. 2nd ed. Nashville: Abingdon Press, 1971. 152 p.

A collection of essays designed to clarify the nature and scope of the psychology of religion in past and present. Essays by James B. Pratt, Seward Hiltner, Paul W. Pruyser, Bernard Spilka, and others.

Thouless, Robert H. "Psychology and Religion." CHURCH QUARTERLY REVIEW 156 (April-June 1955): 137-49.

_____. AN INTRODUCTION TO THE PSYCHOLOGY OF RELIGION. 3rd ed. Cambridge: Cambridge University Press, 1971. 152 p.

A greatly revised version of a work published originally in 1923 and revised in 1961, this edition takes into account statistical and empirical research carried out in the intervening period. Deals with prayer, mysticism, conversion, and religious factors.

Vernon, Glenn M. "Communication between Theologians and Social Scientists in Research." REVIEW OF RELIGIOUS RESEARCH 7, no. 2 (1966): 93-101.

Emphasis on social psychology.

Walker, Ronald E., et al. "An Experimenter Variable: The Psychologist-Clergymen." PSYCHOLOGICAL REPORTS 22 (1968): 709-14.

Wood, Hunter H. "Constructive Collaborators: Religion and Psychology." JOURNAL OF RELIGION AND HEALTH 11 (April 1972): 120-43.

Yinger, Milton J. THE SCIENTIFIC STUDY OF RELIGION. New York: Macmillan, 1970. 593 p.

Proposes that the study of religion include psychological and anthropological perspectives, though the work itself is generally of a sociological nature.

Zunini, Giorgio. MAN AND HIS RELIGION: ASPECTS OF RELIGIOUS PSY-
CHOLOGY. London: Geoffrey Chapman, 1969. xiii, 365 p.

> Written by an Italian psychologist who studied with Gordon All-
> port, this book ranges widely, taking up perspectives from classi-
> cal psychology of religion, psychoanalysis, sociology, anthropology,
> and theology.

A:3 PSYCHOLOGY OF RELIGION PRIOR TO 1950

Allier, Raoul Scipion Philippe. LA PSYCHOLOGIE DE LA CONVERSION
CHEZ LES PEUPLES NONCIVILISES. 2 vols. Paris: Payot, 1925.

Alliott, Richard. PSYCHOLOGY AND THEOLOGY: OR, PSYCHOLOGY AP-
PLIED TO THE INVESTIGATION OF QUESTIONS RELATING TO RELIGION,
NATURAL THEOLOGY, AND REVELATION. London: Jackson and Walford,
1855. 252 p.

Ames, Edward Scribner. "Theology From the Standpoint of Functional Psychology."
AMERICAN JOURNAL OF THEOLOGY 10 (1906): 219-32.

_____. "The Psychological Basis of Religion." MONIST 20 (1910): 242-62.

_____. THE PSYCHOLOGY OF RELIGIOUS EXPERIENCE. New York: Hough-
ton Mifflin Co., 1910. 428 p.

> A functionalist approach which views religious consciousness as the
> highest form of social ideal. Surveys primitive and modern religion
> as well as religious development among "normal" people.

Balmforth, Henry. IS CHRISTIAN EXPERIENCE AN ILLUSION? AN ESSAY
IN THE PHILOSOPHY OF RELIGION. London: Student Christian Movement
Press, 1923. xvi, 139 p.

> Includes annotated bibliography.

Barbour, Clifford Edward. SIN AND THE NEW PSYCHOLOGY. New York:
Abingdon Press, 1930. 369 p.

Barrow, George Alexander. THE VALIDITY OF THE RELIGIOUS EXPERIENCE.
Boston: Sherman, French and Co., 1917. 247 p.

Barry, Frank Russell. CHRISTIANITY AND PSYCHOLOGY. London: Student
Christian Movement Press, 1933. 290 p.

Beck, Frank Orman. "Prayer: A Study in Its History and Psychology." AMER-

ICAN JOURNAL OF RELIGIOUS PSYCHOLOGY AND EDUCATION 2 (1906-7): 107-21.

Berguer, Georges. LA NOTION DE VALEUR, SA NATURE PSYCHIQUE, SON IMPORTANCE EN THEOLOGIE. Geneva: Imprint Romet, 1908. 365 p.

Berkeley-Hill, Owen. "Hindu-Muslim Unity." INTERNATIONAL JOURNAL OF PSYCHOANALYSIS 6 (1925): 282-87.

Bois, Henri. LE SENTIMENT RELIGIEUX. Paris: Librairie Fischbacher, 1902. 64 p.

> A theologian's address to students, drawing mainly on James, Starbuck, and Durkheim.

_____. LA VALEUR DE L'EXPERIENCE RELIGIEUSE. 2nd ed. Paris: E. Nourry, 1908. 215 p.

Bose, R.G. "Religious Concepts of Children." RELIGIOUS EDUCATION 24 (1929): 831-37.

Boutroux, Emile. LA PSYCHOLOGIE DU MYSTICISME. Paris: La Revue Bleu, 1902. 22 p.

Bovet, Pierre. "Le Sentiment religieux: Etude de psychologie." REVUE DE THEOLOGIE ET DE PHILOSOPHIE 7, no. 30 (1919): 149-75.

_____. "Le Sentiment filial et la religion." REVUE DE THEOLOGIE ET DE PHILOSOPHIE 8, no. 34 (1920): 141-53.

Bower, William Clayton. RELIGION AND THE GOOD LIFE. New York: Abingdon Press, 1933. 230 p.

> Emphasizes positive aspects of religion. Discussions of prayer, personality integration, and group participation.

Brabant, Frank Herbert. RELIGION AND THE MYSTERIOUS. London: Longmans, Green and Co., 1930. 97 p.

Bremond, Henri. L'INQUIETUDE RELIGIEUSE. Paris: Perrin, 1919-21 series. 392 p.

Brouwer, Johannes. PSYCHOLOGIE DER SPAANSCHE MYSTIEK. Amsterdam: 1931. xix, 284 p.

Brown, William Adams. IMPERIALISTIC RELIGION AND THE RELIGION OF

DEMOCRACY: A STUDY IN SOCIAL PSYCHOLOGY. New York: Charles Scribner's Sons, 1923. xiv, 223 p.

_____. "Religion and Psychology." HIBBERT JOURNAL 23 (1925): 402-17.

Carpenter, Edward. "On the Connection between Homosexuality and Divination and the Importance of the Intermediate Sexes Generally in Early Civilizations." AMERICAN JOURNAL OF RELIGIOUS PSYCHOLOGY AND EDUCATION 4 (1910-11): 219-43.

Cattell, Raymond B. PSYCHOLOGY AND THE RELIGIOUS QUEST: AN AC-COUNT OF THE PSYCHOLOGY OF RELIGION AND A DEFENCE OF INDIVI-DUALISM. London: Thomas Nelson and Sons, 1938. 195 p.

A noted research psychologist contrasts psychology's support of individualism with religion's "theopsyche," or group mind.

Chamberlain, Alexander F. "New Religions among the North American Indians." JOURNAL OF RELIGIOUS PSYCHOLOGY 6 (1913): 1-49.

Chansou, J. ETUDE DE PSYCHOLOGIE RELIGIEUSE: SUR LES SOURCES ET L'EFFICACITE DE LA PRIERE DANS L'EXPERIENCE CHRETIENNE. Paris: M. Riviere, 1927. 274 p.

Churchill, Winston. THE UNCHARTED WAY: THE PSYCHOLOGY OF THE GOSPEL DOCTRINE. Philadelphia: Dorrance and Co., 1940. 266 p.

Clairer, Henri. L'EXPERIENCE DE LA VIE ETERNELLE: ETUDE DE PSYCHOLO-GIE RELIGIEUSE EN VUE D'UNE SOLUTION PRATIQUE DU PROBLEME DE LA DESTINEE. Paris: Librairie Fischbacher, 1923. 256 p.

Clark, Elmer Talmage. THE PSYCHOLOGY OF RELIGIOUS AWAKENING. New York: Macmillan, 1929. 170 p.

Cock, William Hendy. RELIGIOUS PSYCHOLOGY OF THE CHILD: THE DRIFT FROM ORGANIZED RELIGION. London: The Faith Press, 1928. 113 p.

Coe, George A. THE SPIRITUAL LIFE: STUDIES IN THE SCIENCE OF RELI-GION. New York: Fleming H. Revell Co., 1900. 279 p.

Argues that specific states of consciousness must be empirically ex-amined before drawing theological or philosophical conclusions. Ex-plores the nature of revivalism, conversion, healing, prayer, and other topics.

_____. THE PSYCHOLOGY OF RELIGION. Chicago: University of Chicago Press, 1916. xvii, 365 p.

> An introduction to the basic issues, methods, and data appropriate
> to the psychology of religion.

Conklin, Edmund Smith. THE PSYCHOLOGY OF RELIGIOUS ADJUSTMENT.
New York: Macmillan, 1929. xiv, 340 p.

Cutten, George Barton. THE PSYCHOLOGICAL PHENOMENA OF CHRISTIAN-
ITY. New York: Scribners, 1908. xviii, 497 p.

_____. INSTINCTS AND RELIGION. New York: Harper & Brothers, 1940.
154 p.

> An evolutionary theological perspective on instincts, intelligence,
> morals, and religion.

Dawson, George E. "Suggestions towards an Inductive Study of the Religious
Consciousness." JOURNAL OF RELIGIOUS PSYCHOLOGY 6 (1913): 50-58.

Day, Albert Edward. JESUS AND HUMAN PERSONALITY. New York: Abingdon Press, 1934. 269 p.

de Montmorand, Maxime. PSYCHOLOGIE DES MYSTIQUES CATHOLIQUES
ORTHODOXES. Paris: F. Alcan, 1920. 262 p.

Dewar, Lindsay. MAN AND GOD: AN ESSAY IN THE PSYCHOLOGY AND
PHILOSOPHY OF RELIGIOUS EXPERIENCE. New York: Macmillan, 1935.
244 p.

Dewey, John. PHILOSOPHY, PSYCHOLOGY AND SOCIAL PRACTICE. Edited
by Joseph Ratner. New York: Capricorn, 1965. 315 p.

> A collection of Dewey's earliest articles, centering on his growth
> away from Hegelianism to a philosophical perspective informed by
> the "new psychology."

Dimond, Sydney George. THE PSYCHOLOGY OF THE METHODIST REVIVAL:
AN EMPIRICAL AND DESCRIPTIVE STUDY. London: Oxford University Press,
1926. xv, 296 p.

_____. THE PSYCHOLOGY OF METHODISM. London: Epworth Press, 1932.
154 p.

Dodd, C.H. "The Mind of Paul: A Psychological Approach." BULLETIN OF
THE JOHN RYLANDS LIBRARY (Manchester, England) 17 (1933): 91-105.

> See annotation in section F:3.

Dodds, E.R. "Augustine's Confessions: A Study of Spiritual Maladjustment." HIBBERT JOURNAL 26 (1927-28): 459-73.

See annotation in section F:3.

Dresser, Horatio Willis. OUTLINES OF THE PSYCHOLOGY OF RELIGION. New York: Thomas Y. Crowell Co., 1929. xiii, 451 p.

du Buy, Jean. "Stages of Religious Development." AMERICAN JOURNAL OF RELIGIOUS PSYCHOLOGY AND EDUCATION 1 (1904-5): 7-29.

_____. "Four Types of Protestants: A Comparative Study in the Psychology of Religion." AMERICAN JOURNAL OF RELIGIOUS PSYCHOLOGY AND EDU-CATION 3 (1908-9): 165-209.

Dunlap, Knight. MYSTICISM, FREUDIANISM, AND SCIENTIFIC PSYCHOLO-GY. St. Louis: C.V. Mosby, 1920. 173 p.

Edward, Kenneth. RELIGIOUS EXPERIENCE: ITS NATURE AND TRUTH. Edin-burgh: T. and T. Clark, 1926. 248 p.

Ellis, R.S. "The Attitude Toward Death and the Types of Belief in Immortality: A Study in the Psychology of Religion." JOURNAL OF RELIGIOUS PSYCHOL-OGY 7 (1914-15): 466-510.

Everett, Charles Carroll. THE PSYCHOLOGICAL ELEMENTS OF RELIGIOUS FAITH. New York: Macmillan, 1902. xiii, 215 p.

Faber, Geoffrey Cust. OXFORD APOSTLES: A CHARACTER STUDY OF THE OXFORD MOVEMENT. London: Faber and Faber, 1933.

Employs psychoanalytic concepts in analyzing the character struc-tures of Oxford undergraduates attracted to the Anglo-Catholic movement.

Familler, Ignaz. DAS HEILIGLEBEN IN DER MODERNEN PSYCHOPATHOG-RAPHIE. Regensburg: F. Pustet, 1915. 224 p.

Fisher, Robert Howie. RELIGIOUS EXPERIENCE. New York: George H. Dor-an, 1925. 319 p.

Flower, John Cyril. AN APPROACH TO THE PSYCHOLOGY OF RELIGION. London: K. Paul, Trench, Trubner & Co., 1927. 248 p.

Gardner, Percy. THE INTERPRETATION OF RELIGIOUS EXPERIENCE. London: Williams and Norgate, 1939. 231 p.

Girgensohn, Karl. DER SEELISCHE AUFBAU DES RELIGIOSEN ERLEBENS. 2nd ed. Gutersloh: Bertelsmann, 1930.

Granger, Frank Stephen. THE SOUL OF A CHRISTIAN: A STUDY IN THE RELIGIOUS EXPERIENCE. New York: Macmillan, 1900. 303 p.

Grensted, Laurence William. PSYCHOLOGY AND GOD: A STUDY OF THE IMPLICATIONS OF RECENT PSYCHOLOGY FOR RELIGIOUS BELIEF AND PRACTICE. London: Longmans, Green and Co., 1930. 257 p.

_____. THE PSYCHOLOGY OF RELIGION. New York: Oxford University Press, 1952. 181 p.

> An introduction for the layman to the early classics in the field. While published in 1952, centers almost exclusively on pre-1935 developments.

Hall, G. Stanley. "The Jesus of History and of the Passion versus the Jesus of the Resurrection." AMERICAN JOURNAL OF RELIGIOUS PSYCHOLOGY AND EDUCATION 1 (1904-5): 30-64.

_____. "The Genetic View of Berkeley's Religious Motivation." JOURNAL OF RELIGIOUS PSYCHOLOGY 5 (1912): 137-62.

_____. "The Psychology of the Nativity." JOURNAL OF RELIGIOUS PSYCHOLOGY 7 (1914-15): 421-65.

_____. JESUS, THE CHRIST, IN THE LIGHT OF PSYCHOLOGY. 2 vols. New York: Doubleday, Page and Co., 1917. 650 p.

> Employs an assortment of psychological approaches, including Pavlov, Freud, Frazer, and the author's own work on adolescence.

Halliday, William Fearon. PSYCHOLOGY AND RELIGIOUS EXPERIENCE. London: Hodder and Stoughton, 1929. 320 p.

> A handbook on religion and psychology for the minister.

Harms, Ernest. PSYCHOLOGIE UND PSYCHIATRIE DER CONVERSION. Leiden: A.W. Sijthoff, 1939. 120 p.

Hickman, Franklin Simpson. INTRODUCTION TO THE PSYCHOLOGY OF RELIGION. New York: Abingdon Press, 1926. 558 p.

Hill, Owen Aloysius. PSYCHOLOGY AND NATURAL THEOLOGY. New York: Macmillan, 1921. xiii, 351 p.

Holman, Charles Thomas. THE RELIGION OF A HEALTHY MIND. New York: Round Table Press, 1939. 210 p.

Hopkins, Pryns. "A Critical Survey of the Psychology of Religion." CHARACTER AND PERSONALITY 6 (1937): 16-35.

_____. FROM GODS TO DICTATORS: PSYCHOLOGY OF RELIGIONS AND THEIR TOTALITARIAN SUBSTITUTES. Girard, Kans.: Haldeman-Julius Publishers, 1944. 165 p.

> A search for a common psychological denominator among diverse religious and quasi-religious social phenomena. Includes a chapter comparing the stages of a successful psychoanalysis and "theraeutic" religious practices.

Horton, Walter Marshall. A PSYCHOLOGICAL APPROACH TO THEOLOGY. New York: Harper & Brothers, 1931. xii, 279 p.

> Discusses how personality can be unified, energized, and directed to worthwhile ends, thus demonstrating the relevance of Christianity to the enhancement of human personality.

Howley, John. PSYCHOLOGY AND MYSTICAL EXPERIENCE. London: K. Paul, Trench, Trubner & Co.; St. Louis: B. Herder, 1920. 275 p.

> See annotation in section D:3.

Hughes, Percy. "The Types of Religious Attitude." AMERICAN JOURNAL OF RELIGIOUS PSYCHOLOGY AND EDUCATION 2 (1906-7): 272-81.

Hughes, Thomas Hywel. THE PHILOSOPHIC BASIS OF MYSTICISM. Edinburgh: T. and T. Clark, 1937. 436 p.

_____. PSYCHOLOGY AND RELIGIOUS ORIGINS. New York: Charles Scribner's Sons, 1937. 242 p.

_____. PSYCHOLOGY AND RELIGIOUS TRUTH. London: George Allen and Unwin, 1942. 160 p.

> See annotation in section E:2.

Hylan, John Perham. PUBLIC WORSHIP: A STUDY IN THE PSYCHOLOGY OF RELIGION. Chicago: Open Court Publication Co., 1901. 94 p.

James, William. THE VARIETIES OF RELIGIOUS EXPERIENCE: A STUDY IN HUMAN NATURE. New York: The New American Library Mentor Books, 1958. xviii, 406 p. Paperbound.

> James' Gifford Lectures on Natural Religion delivered at Edinburgh, 1901 to 1902. Considers such topics as religion and neurology, reality of the unseen, healthy and sickmindedness, the divided self, conversion, saintliness, mysticism, and philosophical and aesthetic

characteristics of religion. Copious illustrations from personal documents of religious individuals.

_____. TALKS TO TEACHERS ON PSYCHOLOGY AND TO STUDENTS ON SOME OF LIFE'S IDEALS. New York: Dover Publications, 1962. 146 p.

A series of lectures delivered in 1892. Useful as introduction to James' functional psychology.

Joly, Henri. THE PSYCHOLOGY OF THE SAINTS. London: Duckworth and Co., 1898. xv, 184 p.

Jones, W. Lawson. A PSYCHOLOGICAL STUDY OF RELIGIOUS CONVERSION. London: Epworth Press, 1937. 397 p.

Josey, Charles Conant. THE PSYCHOLOGY OF RELIGION. New York: Macmillan, 1927. 362 p.

Joyce, Gilbert Cunningham. THE INSPIRATION OF PROPHECY: AN ESSAY IN THE PSYCHOLOGY OF REVELATION. New York: H. Frowde, 1910. 195 p.

Kaplan, Jacob H. "Psychology of Prophecy." AMERICAN JOURNAL OF RELIGIOUS PSYCHOLOGY AND EDUCATION 2 (1906-7): 168-203.

Karlson, Karl Johan. "Psychoanalysis and Mythology." JOURNAL OF RELIGIOUS PSYCHOLOGY 7 (1914-15): 137-213.

Kierkegaard, Soren. REPETITION: AN ESSAY IN EXPERIMENTAL PSYCHOLOGY. Translated by Walter Lowrie. New York: Harper & Row, Publishers, 1964. 144 p.

A short study originally published in 1843 by the Danish religious thinker. Anticipates Freud's view of the intimate relation of religion and the repetition compulsion.

King, Irving. THE DEVELOPMENT OF RELIGION: A STUDY IN ANTHROPOLOGY AND SOCIAL PSYCHOLOGY. New York: Macmillan, 1910. xxiii, 371 p.

Kline, L.W. "The Sermon: A Study in Social Psychology." AMERICAN JOURNAL OF RELIGIOUS PSYCHOLOGY AND EDUCATION 1 (1904-5): 288-300.

Knudson, Albert Cornelius. THE VALIDITY OF RELIGIOUS EXPERIENCE. New York: Abingdon Press, 1937. 237 p.

Kupky, Oskar. THE RELIGIOUS DEVELOPMENT OF ADOLESCENTS, BASED UPON THEIR LITERARY PRODUCTIONS. Translated by William Clark Trow. New York: Macmillan, 1928. 138 p.

La Grasserie, Raoul de. DE LA PSYCHOLOGIE DES RELIGIONS. Paris: F. Alcan, 1899. 308 p.

Laufer, Berthold. "The Development of Ancestral Images in China." JOURNAL OF RELIGIOUS PSYCHOLOGY 6 (1913): 111-23.

Leuba, James H. "Studies in the Psychology of Religious Phenomena." AMERICAN JOURNAL OF PSYCHOLOGY 7 (1896): 309-85.

_____. STUDIES IN THE PSYCHOLOGY OF RELIGIOUS PHENOMENA: THE RELIGIOUS MOTIVE, CONVERSION, FACTS, AND DOCTRINES. Worcester, Mass.: J.H. Orpha, 1896. 385 p.

Originally Leuba's Ph.D. dissertation at Clark University.

_____. "Introduction to a Psychological Study of Religion." MONIST 11 (1901): 195-225.

_____. "The Contents of Religious Consciousness." MONIST 11 (1901): 536-73.

_____. "Fundamental Tendencies of the Christian Mystics." REVUE PHILOSOPHIQUE, July 1902, pp. 1-36 and November 1902, pp. 441-87.

_____. "The Stage of Death: An Instance of Internal Adaptation." AMERICAN JOURNAL OF PSYCHOLOGY 14 (July-October 1903): 397-409.

_____. "Faith." AMERICAN JOURNAL OF RELIGIOUS PSYCHOLOGY AND EDUCATION 1 (1904-5): 65-82.

_____. "The Field and the Problems of the Psychology of Religion." AMERICAN JOURNAL OF RELIGIOUS PSYCHOLOGY AND EDUCATION 1 (1904-5): 155-67.

_____. "Fear, Awe and the Sublime in Religion: A Chapter in the Study of Instincts, Impulses and Motives in Religious Life." AMERICAN JOURNAL OF RELIGIOUS PSYCHOLOGY AND EDUCATION 2 (1906-7): 1-23.

_____. "Religion as a Factor in the Struggle for Life." AMERICAN JOURNAL OF RELIGIOUS PSYCHOLOGY AND EDUCATION 2 (1906-7): 307-43.

_____. "The Psychological Origin of Religion." MONIST 19 (1909): 27-35.

_____. THE PSYCHOLOGICAL ORIGIN AND NATURE OF RELIGION. London: A. Constable, 1909. 94 p.

_____. "Dynamism, the Primitive Nature Philosophy, and Its Relation to Religion and Magic." JOURNAL OF RELIGIOUS PSYCHOLOGY 5 (1912): 305-16.

_____. A PSYCHOLOGICAL STUDY OF RELIGION: ITS ORIGIN, FUNCTION, AND FUTURE. New York: Macmillan, 1912. xiv, 371 p.

A general psychology of religion. Topics include magic, morality, conversion, theology, and mythology.

_____. "Religion and Magic: A Reply to Mr. Wallis." JOURNAL OF RELIGIOUS PSYCHOLOGY 6 (1913): 427-30.

Reply to the article of religion and magic by Wilson D. Wallis cited below.

_____. THE BELIEF IN GOD AND IMMORTALITY: A PSYCHOLOGICAL, ANTHROPOLOGICAL AND STATISTICAL STUDY. Boston: Sherman, French and Co., 1916. xvii, 340 p.

_____. "A Modern Mystic." JOURNAL OF ABNORMAL PSYCHOLOGY 15 (1920): 209.

_____. "Psychotherapeutic Cults: Christian Science, Mind Cure, New Thought." MONIST 12 (1922): 348-60.

_____. "Les Grands Mystiques Chretien, l'hysterie et la neurasthenie." JOURNAL DE PSYCHOLOGIE 22 (1925): 236-51.

_____. THE PSYCHOLOGY OF RELIGIOUS MYSTICISM. London: Kegan Paul, 1925. xii, 336 p.

_____. GOD OR MAN? A STUDY OF THE VALUE OF GOD TO MAN. New York: H. Holt and Co., 1933. xii, 338 p.

_____. "The Making of a Psychologist of Religion." RELIGION IN TRANSITION, pp. 173-200. Edited by Vergilius Ferm. London: George Allen and Unwin, 1937.

An autobiographical statement.

Leys, Wayne. THE RELIGIOUS CONTROL OF EMOTION. New York: R. Long and R.R. Smith, 1932. 229 p.

Lindworsky, J. THE PSYCHOLOGY OF ASCETICISM. London: Edwards, 1936.

McComas, Henry Clay. THE PSYCHOLOGY OF RELIGIOUS SECTS: A COMPARISON OF TYPES. New York: Fleming H. Revell Co., 1912. 235 p.

McKenzie, John Grant. PSYCHOLOGY, PSYCHOTHERAPY, AND EVANGELICALISM. London: George Allen and Unwin, 1940. xiii, 238 p.

Mackie, Alexander. THE GIFT OF TONGUES: A STUDY IN PATHOLOGICAL ASPECTS OF CHRISTIANITY. New York: George H. Doran, 1921. xiv, 275 p.

Magni, J.A. "The Ethnological Background of the Eucharist." AMERICAN JOURNAL OF RELIGIOUS PSYCHOLOGY AND EDUCATION 4 (1910-11): 1-47.

Mahoney, Carl K. THE RELIGIOUS MIND: A PSYCHOLOGICAL STUDY OF RELIGIOUS EXPERIENCE. New York: Macmillan, 1927. xxii, 214 p.

Marechal, Joseph. STUDIES IN THE PSYCHOLOGY OF THE MYSTICS. Translated by Algar Thorold. London: Burns, Oates and Washburne, 1927. 344 p.

Martin, Everett Dean. THE MYSTERY OF RELIGION: A STUDY IN SOCIAL PSYCHOLOGY. New York: Harper & Brothers, 1924. xii, 391 p.

Matthews, Walter Robert. THE PSYCHOLOGICAL APPROACH TO RELIGION. New York: Longmans, Green and Co., 1925. 73 p.

_____, ed. PSYCHOLOGY AND THE CHURCH. New York: Macmillan, 1925. 203 p.

> A collection of essays by L.W. Grensted, H.M. Relton, J.A. Hadfield, and others on prayer, religious experience, healing, and moral development.

Mayer-Oakes, F.T. "The Authority of Jesus and Its Meaning for the Modern Mind: A Study in the Psychology of Jesus." Part 1: AMERICAN JOURNAL OF RELIGIOUS PSYCHOLOGY AND EDUCATION 4 (1910-11): 177-218; Part 2: JOURNAL OF RELIGIOUS PSYCHOLOGY 6 (1913): 149-74.

Mellone, Sydney Herbert. THE BEARINGS OF PSYCHOLOGY ON RELIGION. Oxford: B. Blackwell, 1939. 255 p.

Morgan, William Joseph. LA PSYCHOLOGIE DE LA RELIGION DANS L'AMERIQUE D'AUJOURD'HUI. Paris: Jouve and Co., 1928. 223 p.

Morris, Margaretta. "Magic and Morals in Borneo." AMERICAN JOURNAL OF RELIGIOUS PSYCHOLOGY AND EDUCATION 2 (1906-7): 282-94.

Morse, Josiah. "The Pathology of Religions." AMERICAN JOURNAL OF RELIGIOUS PSYCHOLOGY AND EDUCATION 1 (1904-5): 217-47.

_____. "The Psychology and Pedagogy of Doubt." JOURNAL OF RELIGIOUS PSYCHOLOGY 5 (1912): 418-34.

Moxon, Cavendish. "Mystical Ecstasy and Hysterical Dream-States." JOURNAL OF ABNORMAL PSYCHOLOGY 15 (1920-21): 329-34.

Muller, Friedrich Max. THEOSOPHY: OR, PSYCHOLOGICAL RELIGION. London: Longmans, Green and Co., 1893. xxiii, 585 p.

Muller-Freienfels, Richard. PSYCHOLOGIE DER RELIGION. 2 vols. Berlin and Leipzig: Vereinigung Wissenschaftlicher Verlag, 1920. 806 p.

Mumford, Edith E. THE DAWN OF RELIGION IN THE MIND OF THE CHILD. London: Longmans, Green and Co., 1915. 111 p.

Murisier, Ernest. LES MALADIES DU SENTIMENT RELIGIEUX. Paris: F. Alcan, 1901. 174 p.

Neeser, Maurice. LES PRINCIPES DE LA PSYCHOLOGIE DE LA RELIGION ET LA PSYCHANALYSE. Neuchatel: Imprint Attinger Freres, 1920. 24 p.

Odum, Howard W. "Religious Folk-Songs of the Southern Negroes." AMERICAN JOURNAL OF RELIGIOUS PSYCHOLOGY AND EDUCATION 3 (1908-9): 265-365.

Oosterheerdt, A. "Religion as a Matter of Feeling--A Criticism." AMERICAN JOURNAL OF RELIGIOUS PSYCHOLOGY AND EDUCATION 2 (1906-7): 62-75.

_____. "Religion as Functional, Metaphysical, and Normative: An Exposition." AMERICAN JOURNAL OF RELIGIOUS PSYCHOLOGY AND EDUCATION 2 (1906-7): 141-59.

Pacheu, Juleo. INTRODUCTION A LA PSYCHOLOGIE DES MYSTIQUES. Paris: H. Oudin, 1901. 141 p.

_____. L'EXPERIENCE MYSTIQUE ET L'ACTIVITE SUBCONSCIENTE. Paris: Perrin, 1911. 314 p.

Page, F.H. "The Psychology of Religion after Fifty Years." CANADIAN JOURNAL OF PSYCHOLOGY 5 (1951): 60-67.

Povah, John Walter. THE NEW PSYCHOLOGY AND THE HEBREW PROPHETS. London: Longmans, Green and Co., 1925. xiv, 207 p.

_____. THE OLD TESTAMENT AND MODERN PROBLEMS IN PSYCHOLOGY. London: Longmans, Green and Co., 1926. 151 p.

Pratt, James Bissett. "Types of Religious Belief." AMERICAN JOURNAL OF RELIGIOUS PSYCHOLOGY AND EDUCATION 2 (1906-7): 76-94.

_____. "Concerning the Origin of Religion." AMERICAN JOURNAL OF RELIGIOUS PSYCHOLOGY AND EDUCATION 2 (1906-7): 257-71.

_____. THE PSYCHOLOGY OF RELIGIOUS BELIEF. New York: Macmillan, 1907. xii, 327 p.

_____. "The Psychology of Religion." HARVARD THEOLOGICAL REVIEW 1 (1908): 435-54.

_____. "An Empirical Study of Prayer." AMERICAN JOURNAL OF RELIGIOUS PSYCHOLOGY AND EDUCATION 4 (1910-11): 48-67.

_____. "The Psychology of Religion." JOURNAL OF RELIGIOUS PSYCHOLOGY 5 (1912): 383-93.

_____. THE RELIGIOUS CONSCIOUSNESS. New York: Macmillan, 1920. 488 p.

Price, E.J. "The Limitations of the Psychology of Religion." HIBBERT JOURNAL 22 (1924): 664-73.

Ranson, S. Walter. "Studies in the Psychology of Prayer." AMERICAN JOURNAL OF RELIGIOUS PSYCHOLOGY AND EDUCATION 1 (1904-5): 129-42.

Raymond, George Lansing. THE PSYCHOLOGY OF INSPIRATION: AN ATTEMPT TO DISTINGUISH RELIGIOUS FROM SCIENTIFIC TRUTH AND TO HARMONIZE CHRISTIANITY WITH MODERN THOUGHT. New York: Funk and Wagnalls, 1908. xix, 340 p.

Robinson, Charles Frederick. "Some Psychological Elements in Famous Superstitions." AMERICAN JOURNAL OF RELIGIOUS PSYCHOLOGY AND EDUCATION 1 (1904-5): 248-67.

Robinson, V.P. "The Conception of God of College Students: A Study in Religious Psychology." AMERICAN JOURNAL OF RELIGIOUS PSYCHOLOGY AND EDUCATION 3 (1908-9): 247-57.

Royse, Clarence D. "The Psychology of Saul's Conversion." AMERICAN JOURNAL OF RELIGIOUS PSYCHOLOGY AND EDUCATION 1 (1904-5): 143-54.

Sanctis, Sante de. RELIGIOUS CONVERSION: A BIO-PSYCHOLOGICAL STUDY. Translated by Helen Augur. New York: Harcourt, Brace and Co., 1927. 324 p.

Saudreau, Auguste. THE MYSTICAL STATE, ITS NATURE AND PHASES. Translated by D.M.B. London: Burns, Oates and Washbourne, 1924. xvi, 204 p.

Saunders, Kenneth James. ADVENTURES OF THE CHRISTIAN SOUL: BEING CHAPTERS IN THE PSYCHOLOGY OF RELIGION. Cambridge: Cambridge University Press, 1916. xii, 145 p.

Schaub, E.L. "The Present Status of the Psychology of Religion." JOURNAL OF RELIGION 2 (1922): 362-79.

_____. "The Psychology of Religion." PSYCHOLOGICAL BULLETIN 23 (1926): 681-700.

_____. "The Psychology of Religion in America during the Past Quarter-Century." JOURNAL OF RELIGION 6 (1926): 113-34.

Schroeder, Theodore. "Sex-Determinant in Mormon Theology." ALIENIST AND NEUROLOGIST, May 1908, p. 208.

_____. "Religion and Sensualism as Connected by Clergymen." AMERICAN JOURNAL OF RELIGIOUS PSYCHOLOGY AND EDUCATION 3 (1908-9): 16-28.

_____. "Outline for a Study of the Erotogenesis of Religion." JOURNAL OF RELIGIOUS PSYCHOLOGY 5 (1912): 394-401.

_____. "Mathias the Prophet (1788-1837): A Contribution to the Study of the Erotogenesis of Religion." JOURNAL OF RELIGIOUS PSYCHOLOGY 6 (1913): 59-65.

_____. "Adolescence and Religion." JOURNAL OF RELIGIOUS PSYCHOLOGY 6 (1913): 124-48.

_____. "Erotogenesis of Religion: Developing a Working Hypothesis." ALIEN-IST AND NEUROLOGIST, November 1913, p. 330.

_____. "Wildisbuch Crucified Saint." PSYCHOANALYTIC REVIEW 1 (1913): 129-48.

_____. "The Erotogenetic Interpretation of Religion: Its Opponents Reviewed." JOURNAL OF RELIGIOUS PSYCHOLOGY 7 (1914-15): 23-44.

Selbie, William Boothby. THE PSYCHOLOGY OF RELIGION. Oxford: The Clarendon Press, 1924. xii, 310 p.

Sheldon, William Herbert. PSYCHOLOGY AND THE PROMETHEAN WILL: A CONSTRUCTIVE STUDY OF THE ACUTE COMMON PROBLEM OF EDUCA-TION, MEDICINE AND RELIGION. New York: Harper & Brothers, 1936. 265 p.

Shepherd, W.T. "Concerning the Origin of the Ideas of Gods." JOURNAL OF RELIGIOUS PSYCHOLOGY 7 (1914-15): 237-44.

_____. "Concerning the Religion of Childhood." JOURNAL OF RELIGIOUS PSYCHOLOGY 7 (1914-15): 411-16.

Smith, Preserved. "Luther's Early Development in the Light of Psychoanalysis." AMERICAN JOURNAL OF PSYCHOLOGY 24 (1913): 360-77.

Sparkman, C.F. "Satan and His Ancestors, from a Psychological Standpoint." JOURNAL OF RELIGIOUS PSYCHOLOGY 5 (1912): 52-86, 163-94.

Starbuck, Edwin Diller. "Some Aspects of Religious Growth." AMERICAN JOURNAL OF PSYCHOLOGY 9 (1897): 70-124.

_____. "A Study of Conversion." AMERICAN JOURNAL OF PSYCHOLOGY 8 (1898): 268-308.

_____. THE PSYCHOLOGY OF RELIGION: AN EMPIRICAL STUDY OF THE GROWTH OF RELIGIOUS CONSCIOUSNESS. New York: Scribners, 1899. xx, 423 p.

   One of the classics in psychology of religion. Major emphasis on conversion, its origin, context, and effect. Data derived largely from questionnaires.

_____. "The Feelings and Their Place in Religion." AMERICAN JOURNAL OF RELIGIOUS PSYCHOLOGY AND EDUCATION 1 (1904-5): 168-86.

_____. "Religion's Use of Me." In RELIGION IN TRANSITION, pp. 201-

60. Edited by Vergilius Ferm. London: George Allen and Unwin, 1937.
    An autobiographical statement.

Stolz, Karl Ruf. THE PSYCHOLOGY OF RELIGIOUS LIVING. Nashville: Cokesbury Press, 1937. 375 p.

Stratton, George Malcolm. PSYCHOLOGY OF THE RELIGIOUS LIFE. London: George Allen and Co., 1911. xii, 376 p.

Strong, Anna Louise. "The Relation of the Subconscious to Prayer." AMERICAN JOURNAL OF RELIGIOUS PSYCHOLOGY AND EDUCATION 2 (1906-7): 160-67.

Super, Charles W. "The Psychology of Christian Hymns." AMERICAN JOURNAL OF RELIGIOUS PSYCHOLOGY AND EDUCATION 3 (1908-9): 1-15.

Swisher, Walter Samuel. RELIGION AND THE NEW PSYCHOLOGY: A PSYCHO-ANALYTIC STUDY OF RELIGION. London: George Routledge and Sons, n.d. xv, 261 p.

    A work by a minister, dating from the 1930s. Representative of
    an early friendly but somewhat clumsy welcome offered to psycho-
    analysis by students of religion.

Thulie, Henri. LA MYSTIQUE DIVINE, DIABOLIQUE ET NATURELLE CHEZ LES THEOLOGIENS. Paris: Vigot Freres, 1912. 406 p.

Trout, David McCamel. RELIGIOUS BEHAVIOR: AN INTRODUCTION TO THE PSYCHOLOGICAL STUDY OF RELIGION. New York: Macmillan, 1931. xiv, 528 p.

Underhill, Evelyn. THE MYSTIC WAY: A PSYCHOLOGICAL STUDY IN CHRISTIAN ORIGINS. New York: E.P. Dutton, 1913. xiv, 395 p.

Uren, A. Rudolph. RECENT RELIGIOUS PSYCHOLOGY: A STUDY IN THE PSYCHOLOGY OF RELIGION. New York: Charles Scribner's Sons, 1928. 280 p.

    A good summary and critical exposition of the major early work in
    the psychology of religion, including Starbuck, Coe, James, Pratt,
    Ames, and Stratton.

van Teslaar, J.S. "The Problems and Present Status of Religious Psychology." JOURNAL OF RELIGIOUS PSYCHOLOGY 7 (1914-15): 214-36.

Wallis, Wilson D. "The Element of Fear in Religion." JOURNAL OF RELIGIOUS PSYCHOLOGY 5 (1912): 257-304.

_____. "Religion and Magic: Definitions and Relations." JOURNAL OF RELIGIOUS PSYCHOLOGY 6 (1913): 238-72.

_____. "Durkheim's View of Religion." JOURNAL OF RELIGIOUS PSYCHOLOGY 7 (1914-15): 252-67.

Waterhouse, Eric Strickland. PSYCHOLOGY AND RELIGION. London: E. Mathews and Marrot, 1930. xxii, 232 p.

Weatherhead, Leslie Dixon. PSYCHOLOGY AND LIFE. New York: Abingdon Press, 1935. xix, 280 p.

Whatam, Arthur E. "The Origin of Human Sacrifice--Including an Explanation of the Hebrew Asherah." AMERICAN JOURNAL OF RELIGIOUS PSYCHOLOGY AND EDUCATION 2 (1906-7): 24-61.

_____. "The Magic Girdle of Aphrodite." AMERICAN JOURNAL OF RELIGIOUS PSYCHOLOGY AND EDUCATION 3 (1908-9): 368-77.

_____. "The Sign of the Mother-Goddess." AMERICAN JOURNAL OF RELIGIOUS PSYCHOLOGY AND EDUCATION 4 (1910-11): 252-309.

Wheeler, Robert Fulton. A STUDY IN THE PSYCHOLOGY OF THE SPIRIT. Boston: R.G. Badger, 1929. 250 p.

Wieman, Henry Nelson, and Westcott-Wieman, Regina. NORMATIVE PSYCHOLOGY OF RELIGION. New York: Thomas Y. Crowell Co., 1935. 564 p.

> Deals with the practical interests of religious living and teaching. Includes discussion of prayer, faith, mystical experience, and conversion.

Yeaxlee, Basil Alfred. RELIGION AND THE GROWING MIND. London: Nisbet and Co., 1939. 224 p.

Zweig, Stefan. MENTAL HEALERS: FRANZ ANTON MESMER, MARY BAKER EDDY, SIGMUND FREUD. New York: Frederick Ungar, 1932. 363 p.

A:4 DEPTH PSYCHOLOGY AND RELIGION

Adler, Alfred. "Religion and Individual Psychology." In SUPERIORITY AND SOCIAL INTEREST, pp. 271-308. Edited and translated by H.L. Ansbacher and R.R. Ansbacher. New York: Viking Compass Edition, 1973.

Angers, William P. "Clarifications toward the Rapprochement between Religion and Psychology." JOURNAL OF INDIVIDUAL PSYCHOLOGY 16 (1960): 73-76.

Ansbacher, Heinz L. "Religion and Individual Psychology." JOURNAL OF INDIVIDUAL PSYCHOLOGY 27, no. 1 (1971): 3-9.

> Discusses the relation of religion to Alfred Adler's psychology.

Apolito, Arnaldo. "Psychoanalysis and Religion." AMERICAN JOURNAL OF PSYCHOANALYSIS 30, no. 2 (1970): 115-26.

Bakan, David. SIGMUND FREUD AND THE JEWISH MYSTICAL TRADITION. Princeton, N.J.: Van Nostrand, 1958. 326 p.

> Points out certain elements of medieval Kabbalistic movements, the Zohar, and Hasidism as similar to, and possible influences on, aspects of Freud's life and work.

_____. "Science, Mysticism, and Psychoanalysis." CATHOLIC PSYCHOLOGICAL RECORD 4 (1966): 1-9. .

Banks, R. "Religion as Projection: A Re-Appraisal of Freud's Theory." RELIGIOUS STUDIES 9 (December 1973): 401-26.

Bartemeier, Leo H. "Psychoanalysis and Religion." BULLETIN OF THE MENNINGER CLINIC 29 (1965): 237-44.

Becker, Ernest. "A Note on Freud's Primal Horde Theory." PSYCHOANALYTIC QUARTERLY 30 (1961): 413-19.

Berkower, Lary. "The Enduring Effect of the Jewish Tradition upon Freud." AMERICAN JOURNAL OF PSYCHIATRY 125, no. 8 (1969): 1067-75.

Birk, Kasimer. SIGMUND FREUD UND DIE RELIGION. Munsterschwarzach: Vier-Turme-Verlag, 1970. xv, 125 p.

> The first half of the book summarizes Freud's discussions of particular religions and religion in general. The latter and more useful half provides brief synopses of Catholic and non-Catholic interpreters of Freud's psychology of religion.

Bonaparte, Marie. "Psychoanalysis in Relation to Social, Religious, and Natural Forces." INTERNATIONAL JOURNAL OF PSYCHOANALYSIS 39 (1958): 513-15.

Brown, Norman O. LIFE AGAINST DEATH: THE PSYCHOANALYTIC MEANING OF HISTORY. Middletown, Conn.: Wesleyan University Press, 1959.

xii, 366 p.

> Reviews some of Freud's instinct theories and ideas of culture and argues that repression results in social pathology as well as in neurosis. Includes an extended section on the Protestant era and anality, where religion is viewed, contrary to the usual psycho-analytic view as potentially aligned with the "resurrection of the body" against the forces of repression.

Bunker, Henry Alden. "Psychoanalysis and the Study of Religion." PSYCHO-ANALYSIS AND THE SOCIAL SCIENCES 3 (1951): 7-34.

Capps, Donald. "Hartmann's Relationship to Freud: A Reappraisal." JOUR-NAL OF THE HISTORY OF THE BEHAVIORAL SCIENCES 6 (1970): 162-75.

> - Argues in behalf of David Bakan's thesis in SIGMUND FREUD AND THE JEWISH MYSTICAL TRADITION (cited above) by showing links between nineteenth-century German philosophy and Jewish mysti-cism.

Caruso, Igor A. "Is Psychoanalysis Social?" CROSS CURRENTS 12 (1962): 83-98.

Casey, Robert P. "Religion and Psychoanalysis." PSYCHIATRY 6, no. 3 (1943): 291-300.

Choisy, Maryse. SIGMUND FREUD: A NEW APPRAISAL. New York: Cita-del Press, 1963. 141 p.

> Develops the view that Freud cut himself off from the Hassidic mysticism which would have enabled him to achieve a more balanced view of man. Interesting contrast to David Bakan's SIGMUND FREUD AND THE JEWISH MYSTICAL TRADITION cited above.

Croghan, Leo M. "Psychoanalysis: The Future of an Illusion." AMERICAN ECCLESIASTICAL REVIEW 168 (January 1964): 35-42.

Cronbach, A. "Religion and Psychoanalysis." PSYCHOLOGICAL BULLETIN 23 (1926): 701-13.

Dansereau, Michel. FREUD ET L'ATHEISME. Paris: Desclee, 1971. 198 p.

> The work by a psychologist tries to show how psychoanalysis can purify religious belief. Written partly in response to Paul Ricoeur's FREUD AND PHILOSOPHY: AN ESSAY ON INTERPRETATION cited below.

Day, Franklin. "The Future of Psychoanalysis and Religion." PSYCHOANA-LYTIC QUARTERLY 13 (1944): 84-92.

Demos, Raphael. "Jung's Thought and Influence." REVIEW OF METAPHYSICS 9 (1955): 71-89.

Eickhoff, Andrew R. "The Psychodynamics of Freud's Criticism of Religion." PASTORAL PSYCHOLOGY 11 (May 1960): 35-38.

Faber, H. "Importance of the Three Phases of Freud for the Understanding of Religion." ZYGON 4 (December 1969): 356-72.

Feldman, A. Bronson. "Freudian Theology: Part 1." PSYCHOANALYSIS 1 (Winter 1953): 31-52.

_____. "Freudian Theology: Part 2." PSYCHOANALYSIS 1 (Spring 1953): 37-53.

Feldman, Sandor S. "Notes on the 'Primal Horde'." PSYCHOANALYSIS AND THE SOCIAL SCIENCES 1 (1947): 171-93.

Fingarette, Herbert. "Freud and the Standard World." REVIEW OF METAPHYSICS 10 (1956): 258-72.

Flugel, J.C. MAN, MORALS AND SOCIETY: A PSYCHO-ANALYTICAL STUDY. New York: International Universities Press, 1945. 328 p.

    Includes a very good chapter on religion, as well as numerous relevant points throughout the book.

Fortmann, H.M.M. "De Godsdienstpsychologie van Jung." GAWEIN 10, no. 5 (1962): 265-74.

Freud, Sigmund. "The Moses of Michelangelo." In THE STANDARD EDITION OF THE COMPLETE PSYCHOLOGICAL WORKS OF SIGMUND FREUD, vol. 13, pp. 209-38. Edited by James Strachey. London: The Hogarth Press, 1953.

    First published in 1914, this study analyzes the pain, contempt, rage, and restraint portrayed in the statue of Moses at Mt. Sinai.

_____. THE FUTURE OF AN ILLUSION. In THE STANDARD EDITION OF THE COMPLETE PSYCHOLOGICAL WORKS OF SIGMUND FREUD, vol. 21, pp. 3-56. Edited by James Strachey. London: The Hogarth Press, 1961. (Paperback ed. of THE FUTURE OF AN ILLUSION available from New York: Doubleday, Anchor, 1971.)

    Originally published in 1927, this controversial essay is an argument for rationalism; religious ideas are viewed as wishful responses, formerly adaptive, but now outmoded, to helplessness in the face of nature and to unhappiness in the midst of culture.

_____. CIVILIZATION AND ITS DISCONTENTS. In THE STANDARD EDI-
TION OF THE COMPLETE PSYCHOLOGICAL WORKS OF SIGMUND FREUD,
vol. 21, pp. 59-157. Edited by James Strachey. London: The Hogarth Press,
1961. (Paperback ed. of CIVILIZATION AND ITS DISCONTENTS available
from New York: Norton, College Text, 1963.)

> Among more general reflections, this work (originally published in
> 1930) discusses religion not as a remnant of "oceanic" feeling, but
> as a communal form of protection against helplessness and suffering.

Fromm, Erich. PSYCHOANALYSIS AND RELIGION. New Haven, Conn.:
Yale University Press, 1950. 119 p.

> Argues that psychoanalysis is not a foe or ally of religion, but a
> theory and method of dealing with the common human experience
> which underlies all religions. Especially concerned with the re-
> jection of idolatry and generation of human compassion.

_____. "The Philosophy Basic to Freud's Psychoanalysis." PASTORAL PSY-
CHOLOGY 13 (February 1962): 26-32.

Grollman, Earl A. JUDAISM IN SIGMUND FREUD'S WORLD. New York:
Appleton-Century-Crofts, 1965. xxv, 173 p.

> An impressionistic work that does not compare well with David
> Bakan's SIGMUND FREUD AND THE JEWISH MYSTICAL TRADI-
> TION cited above.

Gross, Leonard. GOD AND FREUD. New York: David McKay, 1959.
215 p.

Hall, Robert W. "Alfred Adler's Concept of God." JOURNAL OF INDIVID-
UAL PSYCHOLOGY 27 (May 1971): 10-18.

Held, Rene. "Contribution a l'etude psychoanalytique du phenomene religieux."
REVUE FRANCAISE DE PSYCHANALYSE 26 (1962): 211-66.

Hillman, James. "Psychology: Monotheistic or Polytheistic?" SPRING: AN
ANNUAL OF ARCHETYPAL PSYCHOLOGY AND JUNGIAN THOUGHT, 1971,
pp. 193-208.

Hiltner, Seward. "Religion and Psychoanalysis." PSYCHOANALYTIC REVIEW
37 (1950): 128-39.

Hostie, Raymond. RELIGION AND THE PSYCHOLOGY OF JUNG. Translated
by G.R. Lamb. London and New York: Sheed & Ward, 1957. 249 p.

> A Louvain scholar's expository and critical discussion of Jung's
> work on religious attitude, individuation, and dogma.

Howes, Elizabeth B. "The Contribution of Dr. C.G. Jung to Our Religious Situation and the Contemporary Scene." PASTORAL PSYCHOLOGY 17 (February 1966): 35-46.

Huber, Winfred, et al. LA PSYCHANLYSE, SCIENCE DE L'HOMME. Brussels: Dessart, 1964. 305 p.

> Focuses on the relationship between Freudian theory and competing ideologies in Europe, including Marxism, existentialism, and neo-Catholicism.

Irwin, J.E.G. "Pfister and Freud: The Rediscovery of a Dialogue." JOURNAL OF RELIGION AND HEALTH 12 (October 1973): 315-27.

Jones, Ernest. "The Psychology of Religion." BRITISH JOURNAL OF MEDICAL PSYCHOLOGY 6 (1926): 264-69. Also published in ESSAYS IN APPLIED PSYCHOANALYSIS, vol. 2, pp. 190-97. Edited by Ernest Jones. London: The Hogarth Press, 1951.

> A good exposition of the Freudian view of religion.

_____. "The Psychology of Religion." In PSYCHOANALYSIS TODAY, pp. 315-25. Edited by Sandor Lorand. New York: International Universities Press, 1944.

Jung, C [arl] G. MEMORIES, DREAMS, REFLECTIONS. Edited by Aniela Jaffe. Translated by Richard and Clara Winston. New York: Pantheon Books, 1963. 398 p.

> An autobiographical statement in which Jung's experiences and thoughts on religion figure prominently.
>
> See section B:1 for other works by Jung.

Kaufmann, Walter. "Freud and the Tragic Virtues." AMERICAN SCHOLAR 29 (1960): 469-81.

Klauber, John. "Freuds Ansichten zur Religion aus der Heutigen Sicht." PSYCHE 16, no. 1 (1962): 50-57.

Lee, Roy Stuart. FREUD AND CHRISTIANITY. London: James Clark and Co., 1948. 204 p.

> A brief exposition of psychoanalysis followed by psychological discussion of such topics as atonement, God the father, and the love of Jesus. The basic intent of the book is to show how Freudian insights may purify Christian faith and practice of its infantilisms.

Loewenberg, Peter. "Sigmund Freud as a Jew: A Study in Ambivalence and

Courage." JOURNAL OF THE HISTORY OF THE BEHAVIORAL SCIENCES 7 (1971): 363-69.

Lubin, Albert J. "A Psychoanalytic View of Religion." In CLINICAL PSY-CHIATRY AND RELIGION, pp. 49-60. Edited by E. Mansell Pattison. Boston: Little, Brown and Co., 1969.

Lubin, Marc. "Study of the High Rate of Male Jewish Membership in the Profession of Psychoanalysis." PROCEEDINGS OF THE 77TH ANNUAL CONVENTION OF THE AMERICAN PSYCHOLOGICAL ASSOCIATION 4 (1969): 527-28.

Marcuse, Herbert. EROS AND CIVILIZATION: A PHILOSOPHICAL INQUIRY INTO FREUD. Boston: Beacon Press, 1955. xviii, 256 p.

A critique of Freudian metapsychology and theory of civilization on the basis of political philosophy.

Masih, Y. FREUDIANISM AND RELIGION. Calcutta: Thacker Spink, 1964. 356 p.

Maybaum, Ignaz. CREATION AND GUILT: A THEOLOGICAL ASSESSMENT OF FREUD'S FATHER-SON CONFLICT. London: Vallentine, Mitchell, 1969. 203 p.

Meng, Heinrich, and Freud, Ernst L., eds. PSYCHOANALYSIS AND FAITH: THE LETTERS OF SIGMUND FREUD AND OSKAR PFISTER. Translated by Eric Mosbacher. New York: Basic Books, 1963. 152 p.

A correspondence of one hundred letters, from 1909 to 1939, between Freud and a Protestant minister who remained loyal both to Freud and to his religious faith.

Mitscherlich, Alexander. SOCIETY WITHOUT THE FATHER: A CONTRIBUTION TO SOCIAL PSYCHOLOGY. Translated by Eric Mosbacher. New York: Harcourt, Brace and World, 1969. 329 p.

Originally published in 1963, this study by a distinguished German psychoanalyst probes the psychology of contemporary mass society. "Fatherlessness" refers to the separation of family from work, and the abstractness and diffusion of authority relationships in society. Discusses the role of religion in some of these processes.

Moreno, Antonio. JUNG, GODS, AND MODERN MAN. Notre Dame, Ind.: University of Notre Dame Press, 1970. xiii, 274 p.

Mowrer, O. Hobart. "Comments on Trude Weiss-Rosmarin's 'Adler's Psychology and the Jewish Tradition'." JOURNAL OF INDIVIDUAL PSYCHOLOGY 15 (1959): 128-29.

Response to article by Trude Weiss-Rosmarin cited below.

Nelson, Benjamin N. "The Future of Illusions." PSYCHOANALYSIS 2 (Spring-Summer 1951): 16-37.

Pasche, Francis. "Freud et l'orthodoxie Judeo-Chretienne." REVUE FRANCAISE DE PSYCHANALYSE 25 (1961): 55-88.

Pfister, Oskar Robert. RELIGIONWISSENSCHAFT UND PSYCHOANALYSE. Giessen: A. Topelmann, 1927. 31 p.

A brief essay intended to identify the uses of psychoanalysis for religious studies.

Philp, Howard Littleton. FREUD AND RELIGIOUS BELIEF. London: Rockliff, 1956. 140 p.

Ple, Albert. FREUD ET LA RELIGION. Paris: Les Editions du Cerf, 1968. 144 p.

A French theologian summarizes Freud's statements on religion, separates his anti-Catholic attitudes from psychoanalysis proper, and appropriates some of Freud's notions for theology.

Preuss, Hans Gunter. ILLUSION UND WIRKLICHKEIT; AN DEN GRENZEN VON RELIGION UND PSYCHOANALYSE. Stuttgart: E. Klett, 1971. 201 p.

Progoff, Ira. JUNG'S PSYCHOLOGY AND ITS SOCIAL MEANING. New York: Grove Press, 1955. xviii, 299 p.

_____. DEPTH PSYCHOLOGY AND MODERN MAN. New York: McGraw-Hill, 1959. xii, 277 p.

See annotation in section G:3.

Pruyser, Paul W. "Sigmund Freud and His Legacy: Psychoanalytic Psychology of Religion." In BEYOND THE CLASSICS? ESSAYS IN THE SCIENTIFIC STUDY OF RELIGION, pp. 243-900. Edited by Charles Y. Glock and Phillip E. Hammond. New York: Harper & Row, Publishers, 1973.

A comprehensive summary of the work of Freud and his followers on religion, with recommendations for future clinical work.

Racker, Heinrich. "On Freud's Position towards Religion." AMERICAN IMAGO 13 (1956): 97-121.

Ramnoux, Clemence. "Sur une page de 'Moise et le Monotheisme'." PSYCH-ANALYSE 3 (1957): 165-87.

Rank, Otto. BEYOND PSYCHOLOGY. New York: Dover Publications, 1958. 291 p.

Wide-ranging, provocative essays on the psychological evolution of civilization, including such topics as the double, agape and eros, religious kingship, immortality, the Jews and civilization, and feminine psychology. Originally published in 1941.

Rank, Otto, and Sachs, Hanns. "The Significance of Psychoanalysis for the Humanities." Translated by Charles R. Payne. AMERICAN IMAGO 21 (Spring-Summer 1964): 7-128.

A translation of an early psychoanalytic approach to culture, originally published in 1913. Includes chapters on myth and legend and on religion.

Ricketts, M.L. "Anthropological Psychoanalysis of Religion." HISTORY OF RELIGIONS 11 (August 1971): 147-56.

Ricoeur, Paul. FREUD AND PHILOSOPHY: AN ESSAY ON INTERPRETATION. Translated by Denis Savage. New Haven, Conn.: Yale University Press, 1970. xv, 573 p.

A massive and at times difficult work by a French philosopher of religion. Includes a summary of Freud's views on religion and culture, and develops some of the implications of psychoanalysis for the interpretation of religious symbols.

Rieff, Philip. "The Meaning of History and Religion in Freud's Thought." JOURNAL OF RELIGION 31 (1951): 114-31. Also published in PSYCHO-ANALYSIS AND HISTORY, pp. 23-44. Edited by Bruce Mazlish. Englewood Cliffs, N.J.: Prentice-Hall, 1963.

_____. "The Authority of the Past-Sickness and Society in Freud's Thought." SOCIAL RESEARCH 21 (1954): 428-50.

_____. FREUD: THE MIND OF THE MORALIST. Garden City, N.Y.: Doubleday & Co., 1959. xxvi, 441 p.

An interpretation of the cultural and religious significance of Freud. Probes the moral implications of the replacement of nineteenth-century economic man with the emerging type of "psychological man."

_____. THE TRIUMPH OF THE THERAPEUTIC: USES OF FAITH AFTER FREUD. New York: Harper & Row, Publishers, 1966. 274 p.

Investigates the influence of Freud and his followers on the Western world, particularly in terms of modern man's self-understanding. Specifically criticizes Jung, Reich, and D.H. Lawrence for their deviation from Freud's stoicism, skepticism, and avoidance of comforting religious ideas.

Roheim, Geza. "The Psycho-Analytic Interpretation of Culture." INTERNA-
TIONAL JOURNAL OF PSYCHOANALYSIS 22 (1941): 147-69.

_____. THE ORIGIN AND FUNCTION OF CULTURE. Garden City, N.Y.:
Doubleday & Co., 1971. 146 p.

Originally published in 1943, this essay by a psychoanalytic anthropologist discusses the security-providing function of religion and
culture.

Rubenstein, Richard L. THE RELIGIOUS IMAGINATION; A STUDY OF PSY-
CHOANALYSIS AND JEWISH THEOLOGY. Indianapolis: The Bobbs-Merrill
Co., 1968. xx, 246 p.

Compares psychoanalysis and the rabbinic imagination as revealed
in materials from the Aggadah.

Sauty, Roger. PSYCHANALYSE ET RELIGION: ETUDE PSYCHANALYTIQUE,
PHILOSOPHIQUE ET THEOLOGIQUE DES GRANDS PROBLEMES RELIGIEUX.
Geneva: Perret-Gentil, 1965. 316 p.

Scharfenberg, Joachim. SIGMUND FREUD UND SEINE RELIGIONSKRITIK ALS
HERAUSFORDERUNG FUR DEN CHRISTLICHEN GLAUBEN. Gottingen: Vandenhoeck und Ruprecht, 1968. 221 p.

Addresses Freud's critique of religion from the perspective of his
general theory, his therapeutic concepts, and his specific views on
religion. The therapy chapter, concerned with healing through
speech, has particular importance for theological interpretation.

Schonau, Walter. SIGMUND FREUD'S PROSA: LITERARISCHE ELEMENTE
SEINES STILS. Stuttgart: Metzlersche Verlags Buchhanglung, 1968. 296 p.

Noting the similarity of Freud's prose style to that of Lessing,
the author analyzes the elements of his style, including his
archeological metaphors and allegorical images, in relation
to his theory of culture.

Singer, David. "Ludwig Lewisohn and Freud: The Zionist Therapeutic." PSY-
CHOANALYTIC REVIEW 58 (1971): 169-82.

Singer, June K. "Religion and the Collective Unconscious: Common Ground
of Psychology and Religion." ZYGON 4 (December 1969): 315-32.

Smiley, Blanton. "Freud and Theology." PASTORAL COUNSELOR 1, no. 2
(1963): 3-8.

Steindletz, E. "Hasidism and Psychoanalysis." Translated by A. Holtz. JUDA-
ISM 9 (Summer 1960): 222-28.

Sullivan, John J. "Two Psychologies and the Study of Religion." JOURNAL FOR THE SCIENTIFIC STUDY OF RELIGION 1 (1961-62): 155-64.

A comparison of psychoanalytic and behavioristic orientations in the study of religion.

Taubes, Jacob. "Religion and the Future of Psychoanalysis." PSYCHOANALY-SIS. (Special double issue replacing vol. 4, no. 4 and vol. 5, no. 1, 1956-57): 136-42.

Tiebout, Harry M., Jr. "Freud and Theology." RELIGION IN LIFE 27 (1958): 266-75.

Trilling, Lionel. FREUD AND THE CRISIS OF OUR CULTURE. Boston: Beacon Press, 1955. 55 p.

Weiss-Rosmarin, Trude. "Adler's Psychology and the Jewish Tradition." JOUR-NAL OF INDIVIDUAL PSYCHOLOGY 14 (1958): 142-52.

White, Victor. GOD AND THE UNCONSCIOUS. London: The Harvill Press, 1952. xxv, 277 p.

A collection of essays by a Jungian Catholic theologian.

Wucherer-Huldenfeld, Augustinus. "Was Versteht Freud unter Religion?" JAHR-BUCH FUR PSYCHOLOGIE, PSYCHOTHERAPIE UND MEDIZINISCHE ANTHRO-POLOGIE 15 (1967): 209-16.

Zilboorg, Gregory. "Freud et la religion." SUPPLEMENT DE LA VIE SPIRI-TUELLE 12 (1959): 251-94.

_____. "Psychoanalysis and Religion." PASTORAL PSYCHOLOGY 10 (November 1959): 41-48.

_____. PSYCHOANALYSIS AND RELIGION. New York: Farrar, Straus and Cudahy, 1962. 243 p.

A heterogeneous but solid collection of essays by an analyst.

A:5 EXISTENTIAL, HUMANISTIC, AND PHENOMENOLOGICAL PSYCHOLOGY

Binswanger, Ludwig. BEING-IN-THE-WORLD. Translated by Jacob Needle-man. New York: Basic Books, 1963. 364 p.

A major work by the father of existential psychiatry, with a solid introduction by the translator. Stresses the individual's imbedded-ness in a world or "meaning-matrix" and develops the implications of this emphasis in several clinical papers.

Bregman, Lucy. "Growing Old Together: Temporality, Mutuality, and Performance in the Thought of Alfred Schutz and Erik Erikson." JOURNAL OF RELIGION 53 (April 1973): 195-215.

Bugental, J.F.T. THE SEARCH FOR AUTHENTICITY: AN EXISTENTIAL ANALYTIC APPROACH TO PSYCHOTHERAPY. New York: Holt, Rinehart and Winston, 1965. xix, 437 p.

A theory of existential analysis based on the views of Tillich, Buber, Rogers, May, Fromm, and others.

Caruso, Igor A. EXISTENTIAL PSYCHOLOGY: FROM ANALYSIS TO SYNTHESIS. New York: Herder and Herder, 1964. xx, 227 p.

Criticizes most modern psychology for its failure to take man's "spiritual existence" seriously. Applies existential concepts in the analysis of case materials.

Edie, James M. "William James and the Phenomenology of Religious Experience." In AMERICAN PHILOSOPHY AND THE FUTURE, pp. 247-69. Edited by Michael Novak. New York: Charles Scribner's Sons, 1968.

_____. "The Genesis of a Phenomenological Theory of the Experience of Personal Identity: William James on Consciousness and the Self." MIND AND WORLD 6 (September 1973): 322-40.

Ehman, Robert R. "William James and the Structure of the Self." In NEW ESSAYS IN PHENOMENOLOGY, pp. 256-70. Edited by James M. Edie. Chicago: Quadrangle, 1969.

Ettinger, Ronald F., and Walker, Eugene C. "Behaviorism and Existentialism: Views of Skinner and Tillich." JOURNAL OF RELIGION AND HEALTH 5, no. 2 (1966): 151-57.

Gendlin, Eugene T. EXPERIENCING AND THE CREATION OF MEANING: A PHILOSOPHICAL AND PSYCHOLOGICAL APPROACH TO THE SUBJECTIVE. New York: The Free Press, 1962. xv, 300 p.

A thought-provoking work in philosophical psychology, influenced by both phenomenology and client-centered therapy. Touches only briefly on specifically religious matters, but is of interest for dealing with questions of experience, symbolization, and meaning.

Graves, Clare W. "Levels of Existence: An Open System Theory of Values." JOURNAL OF HUMANISTIC PSYCHOLOGY 10 (1970): 131-56.

Hammes, John A. HUMANISTIC PSYCHOLOGY: A CHRISTIAN INTERPRETATION. New York: Grune & Stratton, 1971. xv, 203 p.

Discusses the compatibility of psychological science and Christian theology, with attention to such topics as guilt, God, and motivation.

Kaam, Adrian van. EXISTENTIAL FOUNDATIONS OF PSYCHOLOGY. Pittsburgh: Duquesne University Press, 1966. xiv, 386 p.

An impressive effort to address psychology from a broad existential perspective. Emphasizes such existentialist categories as freedom, intentionality, and immediate experience.

Klee, James B. "Religion as Facing Forward in Time." EXISTENTIAL INQUIRY 1, no. 2 (1960): 19-32.

Linschofen, Hans. ON THE WAY TOWARD A PHENOMENOLOGICAL PSYCHOLOGY: THE PSYCHOLOGY OF WILLIAM JAMES. Translated by Ameded Giorgio. Pittsburgh: Duquesne University Press, 1968. 319 p.

Originally published in Dutch in 1958, the author argues that James can be recognized as both phenomenologist and Gestaltist.

Lynch, William F. "The Act of Wishing vs. the Willful Act." REVIEW OF EXISTENTIAL PSYCHOLOGY AND PSYCHIATRY 4, no. 3 (1964): 213-24.

McLeod, Robert, ed. WILLIAM JAMES: UNFINISHED BUSINESS. Washington, D.C.: American Psychological Association, 1970. 120 p.

A collection of essays and discussions presented at the seventy-fifth convention of the American Psychological Association. Of special interest to psychologists of religion is the Rollo May essay, "James and Humanism and the Problem of Will."

Maddi, Salvatore R., and Costa, Paul T. HUMANISM IN PERSONOLOGY: ALLPORT, MASLOW, AND MURRAY. Chicago: Aldine-Atherton, 1972. xvii, 200 p.

A study of three humanistic psychologists, with attention to peak experience, prejudice, and projection theory.

May, Rollo. MAN'S SEARCH FOR HIMSELF. New York: W.W. Norton & Co., 1953. 239 p.

See annotation in section G:3.

_____. "Creativity and Encounter." UNION SEMINARY QUARTERLY REVIEW 18 (1962-63): 369-76.

_____. "Creativity and the Unconscious." HUMANITAS 1 (1966): 295-312.

_____. PSYCHOLOGY AND THE HUMAN DILEMMA. New York: Van Nostrand Reinhold Co., 1967. 221 p.

Explores the problems faced by modern man from an existential perspective. The essays "Anxiety and Values" and "A Phenomenological Approach to Psychotherapy" are of particular interest to psychologists of religion.

_____. EXISTENTIAL PSYCHOLOGY. New York: Random House, 1969. 117 p.

_____, ed. EXISTENCE: A NEW DIMENSION IN PSYCHIATRY AND PSYCHOLOGY. New York: Basic Books, 1958. 445 p.

A major attempt to employ existential concepts in psychological theory. Strong Tillichian emphasis.

Meerloo, Joost A.M. CREATIVITY AND ETERNIZATION; ESSAYS ON THE CREATIVE INSTINCT. New York: Humanities Press, 1968. 272 p.

O'Connell, Walter [E.]. "Practicing Christianity and Humanistic Identification." JOURNAL OF HUMANISTIC PSYCHOLOGY 4, no. 2 (1964): 118-29.

Robb, J.W. "Hidden Philosophical Agenda: A Commentary on Humanistic Psychology." JOURNAL OF THE AMERICAN ACADEMY OF RELIGION 37 (March 1969): 3-14.

Royce, Joseph R. "Psychology, Existentialism, and Religion." JOURNAL OF GENERAL PSYCHOLOGY 66 (1962): 3-16.

_____. THE ENCAPSULATED MAN: AN INTERDISCIPLINARY ESSAY ON THE SEARCH FOR MEANING. New York: Van Nostrand Reinhold Co., 1964. 206 p.

A philosopher's effort, through a neo-Kantian perspective, to present an integrated view of the "psychology of man." Special attention to cognition, value, meaning, symbol, and myth.

Ruitenbeck, Hendrik M., ed. PSYCHOANALYSIS AND EXISTENTIAL PHILOSOPHY. New York: E.P. Dutton & Co., 1962. 262 p.

Papers by Paul Tillich, Ludwig Binswanger, Rollo May, and others. Particular emphasis on the existential condition which underlies pathology.

Sadler, William A., Jr. EXISTENCE AND LOVE: A NEW APPROACH IN EXISTENTIAL PHENOMENOLOGY. New York: Charles Scribner's Sons, 1969. xiv, 427 p.

Spiegelberg, Herbert. PHENOMENOLOGY IN PSYCHOLOGY AND PSYCHIA-
TRY: A HISTORICAL INTRODUCTION. Evanston, Ill.: Northwestern University Press, 1972. xxv, 411 p.

> A comprehensive survey of the influence of phenomenology on
> psychology and psychiatry.

Straus, Erwin W. PHENOMENOLOGICAL PSYCHOLOGY. Translated by Er-
ling Eng. New York: Basic Books, 1966. xiii, 353 p.

> Based on a Heideggerian interest in "being-in-the-world," this
> study criticizes modern psychology for understanding psychic events
> as epiphenomena of physiological processes, and recommends a
> psychological understanding of such events as modes of being. Ap-
> plies this view in a series of studies of normal and pathological
> situations.

Strauss, Anselm L. MIRRORS AND MASKS: THE SEARCH FOR IDENTITY.
Glencoe, Ill.: Free Press, 1959. 186 p.

> More in the tradition of George Herbert Mead than Erik Erikson,
> Strauss discusses the strategies and consequences of social inter-
> action: status, control, turning points, and sense of continuity.

Van den Berg, J.H. THE CHANGING NATURE OF MAN: INTRODUCTION
TO A HISTORICAL PSYCHOLOGY. New York: Dell Publishing Co., 1964.
252 p.

> Argues that human nature undergoes real changes, that major dis-
> coveries (Luther's of the inner man, Rousseau's of the child's na-
> ture, and Freud's of the unconscious) are not merely articulations
> of what had always been present but represent genuine alterations
> in human nature.

Wilshire, Bruce. WILLIAM JAMES AND PHENOMENOLOGY: A STUDY OF
"THE PRINCIPLES OF PSYCHOLOGY." Bloomington: Indiana University Press,
1968. 251 p.

Section B

THE MYTHOLOGICAL DIMENSION OF RELIGION

Section B

THE MYTHOLOGICAL DIMENSION OF RELIGION

B:1 GENERAL STUDIES OF MYTH AND SYMBOLS

Abon Zeid, A. "La Psychanalyse des mythes." EGYPTIAN JOURNAL PSY-
CHOLOGY 2 (1946): 233-51.

Abraham, Karl. DREAMS AND MYTHS: A STUDY IN RACE PSYCHOLOGY.
Translated by William A. White. New York: The Journal of Nervous and
Mental Disease Publishing Co., 1913. 74 p. Also published as "Dreams and
Myths: A Study in Race Psychology." In CLINICAL PAPERS AND ESSAYS ON
PSYCHOANALYSIS, vol. 2, pp. 153-209. By Karl Abraham. Translated by
Hilda C. Abraham and D.R. Ellison. London: The Hogarth Press, 1955.

Almansi, Renato J. "Ego-Psychological Implications of a Religious Symbol: A
Cultural and Experimental Study." PSYCHOANALYTIC STUDY OF SOCIETY 3
(1964): 39-70.

Arlow, Jacob A. "Ego Psychology and the Study of Mythology." JOURNAL
OF THE AMERICAN PSYCHOANALYTIC ASSOCIATION 1 (1961): 371-93.

> Correlates different mythological expressions of the same basic theme
> with defenses selected by the cultural needs of given social groups.
> Examples discussed are Jack and the Beanstalk, Prometheus, and
> Moses receiving the law at Sinai.

Bachelard, Gaston. THE PSYCHOANALYSIS OF FIRE. Boston: Beacon Press,
1964. 115 p.

> Noting that fire is no longer of scientific interest, this study seeks
> to understand the continuing primitive or poetic interests which
> prompted its emergence as a scientific datum and now sustain it as
> a symbolic phenomenon.

Barbour, Ian G. MYTHS, MODELS, AND PARADIGMS: A COMPARATIVE
STUDY IN SCIENCE AND RELIGION. New York: Harper & Row, Publishers, 1974. 198 p.

Of special interest to the psychologist of religion is the book's emphasis on mythical language and its role in everyday life.

Baudouin, Charles. PSYCHANALYSE DU SYMBOLE RELIGIEUX. Paris: Librairie Artheme Fayard, 1957. 285 p.

Psychoanalytic studies of French authors, of Don Quixote, Saint John of the Cross, anxiety, festivals, and other topics, around the themes of individuation and communion.

Burke, Kenneth. "Myth, Poetry and Philosophy." JOURNAL OF AMERICAN FOLKLORE 73 (1960): 283-306.

Discusses Freud.

Calogeras, Roy C. "Levi-Strauss and Freud: Their 'Structural' Approaches to Myth." AMERICAN IMAGO 30 (1973): 57-79.

Campbell, Joseph. THE MASKS OF GOD: PRIMITIVE MYTHOLOGY. New York: The Viking Press, 1959. 504 p.

The mythology of primitive hunters and planters, with chapters on shamanism, the psychology of myths, and the function of myths in the stone ages.

_____. THE FLIGHT OF THE GARDEN: EXPLORATIONS IN THE MYTHOLOGICAL DIMENSION. 2nd ed. Chicago: Henry Regnery Co., 1972. 248 p.

A collection of Campbell's essays on fairy tales, the biopsychological function of mythology, theology as mythology, mythogenesis, and secularization.

_____, ed. MYTHS, DREAMS AND RELIGION. New York: E.P. Dutton & Co., 1970. 355 p.

A series of lectures sponsored by the Society for the Arts, Religion and Contemporary Culture. Includes essays of a psychological nature by Rollo May and Ira Progoff.

Cassirer, Ernst. LANGUAGE AND MYTH. Translated by Susanne K. Langer. New York: Harper & Brothers, 1946. 103 p.

_____. MYTHICAL THOUGHT. Translated by Ralph Manheim. The Philosophy of Symbolic Forms, vol. 2. New Haven and London: Yale University Press, 1955.

An important effort by a neo-Kantian philosopher to overcome modern philosophy's bias against mythical modes of thought.

Cox, Howard L. "The Place of Mythology in the Study of Culture." AMERI-

CAN IMAGO 5 (1948): 83-94.

Durand, Gilbert. LES STRUCTURES ANTHROPOLOGIQUES DE L'IMAGINAIRE INTRODUCTION A L'ARCHETYPOLOGIE GENERALE. Paris: Bordas, 1969. 550 p.

Edelheit, Henry. "Mythopoesis and the Primal Scene." PSYCHOANALYTIC STUDY OF SOCIETY 5 (1972): 212-33.

Eliade, Mircea. MYTHS, DREAMS, AND MYSTERIES; THE ENCOUNTER BE-TWEEN CONTEMPORARY FAITHS AND ARCHAIC REALITIES. Translated by Philip Mairet. New York: Harper & Row, Publishers, 1961. 256 p.

Discusses similarities and differences in the ways historians of religion and depth psychologists study and interpret myths.

_____. IMAGES AND SYMBOLS: STUDIES IN RELIGIOUS SYMBOLISM. New York: Sheed and Ward, 1969. 189 p. Paris: Gallimard, 1952.

The opening section presents a critique of psychoanalytic views of symbolism by an historian of religions.

Fontenrose, Joseph Eddy. THE RITUAL THEORY OF MYTH. Berkeley: University of California Press, 1966. 77 p.

Fortes, Meyer. OEDIPUS AND JOB IN WEST AFRICAN RELIGION. New York: Cambridge University Press, 1959. 81 p.

Gargiulo, Gerald J. "Theoretical Models and the Psychological Understanding of Symbols." CROSS CURRENTS 21 (1971): 155-64.

Gedo, John E. "Mythopoesis and Psychoanalysis." AMERICAN IMAGO 27 (1970): 329-37.

Gordon, Rosemary. "Symbols: Content and Process." JOURNAL OF ANALYT-ICAL PSYCHOLOGY 12 (1967): 23-34.

Grotjahn, Martin. THE VOICE OF THE SYMBOL. Los Angeles: Mara Books, 1971. xv, 224 p.

A psychoanalyst's look at the past and future, using the symbol as the key to psychic integration. Includes suggestive discussions of oedipus mythology, medieval Christian art, and television.

Hacker, Frederick J. "The Reality of Myth." INTERNATIONAL JOURNAL OF PSYCHOANALYSIS 45 (1964): 438-43.

Henderson, Joseph L., and Oakes, Maud. THE WISDOM OF THE SERPENT:

THE MYTHS OF DEATH, REBIRTH AND RESURRECTION. New York: George Braziller, 1963. xxiv, 262 p.

> A Jungian approach to myths concerned with the theme of death. Gives special attention to myths related to rites of initiation involving ritual death.

Herzog, Edgar. PSYCHE AND DEATH: ARCHAIC MYTHS AND MODERN DREAMS IN ANALYTICAL PSYCHOLOGY. Translated by David Cox and Eugene Rolfe. New York: G.P. Putnam's Sons, 1967. 224 p.

> See annotation in section G:7.

Hodges, Donald Clark. "Fratricide and Fraternity." JOURNAL OF RELIGION 38 (1958): 240-50.

Jacobsohn, Helmuth, et al. TIMELESS DOCUMENTS OF THE SOUL. Evanston, Ill.: Northwestern University Press, 1968. xii, 263 p.

> Three essays from a Jungian perspective on an ancient Egyptian text, mythological elements in the dreams of Descartes, and a central concept of early Hasidic literature.

Jung, C [arl] G. SYMBOLS OF TRANSFORMATION: AN ANALYSIS OF THE PRELUDE TO A CASE OF SCHIZOPHRENIA. Translated by R.F.C. Hull. COLLECTED WORKS, vol. 5. New York: Pantheon Books, 1956. xxix, 567 p.

> Translated from the fourth edition of 1952, this work, first published in 1912, was Jung's earliest important work in his move away from Freud. He proposes alternative theories of religion. His analysis of the fantasies of a young American woman who became schizophrenic examines closely her use of religious symbolism, including themes of rebirth, the hero, and the Great Mother.

_____. THE ARCHETYPES AND THE COLLECTIVE UNCONSCIOUS. Translated by R.F.C. Hull. COLLECTED WORKS, vol. 9, pt. 1. Princeton, N.J.: Princeton University Press, 1959. 451 p.

> Collects Jung's major statements on the archetypes, including the anima, the mother, the child, and the trickster, as well as essays on fairy tales and mandala symbolism.

_____. AION: RESEARCHES INTO THE PHENOMENOLOGY OF THE SELF. Translated by R.F.C. Hull. COLLECTED WORKS, vol. 9, pt. 2. Princeton, N.J.: Princeton University Press, 1959. 333 p.

> A major statement of the self and its symbolism, Christ as a symbol of the self, fish symbolism, Christian alchemy, and gnosticism.

_____. MYSTERIUM CONIUNCTIONIS; AN INQUIRY INTO THE SEPARATION AND SYNTHESIS OF PSYCHIC OPPOSITES IN ALCHEMY. Translated by R.F.C. Hull. COLLECTED WORKS, vol.14. New York: Pantheon Books, 1963. xix, 704 p.

Jung views alchemy as a "meaningful historical basis" for modern psychology, doing so on the grounds that alchemy, like modern psychology, involved both analysis and synthesis. Includes a wealth of materials on legend, art, religion, physics, and biology.

_____. ALCHEMICAL STUDIES. Translated by R.F.C. Hull. COLLECTED WORKS, vol. 13. Princeton, N.J.: Princeton University Press, 1967. xiii, 444 p.

Essays on a Taoist text, Zosimos, Paracelsus, Mercurius, and the symbol of the tree.

_____. PSYCHOLOGY AND ALCHEMY. 2nd ed. Translated by R.F.C. Hull. COLLECTED WORKS, vol. 12. Princeton, N.J.: Princeton University Press, 1968. xxv, 581 p.

A major text in Jung's later work on religion. Relates dream symbolism to alchemy and the mandala, and examines the psychic nature of alchemical work. Discusses such religious ideas in alchemy as the Lapis-Christ parallel.

_____, ed. MAN AND HIS SYMBOLS. Garden City, N.Y.: Doubleday & Co., 1964. 320 p.

A collection of essays by Jungian analysts which probe the nature and function of symbols in ancient and modern cultures.

Jung, C [arl] G., and Kerenyi, C. ESSAYS ON A SCIENCE OF MYTHOLOGY: THE MYTH OF THE DIVINE CHILD AND THE MYSTERIES OF ELEUSIS. Translated by R.F.C. Hull. New York: Bollingen Foundation, 1963. 200 p.

Essays by a classicist and a psychologist. Includes major essays on the image of the divine child and the Great Mother.

Karlson, Karl Johan. "Psychoanalysis and Mythology." JOURNAL OF RELIGIOUS PSYCHOLOGY 7 (1914): 137-213.

Kirk, G.S. MYTH: ITS MEANING AND FUNCTION IN ANCIENT AND OTHER CULTURES. Berkeley and Los Angeles: University of California Press, 1970. 299 p.

A classicist's discussion of the relations among myth, ritual, and folktale; Levi-Strauss' approach to myths; the distinctive qualities of Greek myths; and the diverse functions of myth. Includes a brief discussion of Freudian and Jungian perspectives.

McCully, Robert S. RORSCHACH THEORY OF SYMBOLISM. Baltimore: The Williams & Wilkins Co., 1971. xxi, 271 p.

A study of Jung and Rorschach on the nature and purpose of symbolism as it relates to personality and culture.

Malinowski, Bronislaw. MYTH IN PRIMITIVE PSYCHOLOGY. New York: W. W. Norton & Co., 1926. 94 p.

> The author contests Freud's Oedipus theory of myth on the basis of anthropological evidence.

_____. "The Role of Myth in Life." PSYCHE 24 (1926): 29–39.

Moloney, James Clark. "The Psychosomatic Aspects of Myths." AMERICAN IMAGO 18 (1961): 57–64.

Moody, Robert. "On Jung's Concept of the Symbol." BRITISH JOURNAL OF MEDICAL PSYCHOLOGY 29 (1956): 9–14.

Moon, Sheila. A MAGIC DWELLS: A POETIC AND PSYCHOLOGICAL STUDY OF THE NAVAHO EMERGENCE MYTH. Middleton, Conn.: Wesleyan University Press, 1970. 206 p.

Murray, Henry A. "The Possible Nature of a 'Mythology' to Come." In MYTH AND MYTHMAKING, pp. 300–52. Edited by Henry A. Murray. New York: George Braziller, 1960. Reprint. Boston: Beacon Press, 1968.

> An important essay, summarizing and criticizing several theories of myth by reducing these to a series of definitional statements of myth.

Neale, Robert E. "Man: The Teller of Tales." UNION SEMINARY QUARTERLY REVIEW 17 (January 1962): 153–61.

Neumann, Erich. THE ORIGINS AND HISTORY OF CONSCIOUSNESS. Translated by R.F.C. Hull. Princeton, N.J.: Princeton University Press, 1954. xxiv, 493 p.

> One of Jung's foremost disciples traces the parallel archetypal stages in the evolution of mythology and the development of personality, emphasizing matriarchal symbolism. Originally published in German in 1949.

Progoff, Ira. THE SYMBOLIC AND THE REAL: A NEW PSYCHOLOGICAL APPROACH TO THE FULLER EXPERIENCE OF PERSONAL EXISTENCE. New York: McGraw-Hill, 1963. xv, 234 p.

> See annotation in section G:3.

Rank, Otto. PSYCHOANALYTISCHE BEITRAGE ZUR MYTHENFORSHUNG AUS DEN JAHREN 1912 BIS 1914. Leipzig: Internationaler Psychoanalytischer Verlag, 1922. 184 p.

_____. THE TRAUMA OF BIRTH. London: Routledge and Kegan Paul, 1929.

xv, 224 p.

Originally published in German in 1924, and republished in America as a Harper paperback in 1973, this work marks the turning point in Rank's career from Freudian loyalty to independence. The chapter on "Religious Sublimation" includes discussions of mysticism, incarnation, crucifixion, and father-god.

_____. THE DOUBLE: A PSYCHOANALYTIC STUDY. Translated by Harry Tucker, Jr. Chapel Hill: University of North Carolina Press, 1971. xxii, 88 p.

This important essay, originally published in 1914 and revised in 1925, presents the views of one of Freud's early followers on a striking phenomenon of literature and primitive mythology.

Reik, Theodor. DER EIGENE UND DER FREMDE GOTT. Leipzig, Vienna, and Zurich: Internationaler Psychoanalytischer Verlag, 1923.

A psychoanalytic study of religious ideas of evil, with special attention to Judas and the Devil.

_____. DOGMA AND COMPULSION: PSYCHOANALYTIC STUDIES OF RELIGION AND MYTHS. Translated by Bernard Miall. New York: International Universities Press, 1951. 332 p.

This study continues Reik's interest in the development of religion by focusing on the psychological processes in the transition from myth to dogma.

_____. MYTH AND GUILT: THE CRIME AND PUNISHMENT OF MANKIND. New York: George Braziller, 1957. xiii, 432 p.

A reinterpretation of the myth of the Fall inspired by Freud's TOTEM AND TABOO cited in section C:4.

Roheim, Geza. "Myth and Folk-Tale." AMERICAN IMAGO 2 (1941): 266-79.

_____. THE ETERNAL ONES OF THE DREAM: A PSYCHOANALYTIC INTERPRETATION OF AUSTRALIAN MYTH AND RITUAL. New York: International Universities Press, 1970. xiii, 270 p.

A wide-ranging study of primitive myths and rituals, with particular emphasis on their sexual symbolism.

_____. THE PANIC OF THE GODS AND OTHER ESSAYS. New York: Harper & Row, Publishers, 1972. xxiii, 227 p.

Rosolato, Guy. "Trois Generations d'hommes dans le mythe religieux et la genealogie." L'INCONSCIENT, no. 1, January-March 1967, pp. 71-108.

> A French psychoanalyst's model of sacrificial myths in three great monotheistic religions (Judaism, Islam, and Christianity) as a masculine trinity of three generations.

Royce, Joseph R., ed. PSYCHOLOGY AND THE SYMBOL: AN INTERDISCI-PLINARY SYMPOSIUM. New York: Random House, 1965. 117 p.

Schmidbauer, Wolfgang. MYTHOS UND PSYCHOLOGIE. Munich and Basel: Ernst Reinhardt Verlag, 1970. 181 p.

> A comprehensive study of psychological theories of myth, including theories developed by the Wundtian, Freudian, and Jungian schools, with special attention to interpretations of the Oedipus myth.

Scott, W. Clifford M. "The Psychoanalytic View of Mandala Symbols." BRITISH JOURNAL OF MEDICAL PSYCHOLOGY 22 (1949): 23-25.

Shumaker, Wayne. LITERATURE AND THE IRRATIONAL. New York: Washington Square Press, 1966. 279 p.

> Originally published in 1960, this study develops the view that literary creativity involves an unconscious appropriation of primitive myths and symbols.

Stern, Max M. "Ego Psychology, Myth and Rite: Remarks about the Relationship of the Individual and the Group." PSYCHOANALYTIC STUDY OF SOCIETY 3 (1964): 71-93.

Watts, Alan W. THE TWO HANDS OF GOD: THE MYTHS OF POLARITY. New York: George Braziller, 1963. xx, 261 p.

> Focuses on myths which have as their central meaning the ultimate reconciliation of such polar experiences as good and evil, life and death, pleasure and pain.

Wheelwright, Joseph, ed. THE REALITY OF THE PSYCHE. Proceedings of the Third International Congress for Analytical Psychology. New York: G.P. Putnam's Sons, 1968. 304 p.

> A collection of papers by Jungian psychologists, with considerable attention to myth and symbolism.

Wundt, Wilhelm Max. VOLKERPSYCHOLOGIE: EINE UNTERSUCHUNG DER ENTWICKLUNGSGESETZE VON SPRACE, MYTHUS UND SITTE. 10 vols. Leipzig: W. Engleman, 1900-20.

> A major study of folk psychology and myth by the father of modern psychology. Develops notions similar to Jung's archetype and collective unconscious.

Wysling, Hans. "MYTHOS UND PSYCHOLOGIE" BEI THOMAS MANN. Zurich: Polygraphischer Verlag, 1969. 23 p.

B:2 GREEK MYTHOLOGY

Abadi, Mauricio. "Psychoanalytic Study of the Dionysian Myth and Cult." REVISTA DE PSICOANALISIS 12 (1955): 18-39.

Borkenau, Franz. "Zwei Abhandlungen zur Griechischen Mythologie" [Two treatises on Greek mythology]. PSYCHE 11 (1957): 1-27.

Bunker, Henry Alden. "Narcissus: A Psychoanalytic Note." PSYCHOANALY-SIS AND THE SOCIAL SCIENCES 1 (1947): 159-62.

_____. "The Feast of Tantalus." PSYCHOANALYTIC QUARTERLY 21 (1952): 355-72.

_____. "Tantalus: A Preoedipal Figure of Myth." PSYCHOANALYTIC QUARTERLY 22 (1953): 159-73.

Carlisky, Mario. "Oedipus, beyond Complex." PSYCHOANALYTIC REVIEW 54 (1967): 100-106.

Chassequet-Smirgel, J. "Oedipe et religion." REVUE FRANCAISE DE PSY-CHANALYSE 31 (1967): 875-82.

Coriat, Isador H. "A Note on Medusa Symbolism." AMERICAN IMAGO 2 (1941): 281-85.

Deutsch, Helene. A PSYCHOANALYTIC STUDY OF THE MYTH OF DIONY-SUS AND APOLLO. New York: International Universities Press, 1969. 101 p.

> This psychoanalytic study addresses the myths of Dionysus and Apollo as two variants of the son-mother relationship.

Devereux, George. "Why Oedipus Killed Laius." INTERNATIONAL JOURNAL OF PSYCHOANALYSIS 34 (1953): 132-41.

_____. "Sociopolitical Function of the Oedipus Myth in Early Greece." PSYCHOANALYTIC QUARTERLY 32, no. 2 (1963): 205-14.

Eberz, Jakob. SOPHIA UND LOGOS: ODER, DIE PHILOSOPHIE DEN WIEDER-HESTELLUNG. Munich: E. Reinhardt, 1967. 615 p.

Ehrenzweig, Anton. "The Origin of the Scientific and Heroic Urge (the Guilt of Prometheus)." INTERNATIONAL JOURNAL OF PSYCHOANALYSIS 30 (1949): 108-23.

Fingarette, Herbert. "Orestes: Paradigmatic Hero of Contemporary Ego Psychology." PSYCHOANALYTIC REVIEW 50 (1963): 437-61.

Freud, Sigmund. "The Acquisition of Power over Fire". Translated by Joan Riviere. INTERNATIONAL JOURNAL OF PSYCHOANALYSIS 13 (1932): 405.

  Freud's interpretation of the myth of Prometheus.

Friedman, Joel, and Gassel, Sylvia. "Odysseus: The Return of the Primal Father." PSYCHOANALYTIC QUARTERLY 21 (1952): 215-23.

Fromm, Erich. THE FORGOTTEN LANGUAGE: AN INTRODUCTION TO THE UNDERSTANDING OF DREAMS, FAIRY TALES, AND MYTHS. New York: Grove Press, 1957. 263 p.

  In addition to general discussion of the similarity of dream and myth interpretation, this book contains an extended study of the Oedipus myth. Develops the argument that the Oedipus myth concerns political conflict between matriarchal and patriarchal societies.

Garma, Angel. "The Indoamerican Winged or Feathered Serpent, the Step Coil and the Greek Neander: The Unconscious Meaning of Serpentine Ornamentation." AMERICAN IMAGO 11 (1954): 113-45.

Golden, Lester M. "Freud's Oedipus: Its Mytho-Dramatic Basis." AMERICAN IMAGO 24 (1967): 271-82.

Hadas, Moses, and Smith, Morton. HEROES AND GODS: SPIRITUAL BIOGRAPHY IN ANTIQUITY. New York: Harper & Row, Publishers, 1965. xiv, 266 p.

  Based largely on Greek myth. Important for its reflections on the relation of myth to biography.

Harrison, Jane Ellen. EPILEGOMENA TO THE STUDY OF GREEK RELIGION AND THEMIS: A STUDY OF THE SOCIAL ORIGINS OF GREEK RELIGION. New Hyde Park, N.Y.: University Books, 1962. 600 p.

  An important study by a classicist whose work has influenced the psychological study of myth.

Herskovits, Melville, and Herskovits, Frances. "Sibling Rivalry, the Oedipus Complex, and Myth." JOURNAL OF AMERICAN FOLKLORE 71 (1958): 1-15.

Huckel, Helen. "The Tragic Guilt of Prometheus." AMERICAN IMAGO 12

(1955): 325-36.

Kerenyi, C. PROMETHEUS: ARCHETYPAL IMAGE OF HUMAN EXISTENCE.
Translated by Ralph Manheim. New York: Bollingen Foundation, 1963. xxvi,
152 p.

> Examines the Prometheus myth as formulated by Hesiod, Aeschylus,
> Shelley, and Goethe. Uses the figure of Prometheus as informing
> man's image of himself from earliest antiquity to the modern age.

Kleinschmidt, Hans J. "The Death of Elpenor." JOURNAL OF THE HILLSIDE
HOSPITAL 5 (1956): 320-27.

Kouretas, D. "Psychanalyse et mythologie: la neurose sexuelle des Danaides"
[Sexual neurosis of the Danaides]. REVUE FRANCAISE DE PSYCHANALYSE 21
(1957): 597-602.

Kursh, Charlotte O. "Heracles and the Centaur." PSYCHOANALYTIC REVIEW
55 (1968): 387-99.

Lederer, Wolfgang. "Oedipus and the Serpent." PSYCHOANALYTIC REVIEW
51 (1964): 619-44.

Marcus, Ned N. "Prometheus Reconsidered: Sublimation and Vicissitudes of
the Symbolic Ego." PSYCHOANALYTIC REVIEW 54, no. 3 (1967): 475-98.

Moloney, James Clark. "Oedipus Rex, Cu Chulain, Khepri and the Ass."
PSYCHOANALYTIC REVIEW 54 (1967): 201-47.

Mullahy, Patrick. OEDIPUS: MYTH AND COMPLEX. New York: Grove
Press, 1955. xii, 370 p.

> Not a thoroughgoing study of the Oedipus myth, but an effort to
> employ the myth as a metaphor for differences between psychologi-
> cal schools. Written by a student of Harry Stack Sullivan.

Posinsky, S.H. "Oedipal Gods and Moral Men." AMERICAN IMAGO 19
(1962): 101-25.

Schneiderman, Leo. "The Death of Apsyrtus." PSYCHOANALYTIC REVIEW
54 (1962): 159-76.

Seidenberg, Robert, and Papathomopoulos, Evangelos. "Sophocles Ajax--Mo-
rality for Madness." PSYCHOANALYTIC QUARTERLY 30 (1961): 404-12.

Spotnitz, Hyman, and Resnikoff, Philip. "The Myths of Narcissus." PSYCHO-

ANALYTIC REVIEW 41 (1954): 173-81.

_____. "The Prophecies of Tiresias." PSYCHOANALYSIS 4 (Winter 1955–56): 37–43.

Stewart, Harold. "Jocasta's Crimes." INTERNATIONAL JOURNAL OF PSY-CHOANALYSIS 42 (1961): 424-30.

Stokes, Adrian. GREEK CULTURE AND THE EGO: A PSYCHOANALYTIC SURVEY OF AN ASPECT OF GREEK CIVILIZATION AND ART. London: Tavistock Publications, 1958. 101 p.

Explores Greek art, philosophy, and religion.

Thass-Thienemann, Theodore. "Oedipus and the Sphinx." PSYCHOANALYTIC REVIEW 44 (1957): 10-33.

Vernant, Jean-Piere. MYTHE ET PENSEE CHEZ LES GRECS: ETUDES PSY-CHOLOGIE HISTORIQUE. Paris: F. Maspero, 1965. 331 p.

Ware, J.G. "Greater Still is Diana of the Ephesians." AMERICAN IMAGO 19 (1962): 253-75.

Wayne, Robert. "Prometheus and Christ." PSYCHOANALYSIS AND THE SO-CIAL SCIENCES 3 (1951): 201-19.

B:3   SEMITIC MYTHS AND LEGENDS

Abraham, Karl. "Amenhotep IV: A Psychoanalytic Contribution to the Understanding of His Personality and the Monotheistic Cult of Aton." PSYCHOAN-ALYTIC QUARTERLY 4 (1935): 537-69.

Beck, Samuel J. "Abraham's Ordeal: Creation of a New Reality." PSYCHO-ANALYTIC REVIEW 50, no. 2 (1963): 334-49.

_____. "Cosmic Optimism in Some Genesis Myths." AMERICAN JOURNAL OF ORTHOPSYCHIATRY 41 (April 1971): 380-89.

Bobroff, Alvin J. "Biblical Psychodrama." GROUP PSYCHOTHERAPY 15, no. 2 (1962): 129-31.

An interpretation of the story of Joseph and his brothers.

Brenner, Arthur B. "The Covenant with Abraham." PSYCHOANALYTIC REVIEW 39 (1952): 34-52.

_____. "Onan, the Levirate Marriage, and the Genealogy of the Messiah." JOURNAL OF THE AMERICAN PSYCHOANALYTIC ASSOCIATION 10 (1962): 701-21.

Chandler, Tertius. "Ikhnaton and Moses." AMERICAN IMAGO 19 (1962): 127-39.

Cohen, Sheldon. "The Ontogenesis of Prophetic Behavior: A Study in Creative Conscience Formation." PSYCHOANALYSIS AND THE PSYCHOANALYTIC REVIEW 49, no. 1 (1962): 100-22.

de Monchy, S.J.R. "Adam-Cain-Oedipus." AMERICAN IMAGO 19 (1962): 3-17.

Desmonde, William H. "The Murder of Moses." AMERICAN IMAGO 7 (1950): 351-67.

Dreifuss, Gustav. "Isaac, the Sacrificial Lamb: A Study of Some Jewish Legends." JOURNAL OF ANALYTICAL PSYCHOLOGY 16, no. 1 (1971): 69-78.

_____. "The Figures of Satan and Abraham: In the Legends on Genesis 22, the Akedah." JOURNAL OF ANAYLTICAL PSYCHOLOGY 17 (July 1972): 166-78.

Feldman, A. Bronson. "The Word in the Beginning." PSYCHOANALYTIC REVIEW 51 (1964): 79-98.

Feldman, Arthur A. "The Davidic Dynasty and the Davidic Messiah." AMERICAN IMAGO 17 (1960): 163-78.

Feldman, Sandor S. "The Sin of Reuben, First-Born of Jacob." PSYCHOANALYSIS AND THE SOCIAL SCIENCES 4 (1955): 282-87.

_____. "Patterns in Obedience and Disobedience." AMERICAN IMAGO 26 (1969): 21-36.

Fingert, Hyman H. "Psychoanalytic Study of the Minor Prophet, Jonah." PSYCHOANALYTIC REVIEW 41 (1954): 55-65.

Fodor, A. "Was Moses an Egyptian?" PSYCHOANALYSIS AND THE SOCIAL SCIENCES 3 (1951): 189-200.

_____. "The Fall of Man in the Book of Genesis." AMERICAN IMAGO 11 (1954): 203-31.

Freud, Sigmund. MOSES AND MONOTHEISM. In THE STANDARD EDITION OF THE COMPLETE PSYCHOLOGICAL WORKS OF SIGMUND FREUD, vol. 23, pp. 3-137. Edited by James Strachey. London: The Hogarth Press, 1964. (Paperback ed. of MOSES AND MONOTHEISM available from New York: Random, Vintage, 1955.)

See annotation in section E:1.

Goitein, Lionel. "The Importance of the Book of Job for Analytic Thought." AMERICAN IMAGO 11 (1954): 407-15.

_____. "Green Pastures: Psalm XXIII, Analytically Interpreted." AMERICAN IMAGO 13 (1956): 409-14.

Gonen, Jay Y. "Then Men Said, 'Let Us Make God in Our Image, after Our Likeness'." LITERATURE AND PSYCHOLOGY 21, no. 2 (1971): 69-79.

An analysis of the imagery of the creation and Eden myths, of the masculine-feminine duality in God and man, and of God as the projection of man's unattainble wishes.

Isaac-Edersheim, E. "Messias, Golem, Ahasver: Three Mythical Figures in the Hebrew Culture." Part I. INTERNATIONALE ZEITSCHRIFT FUR PSYCHOANALYSE UND IMAGO 26 (1941): 50-80.

_____. "Messias, Golem, Ahasver: Three Mythical Figures in the Hebrew Culture." Part 2. INTERNATIONAL ZEITSCHRIFT FUR PSYCHOANALYSE UND IMAGO 26 (1941): 179-213.

_____. "Messias, Golem, Ahasver: Three Mythical Figures in the Hebrew Culture." Part 3. INTERNATIONALE ZEITSCHRIFT FUR PSYCHOANALYSE UND IMAGO 26 (1941): 286-315.

Katz, Joseph. "The Joseph Dreams Anew." PSYCHOANALYTIC REVIEW 50 (1963): 252-78.

Kluger, Rivkah Scharf. SATAN IN THE OLD TESTAMENT. Translated by Hildegard Nagel. Evanston, Ill.: Northwestern University Press, 1967. xvii, 173 p.

A careful historical study influenced by Jungian psychology; translated from the original German, it was originally a 1947 Ph.D. dissertation from Zurich.

Laughlin, Henry P. "King David's Anger." PSYCHOANALYTIC QUARTERLY 23 (1954): 87-95.

Leschnitzer, Adolf F. "Faust and Moses." AMERICAN IMAGO 6 (December 1949): 229-43.

Levin, A.J. "Oedipus and Samson, the Rejected Hero-Child." INTERNA-
TIONAL JOURNAL OF PSYCHOANALYSIS 38 (1957): 105-16.

Levy, Ludwig. "Die Sexual Symbolik des Ackerbaus im Bibel und Talmud."
ZEITSCHRIFT FUR SEXUALWISSENSCHAFT 2 (1916): 437-44.

Locke, Norman. "A Myth of Ancient Egypt." AMERICAN IMAGO 18 (1961):
105-28.

Lynch, Thomas H. "Corroboration of Jungian Psychology in the Biblical Story
of Abraham." PSYCHOTHERAPY: THEORY, RESEARCH AND PRACTICE 8
(Winter 1971): 315-18.

Micklem, Nathaniel. PROPHECY AND ESCHATOLOGY. London: George
Allen and Unwin, 1926. 248 p.

   A psychological study of Elijah, Amos, Hosea, and other Hebrew
   prophets.

More, Joseph. "The Prophet Jonah: The Story of an Intrapsychic Process."
AMERICAN IMAGO 27 (1970): 3-11.

Niederland, William G. "Jacob's Dream: With Some Remarks on Ladder and
River Symbolism." JOURNAL OF THE HILLSIDE HOSPITAL 3 (1954): 73-97.

Petrus, Earl P. "The Golem: Significance of the Legend." PSYCHOANALY-
TIC REVIEW 53 (1966): 63-68.

Pruyser, Paul W. "Nathan and David: A Psychological Footnote." PASTORAL
PSYCHOLOGY 13 (February 1962): 14-18.

Reik, Theodor. "The Face of God." PSYCHOANALYSIS 3 (Winter 1955): 3-26.

_____. THE TEMPTATION. New York: George Braziller, 1961. 256 p.

   A psychoanalytic interpretation of the story of Abraham and Isaac
   in terms of initiation rites.

Reisner, Erwin. LE DEMON ET SON IMAGE. Translated by Jean Viret.
Bruges: Desclee de Brouwer, 1961. 237 p.

Roheim, Geza. "The Covenant of Abraham." INTERNATIONAL JOURNAL
OF PSYCHOANALYSIS 20 (1939): 452-59.

Rosenfeld, Eva M. "The Pan-Headed Moses--A Parallel." INTERNATIONAL
JOURNAL OF PSYCHOANALYSIS 32 (1951): 83-93.

Rosenzweig, Efraim M. "Some Notes, Historical and Psychoanalytical, on the People of Israel and the Land of Israel with Special Reference to Deuteronomy." AMERICAN IMAGO 1 (1939-40): 50-64.

Rubenstein, Richard L. "Psychoanalysis and the Origins of Judaism." RECONSTRUCTIONIST 26 (December 2, 1960): 11-20.

_____. "The Significance of Castration Anxiety in Rabbinic Mythology." PSYCHOANALYTIC REVIEW 50 (1963): 289-312.

Sachs, Hanns. "At the Gates of Heaven." AMERICAN IMAGO 4 (April 1947): 15-32.

Schlossman, Howard H. "God the Father and His Sons." AMERICAN IMAGO 29 (1972): 35-52.

Schnaper, Nathan, and Schnaper, William H. "A Few Kind Words for the Devil." JOURNAL OF RELIGION AND HEALTH 8 (1969): 108-22.

Compares role of devil in Jewish lore and in psychotherapy.

Szondi, L. "Thanatos and Cain." AMERICAN IMAGO 21 (Fall-Winter 1964): 52-63.

Theodoropoulos, Jane. "Adam's Rib." PSYCHOANALYTIC REVIEW 54, no. 3 (1967): 150-52.

Trevett, Laurence D. "Origin of the Creation Myth: A Hypothesis." JOURNAL OF THE AMERICAN PSYCHOANALYTIC ASSOCIATION 5 (1957): 461-68.

Weiss, Samuel A. "The Biblical Story of Ruth: Analytic Implications of the Hebrew Masoretic Text." AMERICAN IMAGO 16 (1959): 195-209.

Wilbur, George B. "The Reciprocal Relationship of Man and His Ideological Milieu: A Primal Scene from Ancient Egypt and Its Role in the Genesis of a Cosmology." AMERICAN IMAGO 3 (February 1946): 3-48.

Wolff, Werner. CHANGING CONCEPTS OF THE BIBLE: A PSYCHOLOGICAL ANALYSIS OF ITS WORDS, SYMBOLS AND BELIEFS. New York: Hermitage House, 1951. 463 p.

Uses an amalgam of depth psychological approaches, principally Jungian, to develop an understanding of the story of creation in comparison with other myths and symbols.

Zeligs, Dorothy F. "Two Episodes in the Life of Jacob." AMERICAN IMAGO

10 (1953): 181-203.

_____. "Abraham and Monotheism." AMERICAN IMAGO 11 (1954): 293-316.

_____. "The Personality of Joseph." AMERICAN IMAGO 12 (1955): 47-69.

_____. "A Character Study of Samuel." AMERICAN IMAGO 12 (1955): 355-85.

_____. "A Psychoanalytic Note on the Function of the Bible." AMERICAN IMAGO 14 (1957): 57-60.

_____. "Saul, the Tragic King." AMERICAN IMAGO 14 (1957): 61-85, 165-84.

_____. "The Role of the Mother in the Development of Hebraic Monotheism: As Exemplified in the Life of Abraham." PSYCHOANALYTIC STUDY OF SO-CIETY 1 (1960): 287-310.

_____. "A Study of King David." AMERICAN IMAGO 17 (1950): 179-99.

_____. "Abraham and the Covenant of the Pieces: A Study in Ambivalence." AMERICAN IMAGO 18 (1961): 173-86.

_____. "Solomon: The Man and the Myth." PSYCHOANALYSIS AND THE PSYCHOANALYTIC REVIEW 48, no. 1 (1961): 77-103; 48, no. 2 (1961): 91-110.

_____. "The Family Romance of Moses." AMERICAN IMAGO 23 (1966): 110-31.

_____. "Moses in Midian: The Burning Bush." AMERICAN IMAGO 26 (1969): 379-400.

_____. "Moses Encounters the Daemonic Aspect of God." AMERICAN IMAGO 27 (1970): 379-91.

_____. "Moses and Pharaoh: A Psychoanalytic Study of Their Encounter." AMERICAN IMAGO 30 (1973): 192-220.

Zimmerman, Frank. "The Book of Ecclesiastes in the Light of Some Psychoanalytic Observations." AMERICAN IMAGO 5 (1948): 301-5.

B:4   CHRISTIAN MYTHS AND LEGENDS

Bonaparte, Marie. "Saint Christopher, Patron Saint of the Motor-Car Driver."
AMERICAN IMAGO 4 (July 1947): 49-77.

deGroot, Adriaan D. SAINT NICHOLAS: A PSYCHOANALYTIC STUDY OF
HIS HISTORY AND MYTH. Translated by Miriam Gallaher. New York: Basic
Books; The Hague: Mouton, 1965. 211 p.

>   Contains a good history of the evolution of the Saint Nicholas
>   legends, an account of Freudian and Jungian symbol interpretation,
>   and their application to the myths, in which motifs of fertility,
>   rebirth, and regulation of commerce predominate. Proposes the
>   use of psychological interpretation to make myths meaningful to
>   modern man.

Fodor, Nandor. "The Hound of Heaven." PSYCHOANALYSIS 3 (Summer
1955): 45-49.

Freemantle, Anne. "The Oedipal Legend in Christian Hagiology." PSYCHO-
ANALYTIC QUARTERLY 19 (1950): 408-9.

>   Discusses Judas Iscariot as oedipal figure.

Jacobs, Leon I. "The Primal Crime." PSYCHOANALYTIC REVIEW 52 (1965):
456-84.

>   The Jesus-myth interpreted in terms of preoedipal matricidal, rather
>   than patricidal, impulses.

Lodge, Ann. "Satan's Symbolic Syndrome: A Psychological Interpretation of
Milton's Satan." PSYCHOANALYTIC REVIEW 43 (1956): 411-22.

Lowenfeld, Henry. "Uber den Niedergang des Teufelsglaubens und seine Folgen
fur die Massenpsychologie." PSYCHE 21 (1967): 513-19.

>   The decline in the belief in the devil and its consequences for
>   mass society.

Nicole, Albert. JUDAS THE BETRAYER: A PSYCHOLOGICAL STUDY OF
JUDAS ISCARIOT. Grand Rapids, Mich.: Baker Book House, 1957. 81 p.

Parcells, Frank H., and Segel, Nathan P. "Oedipus and the Prodigal Son."
PSYCHOANALYTIC QUARTERLY 28 (1959): 213-27.

Reider, Norman. "Medieval Oedipal Legends about Judas." PSYCHOANALY-
TIC QUARTERLY 29 (1960): 515-27.

Roheim, Geza. "Saint Agatha and the Tuesday Women." INTERNATIONAL

JOURNAL OF PSYCHOANALYSIS 27 (1946): 119-26.

Schendler, David. "Judas, Oedipus and Various Saints." PSYCHOANALYSIS 2 (Winter 1954): 41-46.

Schnier, Jacques. "The Symbolic Bird in Medieval and Renaissance Art." AMERICAN IMAGO 9 (1952): 89-126.

Skeels, Dell R. "Guingamor and Guerrehes: Psychological Symbolism in a Medieval Romance." JOURNAL OF AMERICAN FOLKLORE 79 (1966): 52-83.

Tarachow, Sidney. "Judas, the Beloved Executioner." PSYCHOANALYTIC QUARTERLY 29 (1960): 528-54.

Ulanov, Ann Belford. "The Two Strangers (Ephesians 2:11-22) in the Perspectives of Psychiatry and Religion." UNION SEMINARY QUARTERLY REVIEW 28 (Summer 1973): 273-83.

Wittels, Fritz. "Psychoanalysis and History: The Nibelungs and the Bible." PSYCHOANALYTIC QUARTERLY 15 (1946): 88-103.

Wolf, Roland. "Castration Symbolism in Patristic Thought: Preliminary Studies in the Development of Christianity." PSYCHOANALYSIS AND THE PSYCHO-ANALYTIC REVIEW 49, no. 3 (1962): 26-38.

B:5   HERO MYTHS

Allen, John Alexander, ed. HERO'S WAY: CONTEMPORARY POEMS IN THE MYTHIC TRADITION. Englewood Cliffs, N.J.: Prentice-Hall, 1971. lii, 473 p.

> Contemporary poems organized thematically according to Joseph Campbell's analysis of the heroic pattern in THE HERO WITH A THOUSAND FACES cited below. Has excellent bibliography on myth.

Bodkin, Maud. ARCHETYPAL PATTERNS IN POETRY: PSYCHOLOGICAL STUDIES OF IMAGINATION. London: Oxford University Press, 1963. xii, 340 p.

> First published in 1934, this wide-ranging but extremely learned work has served as a model for Jungian studies of myth in general and hero myths in particular. Among specific hero myths addressed in the book, the most fully developed are the ancient mariner, Satan as Promethean hero, Dante's DIVINE COMEDY, and Shakespeare's tragedies.

Campbell, Joseph. THE HERO WITH A THOUSAND FACES. New York: Bollingen Foundation, 1949. xxiii, 416 p.

A view of the mono-myth of the hero, and its corresponding cosmology, with reflections on the place of hero myths in modern culture.

Czarnowski, Stefan. LA CULTE DES HEROS ET SES CONDITIONS SOCIALES: SAINT PATRICK, HEROS NATIONAL D'IRLANDE. Paris: F. Alcan, 1919. 369 p.

Feldman, Harold. "How We Create 'Fathers' and Make Them 'Sons'." AMERICAN IMAGO 12 (1955): 71-86.

A study of hero myths.

_____. "Some Distinctions in Hero Psychology." PSYCHOANALYSIS 4 (Fall 1955): 43-52.

Fodor, Nandor. "The Hero's Rebirth." PSYCHOANALYTIC REVIEW 32 (1945): 481-98.

Lourie, Anton. "The Jewish God and the Greek Hero." AMERICAN IMAGO 5 (1948): 152-66.

Macwatters, M.R.C. "A Birth of the Hero Myth from Kashmir." INTERNATIONAL JOURNAL OF PSYCHOANALYSIS 2 (1921): 416-19.

Moloney, James Clark. "The Origin of the Rejected and Crippled Hero Myths." AMERICAN IMAGO 16 (1959): 271-328.

Norman, Dorothy. THE HERO, MYTH, IMAGE, AND SYMBOL. New York: World Publishing Co., 1969. xvii, 238 p.

Perry, John Weir. LORD OF THE FOUR QUARTERS: MYTHS OF THE ROYAL FATHER. New York: George Braziller, 1966. xvi, 272 p.

A Jungian perspective on mythology and rituals of archaic kingship.

_____. "The Messianic Hero." JOURNAL OF ANALYTICAL PSYCHOLOGY 17 (July 1972): 184-98.

Posinsky, S.H. "The Death of Mani." JOURNAL OF THE AMERICAN PSYCHOANALYTIC ASSOCIATION 5 (1957): 485-89.

Radin, Paul. THE TRICKSTER: A STUDY IN AMERICAN INDIAN MYTHOLOGY. With commentaries by C.G. Jung and Carl Kerenyi. New York: Philosophical Library, 1956. 211 p.

Raglan, F.R.R.S. THE HERO: A STUDY IN TRADITION, MYTH, AND DRAMA. London: Methuen, 1936. xi, 311 p.

A proponent of the myth-ritual school argues that hero myths are based on ritual patterns. Analyzes the mythic pattern by isolating twenty-two events in the life of the prototypical hero.

Rank, Otto. THE MYTH OF THE BIRTH OF THE HERO, AND OTHER WRITINGS. Edited by Philip Freund. New York: Alfred A. Knopf, 1959. xv, 315 p.

The title essay, originally published in 1914, is one of the earliest and most influential psychoanalytic interpretations of myth, and brings out the motifs of family romance and the mechanisms of representation in a range of heroic legends.

B:6 MYTHS OF MOTHER FIGURES AND OTHER FEMININE TYPES

Arlow, Jacob A. "The Madonna's Conception through the Eyes." PSYCHO-ANALYTIC STUDY OF SOCIETY 3 (1964): 13-25.

Bachofen, Johann Jakob. MYTH, RELIGION, AND MOTHER RIGHT: SELECTED WRITINGS OF J.J. BACHOFEN. Translated by Ralph Manheim. Princeton, N.J.: Princeton University Press, 1967. lvii, 309 p.

A nineteenth-century classical historian's controversial interpretation of the primacy of matriarchal societies. This study is important to the psychology of religion because Erich Fromm employs Bachofen's theories in his analysis of the Oedipus myth. See Fromm's THE FORGOTTEN LANGUAGE: AN INTRODUCTION TO THE UNDERSTANDING OF DREAMS, FAIRY TALES, AND MYTHS in section B:2.

Balter, Leon. "The Mother as a Source of Power: A Psychoanalytic Study of Three Greek Myths." PSYCHOANALYTIC QUARTERLY 38 (1969): 217-74.

Barag, G.G. "The Mother in the Religious Concepts of Judaism." AMERICAN IMAGO 4 (August (1946): 32-53.

Bradley, Noel. "The Vulture as Mother Symbol: A Note on Freud's Leonardo." AMERICAN IMAGO 22 (1965): 47-56.

Bunker, Henry Alden. "Mother-Murder in Myth and Legend." PSYCHOANALYTIC QUARTERLY 13 (1944): 198-207.

Chaudhuri, Arum Kumar Ray. "A Psycho-Analytic Study of the Hindu Mother

Goddess (Kali) Concept." AMERICAN IMAGO 13 (1956): 123-45.

Fodor, A. "Asherah of Ugarit." AMERICAN IMAGO 9 (1952): 127-46.

Grollman, Earl A. "Some Sights and Insights of History, Psychology and Psychoanalysis Concerning the Father-God and Mother-Goddess Concepts of Judaism and Christianity." AMERICAN IMAGO 20 (1963): 187-209.

Harding, M. Esther. WOMEN'S MYSTERIES, ANCIENT AND MODERN: A PSYCHOLOGICAL INTERPRETATION OF THE FEMININE PRINCIPLE AS PORTRAYED IN MYTH, STORY, AND DREAMS. New York: Pantheon Books, 1955. New York: G.P. Putnam's Sons, 1972. xvi, 256 p.

> A Jungian perspective on women in folk-lore, moon symbolism, and religion.

_____. THE PARENTAL IMAGE: ITS INJURY AND RECONSTRUCTION. New York: G.P. Putnam's Sons, 1965. xviii, 238 p.

> A Jungian study of the archetypal complexes of the mother and father. Emphasis on the healing value of myth.

Jones, Ernest. "The Madonna's Conception through the Ear." In ESSAYS IN APPLIED PSYCHOANALYSIS, vol. 2, pp. 266-357. Edited by Ernest Jones. London: The Hogarth Press, 1951.

Kohen, Max. "The Venus of Willendorf." AMERICAN IMAGO 3 (Feburary 1946): 49-60.

Lederer, Wolfgang. THE FEAR OF WOMEN. New York: Grune & Stratton, 1968. 360 p.

> Discusses various myths from a wide range of cultures to demonstrate the view that women, as carriers of the life force, are feared as well as revered.

Lorand, Sandor. "The Anathema of the Dead Mother." PSYCHOANALYSIS AND THE SOCIAL SCIENCES 1 (1947): 235-44.

Moloney, James Clark. "Mother, God and Superego." JOURNAL OF THE AMERICAN PSYCHOANALYTIC ASSOCIATION 2 (1954): 120-51.

Neumann, Erich. THE GREAT MOTHER: AN ANALYSIS OF THE ARCHETYPE. New York: Pantheon Books, 1955. xliii, 380 p.

> An important Jungian psychohistory of the feminine as it is expressed in the myths and symbols of primitive religions.

_____. AMOR AND PSYCHE: THE PSYCHIC DEVELOPMENT OF THE FEMININE. Translated by Ralph Manheim. New York: Pantheon Books, 1956. 181 p.

Peto, Andrew. "The Demonic Mother Imago in the Jewish Religion." PSYCHOANALYSIS AND THE SOCIAL SCIENCES 5 (1958): 280-87.

Reider, Norman. "Chess, Oedipus, and the Mater Dolorosa." INTERNATIONAL JOURNAL OF PSYCHOANALYSIS 40 (1959): 320-33.

Reik, Theodor. THE CREATION OF WOMAN. New York: George Braziller, 1960. 159 p.

A psychoanalytic interpretation of the story of Adam and Eve and other myths of the origin of women.

Roellenbleck, Ewald. MAGNA MATER IN ALTEN TESTAMENT: EINE PSY-. CHOANALYTISCHE UNTERSUCHUNG. Darmstadt: Claassen and Roether, 1949. 187 p.

Schnier, Jacques. "Dragon Lady." AMERICAN IMAGO 4 (July 1947): 78-98.

Schoenfeld, C.G. "God the Father--and Mother: Study and Extension of Freud's Conception of God as an Exalted Father." AMERICAN IMAGO 19 (1962): 214-34.

Ulanov, Ann Belford. THE FEMININE IN JUNGIAN PSYCHOLOGY AND IN CHRISTIAN THEOLOGY. Evanston, Ill.: Northwestern University Press, 1971. 347 p.

Weigert-Vowinkel, Edith. "The Cult and Mythology of the Magna Mater from the Standpoint of Psychoanalysis." PSYCHIATRY 1 (1938): 347-78.

B:7 LEGENDS AND FOLKLORE

Barnouw, V. "A Psychological Interpretation of a Chippewa Origin Legend." JOURNAL OF AMERICAN FOLKLORE 68, no. 267 (1955): 73-85.

_____. "A Psychological Interpretation of a Chippewa Origin Legend." JOURNAL OF AMERICAN FOLKLORE 68, no. 268 (1955): 211-23.

_____. "A Psychological Interpretation of a Chippewa Origin Legend." JOURNAL OF AMERICAN FOLKLORE 68, no. 269 (1955): 341-55.

Beidelman, T.O. "The Ox and Nuer Sacrifice: Some Freudian Hypotheses about Nuer Symbolism." MAN 1 (1966): 453-67.

Berne, Eric. "The Mythology of Dark and Fair: Psychiatric Use of Folklore." JOURNAL OF AMERICAN FOLKLORE 72 (1959): 1-13.

Bonaparte, Marie. "The Legend of the Unfathomable Waters." AMERICAN IMAGO 4 (August 1946): 20-31.

Bustamente, Jose Angel. "Folklore and Psychiatry." REVISTA PSIQUIATRICA PERUAVA 3 (1960): 110-24.

Desmonde, William H. "The Eternal Fire as a Symbol of the State." JOURNAL OF THE HILLSIDE HOSPITAL 2 (1953): 143-47.

Drake, Carlos C. "Jungian Psychology and Its Uses in Folklore." JOURNAL OF AMERICAN FOLKLORE 82 (1969): 122-31.

Dundes, Alan. "The Folklore of Wishing Wells." AMERICAN IMAGO 19 (1962): 27-34.

Fischer, John L. "The Sociopsychological Analysis of Folktales." CURRENT ANTHROPOLOGY 4 (1963): 235-96.

_____. "A Ponapean Oedipus Tale: Structural and Sociopsychological Analysis." JOURNAL OF AMERICAN FOLKLORE 79 (1966): 109-29.

Freeman, Derek. "Thunder, Blood, and the Nicknaming of God's Creatures." PSYCHOANALYTIC QUARTERLY 37 (1968): 353-99.

Gennep, Arnold van. LA FORMATION DES LEGENDES. Paris: Flammarion, 1910. 1, 326 p.

Jones, Ernest. ESSAYS IN FOLKLORE, ANTHROPOLOGY AND RELIGION. Essays in Applied Psycho-Analysis, vol. 2. London: The Hogarth Press, 1951. 383 p.

A collection of some of the most important essays on religion and folklore by an early associate of Freud. Includes psychoanalytic interpretations of superstitions concerning salt and its illegitimate use in the Christian eucharist, Christmas, the Holy Ghost, and other topics.

_____. ON THE NIGHTMARE. London: Liveright, 1951. 374 p.

A Freudian perspective on nightmares and their relation to medieval superstitions about witches, the devil, vampires, and werewolves. Originally published in 1931.

Kaplan, Bert. "Psychological Themes in Zuni Mythology and Zuni TAT's." PSYCHOANALYTIC STUDY OF SOCIETY 2 (1962): 255-62.

Lestavel, Jean. "Le Vent et les mythes." PSYCHE-PARIS 9 (1954): 256-66.

Link, Margaret S. THE POLLEN PATH: A COLLECTION OF NAVAJO MYTHS. Stanford, Calif.: Stanford University Press, 1956. 205 p.

> Contains a psychological commentary by Jungian analyst J.L. Henderson.

Lorand, Sandor. "Fairy Tales and Neurosis." PSYCHOANALYTIC QUARTERLY 4 (1935): 234-43.

Moller, Herbert. "The Meaning of Courtly Love." JOURNAL OF AMERICAN FOLKLORE 73 (1960): 39-52.

Moloney, James Clark. "Carnal Myths Involving the Sun." AMERICAN IMAGO 20 (1963): 93-103.

Reik, Theodor. "Freud and Jewish Wit." PSYCHOANALYSIS 2 (Winter 1959): 12-20.

Roheim, Geza. "Primitive High Gods." PSYCHOANALYTIC QUARTERLY 3, no. 1, pt. 2 (1934): 1-133.

Sarnoff, Charles A. "Mythic Symbols in Two Precolumbian Myths." AMERICAN IMAGO 26 (1969): 3-20.

Schnier, Jacques. "Morphology of a Symbol: The Octopus." AMERICAN IMAGO 13 (1956): 3-31.

Skeels, Dell R. "The Function of Humor in Three Nez Perce Indian Myths." AMERICAN IMAGO 11 (1954): 249-61.

_____. "Eros and Thanatos in Nez Perce River Mythology." AMERICAN IMAGO 21 (Fall-Winter 1964): 103-10.

Stern, Theodore. "Ideal and Expected Behavior as Seen in Klamath Mythology." JOURNAL OF AMERICAN FOLKLORE 76 (1963): 21-30.

Swanson, Chang-Su. "Problems and Solutions: Korean Folktales and Personality." JOURNAL OF AMERICAN FOLKLORE 81 (1968): 121-32.

Upadhyaya, Hari S. "Patterns of Mother-Son Behavior in the Hindu Family as

Depicted in the Bhojpuri Folksongs of India." ANTHROPOLOGICA 11 (1969): 203-14.

Veszy-Wagner, Lilla. "Le Symbolisme de l'oiseau." INTERPRETATION 5, no. 2-3 (1971): 3-21.

Section C

THE RITUAL DIMENSION OF RELIGION

Section C

THE RITUAL DIMENSION OF RELIGION

C:1   GENERAL STUDIES OF RITUAL

Caillois, Roger. MAN AND THE SACRED. Translated by Meyer Barash. Glencoe, Ill.: Free Press, 1960. 190 p.

> Written by a French sociologist in the tradition of Durkheim and Mauss, this study employs the sacred-profane distinction in the study of fertility, play, festivals, and war.

Crumrine, N. Ross. "Ritual Drama and Culture Change." COMPARATIVE STUDIES IN SOCIETY AND HISTORY 12 (1970): 361-72.

Deshen, Shlomo. "The Varieties of Abandonment of Religious Symbols." JOURNAL FOR THE SCIENTIFIC STUDY OF RELIGION 11 (March 1972): 33-41.

> Comparison of a Jewish and a Tunisian ritual.

Desmonde, William H. "Compulsive Aspects to Ancient Law." AMERICAN IMAGO 11 (1954): 85-110.

_____. "The Ritual Origin of Plato's Dialogues: A Study of Argumentation and Conversation among Intellectuals." AMERICAN IMAGO 17 (1960): 389-406.

Douglas, Mary. PURITY AND DANGER: AN ANALYSIS OF CONCEPTS OF POLLUTION AND TABOO. London: Routledge and Kegan Paul, 1966. viii, 188 p. Baltimore: Pelican Publishing Co., 1970. 220 p.

> A well-written anthropological discussion of the symbolic ordering systems involved in any cultural handling of dirt, defilement, and boundaries. Attempts to correct the common distinctions between magic and religion, primitive and advanced cultures.

El-Islam, Mohamed F [akhr]. "The Psychotherapeutic Basis of Some Arab Rituals." PSYCHOTHERAPY AND PSYCHOSOMATICS 15 (1967): 18.

Erikson, Erik H. "Ontogeny of Ritualization." In PSYCHOANALYSIS--A GENERAL PSYCHOLOGY: ESSAYS IN HONOR OF HEINZ HARTMANN, pp. 601-21. Edited by Rudolph Loewenstein, et al. New York: International Universities Press, 1966.

> An important essay which argues for the expansion of the clinical approach to ritual through the appropriation of anthropological perspectives. Stresses the mutual activation of care and trust, as exemplified in the mother-infant relationship, and in the interaction of generations and social groups.

Feldman, Sandor S. "Notes on Some Religious Rites and Ceremonies." JOURNAL OF THE HILLSIDE HOSPITAL 8 (January-April 1959): 36-41.

> Contrasts religious and neurotic rituals, and denies that therapy destroys religious faith.

Freud, Sigmund. "Obsessive Actions and Religious Practices." In THE STANDARD EDITION OF THE COMPLETE PSYCHOLOGICAL WORKS OF SIGMUND FREUD, vol. 9, pp. 115-27. Edited by James Strachey. London: The Hogarth Press, 1959.

> Freud's first essay on the psychology of religion compares the defensive ceremonials and sense of guilt in obsessional neurotics and religious rituals.

Goffman, Erving. INTERACTION RITUAL: ESSAYS ON FACE-TO-FACE BEHAVIOR. Chicago: Aldine Publishing Co., 1968. 270 p.

> Essays by a sociologist in the tradition of George Herbert Mead dealing with the ritual aspects of social behavior and their implications for self-definition and social equilibrium. Includes intriguing discussion of "fateful moments" in various social rituals, e.g., bull-fighting, automobile racing.

Goody, Jack. "Religion and Ritual: The Definitional Problem." BRITISH JOURNAL OF SOCIOLOGY 12 (1961): 142-64.

Henke, Frederick Goodrich. A STUDY IN THE PSYCHOLOGY OF RITUALISM. Chicago: University of Chicago Press, 1910. 96 p.

Klapp, Orrin E. RITUAL AND CULT: A SOCIOLOGICAL INTERPRETATION. Washington, D.C.: Public Affairs Press, 1956. 40 p.

> Written by a sociologist who addresses contemporary American forms of social drama. Also see his studies of leaders in section F:3.

Kluckhohn, Richard, ed. CULTURE AND BEHAVIOR: THE COLLECTED ESSAYS OF CLYDE KLUCKHOHN. New York: Free Press of Glencoe, 1962. 402 p.

> A collection of essays by the celebrated anthropologist. Of partic-

ular interest to the psychology of religion are the studies which develop a psychoanalytic approach to Navaho ritual practices (witchcraft, songs, and ceremonies).

Krishnamurthy, N. "Social and Psychological Significance of the Indian Rites and Rituals on the Indian Mind." TRANSACTIONS OF THE ALL-INDIA INSTITUTE OF MENTAL HEALTH 5 (1965): 86-93.

Le Coeur, Charles. LE RITE ET L'OUTIL: ESSAI SUR LA RATIONALISME ET LA PLURALITE DES CIVILISATIONS. 2nd ed. Paris: Presses Universitaires de France, 1969. 248 p.

Lee, Roy Stuart. PSYCHOLOGY AND WORSHIP. New York: Philosophical Library, 1956. 110 p.

Interesting Freudian account of the efficacy of prayer and the meaning of the Christian communion service.

Metheny, Eleanor. MOVEMENT AND MEANING. New York: McGraw-Hill, 1968. 126 p.

Discusses structural and functional meanings of the forms and movements of preliterate and ancient people. Considers a range of nonverbal expressions, from the learning of skills to complex ritual and athletic interactions.

Moberg, David O. "Religious Practices." In RESEARCH ON RELIGIOUS DEVELOPMENT: A COMPREHENSIVE HANDBOOK, pp. 551-98. Edited by Merton P. Strommen. New York: Hawthorn Books, 1971.

Nagendra, S.P. THE CONCEPT OF RITUAL IN MODERN SOCIOLOGICAL THEORY. New Delhi: Academic Journals of India, 1971. xvi, 199 p.

Narramore, S. Bruce. "Psychological Dynamics in Christian Worship: A Beginning Inquiry." JOURNAL OF PSYCHOLOGY AND THEOLOGY 1 (October 1973): 10-19.

Norbeck, Edward. "African Rituals of Conflict." AMERICAN ANTHROPOLOGIST 65 (1963): 1254-79.

Posinsky, S.H. "Ritual, Neurotic and Social." AMERICAN IMAGO 19 (1962): 375-90.

Rappaport, Roy A. "Ritual, Sanctity, and Cybernetics." AMERICAN ANTHROPOLOGIST 73 (1971): 59-76.

Reik, Theodor. RITUAL: PSYCHOANALYTIC STUDIES OF RELIGION. New

York: Farrar, Straus, 1946. 367 p.

> Studies of couvade, puberty rites, and shofar.

_____. PAGAN RITES IN JUDAISM. New York: The Noonday Press, 1964. 206 p.

> Recognizing the persistence of pagan rituals in modern Judaism, the author addresses the task of discovering their meaning psychoanalytically. Chapters concern gravestones, the Kaddish, prayer shawls and phylacteries, the mother-goddess, priestly blessings, and other topics.

Skublics, E. "Psychologically Living Symbolism and Liturgy." EGLISE ET THEOLOGIE 1 (May 1970): 205-28.

Turner, Victor W. DRAMAS, FIELDS, AND METAPHORS: SYMBOLIC ACTION IN HUMAN SOCIETY. Ithaca, N.Y.: Cornell University Press, 1974. 309 p.

> A collection of essays by a social anthropologist concerned with symbolism in social action and in individual and collective performance. Includes essays on the confrontation of Thomas Becket and Henry II and on pilgrimages, as well as more general topics such as symbols of communitas, metaphors of anti-structure, and social drama.

Wallace, Anthony F.C. RELIGION: AN ANTHROPOLOGICAL VIEW. New York: Random House, 1966. xv, 300 p.

> Stresses the centrality of ritual in the anthropology of religion. Discusses ritual as therapy, ideology, and salvation.

Winter, Gibson. "Ritual and Worship in Family Life." PASTORAL PSYCHOLOGY 11 (March 1960): 29-34.

C:2   INITIATION AND TRANSITION RITES

Arlow, Jacob A. "A Psychoanalytic Study of a Religious Initiation Rite: Bar Mitzvah." PSYCHOANALYTIC STUDY OF THE CHILD 6 (1951): 353-74.

_____. "The Consecration of the Prophet." PSYCHOANALYTIC QUARTERLY 20 (1951): 374-97.

Bardis, Panos D. "Aspetti soliali dell'onomastica personale tra gli antichi Ebrei" [Social aspects of personal onomatology among the ancient Hebrews]. RASSEGNA ITALIANA DI DOSIOLOGIA 11 (January 1970): 81-98.

> A study of name-giving practices.

Bettelheim, Bruno. SYMBOLIC WOUNDS: PUBERTY RITES AND THE ENVIOUS MALE. Rev. ed. Glencoe, Ill.: Free Press, 1954. 286 p.; New York: Collier Books, 1962. 194 p.

Develops the argument that primitive initiation rituals are essentially spurious efforts by males to appropriate the procreative powers of women. On the strength of this argument, challenges the traditional Freudian interpretation of initiation rites as concerned with castration anxiety, maintaining instead that they concern the duality of the sexes.

Bouhdiba, Abdouhwahab. "Der Hammans: Beitrag zu einer Psycoanalyse des Islam." KOLNER ZEITSCHRIFT FUR SOZIOLOGIE UND SOZIALPSYCHOLOGIE 22 (1970): 463-72.

On ritual bathing in Islam.

Cohen, Yehudi. THE TRANSITION FROM CHILDHOOD TO ADOLESCENCE: CROSS-CULTURAL STUDIES OF INITIATION CEREMONIES, LEGAL SYSTEMS AND INCEST TABOOS. Chicago: Aldine Publishing Co., 1964. 254 p.

A study of sixty-five societies and the way they handle the transition from childhood to adolescence. Distinguishes societies which stress sociological independence from those which emphasize sociological interdependence, and contends that the latter institute initiation rites at an earlier age.

Dreifuss, Gustav. "A Psychological Study of Circumcision in Judaism." JOURNAL OF ANALYTICAL PSYCHOLOGY 10 (1965): 5-22.

Gennep, Arnold van. THE RITES OF PASSAGE. Translated by Monika B. Vizedom and Gabrielle L. Caffee. Chicago: University of Chicago Press, 1960. xix, 198 p.

Originally published in 1909, this classic study by a Dutch sociologist analyzes birth, puberty, marriage, and death rituals according to their three phases: separation, transition, and incorporation.

Glaser, Barney G., and Strauss, Anselm L. "Temporal Aspects of Dying as a Non-Scheduled Status Passage." AMERICAN JOURNAL OF SOCIOLOGY 71 (1965-66): 48-60.

Granzberg, Gary. "Hopi Initiation Rites: A Case Study of the Validity of the Freudian Theory of Culture." JOURNAL OF SOCIAL PSYCHOLOGY 87 (1972): 189-95.

_____. "The Psychological Integration of Culture: A Cross-Cultural Study of Hopi-Type Initiation Rites." JOURNAL OF SOCIAL PSYCHOLOGY 90 (1973): 3-9.

Henderson, Joseph L. THRESHOLDS OF INITIATION. Middletown, Conn.: Wesleyan University Press, 1967. 260 p.

Leemon, Thomas A. THE RITES OF PASSAGE IN A STUDENT CULTURE: A STUDY OF THE DYNAMICS OF TRANSITION. New York: Teachers College Press, 1972. 215 p.

A study of Greek letter fraternity initiation on a contemporary campus.

Lomas, Peter. "Ritualistic Elements in the Management of Childbirth." BRITISH JOURNAL OF MEDICAL PSYCHOLOGY 39 (1966): 207-13.

Maler, Milton. "The Jewish Orthodox Circumcision Ceremony: Its Meaning from Direct Study of the Rite." JOURNAL OF THE AMERICAN PSYCHOAN-ALYTIC ASSOCIATION 14 (1966): 510-17.

Reik, Theodor. MYSTERY ON THE MOUNTAIN: THE DRAMA OF THE SINAI REVELATION. New York: Harper & Brothers, 1959. 210 p.

Differing from Freud's views, an interpretation of Moses and the events at Sinai as a return to earlier customs, especially initiation rites.

Roheim, Geza. "Transition Rites." PSYCHOANALYTIC QUARTERLY 11 (1942): 336-74.

Schlossman, Howard H. "Circumcision as Defense: A Study in Psychoanalysis and Religion." PSYCHOANALYTIC QUARTERLY 35 (1966): 340-56.

Schneiderman, Leo. "The Cult of Osiris in Relation to Primitive Initiation Rites." PSYCHOANALYTIC REVIEW 52, no. 1 (1965): 38-50.

_____. "A Theory of Repression in the Light of Archaic Religion." PSYCHO-ANALYTIC REVIEW 53, no. 2 (1966): 56-68.

Discussion based on ancient fertility rites.

Schnier, Jacques. "The Tibetan Lamaist Ritual: Chod." INTERNATIONAL JOURNAL OF PSYCHOANALYSIS 38 (1957): 402-7.

Schwartz, Gary, and Merten, Don. "Social Identity and Expressive Symbols: The Meaning of an Initiation Ritual." AMERICAN ANTHROPOLOGIST 70 (1968): 1117-31.

Segy, Ladislas. "Initiation Ceremonies and African Sculpture." AMERICAN IMAGO 10 (1953): 57-82.

Turner, Victor W. THE RITUAL PROCESS. Chicago: Aldine Publishing Co., 1969. 213 p.

An extensive study of the transition rituals of the Ndembu, particularly rituals involving pregnancy and childbirth, and a theoretical statement on the nature and function of ritual. Ritual is viewed as an agent in the maintenance and transformation of social and psychic structures. Pays some attention to rituals in Christianity, Hinduism, and modern cults.

Whiting, John W.M., et al. "The Function of Male Initiation Ceremonies at Puberty." In READINGS IN SOCIAL PSYCHOLOGY, pp. 359-70. Edited by E.E. Maccoby, et al. New York: Holt, 1958.

Young, Frank W. "The Function of Male Initiation Ceremonies: A Cross Cultural Test of an Alternative Hypothesis." AMERICAN JOURNAL OF SOCIOLOGY 67 (1961-62): 379-90.

_____. INITIATION CEREMONIES: A CROSS-CULTURAL STUDY OF STATUS DRAMATIZATION. Indianapolis: The Bobbs-Merrill Co., 1965. xiv, 199 p.

C:3   FESTIVALS AND CEREMONIES

Barnett, James H. "Christmas in American Culture." PSYCHIATRY 9 (1946): 51-66.

Birner, Louis. "The First Foreign Land." PSYCHOANALYTIC REVIEW 58 (1971): 303-9.

Boyer, L. Bryce. "Christmas 'Neurosis'." JOURNAL OF AMERICAN PSYCHOANALYTIC ASSOCIATION 3 (1955): 467-88.

Cattell, James P. "The Holiday Syndrome." PSYCHOANALYTIC REVIEW 42 (1955): 39-43.

Crumrine, N. Ross. "Capakoba, the Maya Easter Ceremonial Impersonation: Explanations of Ritual Clowning." JOURNAL FOR THE SCIENTIFIC STUDY OF RELIGION 8 (1969): 1-22.

deGroot, Adriaan D. SAINT NICHOLAS: A PSYCHOANALYTIC STUDY OF HIS HISTORY AND MYTH. Translated by Miriam Gallaher. New York: Basic Books; The Hague: Mouton, 1965. 211 p.

See annotation in section B:4.

Desmonde, William H. "The Bull-Fight as a Religious Ritual." AMERICAN IMAGO 9 (1952): 173-95.

Eder, M.D. "The Jewish Phylacteries and Other Jewish Ritual Observances." INTERNATIONAL JOURNAL OF PSYCHOANALYSIS 14 (1933): 341-75.

Eisenbud, Jule. "Negative Reactions to Christmas." PSYCHOANALYTIC QUARTERLY 10 (1941): 639-45.

Feldman, Sandor [S.]. "The Blessing of the Kohenites." AMERICAN IMAGO 2 (1941): 296-322.

Fraiberg, Louis, and Fraiberg, Selma. "Hallowe'en: Ritual and Myth in a Children's Holiday." AMERICAN IMAGO 7 (1950): 289-327.

Geertz, Clifford. "Deep Play: Notes on the Balinese Cockfight." DAEDALUS 101, no. 1 (1972): 1-38.

Grotjahn, Martin. "On Bullfighting and the Future of Tragedy." INTERNATIONAL JOURNAL OF PSYCHOANALYSIS 40 (1959): 238-39.

Jekels, Ludwig. "The Psychology of the Festival of Christmas." INTERNATIONAL JOURNAL OF PSYCHOANALYSIS 17 (1936): 57-72.

Levitt, M., and Rubenstein, B. "The Children's Crusade." AMERICAN JOURNAL OF ORTHOPSYCHIATRY 38 (1968): 591-98.

Meerloo, Joost A.M. "The Monument as a Delusional Token." AMERICAN IMAGO 11 (1954): 363-74.

Meyerson, Bernard G., and Stollar, Louis. "A Psychoanalytical Interpretation of the Crucifixion." PSYCHOANALYSIS AND THE PSYCHOANALYTIC REVIEW 49 (Winter 1962): 117-18.

Mitchell, John D. "The Sanskrit Drama SHAKUNTALA: A Psychologic Sounding Board for Hindu Culture." AMERICAN IMAGO 16 (1959): 327-48.

Pollock, George H. "On Mourning and Anniversaries: The Relationship of Culturally Constituted Defensive Systems to Intra-Psychic Adaptive Processes." ISRAEL ANNALS OF PSYCHIATRY AND RELATED DISCIPLINES 10 (March 1972): 9-40.

An important study by a distinguished psychoanalyst.

Reidy, J.J. "Psychoanalyst Looks at Religious Celebration." WORSHIP 43 (November 1969): 557-61.

Reik, Theodor. "A Booth Away from the House." PSYCHOANALYTIC REVIEW

50 (1963): 167-86.

> On the Jewish festival of Sukkoth.

Schnier, Jacques. "The Cornerstone Ceremony." PSYCHOANALYTIC REVIEW 34 (1947): 357-69.

Sereno, Renzo. "Some Observations on the Santa Claus Custom." PSYCHIATRY 14 (1951): 387-96.

Snyder, C.R. ALCOHOL AND THE JEWS. Monographs of the Yale Center of Alcohol Studies, no. 1. Glencoe, Ill.: The Free Press, 1958. 226 p.

> Attributes the unusually low incidence of alcoholism among Jews to the fact that many of their religious rituals instill a ritualistic attitude toward alcohol consumption.

Sterba, Richard. "A Dutch Celebration of a Festival." AMERICAN IMAGO 2 (1941): 205-8.

_____. "On Christmas." PSYCHOANALYTIC QUARTERLY 13 (1944): 79-83.

_____. "On Hallowe'en." AMERICAN IMAGO 5 (1948): 213-24.

Verlynde, Noelle. "The Child and Festivities: A Psychological Study." LUMEN VITAE 18 (1963): 624-38.

Walsh, Maurice N. "A Psychoanalytic Interpretation of a Primitive Dramatic Ritual." JOURNAL OF THE HILLSIDE HOSPITAL 11 (1962): 3-20.

Wayne, Robert. "A Little Religious Ceremonial." AMERICAN IMAGO 11 (1954): 191-202.

C:4   SUPERSTITION, MAGIC, AND TABOO

Bachrach, Arthur J. "An Experimental Approach to Superstitious Behavior." JOURNAL OF AMERICAN FOLKLORE 75 (1962): 1-9.

Bakan, David. DISEASE, PAIN, AND SACRIFICE: TOWARD A PSYCHOLOGY OF SUFFERING. Chicago: University of Chicago Press, 1968. 134 p.

> In addition to two essays concerned with the effect of the threat of separation-estrangement in precipitating physiological symptoms, the book contains a major chapter on child sacrifice as the historical and psychological background of the sufferings of Job.

Brehm, Felix. "Anthropophagy: Its Forms and Motives." INTERNATIONAL

JOURNAL OF PSYCHOANALYSIS 16 (1935): 9-21.

A study of cannibalism.

Bunker, Henry Alden. "The Bouphonia, or Ox-Murder: A Footnote to 'Totem and Taboo'." PSYCHOANALYSIS AND THE SOCIAL SCIENCES 1 (1947): 165-69.

Bychowski, Gustav. "Art, Magic and the Creative Ego." PSYCHOANALYSIS. (Special double issue replacing vol. 4, no. 4 and vol. 5, no. 1, 1956-57): 125-35.

Cook de Leonard, Carmen. "Psicodinamia de un sacrificio" [Psychodynamics of a sacrifice]. REVISTA MEXICANA DE PSICOLOGIA 2, no. 9 (1966): 763-74.

Crabbe, Brian D. "Behavior Change in Response to a Changed Church Rule." JOURNAL OF SOCIAL PSYCHOLOGY 84 (1971): 311-12.

A study of Roman Catholics and meat-eating.

Desmonde, William H. MAGIC, MYTH AND MONEY: THE ORIGIN OF MONEY IN RELIGIOUS RITUAL. New York: The Free Press of Glencoe, 1962. 208 p.

A provocative history of money's origin in the communal meals of Graeco-Roman culture. Employs some of Freud's views on totemism and the primal horde.

Devereux, George. "Belief, Superstition, and Symptom." SAMIKSA 8 (1954): 210-15.

Dundes, Alan. "Summoning Deity through Ritual Fasting." AMERICAN IMAGO 20 (1963): 213-20.

Durkheim, Emile, and Ellis, Albert. INCEST: THE NATURE AND ORIGIN OF THE TABOO; THE ORIGINS AND THE DEVELOPMENT OF THE INCEST TABOO. New York: Lyle Stuart, 1963. 186 p.

Combines Durkheim's classic essay on incest and a supplementary essay by Ellis, a clinical psychologist. Ellis' essay is especially concerned with the persistence of the incest taboo in modern societies.

Eckstein, Jerome. "The Incest Taboo: Maimonides, Freud, and Reik." PSYCHOANALYSIS 5 (Fall 1957): 3-15.

Fischer, John L., et al. "Totemism and Allergy." INTERNATIONAL JOURNAL OF SOCIAL PSYCHIATRY 5 (1959): 33-40.

Fodor, A. "The Origin of the Mosaic Prohibition Against Cooking the Suckling in Its Mother's Milk." INTERNATIONAL JOURNAL OF PSYCHOANALYSIS 27 (1946): 140-44.

Fodor, Nandor. "A Personal Analytic Approach to the Problem of the Holy Name." PSYCHOANALYTIC REVIEW 31 (1944): 165-80.

Fox, Robin. "TOTEM AND TABOO Reconsidered." In THE STRUCTURAL STUDY OF MYTH AND TOTEMISM, pp. 161-78. Edited by Edmund Leach. London: Tavistock Publishers, 1967.

   A reappraisal of Freud's TOTEM AND TABOO (cited below) from a
   sociological perspective.

Freud, Sigmund. TOTEM AND TABOO. In THE STANDARD EDITION OF THE COMPLETE PSYCHOLOGICAL WORKS OF SIGMUND FREUD, vol. 13, pp. 1-162. Edited by James Strachey. London: The Hogarth Press, 1953. (Paperback ed. of TOTEM AND TABOO available from New York: Random, Vintage, 1960.)

   Still controversial among anthropologists, this work (originally published in 1913-14) discusses incest, ambivalence, attitudes toward rulers, animism, magic, exogamy, animal phobias, totem
   meals, and the primal horde. Employs clinical findings in the
   analysis of social and religious rituals and taboos.

Goffman, Erving. STIGMA: NOTES ON THE MANAGEMENT OF SPOILED IDENTITY. Englewood Cliffs, N.J.: Prentice-Hall, 1963. 147 p.

   While a sociological essay, this study of persons who possess some
   physical or other characteristic which sets them off as abnormal
   holds special interest for the psychologist. Considers deaf, blind,
   crippled, and other "tabooed" persons and shows how social rituals
   have been erected to neutralize their effects on "normal" society.

Grinberg, Leon. "Psychoanalytic Considerations on the Jewish Passover: Totem-ic Sacrifice and Meal." AMERICAN IMAGO 19 (1962): 391-424.

Jahoda, Gustav. THE PSYCHOLOGY OF SUPERSTITION. Baltimore: Penguin Books, 1969. 158 p.

   Argues that superstitions, such as witchcraft, sorcery, and other
   religious beliefs, are typically socially transmitted and not solely
   a matter of the psychology of individuals.

Jarvie, I.C., and Agassi, Joseph. "The Problem of the Rationality of Magic." BRITISH JOURNAL OF SOCIOLOGY 18 (1967): 55-74.

Kiev, Ari. "Ritual Goat Sacrifice in Haiti." AMERICAN IMAGO 19 (1962): 349-59.

Kortmulder, K. "An Ethological Theory of the Incest Taboo and Exogamy." CURRENT ANTHROPOLOGY 9 (1968): 437-49.

Layard, John. "Boar-Sacrifice." JOURNAL OF ANALYTICAL PSYCHOLOGY 1 (1955): 7-32.

Lewis, Lionel S. "Knowledge, Danger, Certainty, and the Theory of Magic." AMERICAN JOURNAL OF SOCIOLOGY 69 (1963-64): 7-13.

Lomas, Peter. "Taboo and Illness." BRITISH JOURNAL OF MEDICAL PSY- CHOLOGY 42 (1969): 33-39.

Lord, Richard A. "A Note on Stigmata." AMERICAN IMAGO 14 (1957): 299-302.

Mauss, Marcel. A GENERAL THEORY OF MAGIC. Translated by Robert Brain. London: Routledge and Kegan Paul, 1972. 148 p.

> Originally published in the early part of the century, this work by an anthropologist who worked with Durkheim and influenced Levi- Strauss discusses some of the quasi-religious collective forces that operate in magic acts and representations.

Parsons, Anne. BELIEF, MAGIC, AND ANOMIE. ESSAYS IN PSYCHOSOCIAL ANTHROPOLOGY. New York: The Free Press, 1969. xvi, 376 p.

> A collection of essays, published posthumously, which utilizes Freudian perspectives interlaced with contemporary social scientific theories. Topics include family dynamics, religion, symbolism, magic, and mental illness.

Rawcliffe, D.H. ILLUSIONS AND DELUSIONS OF THE SUPERNATURAL AND THE OCCULT. New York: Dover Publications, 1960. 551 p.

Reik, Theodor. "From Spell to Prayer." PSYCHOANALYSIS 3 (Summer 1955): 3-26.

Roheim, Geza. AUSTRALIAN TOTEMISM: A PSYCHO-ANALYTIC STUDY IN ANTHROPOLOGY. London: George Allen and Unwin, 1925. 487 p.

_____. ANIMISM, MAGIC AND THE DIVINE KING. London: Kegan Paul, Trench, Trubner and Co.; New York: A. Knopf, 1930. xviii, 390 p.

> Applies the psychological views put forward by Ferenczi in THALAS- SA to religious phenomena.

_____. "The Oedipus Complex, Magic and Culture." PSYCHOANALYSIS AND THE SOCIAL SCIENCES 2 (1950): 173-228.

_____. "The Evil Eye." AMERICAN IMAGO 9 (1952): 351-63.

_____. MAGIC AND SCHIZOPHRENIA. Edited by Warner Muensterberger and S.H. Posinsky. New York: International Universities Press, 1955. 230 p.

> Contains two essays, "The Origin and Function of Magic" and "Fantasies and Dreams in Schizophrenia."

Rosenman, Stanley. "Black Magic and Superego Formation." PSYCHOANALYTIC REVIEW 43 (1956): 272-319.

Roth, Julius A. "Ritual and Magic in the Control of Contagion." AMERICAN SOCIOLOGICAL REVIEW 22 (1957): 310-15.

Seidenberg, Robert. "Sacrificing the First You See." PSYCHOANALYTIC REVIEW 53 (1966): 49-62.

Simoons, Frederick J. EAT NOT THIS FLESH: FOOD AVOIDANCES IN THE OLD WORLD. Madison: University of Wisconsin Press, 1961. xiii, 241 p.

Skinner, John. "Ritual Matricide: A Study of the Origins of Sacrifice." AMERICAN IMAGO 18 (1961): 71-102.

Steiner, Franz. TABOO. New York: Philosophical Library, 1956. 154 p.

Tourney, Garfield, and Plazak, Dean J. "Evil Eye in Myth and Schizophrenia." PSYCHIATRIC QUARTERLY 28 (1954): 478-95.

Vetter, George B. MAGIC AND RELIGION: THEIR PSYCHOLOGICAL NATURE, ORIGIN, AND FUNCTION. New York: Philosophical Library, 1958. 555 p.

Woolf, M. "Prohibitions against the Simultaneous Consumption of Milk and Flesh in Orthodox Jewish Law." INTERNATIONAL JOURNAL OF PSYCHO-ANALYSIS 26 (1945): 169-77.

C:5   WITCHCRAFT, SHAMANISM, AND POSSESSION

Alland, Alexander. "'Possession' in a Revivalistic Negro Church." JOURNAL FOR THE SCIENTIFIC STUDY OF RELIGION 1 (1961-62): 204-13.

Anderson, Robert D. "The History of Witchcraft: A Review with Some Psychiatric Concepts." AMERICAN JOURNAL OF PSYCHIATRY 126 (1970): 1727-35.

Baroja, Julio Caro. THE WORLD OF THE WITCHES. Translated by O.N.V.

Glendinning. Chicago: University of Chicago Press, 1966. xiv, 313 p.

>A study based on the thesis that "witches tend to be much the
>same whenever and wherever they happen to be," it attempts to
>isolate persistent themes in witchcraft and focuses in this regard
>on the mythical role of the devil in witchcraft. Somewhat naive
>in its effort to penetrate the psychological motivations of witches.

Baruk, H. "Societe moreau de Tours: Le Probleme des sorcieres est-il un probleme purement psycho-pathologigue?" ANNALES MEDICO-PSYCHOLOGI-
GUES 2 (1968): 591-93.

Beattie, John, and Middleton, John. SPIRIT MEDIUMSHIP AND SOCIETY IN
AFRICA. New York: Africana, 1969. xxx, 310 p.

Boyer, L. Bryce. "Notes on the Personality Structure of a North American Indian Shaman." JOURNAL OF THE HILLSIDE HOSPITAL 10 (1961): 14-33.

_____. "Remarks on the Personality of Shamans, with Special Reference to
the Apache of the Mescalero Indian Reservation." PSYCHOANALYTIC STUDY
OF SOCIETY 2 (1962): 233-54.

Diethelm, Oskar. "The Medical Teaching of Demonology in the 17th and 18th
Centuries." JOURNAL OF THE HISTORY OF THE BEHAVIORAL SCIENCES 6
(1970): 3-15.

Fahd, Tawfig. LA DIVINATION ARABE: ETUDES RELIGIEUSES, SOCIOLO-
GIGUES ET FOLKLORIQUES SUR LE MILIEU NATIF D'ISLAM. Leiden: E.J.
Brill, 1966. xi, 617 p.

Freud, Sigmund. "A Seventeenth-Century Demonological Neurosis." In
THE STANDARD EDITION OF THE COMPLETE PSYCHOLOGICAL WORKS OF
SIGMUND FREUD, vol. 19, pp. 61-105. Edited by James Strachey. London:
The Hogarth Press, 1961.

>A study of Christopher Haizmann, the painter, and his pact with
>the devil.

Handelman, Don. "The Development of a Washo Shaman." ETHNOLOGY 6
(1967): 444-64.

>A psychological study of the last Washo shaman. Argues that the
>shaman, Henry Rupert, made a satisfactory adjustment to the incur-
>sion of alien religious and cultural traditions through a synthesis
>of these and his traditional belief system.

Harner, Michael J., ed. HALLUCINOGENS AND SHAMANISM. London
and New York: Oxford University Press, 1973. xv, 200 p.

>Ten field studies about the use of drugs in religious ceremonies

presided over by shamans and other religious leaders. See annotation in section D:3.

Kanzer, Mark. "Freud and the Demon." JOURNAL OF THE HILLSIDE HOS-PITAL 10 (1961): 190-202.

Kim, Wonsik. "Korean Shamanism and Hypnosis." AMERICAN JOURNAL OF CLINICAL HYPNOSIS 9 (1967): 193-97.

_____. "A Further Study of Korean Shamanism and Hypnosis." AMERICAN JOURNAL OF CLINICAL HYPNOSIS 11, no. 3 (1969): 183-90.

Klopfer, Bruno, and Boyer, L. Bryce. "Notes of the Personality Structure of a North American Shaman: Rorschach Interpretation." JOURNAL OF PRO-JECTIVE TECHNIQUES 25 (1961): 169-78.

Kluckhohn, Clyde. NAVAHO WITCHCRAFT. Boston: Beacon Press, 1967. xxii, 254 p.

Kraus, Robert F. "A Psychoanalytic Interpretation of Shamanism." PSYCHO-ANALYTIC REVIEW 59 (Spring 1972): 19-32.

La Barre, Weston. THE PEYOTE CULT. 2nd ed. New York: Schocken Books, 1969. xvii, 260 p.

Republication of the original study by a psychoanalytically-trained anthropologist of the North American Indian ritual. This edition includes an extensive bibliography, a review of recent literature, and reflections on the native American church.

_____. THE GHOST DANCE: ORIGINS OF RELIGION. Garden City, N.Y.: Doubleday & Co., 1970. xvi, 677 p.

See annotation in section F:3.

Lester, David. "Voodoo Death: Some New Thoughts on an Old Phenomenon." AMERICAN ANTHROPOLOGIST 74 (June 1972): 386-90.

Lewis, I.M. ECSTATIC RELIGION: AN ANTHROPOLOGICAL STUDY OF SPIRIT POSSESSION AND SHAMANISM. Baltimore: Penguin Books, 1971. 211 p.

Contains strong chapter on the subject of possession and psychiatry.

Lieban, Richard W. CEBUANO SORCERY: MALIGN MAGIC IN THE PHILIP-PINES. Berkeley: University of California Press, 1967. 163 p.

An analysis of sorcery among Christians on the island of Cebu.

Lommel, Andress. SHAMANISM: THE BEGINNINGS OF ART. Translated by Michael Bulloch. New York: McGraw-Hill, 1967. 175 p. Illustrated.

Argues that prehistoric cave art was produced in the process of cure from severe psychopathological states.

Middlemore, Merell. "The Treatment of Bewitchment in a Puritan Community." INTERNATIONAL JOURNAL OF PSYCHOANALYSIS 15 (1934): 41-58.

Mischel, Walter, and Mischel, Frances. "Psychological Aspects of Spirit Possession in Trinidad." AMERICAN ANTHROPOLOGIST 60 (1958): 249-60.

Nelson, Cynthia. "Self, Spirit Possession and World View: An Illustration from Egypt." INTERNATIONAL JOURNAL OF SOCIAL PSYCHIATRY 17 (1971): 194-209.

Oesterreich, T.K. POSSESSION, DEMONIACAL AND OTHER AMONG PRIMITIVE RACES, IN ANTIQUITY, THE MIDDLE AGES, AND IN MODERN TIMES. New York: University Books, 1966.

Originally published in 1922.

Progoff, Ira. THE IMAGE OF AN ORACLE: A REPORT ON RESEARCH INTO THE MEDIUMSHIP OF EILEEN J. GARRETT. New York: Garrett Publications, 1964. 372 p.

Ravenschroft, Kent. "Voodoo Possession: A Natural Experiment in Hypnosis." INTERNATIONAL JOURNAL OF CLINICAL AND EXPERIMENTAL HYPNOSIS 13, no. 3 (1965): 157-82.

Roche, Jean L. "Posession et delivrance chez les Lebous de Cap-Vert et du Diander (Senegal)" [Possession and deliverance among the Lebous of Cap-Vert and of Diander]. BULLETIN DE PSYCHOLOGIE 25, no. 18 (1971-72): 1057-62.

Roheim, Geza. "Hungarian Shamanism." PSYCHOANALYSIS AND THE SOCIAL SCIENCES 3 (1951): 131-69.

Rosenman, Stanley. "The Witch Hunter." PSYCHOANALYSIS 3 (Fall 1954): 3-18.

Silverman, Julian. "Shamans and Acute Schizophrenia." AMERICAN ANTHROPOLOGIST 69 (1967): 21-31.

Songer, Harold S. "Demonic Possession and Mental Illness." RELIGION IN LIFE 36 (1967): 119-27.

Spiro, Melford E.   BURMESE SUPERNATURALISM: A STUDY IN THE EXPLANA-
TION AND REDUCTION OF SUFFERING. Englewood Cliffs, N.J.: Prentice-
Hall, 1967. 300 p.

> Focuses on the functions of belief in witches, ghosts, demons, and
> similar phenomena among the Theravada Buddhist population in Up-
> per Burma. Utilizes a wide range of social, psychological, and
> historical evidence.

Spitz, Rene A.   "The Genesis of Magical and Transcendent Cults." AMERICAN
IMAGO 29 (1973): 1-10.

Torrey, E. Fuller.   "The Zar Cult in Ethiopia." INTERNATIONAL JOURNAL
OF SOCIAL PSYCHIATRY 13 (1967): 216-23.

> A study of spirit possession.

Witthower, E.D.   "Trance and Possession States." INTERNATIONAL JOURNAL
OF SOCIAL PSYCHIATRY 16 (1970): 153-60.

> Discusses cult saviors in Haiti, Liberia, and Brazil.

Yap, P.M.   "The Possession Syndrome--A Comparison of Hong Kong and French
Findings." JOURNAL OF MENTAL SCIENCE 106 (1960): 114-37.

Section D

THE EXPERIENTIAL DIMENSION OF RELIGION

Section D

THE EXPERIENTIAL DIMENSION OF RELIGION

D:1 GENERAL STUDIES OF RELIGIOUS EXPERIENCE

Bartlett, Sir Frederic. RELIGION AS EXPERIENCE, BELIEF, ACTION. London: Oxford University Press, 1950. 38 p.

> From the perspective of an experimental psychologist.

Benassy, M. "Psychanalyses didactiques et experiences religieuses" [Didactic analyses and religious experiences]. REVUE FRANCAISE DE PSYCHO-ANALYSE 29, no. 1 (1965): 31-41.

Berthold, Fred, Jr. "The Meaning of Religious Experience." JOURNAL OF RELIGION 32 (1952): 263-71.

Bertocci, Peter A. "Psychological Interpretations of Religious Experience." In RESEARCH ON RELIGIOUS DEVELOPMENT: A COMPREHENSIVE HANDBOOK, pp. 3-41. Edited by Merton P. Strommen. New York: Hawthorn Books, 1971.

Biernaert, Louis. EXPERIENCE CHRETIENNE ET PSYCHOLOGIE. Paris: Editions de l'Epi, 1964. 435 p.

Bindl, Maria Frieda. DAS RELIGIOSE ERLEBEN IM SPIEGEL DER BILD-GESTALTUNG: EINE ENTWICKLUNGS-PSYCHOLOGISCHE UNTERSUCHUNG. Freiburg: Herder, 1965. 287 p.

> An extremely comprehensive analysis of major theories of religious experience, including discussions of depth psychology, genetic theories, classical psychology of religion, and structural theorists. Illustrations from case studies.

Boisen, Anton T. "Religious Experience and Psychological Conflict." AMERICAN PSYCHOLOGIST 13 (1958): 568-70.

Bouquet, Alan Coates. RELIGIOUS EXPERIENCE: ITS NATURE, TYPES AND

VALIDITY. 2nd ed., rev. Cambridge, England: W. Heffer and Sons, 1968.
140 p.

An analysis of the origin and development of religious experiences,
especially those of Christianity. Includes discussions of sin, grace,
and conversion.

Brody, Nathan. "Psychology of the Scientist: Scientific and Religious Experiences Distinguished by Their Affect." PSYCHOLOGICAL REPORTS 16, no. 3,
pt. 1 (1965): 737-44.

Bucke (R.M.) Memorial Society. CONFERENCE ON PERSONALITY CHANGE
AND RELIGIOUS EXPERIENCE. (Proceedings of the First Annual Conference.)
Edited by Raymond [H.] Prince. Montreal: 1965. 86 p.

Discussion of personality change and religious experience.

_____. DO PSYCHEDELICS HAVE RELIGIOUS IMPLICATIONS? (Proceedings
of the Third Annual Conference.) Edited by D.H. Salman and R[aymond] H.
Prince. Montreal: 1968. 81 p.

Discussion of the religious implications of psychedelic drugs. See
listing in section D:3.

_____. TRANCE AND POSSESSION STATES. (Proceedings of the Second
Annual Conference.) Edited by Raymond [H.] Prince. Montreal: 1966. 200 p.

Papers on trance and possession states. See listing in section D:3.

Buscarlet, Jean Marc. CHEMINS INTERIEURS, PSYCHOLOGIE DE LA GRACE.
Neuchatel: Delachaux et Niestle, 1965. 174 p.

Bychowski, Gustav. "The Ego and the Introjects: Origins of Religious Experience." PSYCHOANALYSIS AND THE SOCIAL SCIENCES 5 (1958): 246-79.

Cailliet, Emile. "Personal Religious Experiences." RELIGION IN LIFE 19
(1950): 380-88.

Campbell, Peter A., and McMahon, Edwin M. "Religious-Type Experience in
the Context of Humanistic and Transpersonal Psychology." THE JOURNAL OF
TRANSPERSONAL PSYCHOLOGY 6, no. 1 (1974): 11-17.

Chamberlain, Gary L. "The Drive for Meaning in William James' Analysis of
Religious Experience." JOURNAL OF VALUE INQUIRY 5 (Summer 1971): 194-
206.

Clark, Walter Houston. "The Psychology of Religious Experience." PSYCHOL-
OGY TODAY 1, no. 9 (1968): 42-47, 68-69.

_____, et al. RELIGIOUS EXPERIENCE: ITS NATURE AND FUNCTION IN THE HUMAN PSYCHE. Springfield, Ill.: Charles C Thomas, 1973. 151 p.

>   Lectures by Clark on ecstasy, mysticism, and conversion; with responses by a theologian, an anthropologist, and a psychologist.

Elkind, David, and Elkind, Sally. "Varieties of Religious Experience in Young Adolescents." JOURNAL FOR THE SCIENTIFIC STUDY OF RELIGION 2 (1962-63): 102-12.

England, F.E. THE VALIDITY OF RELIGIOUS EXPERIENCE. New York and London: Harper & Brothers, 1938. 288 p.

>   Philosophical reflections on the psychological experience of "the fear that exalts."

Ferrater-Mora, Jose. "The Language of Religious Experience." INTERNATIONAL JOURNAL FOR PHILOSOPHY OF RELIGION 1 (1970): 22-33.

Forest, Aime. "Concerning the Esthetic and Religious Experience." HUMANITAS 4, no. 2 (1968): 151-60.

Goodenough, E.R. THE PSYCHOLOGY OF RELIGIOUS EXPERIENCES. New York: Basic Books, 1965. 192 p.

>   A scholar of Hellenistic religion here turns to psychology and, in an unusual mixture of Freud, Otto, and others, develops a unique theory of the way types of religious experiences participate in and protect man from "the tremendum."

Gorlow, Leon, and Schroeder, Harold E. "Motives for Participating in the Religious Experience." JOURNAL FOR THE SCIENTIFIC STUDY OF RELIGION 7 (1968): 241-51.

Guirdham, Arthur. CHRIST AND FREUD: A STUDY OF RELIGIOUS EXPERIENCE AND OBSERVANCE. London: George Allen and Unwin, 1959. 193 p.

Gusmer, Charles W. "Worship and Religious Experience." AMERICAN ECCLESIASTICAL REVIEW 168 (January 1974): 62-69.

Haddox, Bruce. "Religious Language as Religious Experience." INTERNATIONAL JOURNAL FOR PHILOSOPHY OF RELIGION 2 (1971): 222-27.

Hitschmann, Edward. "New Varieties of Religious Experience." In GREAT MEN: PSYCHOANALYTIC STUDIES, pp. 232-64. By Edward Hitschmann. New York: International Universities Press, 1956.

>   An essay which recounts the religious experiences of William James,

Franz Werfel, Albert Schweitzer, Auguste Comte, Mahatma Gandhi, Samuel Johnson, and others. These examples are intended to show the "regularity of occurrences" in religious experiences, and the essay in general seeks to unify Freudian and Jamesian perspectives. See listing for book in section F:3.

Hopkins, Pryns. THE SOCIAL PSYCHOLOGY OF RELIGIOUS EXPERIENCE. New York: Paine-Whitman Publishers, 1962. 135 p.

Considers the dynamics of salvation, propitiation, and the paradox of good and evil in Buddhism as well as Christianity.

Lee, Harry B. "Spirituality and Beauty in Artistic Experiences." PSYCHO-ANALYTIC QUARTERLY 17 (1948): 507-23.

McBride, Alfred. "Religious Experience: Public Utterance and Dogma Development." AMERICAN ECCLESIASTICAL REVIEW 168 (March 1974): 162-76.

Martin, F. David. "The Aesthetic in Religious Experience." RELIGIOUS STUDIES 4 (1968): 1-24.

Needleman, Jacob. "Religion and the Recovery of Experience." REVIEW OF METAPHYSICS 23 (1969): 102-13.

Neumann, Erich. "Stages of Religious Experience and the Path of Depth Psychology." ISRAEL ANNALS OF PSYCHIATRY AND RELATED DISCIPLINES 8 (1970): 232-54.

Norborg, Sverre. VARIETIES OF CHRISTIAN EXPERIENCE. Minneapolis: Augsburg Publishing House, 1937. 289 p.

Owen, H.P. "Our Experience of God." RELIGIOUS STUDIES 7 (1971): 175-84.

Potempa, P. Rudolf. PERSONLICHKEIT UND RELIGIOSITAT: VERSUCH EINER PSYCHOLOGISCHEN SCHAU. Gottingen: Verlag fur Psychologie, 1958. 116 p.

Recognizing that classical psychology of religion was primarily concerned with religious experience, this study demonstrates the importance of personality in religious experiences.

Salman, D.H. "The Psychology of Religious Experience." JOURNAL OF RELIGION AND HEALTH 4 (1965): 387-97.

Sevigny, Robert. L'EXPERIENCE RELIGIEUSE CHEZ LES JEUNES: UNE ETUDE PSYCHO-SOCIOLOGIQUE DE L'ACTUALIZATION DE SOI. Montreal: Les

Presses de l'Universite de Montreal, 1971. xxii, 323 p.

> Uses the theories of Carl Rogers to study empirically religious experiences in relation to God, the church, mass, and ethics. Interesting discussions of distinct types of religious experience, reference groups, and self-image, with statistical analysis. Also listed in section G:3.

Singer, Jerome L. DAYDREAMING: AN INTRODUCTION TO THE EXPERIMENTAL STUDY OF INNER EXPERIENCE. New York: Random House, 1966. xxi, 234 p.

> A major study designed to revive the problem of introspection in psychology. Argues that daydreaming is an important dimension of personality, affecting cognitive style, sensitivity, and adjustment.

Smith, Leona J. "Religion in Living." CHARACTER POTENTIAL 2, no. 1 (1963): 26-39.

> Considers the effect of religious experiences on conviction, thought, feeling, and action.

Stark, Rodney. "A Taxonomy of Religious Experience." JOURNAL FOR THE SCIENTIFIC STUDY OF RELIGION 5 (1965-66): 97-116.

Tyson, Herbert A. "Elements of Religious Experience." JOURNAL OF RELIGION AND HEALTH 4 (1965): 441-47.

Vergote, Antoine. "Religious Experience." LUMEN VITAE 19 (1964): 205-20.

Weininger, Benjamin. "The Interpersonal Factor in the Religious Experience." PSYCHOANALYSIS 3 (Summer 1955): 27-44.

Weiss, Paul. "Religious Experience." REVIEW OF METAPHYSICS 17 (1963): 3-17.

Winnicott, D.W. PLAYING AND REALITY. New York: Basic Books, 1971. 169 p.

> Original and imaginative work of a British child analyst. Points to the important realm of the potential space between subject and object, which is psychologically neither inside nor outside the individual, as the place of esthetic, religious, and creative experience.

Wolf, Arnold Jacob. "Psychoanalysis and Religious Experience." JOURNAL OF RELIGION AND HEALTH 2 (1962): 74-80.

D:2 CONVERSION EXPERIENCE

Allison, Gerda E. "Psychiatric Implications of Religious Conversion." CANA-
DIAN PSYCHIATRIC ASSOCIATION JOURNAL 12, no. 1 (1967): 55-61.

Allison, Joel. "Recent Empirical Studies in Religious Conversion Experiences."
PASTORAL PSYCHOLOGY 17 (September 1966): 21-34.

_____. "Adaptive Regression and Intense Religious Experiences." JOURNAL
OF NERVOUS AND MENTAL DISEASE 145 (1968): 452-63.

_____. "Religious Conversion: Regression and Progression in an Adolescent
Experience." JOURNAL FOR THE SCIENTIFIC STUDY OF RELIGION 8 (1969):
23-38.

Annett, Edward A. CONVERSION IN INDIA: A STUDY IN RELIGIOUS PSY-
CHOLOGY. Calcutta: Christian Literature Society for India, 1920. xiii,
105 p.

> Seeks to explain why the conversion experience of the Indian is
> different from that of the Westerner.

Bagwell, H. Roberts. "The Abrupt Religious Conversion Experience." JOUR-
NAL OF RELIGION AND HEALTH 8 (1969): 163-78.

Beck, Robert N. "Hall's Genetic Psychology and Religious Conversion." PAS-
TORAL PSYCHOLOGY 16 (September 1965): 45-52.

Brock, Timothy C. "Implications of Conversion and Magnitude of Cognitive
Dissonance." JOURNAL FOR THE SCIENTIFIC STUDY OF RELIGION 1 (1961-
62): 198-203.

Christensen, Carl W. "Religious Conversion." ARCHIVES OF GENERAL PSY-
CHIATRY 9 (1963): 207-16.

_____. "Religious Conversion in Adolescence." PASTORAL PSYCHOLOGY
16 (September 1965): 17-29.

Clark, Walter Houston. "William James: Contributions to the Psychology of
Religious Conversion." PASTORAL PSYCHOLOGY 16 (September 1965): 29-36.

_____. "Intense Religious Experience." In RESEARCH ON RELIGIOUS DE-
VELOPMENT: A COMPREHENSIVE HANDBOOK, pp. 521-50. Edited by Merton
P. Strommen. New York: Hawthorn Books, 1971.

Dewhurst, Kenneth, and Beard, A.W. "Sudden Religious Conversions in Temporal Lobe Epilepsy." BRITISH JOURNAL OF PSYCHIATRY 117 (November 1970): 497-507.

Feuer, Lewis S [amuel]. "The Dream of Benedict Spinoza." AMERICAN IMAGO 14 (Fall (1957): 225-42.

An interpretation of Spinoza's dream in the wake of his apostasy from the jewish faith.

_____. "Anxiety and Philosophy: The Case of Descartes." AMERICAN IMAGO 20 (Winter 1963): 411-49.

A study of the relation of emotional conflicts and philosophical thought as revealed in Descartes' account of his "enlightenment" experience in which he recognized man as a reflective self.

Freud, Sigmund. "A Religious Experience." In THE STANDARD EDITION OF THE COMPLETE PSYCHOLOGICAL WORKS OF SIGMUND FREUD, vol. 21, pp. 167-72. Edited by James Strachey. London: The Hogarth Press, 1961.

Discusses a religious experience of conversion in terms of the oedipal conflict.

Furgeson, Earl H. "The Definition of Religious Conversion." PASTORAL PSYCHOLOGY 16 (September 1965): 8-16.

Harms, Ernest. "Ethical and Psychological Implications of Religious Conversion." REVIEW OF RELIGIOUS RESEARCH 3 (1962): 122-31.

Also see his article on conversion in section A:3.

Hiltner, Seward. "Toward a Theology of Conversion in the Light of Psychology." PASTORAL PSYCHOLOGY 17 (September 1966): 35-42.

Hitschmann, Edward. "Swedenborg's Paranoia." In GREAT MEN: PSYCHO-ANALYTIC STUDIES, pp. 225-31. By Edward Hitschmann. New York: International Universities Press, 1956.

Attributes Swedenborg's abrupt conversion in middle age to religious paranoia. See listing for book in section F:3.

Hood, Ralph W., Jr. "Religious Orientation and the Report of Religious Experience." JOURNAL FOR THE SCIENTIFIC STUDY OF RELIGION 9 (Winter 1970): 285-92.

_____. "Forms of Religious Commitment and Intense Religious Experience." REVIEW OF RELIGIOUS RESEARCH 15 (Fall 1973): 29-36.

Kietzig, Ottfried. "Einmaligkeit und Allgemeine Gultigkeit von Bekehrung: Dargestellt an der Bekehrung des Paulus." ARCHIV FUR RELIGION PSYCHOLO-GIE 7 (1962): 105-34.

> A study of the validity and permanence of religious conversions as exemplified in Saint Paul.

Kildahl, John [P]. "Religious Conversions." DIALOG 2 (Summer 1963): 240-41.

_____. "The Personalities of Sudden Religious Converts." PASTORAL PSY-CHOLOGY 16 (September 1965): 37-44.

Lebra, Takie S. "Logic of Salvation: The Case of a Japanese Sect in Hawaii." INTERNATIONAL JOURNAL OF SOCIAL PSYCHIATRY 16 (1969): 45-53.

_____. "Religious Conversion as a Breakthrough for Transculturation: A Japanese Sect in Hawaii." JOURNAL FOR THE SCIENTIFIC STUDY OF RELI-GION 9 (Fall 1970): 181-96.

> On the basis of a Weberian analysis of a Japanese-American religious sect in Hawaii (Tensho), the author concludes that conversion is "a trigger for releasing a wider range of behavioral options suited for trans-cultural environment."

Levin, Theodore M., and Zegano, Leonard S. "Adolescent Identity Crisis and Religious Conversion: Implications for Psychotherapy." BRITISH JOURNAL OF MEDICAL PSYCHOLOGY 47 (1974): 73-82.

Lofland, John, and Stark, Rodney. "Becoming a World-Saver: A Theory of Conversion to a Deviant Perspective." AMERICAN SOCIOLOGICAL REVIEW 30 (1965): 862-75.

_____. DOOMSDAY CULT: A STUDY OF CONVERSION, PROSELYTIZA-TION, AND MAINTENANCE OF FAITH. Englewood Cliffs, N.J.: Prentice-Hall, 1966. 276 p.

> A sociological study of a millenarian religious group. Its special appeal to the psychologist is its analysis of the "maintenance of faith" following conversion to the sect.

Maves, Paul B. "Conversion: A Behavioral Category." REVIEW OF RELIGIOUS RESEARCH 5 (1963): 41-48.

Moore, Robert L. "Justification without Joy: Psychohistorical Reflections on John Wesley's Childhood and Conversion." HISTORY OF CHILDHOOD QUAR-TERLY: A JOURNAL OF PSYCHOHISTORY 2 (1974): 31-52.

Nock, Arthur Darby. CONVERSION: THE OLD AND NEW IN RELIGION

FROM ALEXANDER THE GREAT TO AUGUSTINE OF HIPPO. New York: Oxford University Press, 1961. xii, 309 p.

> An historical study of religious conversion which places considerable emphasis on the social and psychological context of large-scale religious conversion.

Oates, Wayne E [dward]. "Conversion and Mental Health." PASTORAL PSYCHOLOGY 17 (September 1966): 43-48.

Pitts, John. "Conversion: Its Nature and Necessity." RELIGION IN LIFE 22 (1953): 261-72.

Roberts, F.J. "Some Psychological Factors in Religious Conversion." BRITISH JOURNAL OF SOCIAL AND CLINICAL PSYCHOLOGY 4, no. 3 (1965): 185-87.

Salzman, Leon. "The Psychology of Religious and Ideological Conversion." PSYCHIATRY 16 (1953): 177-87.

_____. "Types of Religious Conversion." PASTORAL PSYCHOLOGY 17 (September 1966): 8-20.

Sarbin, Theodore R., and Adler, Nathan. "Self-Reconstitution Processes: A Preliminary Report." PSYCHOANALYTIC REVIEW 57 (1970-71): 599-616.

> Views religious conversion as a self-reconstitution process.

Sargant, William. BATTLE FOR THE MIND: HOW EVANGELISTS, PSYCHIATRISTS, POLITICIANS AND MEDICINE MEN CAN CHANGE YOUR BELIEFS AND BEHAVIOR. Garden City, N.Y.: Doubleday & Co., 1957. 263 p.

> A psychiatrist's investigation of the stress and emotional collapse involved in ideological and religious conversion and belief-reversal. An extended section on the conversion techniques of John Wesley.

Scroggs, James R., and Douglas, William G.T. "Issues in the Psychology of Religious Conversion." JOURNAL OF RELIGION AND HEALTH 6 (1967): 204-16.

Sedman, G., and Hopkinson, G. "The Psychopathology of Mystical and Religious Conversion Experiences in Psychiatric Patients." CONFINIA PSYCHIATRICA 9 (1966): 1-19.

Seggar, John, and Kenny, Phillip. "Conversion: Evaluation of a Step-Like Process for Problem-Solving." REVIEW OF RELIGIOUS RESEARCH 13 (1972): 178-84.

Siegel, Lawrence M. "A Bar to Conversion." PSYCHOANALYTIC REVIEW 53 (1966): 16–23.

Spellman, Charles M., et al. "Manifest Anxiety as a Contributing Factor in Religious Conversion." JOURNAL OF CONSULTING AND CLINICAL PSY-CHOLOGY 36 (April 1971): 245–47.

Stanley, Gordon. "Personality and Attitude Correlates of Religious Conversion." JOURNAL FOR THE SCIENTIFIC STUDY OF RELIGION 4, no. 1 (1964); 60–63.

Tremmel, William C. "The Converting Choice." JOURNAL FOR THE SCIEN-TIFIC STUDY OF RELIGION 10 (1971): 17–25.

> An interpretation of conversion as the choice available to the indi-vidual for changing the "psychic set" which dominates all critical choices. See also entries on conversion in section A:3.

D:3 MYSTICAL AND OTHER ALTERED STATES OF CONSCIOUSNESS

Aaronson, Bernard S. "Mystic and Schizophreniform States and the Experience of Depth." JOURNAL FOR THE SCIENTIFIC STUDY OF RELIGION 6 (1967): 246–52.

Abe, T. "The Relation between Emotions and Bodily Sensations." PSYCHOLO-GIA 8 (1965): 187–90.

> Based on Zen Buddhist meditation.

Angoff, Allan. "The Literature of Religion and Parapsychology." INTERNA-TIONAL JOURNAL OF PARAPSYCHOLOGY 8, no. 2 (1966): 321–34.

Arieti, Silvano. "The Loss of Reality." PSYCHOANALYSIS AND THE PSY-CHOANALYTIC REVIEW 48, no. 3 (1961): 3–24.

> Includes a discussion of religious mystical experiences, with histori-cal examples.

Assagioli, Roberto. "Symbols of Transpersonal Experiences." JOURNAL OF TRANSPERSONAL PSYCHOLOGY 1 (1969): 33–46.

Banquet, J.P. "Spectral Analysis of the EEG in Meditation." ELECTROEN-CEPHALOGRAPHY CLINICAL AND NEUROPHYSIOLOGY 35 (August 1963): 143–51.

Barber, Theodore X. LSD, MARIHUANA, YOGA, AND HYPNOSIS. Chicago: Aldine Publishing Co., 1970. xii, 337 p.

Bastide, Roger. THE MYSTICAL LIFE. Translated by H.F. Kynaston-Snell and David Waring. London: J. Cape, 1934. 256 p.

Discusses Christian mysticism in terms of its pathological and non-pathological manifestations.

Bazak, Jacob. "ESP and Judaism." PARAPSYCHOLOGY REVIEW 1 (September 1970): 9-13.

Benzi, M. "Visions des huichols sous l'effet du peyote." HYGIENE MENTALE 58, no. 3 (1969): 61-97.

Bolley, Alfons. "Recent Research into the Psychology of God Consciousness in Meditation." LUMEN VITAE 16 (1961): 223-32.

_____. "Die Bedeutung von Einsfuhlungs- und Einfuhlungs-erlebnissen in der Meditation." ARCHIV FUR RELIGIONS-PSYCHOLOGIE 8 (1964): 145-52.

Boudreau, Leonce. "Transcendental Meditation and Yoga as Reciprocal Inhibitors." JOURNAL OF BEHAVIOR THERAPY AND EXPERIMENTAL PSYCHIATRY 3 (June 1972): 97-98.

Bourguignon, Erika, ed. RELIGION, ALTERED STATES OF CONSCIOUSNESS, AND SOCIAL CHANGE. Columbus: Ohio State University Press, 1973. 389 p.

Essays by anthropologists, with some attention to psychological considerations. Field reports of native movements from Mexico, South America, and the Caribbean, as well as several papers which attempt a framework for comparative study.

Bourque, Linda B., and Back, Kurt W. "Values and Transcendental Experiences." SOCIAL FORCES 47 (1968): 34-38.

Breed, George, and Fagan, Joen. "Religious Dogmatism and Peak Experiences: A Test of Maslow's Hypothesis." PSYCHOLOGICAL REPORTS 31 (December 1972): 866.

Bryan, William J., Jr. RELIGIOUS ASPECTS OF HYPNOTISM. Springfield, Ill.: Charles C Thomas, 1962. 77 p.

Bucke (R.M.) Memorial Society. TRANCE AND POSSESSION STATES. (Proceedings of the Second Annual Conference.) Edited by Raymond [H.] Prince. Montreal: 1966. 200 p.

Includes, in addition to demographic and sociological analyses, essays from the perspectives of ego psychology, Rorschach interpretation, and psychotherapy. See listing in section D:1.

_____. DO PSYCHEDELICS HAVE RELIGIOUS IMPLICATIONS? (Proceedings of the Third Annual Conference.) Edited by D.H. Salman and R[aymond] H. Prince. Montreal: 1968. 81 p.

Essays on LSD, folk healing, psychedelic therapy, and related topics. See listing in section D:1.

Cheek, John L. "Paul's Mysticism in the Light of Psychedelic Experience." JOURNAL OF THE AMERICAN ACADEMY OF RELIGION 38 (1970): 381-89.

Clark, Robert A. "Cosmic Consciousness in Catatonic Schizophrenia." PSYCHOANALYTIC REVIEW 33 (1946): 460-504.

Clark, Walter Houston. "Mysticism as a Basic Concept in Defining the Religious Self." LUMEN VITAE 19 (1964): 221-32.

_____. "Religious Aspects of the Psychedelic Substances and the Law." INTERNATIONAL JOURNAL OF PARAPSYCHOLOGY 9, no. 1 (1967): 32-36.

_____. "The Religious Significance of Psychedelic Substances." RELIGION IN LIFE 36 (1967): 393-403.

_____. CHEMICAL ECSTASY: PSYCHEDELIC DRUGS AND RELIGION. New York: Sheed & Ward, 1969. 179 p.

An argument for the positive uses of psychedelic drugs in the inducement of religious experience. Includes some discussion of classic cases of ecstasy not drug induced, e.g., Isaiah, Pascal.

_____. "The Mystical Consciousness and Its Contribution to Human Understanding." HUMANITAS 6 (1971): 311-24.

_____, ed. "Religion and Parapsychology." PASTORAL PSYCHOLOGY 21 (September 1970): 1-54.

Issue devoted to parapsychology.

Crookall, Robert. THE INTERPRETATION OF COSMIC AND MYSTICAL EXPERIENCES. Cambridge, England: James Clarke, 1969. xii, 175 p.

Dabrowski, Kazimierz. POSITIVE DISINTEGRATION. Boston: Little, Brown and Co., 1964. xxviii, 132 p.

Emphasizes the positive aspects of personal disintegration, understood here as the "loosening of structures, the dispersion and breaking up of psychic forces.

_____. PERSONALITY SHAPING THROUGH POSITIVE DISINTEGRATION.
Boston: Little, Brown and Co., 1967. 304 p.

Discusses the personality disintegration, leading to higher integration, of various figures, including Saint Augustine.

Dalal, A.S., and Barber, T[heodore] X. "Yoga, 'Yoga Feats', and Hypnosis
in the Light of Empirical Research." AMERICAN JOURNAL OF CLINICAL
HYPNOSIS 11, no. 3 (1969): 155-66.

Deikman, Arthur J. "De-Automatization and the Mystic Experience." PSY-
CHIATRY 29, no. 4 (1966): 324-38. Reprinted in ALTERED STATES OF CON-
SCIOUSNESS: A BOOK OF READINGS, pp. 23-43. Edited by Charles T.
Tart. New York: John Wiley & Sons, 1969. (See below for book listing.)

An extremely influential essay in the study of the religious aspects
of altered states of consciousness.

De Ropp, Robert S. THE MASTER GAME: PATHWAYS TO HIGHER CON-
SCIOUSNESS BEYOND THE DRUG EXPERIENCE. New York: Delacarte, 1968.
252 p.

Summary of the strategies mystics have employed in achieving higher
states of consciousness.

Douglas-Smith, Basil. "An Empirical Study of Religious Mysticism." BRITISH
JOURNAL OF PSYCHIATRY 118 (1971): 549-54.

Contends that data do not support the view of mysticism as due to
pathology.

Faure, Henri. HALLUCINATIONS ET REALITE PERCEPTIVE. Paris: Presses
Universitaires de France, 1965. 255 p.

A study of the psychopathology of hallucinations, with an extremely
useful account of such experiences in myth, folklore, superstitions,
and mysticism.

Fedi, Remo. "La Manifestazioni del Transcendente." RICERCHE BIOPSICHICHE
11 (1967): 121-29.

Fingarette, Herbert. "The Ego and Mystic Selflessness." PSYCHOANALYSIS
AND THE PSYCHOANALYTIC REVIEW 45 (Spring-Summer 1958): 5-40.

Furst, Peter J., ed. FLESH OF THE GODS: THE RITUAL USES OF HALLUCI-
NOGENS. New York: Praeger Publishers, 1972. xvi, 304 p.

Essays by anthropologists and botanists, including a paper by Weston

Barre, on hallucinogens and the shamanic origins of religions; fairly extensive bibliography.

Gellhorn, Ernest, and Kiely, William F. "Mystical States of Consciousness: Neurophysiological and Clinical Aspects." JOURNAL OF NERVOUS AND MENTAL DISEASE 154 (June 1972): 399-405.

Gibbons, Don, and de Jarnette, James. "Hypnotic Susceptibility and Religious Experience." JOURNAL FOR THE SCIENTIFIC STUDY OF RELIGION 11 (June 1972): 152-56.

Gilbert, Albin R. "Identifying the Mystic Variable." PSYCHOLOGIA: AN INTERNATIONAL JOURNAL OF PSYCHOLOGY IN THE ORIENT 12 (December 1969): 139-46.

_____. "Pseudo Mind-Expansion through Psychedelics and Brain-Wave-Programming versus True Mind-Expansion through Life Conditioning to the Absolute." PSYCHOLOGIA: AN INTERNATIONAL JOURNAL OF PSYCHOLOGY IN THE ORIENT 14 (December 1971): 187-92.

Goleman, Daniel. "The Buddha on Meditation and States of Consciousness. Part 1: The Teachings." JOURNAL OF TRANSPERSONAL PSYCHOLOGY 4 (1972): 1-44.

_____. "The Buddha on Meditation and States of Consciousness. Part 2: Typology of Meditation Techniques." JOURNAL OF TRANSPERSONAL PSYCHOLOGY 4 (1972): 151-210.

Goodman, Felicitas D., et al. TRANCE, HEALING AND HALLUCINATION: THREE FIELD STUDIES IN RELIGIOUS EXPERIENCE. New York: John Wiley & Sons, 1974. xxiii, 388 p.

Field studies in the Caribbean, Brazil, and Mexico of the social and cultic context, mode of occurence, perpetuation, and religious significance of trance-states.

Grace, Roy E. "Parapsychology and Biblical Religion." PASTORAL PSYCHOLOGY 21 (September 1970): 8-12.

Greeff, Etienne de. L'HOMME ET SON JUGE. Brussels: Editions Desclee De Brouwer, 1962. 182 p.

Based on Jungian psychology, phenomenological analysis, and existential philosophy, this study addresses the experience of "the presence of being" which precedes conscious awareness. This experience is analyzed with respect to its "expansive" quality.

Greeley, Andrew M. ECSTASY: A WAY OF KNOWING. Englewood

Cliffs, N.J.: Prentice-Hall, 1974. 150 p.

> A research sociologists's nontechnical discussion of mystical experi-
> ence as a kind of knowledge that is not limited to an esoteric
> elite but may occur in up to 35 percent of the American popula-
> tion. In addition to reporting preliminary research findings and
> plans for further research, Greeley includes brief chapters on the
> psychology of ecstasy, sex and ecstasy, ecstatic politics, and
> faddism.

Greene, Thayer A. "The Dream: Clinical Aid and Theological Catalyst."
UNION SEMINARY QUARTERLY REVIEW 24, no. 2 (1969): 171-80.

> Also listed in section G:2.

Grof, Stanislav. "Beyond Psychoanalysis: Implications of LSD Research for
Understanding Dimensions of Human Personality." DARSHANA INTERNATION-
AL 10 (July 1970): 55-73.

_____. "Varieties of Transpersonal Experiences: Observations from LSD Psy-
chotherapy." JOURNAL OF TRANSPERSONAL PSYCHOLOGY 4 (1972): 45-80.

Hardy, Alister. "Parapsychology in Relation to Religion." PARAPSYCHOLOGY
REVIEW 2, no. 3 (1971): 3-6, 21.

Harner, Michael J., ed. HALLUCINOGENS AND SHAMANISM. London and
New York: Oxford University Press, 1973. xv, 200 p.

> Anthropological and psychological participant-observer studies of
> psychotropic drug use and shamanism in South America, Westerniz-
> ing areas, and in the West. Two essays on the question of a
> transcultural experience. See annotation in section C:5.

Havens, Joseph. "Memo on the Religious Implications of the Consciousness-
Changing Drugs." JOURNAL FOR THE SCIENTIFIC STUDY OF RELIGION 3,
no. 2 (1964): 216-26.

Hayman, Max. "Science, Mysticism and Psychopharmacology." CALIFORNIA
MEDICINE 101 (October 1964): 266-71.

Hefner, Lawrence S. "Beyond the Limits of Sense Perception." PASTORAL
PSYCHOLOGY 10 (November 1959): 31-40.

Hood, Ralph W., Jr. "Forms of Religious Commitment and Intense Religious
Experience." REVIEW OF RELIGIOUS RESEARCH 15 (Fall 1973): 29-36.

_____. "Hypnotic Susceptibility and Reported Religious Experience." PSYCHO-
LOGICAL REPORTS 33 (October 1973): 549-50.

_____. "Religious Orientation and the Experience of Transcendence." JOURNAL FOR THE SCIENTIFIC STUDY OF RELIGION 12 (December 1973): 441-48.

_____. "Psychological Strength and the Report of Intense Religious Experience." JOURNAL FOR THE SCIENTIFIC STUDY OF RELIGION 13 (March 1974): 65-72.

Howley, John. PSYCHOLOGY AND MYSTICAL EXPERIENCE. London: K. Paul, Trench, Trubner & Co.; St. Louis: B. Herder, 1920. 275 p.

Discussions of retreat, conversion, revivals, and varieties of mysticism from a Catholic perspective.

Jordan, G. Ray. "Reflections on LSD, Zen Meditation and Satori." PSYCHOLOGIA 5 (1961): 124-30.

_____. "LSD and Mystic Experience." JOURNAL OF BIBLE AND RELIGION 31 (1963): 114-23.

Kanzer, Mark. "The Vision of Father Zossina from the Brothers Karamazov." AMERICAN IMAGO 8 (1951): 329-35.

Kasamatsu, A., and Hirai, T. "Science of Zazen." PSYCHOLOGIA 6 (1963): 86-91.

Physiological and psychological study of Zen meditation.

_____. "An Electroencephalographic Study on the Zen Meditation (Zazen)." PSYCHOLOGIA: AN INTERNATIONAL JOURNAL OF PSYCHOLOGY IN THE ORIENT 12 (December 1969): 205-25.

Kelman, Harold. "Oriental Psychological Processes and Creativity." AMERICAN JOURNAL OF PSYCHOANALYSIS 23 (1963): 67-84.

Kelsey, Morton T. DREAMS: THE DARK SPEECH OF THE SPIRIT: A CHRISTIAN INTERPRETATION. New York: Doubleday & Co., 1968. 326 p.

Kondo, Akihisa. "Intuition in Zen Buddhism." AMERICAN JOURNAL OF PSYCHOANALYSIS 12 (1952): 10-14.

Krippner, Stanley, and Davidson, Richard. "Religious Implications of Para-Normal Events Occurring during Chemically Induced 'Psychedelic' Experiences." PASTORAL PSYCHOLOGY 21 (September 1970); 27-34.

Kurty, Paul S. "Similarities and Differences between Religious Mysticism and Drug Induced Experiences." JOURNAL OF HUMANISTIC PSYCHOLOGY 3 (1963): 146-54.

La Barre, Weston. "Religions, Rorschachs and Tranquilizers." AMERICAN JOURNAL OF ORTHOPSYCHIATRY 29 (1959): 688-98.

Larson, Gerald J. "Mystical Man in India." JOURNAL FOR THE SCIENTIFIC STUDY OF RELIGION 12 (March 1973): 1-16.

Develops typology of mystical experience as unitive, isolative, copulative, and nihilative.

Laski, Margharita. ECSTASY: A STUDY OF SOME SECULAR AND RELIGIOUS EXPERIENCES. Bloomington: Indiana University Press, 1961. xii, 544 p.

A novelist's attempt to isolate some characteristics of ecstasy on the basis of questionnaires and literary and religious texts.

Leary, Timothy, and Clark, Walter Houston. "Religious Implications of Consciousness Expanding Drugs." RELIGIOUS EDUCATION 58 (1963): 251-56.

A study of openness to religious stimuli of 400 subjects to whom psilocybin was administered.

Levy-Bruhl, Lucien. THE "SOUL" OF THE PRIMITIVE. Translated by Lilian A. Clare. London: George Allen and Unwin, 1966; Chicago: Henry Regnery Co., 1971. 351 p.

A translation of a 1927 work by a French scholar who influenced Freud, Jung, and other psychologists. Discusses the pre-logical and mystical participation in primitive views of the individual, of social solidarity, and of death and reincarnation.

Lidz, Theodore, and Rothenberg, Albert. "Psychedelism: Dionysius Reborn." PSYCHIATRY 31 (1968): 116-25.

Magnino, Leo. "Zen e Spontaneita." RASSEGNA ITALIANA DI RICERCA PSICHICA, nos. 2-3, 1966, pp. 37-46.

Maraczewski, Albert. "Psychedelic Agents and Mysticism." PSYCHOSOMATICS 12, no. 2 (1971): 94-100.

Marechal, Joseph. STUDIES IN THE PSYCHOLOGY OF THE MYSTICS. Translated by Algar Thorold. London: Burns, Oates and Washburne, 1927. 344 p.

Margetts, E.L. "The Concept of Levels of Consciousness in the Upanishads." CANADIAN MEDICAL ASSOCIATION JOURNAL 65 (1951): 391.

Maslow, Abraham H. "Cognition of Being in the Peak Experience." JOURNAL OF GENETIC PSYCHOLOGY 94 (1959): 43-67.

_____. TOWARD A PSYCHOLOGY OF BEING. Princeton, N.J.: D. Van Nostrand, 1962. 214 p.

Maslow's classic study of peak experiences, with chapters on the relation of peak experience to cognition, identity, creativity, and values.

_____. RELIGIONS, VALUES AND PEAK-EXPERIENCES. Columbus: Ohio State University Press, 1964. xx, 123 p.

Argues for the self-validating character of peak-experiences and being-values.

_____. "The Farther Reaches of Human Nature." JOURNAL OF TRANSPERSONAL PSYCHOLOGY 1 (1969): 1-10.

Massoon, Harold. "Gates of Eden." PSYCHEDELIC REVIEW, no. 10, 1969, pp. 65-69.

A study of LSD and ecstasy.

Moller, Herbert. "Affective Mysticism in Western Civilization." PSYCHOANALYTIC REVIEW 52 (1965): 259-72.

Mukerjee, Radhakamal. THE THEORY AND ART OF MYSTICISM. 2nd ed. New York: Asia Publishing House, 1961. xx, 352 p.

Murphy, Gardner. "The Natural, the Mystical and the Paranormal." PASTORAL PSYCHOLOGY 15 (January 1965): 42-59.

Muses, Charles, and Young, Arthur M., eds. CONSCIOUSNESS AND REALITY: THE HUMAN PIVOT POINT. New York: Outerbridge and Lazard, 1972. xii, 472 p.

A collection of readings on such diverse subjects as telepathy, reincarnation, and myth.

Myer, John C. "Two Types of Mystical Response." PSYCHOLOGY 6 (1969): 53-60.

Mynard, Jacques. "Remarques introductives a l'etude de fantasmes mystiques." REVUE FRANCAISE DE PSYCHANALYSE 35 (1971): 365-68.

Onda, A. "Zen and Creativity." PSYCHOLOGIA 5 (1962): 13-20.

Orme-Johnson, David W. "Autonomic Stability and Transcendental Meditation." PSYCHOSOMATIC MEDICINE 35 (July 1973): 341-49.

Osis, Karlis. "Informal Methods of Research in Psychic Phenomena for Religious Believers." PASTORAL PSYCHOLOGY 21 (September 1970): 35-40.

_____, et al. "Dimensions of Meditative Experience." JOURNAL OF TRANS-PERSONAL PSYCHIATRY 5, no. 2 (1973): 109-35.

Pahnke, Walter N., and Richards, William A. "Implications of LSD and Experimental Mysticism." JOURNAL OF RELIGION AND HEALTH 5, no. 3 (1966): 175-208.

Penner, Wes. "Hippies' Attraction to Mysticism." ADOLESCENCE 7 (Summer 1972): 199-210.

Quercy, Pierre. L'HALLUCINATION. 2 vols. Paris: F. Alcan, 1930.

   Studies in the theories of perception, image, and hallucination of
   Spinoza, Leibniz, and Bergson; the suffering and visions of St.
   Theresa; and clinical studies.

Rogers, A.H. "Zen and LSD: An Enlightening Experience." PSYCHOLOGIA 7 (1964): 150-51.

Rugg, Harold. IMAGINATION. New York: Harper & Row, Publishers, 1963. xxii, 361 p.

   Draws on Eastern and Western mysticism to illustrate techniques
   for emptying the conscious mind in order to facilitate the creative
   process which occurs in the "trans-liminal" or "off-conscious"
   mind.

Sargant, William. "The Physiology of Faith." BRITISH JOURNAL OF PSYCHIATRY 118 (1969): 505-18.

_____. THE MIND POSSESSED: A PHYSIOLOGY OF POSSESSION, MYSTICISM, AND FAITH HEALING. Philadelphia: J.B. Lippincott Co., 1974. xii, 212 p.

   A psychiatric approach to the physiological mechanisms underlying
   religious phenomena in different cultures.

Sasamoto, K. "Samadhi and Hypnotism." PSYCHOLOGIA 5 (1962): 73-74.

Scharfstein, Ben-Ami. MYSTICAL EXPERIENCE. Indianapolis: The Bobbs-Merrill Co., 1973. 195 p.

A good discussion of mysticism by a philosopher who includes one chapter comparing Freud's psychoanalysis with Patanjali's yoga and another chapter on psychotic mysticism.

Schneiderman, Leo. "Psychological Notes on the Nature of Mystical Experience." JOURNAL FOR THE SCIENTIFIC STUDY OF RELIGION 6 (1967): 91-100.

Schroeder, Theodore. "Prenatal Psychisms and Mystical Pantheism." INTERNATIONAL JOURNAL OF PSYCHOANALYSIS 3 (1922): 445-66.

Setzer, J. Schoneberg. "Parapsychology: Religion's Basic Science." RELIGION IN LIFE 39 (1970): 595-607.

Silberer, Herbert. PROBLEMS OF MYSTICISM AND ITS SYMBOLISM. Translated by Smith Ely Jeliffe. New York: Moffat, Yard, 1917. Reprinted as HIDDEN SYMBOLISM OF ALCHEMY AND THE OCCULT ARTS. New York: Dover Publications, 1971. 451 p.

One of the earliest and most extended psychoanalytic studies of mysticism, this work deals with one parable from an eighteenth-century alchemical text, but develops a comprehensive perspective on many different symbols, on other alchemists, and on the relation between depth psychology and mysticism.

Smith, Alson J. RELIGION AND THE NEW PSYCHOLOGY. New York: Doubleday & Co., 1951. 192 p.

Deals largely with the religious implications of the work of Joseph B. Rhine, the parapsychologist, at Duke University. Argues that parapsychology "can make religion intellectually respectable and science emotionally satisfying."

Stendahl, Krister. "Religion, Mysticism, and the Institutional Church." DAEDALUS 96 (1967): 854-59.

Sterba, Richard. "Remarks on Mystic States." AMERICAN IMAGO 25 (1968): 77-85.

Tart, Charles T., ed. ALTERED STATES OF CONSCIOUSNESS: A BOOK OF READINGS. New York: John Wiley & Sons, 1969. 575 p.

A collection of readings generally credited with unifying the field of altered states research. Includes theoretical and research papers, contemporary and historical.

_____. "A Psychologist's Experience with Transcendental Meditation." JOURNAL OF TRANSPERSONAL PSYCHOLOGY 3 (1972): 135-40.

Thorner, Isidor. "Prophetic and Mystic Experience: Comparison and Consequences." JOURNAL FOR THE SCIENTIFIC STUDY OF RELIGION 5 (1965-66): 82-96.

von Grunebaum, G.E. "The Place of Parapsychological Phenomena in Islam." INTERNATIONAL JOURNAL OF PARAPSYCHOLOGY 8, no. 2 (1966): 264-80.

   The author is a noted Islamicist.

Wainwright, W.J. "Mysticism and Sense Perception." RELIGIOUS STUDIES 9 (September 1973): 257-78.

Walther, Gerda. PHANOMENOLOGIE DE MYSTIK. Olten: Walter, 1955. 264 p.

Wapnick, Kenneth. "Mysticism and Schizophrenia." JOURNAL OF TRANS-PERSONAL PSYCHOLOGY 1 (1969): 49-68.

Watts, Alan W. THE JOYOUS COSMOLOGY: ADVENTURES IN THE CHEMISTRY OF CONSCIOUSNESS. New York: Pantheon Books, 1962. xix, 94 p.

   A description of the author's drug-induced experiences. Stresses
   the implications of such experiences for the evolution of a new
   image of man.

Weil, Andrew. THE NATURAL MIND: A NEW WAY OF LOOKING AT DRUGS AND THE HIGHER CONSCIOUSNESS. Boston: Houghton Mifflin Co., 1973. 229 p.

Weinpahl, P. "Zazen and Identity." PSYCHOLOGIA 8 (1965): 135-44.

White, John, ed. THE HIGHEST STATE OF CONSCIOUSNESS. New York: Doubleday & Co., 1972. xxi, 484 p.

   A collection of essays on altered states of consciousness, mysticism,
   Zen, LSD, biofeedback, and trance.

Wolff, Werner. THE DREAM, MIRROR OF CONSCIENCE: A HISTORY OF DREAM INTERPRETATION FROM 2000 B.C. AND A NEW THEORY OF DREAM SYNTHESIS. New York: Grune & Stratton, 1952. 348 p.

Wolstein, Benjamin. "On the Limitations of Mysticism in Psychoanalysis." PSYCHOLOGIA 5 (1962): 140-45.

Zaehner, Robert Charles. MYSTICISM SACRED AND PROFANE: AN INQUIRY INTO SOME VARIETIES OF PRAETERNATURAL EXPERIENCE. New York: Oxford University Press, 1957. xviii, 256 p.

   The author is a noted historian of religions.

_____. DRUGS, MYSTICISM, AND MAKE-BELIEVE. London: Collins, 1972. 223 p.

D:4 GLOSSOLALIA

Bryant, Ernest, and O'Connell, Daniel C. "A Phonemic Analysis of Nine Samples of Glossolalic Speech." PSYCHONOMIC SPEECH 22, no. 2 (1971): 81-83.

Goodman, Felicitas D. "Glossolalia: Speaking in Tongues in Four Cultural Settings." CONFINA PSYCHIATRICA 12, nos. 2-4 (1969): 113-29.

_____. "Phonetic Analysis of Glossolalia in Four Cultural Settings." JOURNAL FOR THE SCIENTIFIC STUDY OF RELIGION 8 (Fall 1969): 227-39.

_____. SPEAKING IN TONGUES: A CROSS-CULTURAL STUDY OF GLOSSOLALIA. Chicago: University of Chicago Press, 1972. xxii, 175 p.

> An ethnographic, linguistic approach which takes into account psychological perspectives on ecstasy and glossolalia. Argues that speech behavior is modified by the way the body acts in particular mental states, e.g., trance.

_____. "Glossolalia and Hallucination in Pentecostal Congregations." PSYCHIATRIA CLINICA 6, no. 2 (1973): 97-103.

Hine, Virginia H. "Pentecostal Glossolalia: Toward a Functional Interpretation." JOURNAL FOR THE SCIENTIFIC STUDY OF RELIGION 8 (1969): 211-26.

Jaquith, James R. "Toward a Typology of Formal Communicative Behaviors: Glossolalia." ANTHROPOLOGICAL LINGUISTICS 9, no. 8 (1967): 1-8.

Kildahl, John P. THE PSYCHOLOGY OF SPEAKING IN TONGUES. New York: Harper & Row, Publishers, 1972. xii, 110 p.

> A clinical psychologist's report on an extensive research effort, involving field work and psychological testing in groups across the United States. Includes a brief history of glossolalia, a summary of different psychological explanations, and an extensive bibliography.

Lapsley, James N., and Simpson, John H. "Speaking in Tongues: Token of Group Acceptance and Divine Approval." PASTORAL PSYCHOLOGY 15 (May 1964): 48-56.

_____. "Speaking in Tongues: Infantile Babble or Song of the Self?" PASTORAL PSYCHOLOGY 15 (September 1964): 16-24.

Martin, Ira. GLOSSOLALIA IN THE APOSTOLIC CHURCH, A SURVEY STUDY OF TONGUE-SPEECH. Berea, Ky.: Berea College Press, 1960. 100 p.

May, L. Carlyle. "A Survey of Glossolalia and Related Phenomena in Non-Christian Religions." AMERICAN ANTHROPOLOGIST 58 (1956): 75-96.

Osser, H.A., et al. "Glossolalic Speech from a Psycholinguistic Perspective." JOURNAL OF PSYCHOLINGUISTIC RESEARCH 2 (January 1973): 9-19.

Pattison, E. Mansell. "Behavioral Science Research on the Nature of Glosso-lalia." JOURNAL OF THE AMERICAN SCIENTIFIC AFFILIATION, September 1968, pp. 73-86.

Qualben, Paul A., and Kildahl, John P. RELATIONSHIPS BETWEEN GLOS-SOLALIA AND MENTAL HEALTH. Bethesda, Md.: National Institute of Mental Health, 1971.

> The report of extensive research by a psychiatrist and a clinical psychologist who find no differences in the mental health of tongue-speakers and non-tongue-speakers.

Richardson, James T. "Psychological Interpretations of Glossolalia: A Reexamination of Research." JOURNAL FOR THE SCIENTIFIC STUDY OF RELIGION 12 (June 1973): 199-208.

Sadler, A.W. "Glossolalia and Possession: An Appeal to the Episcopal Study Commission." JOURNAL FOR THE SCIENTIFIC STUDY OF RELIGION 4, no. 1 (1964): 84-90.

Samarin, William J. "The Linguisticality of Glossolalia." HARTFORD QUAR-TERLY 8, no. 4 (1968): 49-75.

_____. "Variation and Variables in Religious Glossolalia." LANGUAGE IN SOCIETY 1 (April 1972): 121-30.

_____. "Glossolalia as Regressive Speech." LANGUAGE AND SPEECH 16 (January 1973): 77-89.

Spoerri, Th. "Ekstatische Rede und Glossolalie." In BEITRAGE ZUR EKSTASE, pp. 137-52. Edited by Th. Spoerri. Basel: S. Karger, 1968.

Vivier, L.M. "The Glossolalic and His Personality." In BEITRAGE ZUR EK-STASE, pp. 153-75. Edited by Th. Spoerri. Basel: S. Karger, 1968.

Section E

THE DISPOSITIONAL DIMENSION OF RELIGION

Section E

THE DISPOSITIONAL DIMENSION OF RELIGION

E:1 WORLD RELIGIONS AND SYSTEMS OF MEANING

Akhilananda, Swami. HINDU PSYCHOLOGY: ITS MEANING FOR THE WEST.
London: Routledge and Kegan Paul, 1946. xviii, 241 p.

Ali Beg, Moazziz. "The Theory of Personality in the Bhagavad Gita: A Study
in Transpersonal Psychology." PSYCHOLOGIA: AN INTERNATIONAL JOUR-
NAL OF PSYCHOLOGY IN THE ORIENT 13 (March 1970): 12-17.

Amsel, Abraham. JUDAISM AND PSYCHOLOGY. New York: Philipp Feld-
heim, 1969. 213 p.

> Attempts to develop a Jewish psychology which is more in conso-
> nance with traditional Jewish concepts than psychoanalysis is gen-
> erally considered to be.

Arapura, J.G. RELIGION AS ANXIETY AND TRANQUILITY: AN ESSAY IN
COMPARATIVE PHENOMENOLOGY OF THE SPIRIT. Paris and The Hague:
Mouton, 1972. 146 p.

> Discussions of the reflection in consciousness of two constant motifs
> as they appear especially in Christianity and Hinduism-Buddhism.

Barag, G.G. "Question of Jewish Monotheism." AMERICAN IMAGO 4
(July 1947): 8-25.

Becker, Ernest. ZEN: A RATIONAL CRITIQUE. New York: W.W. Norton
& Co., 1961. 192 p.

> The first book by Becker, an anthropologist who works with psy-
> chological materials. Criticizes Zen along with psychoanalysis as
> being a subversive force on the Western tradition of autonomy and
> individualism.

Bellah, Robert N. "Father and Son in Christianity and Confucianism." PSY-

CHOANALYTIC REVIEW 52 (1965): 236-58. Also published in BEYOND BE-
LIEF: ESSAYS ON RELIGION IN A POST-TRADITIONAL WORLD, pp. 76-99.
Edited by Robert N. Bellah. New York: Harper & Row, Publishers, 1970.

Bellet, Maurice. LA DEPLACEMENT DE LA RELIGION. Paris: Desclee de
Brouwer, 1972. 256 p.

Benoit, Hubert. THE SUPREME DOCTRINE: PSYCHOLOGICAL STUDIES IN
ZEN THOUGHT. New York: Pantheon Books, 1955. xv, 248 p.

Berenda, C.W. WORLD VISIONS AND THE IMAGE OF MAN. New York:
Vantage, 1965. 233 p.

Berkeley-Hill, Owen. "The Anal-Erotic Factor in the Religion, Philosophy and
Character of the Hindus." INTERNATIONAL JOURNAL OF PSYCHOANALY-
SIS 2 (1921): 306-38.

Dalman, Carlos J. "Anthropocentric Aspects of Religion." PSYCHOANALY-
TIC REVIEW 54 (1967): 679-87.

Daujat, Jean. PSYCHOLOGIE CONTEMPORAINE ET PENSEE CHRETIENNE.
Tournai: Desclee, 1962. 335 p.

de Bont, Walter. "Psychologie van de Sekulariserung." SOCIALE WETENS-
CHAPPEN 11, no. 3 (1968): 207-35.

_____. "Le Secularisation de l'eschaton." VIE SPIRITUELLE SUPPLEMENT
22 (November 1969): 462-82.

Dodds, E.R. PAGAN AND CHRISTIAN IN AN AGE OF ANXIETY. New
York: W.W. Norton & Co., 1965. xii, 144 p.

    Probes the "spiritual climate" of the ancient world (Marcus Aurelius
    to Constantine) in order to show why Christianity emerged as a
    pervasive religious force. Strongly influenced by Jamesian psychol-
    ogy of religion.

Feldman, Arthur A. "Freud's MOSES AND MONOTHEISM and the Three
Stages of Israelitish Religion." PSYCHOANALYTIC REVIEW 31 (1944): 361-
418.

Freeman, Thomas. "Some Notes on a Forgotten Religion." PSYCHOANALY-
TIC REVIEW 41 (1954): 9-27.

    A study of Mithraism.

Freud, Sigmund. MOSES AND MONOTHEISM. In THE STANDARD EDITION

OF THE COMPLETE PSYCHOLOGICAL WORKS OF SIGMUND FREUD, vol. 23, pp. 3-137. Edited by James Strachey. London: The Hogarth Press, 1964. (Paperback ed. of MOSES AND MONOTHEISM available from New York: Random, Vintage, 1955.)

> Continuing his work in TOTEM AND TABOO and GROUP PSYCHOL- OGY AND THE ANALYSIS OF THE EGO on group formation, Freud here turns to a psychological reconstruction of Jewish history and Moses, who is seen as an Egyptian, murdered after bringing monotheism to the Semites. Discussions of the increase in self- esteem and intellectuality deriving from monotheism.

Fromm, Erich. "Psychoanalysis and Zen Buddhism." In ZEN BUDDHISM AND PSYCHOANALYSIS, pp. 77-141. Edited by D.T. Suzuki, et al. New York: Grove Press, 1963.

Gilbert, Rabbi Arthur. "A Rabbinic Theory of Instincts." PSYCHOANALYSIS 3 (Spring 1955): 36-43.

Harms, Ernest. "Five Basic Types of Theistic Worlds in the Religions of Man." NUMEN: INTERNATIONAL REVIEW FOR THE HISTORY OF RELIGIONS 13 (1966): 205-40.

Hart, Joseph. "The Zen of Hubert Benoit." JOURNAL OF TRANSPERSONAL PSYCHOLOGY 2 (1970): 141-67.

> See Hubert Benoit's THE SUPREME DOCTRINE: PSYCHOLOGICAL STUDIES IN ZEN THOUGHT cited above.

Hirschberg, H.H. "Eighteen Hundred Years before Freud: A Re-Evaluation of the Term Yetzer Ha-ra." JUDAISM 10 (Spring 1961): 129-41.

Hoffman, Robert. "Theistic Religion as Regression." INSIGHT QUARTERLY REVIEW OF RELIGION AND MENTAL HEALTH 4, no. 3 (1966): 31-33.

Jaiswal, Sita Ram. "The Psychology of Bhagavad Gita." RESEARCH JOURNAL OF PHILOSOPHY AND SOCIAL SCIENCES 1, no. 2 (1964): 23-33.

Javadekar, A.G. "Some Aspects of the Vedanta Psychology." RESEARCH JOURNAL OF PHILOSOPHY AND SOCIAL SCIENCES 1, no. 2 (1964): 93-101.

Jones, W.T. "World Views: Their Nature and Their Functions." CURRENT ANTHROPOLOGY 13 (1972): 79-109.

Jung, C [arl] G. PSYCHOLOGY AND RELIGION: WEST AND EAST. Trans- lated by R.F.C. Hull. COLLECTED WORKS, vol. 11. Princeton, N.J.: Princeton University Press, 1958. xii, 699 p.

> Collects some of Jung's major works on religious systems, including

his Terry lectures on psychology and religion, ANSWER TO JOB, essays on the Trinity and the Mass, as well as commentaries on the TIBETAN BOOK OF THE DEAD, Zen, and the I CHING.

_____. THE STRUCTURE AND DYNAMICS OF THE PSYCHE. Translated by R.F.C. Hull. COLLECTED WORKS, vol. 8. New York: Pantheon Books, 1960. 596 p.

Includes essays on the transcendent function, belief in spirits, the soul and death, and synchronicity.

Kalghatgi, T.G. "Some Problems in Jaina Psychology." RESEARCH JOURNAL OF PHILOSOPHY AND SOCIAL SCIENCES 1, no. 2 (1964): 41-72.

Kirsch, J. "Affinities Between Zen and Analytical Psychology." PSYCHOLO-GIA 3 (1960): 85-91.

Kuppuswamy, B. "Bhagavad-Gita and Mental Health." PRATIBHA 2, no. 1 (1959): 107-11.

Lantis, Margaret. "The Symbol of a New Religion." PSYCHIATRY 13, no. 1 (1950): 101-13.

Mehta, Mohan Lal. JAINA PSYCHOLOGY: A PSYCHOLOGICAL ANALYSIS OF THE JAINA DOCTRINE OF KARMA. Amritsar: Sohanlal Jaindharma Pracharak Samiti, 1957. xvi, 220 p.

Meissner, W [illiam] W. "Notes on Monotheism: The Argument." JOURNAL OF RELIGION AND HEALTH 6 (1967): 269-79.

_____. "Notes on Monotheism: Origins." JOURNAL OF RELIGION AND HEALTH 7 (1968): 43-60.

_____. "Notes on Monotheism: Psychodynamic Aspects." JOURNAL OF RELIGION AND HEALTH 7 (1968): 151-63.

Murphy, Gardner, and Murphy, Lois, eds. ASIAN PSYCHOLOGY. New York: Basic Books, 1968. xv, 238 p.

Brief introductions and selections from the national literatures of India, China, and Japan. The selections place particular emphasis on the psychological concepts in the religious traditions of these three nations.

Parrinder, Edward Geoffrey. WEST AFRICAN PSYCHOLOGY: A COMPARATIVE STUDY OF PSYCHOLOGICAL AND RELIGIOUS THOUGHT. London: Lutterworth Press, 1951. 229 p.

Peto, Andrew. "The Development of Ethical Monotheism." In THE PSYCHO-
ANALYTIC STUDY OF SOCIETY, vol. 1, pp. 311-76. Edited by W. Muensterberger and S. Axelrod. New York: International Universities Press, 1960.

Pfister, Oskar [Robert]. "Abolishment and Stimulus of Fear and Restraint in
the Israelitic-Christian Religion. INTERNATIONAL ZEITSCHRIFT FUR PSYCHO-
ANALYSE UND IMAGO 25, pt. 2 (1940): 206-13.

_____. CHRISTIANITY AND FEAR: A STUDY IN HISTORY AND IN THE
PSYCHOLOGY AND HYGIENE OF RELIGION. Translated by W.H. Johnston.
London: George Allen and Unwin, 1948. 589 p.

> A Swiss pastor who practiced psychoanalysis and entered into lengthy
> correspondence with Freud writes here of love and faith as inherent
> in the treatment of compulsion and fear. Both elements are traced
> in historical developments of Christianity and related to normal and
> neurotic fear. Originally published in 1944.

Rao, S.K. Ramachandra. DEVELOPMENT OF PSYCHOLOGICAL THOUGHT
IN INDIA. Mysore, India: Kavyalaya Publishers, 1962. 225 p.

> A survey in ten chapters of Indian psychology as it has developed
> over the past 3000 years. Demonstrates that practice, as in yoga,
> has had greater constancy than thought, which tends toward greater
> alteration in the same time frame.

Reid, Stephen. "Moses and Monotheism: Guilt and the Murder of the Primal
Father." AMERICAN IMAGO 29 (1972): 11-34.

Ritsema, Rudolf. "Notes for Differentiating Some Terms in the I CHING."
SPRING: AN ANNUAL OF ARCHETYPAL PSYCHOLOGY AND JUNGIAN
THOUGHT, 1970, pp. 111-25.

Roheim, Geza. "Some Aspects of Semitic Monotheism." PSYCHOANALYSIS
AND THE SOCIAL SCIENCES 4 (1955): 169-222.

Satya Nand, D. DYNAMIC PSYCHOLOGY OF THE GITA OF HINDUISM.
New Delhi: Oxford & IBH Publishing Co., 1972. xvii, 150 p.

Schneiderman, Leo. "Psychological Evolution from Polytheism to Monotheism."
PSYCHOANALYTIC REVIEW 51 (1964): 274-84.

Schultz, J.P. "Religious Psychology of Jonathan Edwards and the Hassidic Mas-
ters of Habad." JOURNAL OF ECUMENICAL STUDIES 10 (Fall 1973): 716-
27.

Sillman, Leonard R. "Monotheism and the Sense of Reality." INTERNATION-
AL JOURNAL OF PSYCHOANALYSIS 30 (1949): 124-32.

Sinha, Ajit Kumar. "Yoga and Western Psychology." RESEARCH JOURNAL OF PHILOSOPHY AND SOCIAL SCIENCES 1, no. 2 (1964): 80-92.

Sinha, H.S. "Psychological Bipolarity in Sankhya System." RESEARCH JOURNAL OF PHILOSOPHY AND SOCIAL SCIENCES 1, no. 2 (1964): 73-79.

Siu, R.G.H. THE TAO OF SCIENCE: AN ESSAY ON WESTERN KNOWLEDGE AND EASTERN WISDOM. Cambridge, Mass.: The MIT Press, 1957. xvi, 180 p.

Smith, Noel W. "Belief Systems and Psychological Concepts in Ancient Egypt to the End of the Old Kingdom (220 BC)." PROCEEDINGS OF THE 79TH ANNUAL CONVENTION OF THE AMERICAN PSYCHOLOGICAL ASSOCIATION 6, part 2 (1971): 721-22.

Stunkard, Albert. "Some Interpersonal Aspects of an Oriental Religion." PSYCHIATRY 14 (1951): 419-32.

    Zen Buddhism in the light of Harry S. Sullivan.

Subbannachar, N.V. "The Problem of Consciousness: Modern Psychology and Sri Aurobindo." RESEARCH JOURNAL OF PHILOSOPHY AND SOCIAL SCIENCES 1, no. 2 (1964): 102-20.

Swanson, Guy E. THE BIRTH OF THE GODS: THE ORIGIN OF PRIMITIVE BELIEFS. Ann Arbor: University of Michigan Press, 1960. 225 p.

    A methodologically rigorous study by a sociologist who correlates social experience and such religious beliefs as a monotheistic "High God."

Terry, Roger L. "Dependence, Nurturance and Monotheism." JOURNAL OF SOCIAL PSYCHOLOGY 84 (1971): 175-81.

Vasavada, A.U. "Analytical Psychology of C.G. Jung and Indian Wisdom." JOURNAL OF ANALYTICAL PSYCHOLOGY 13 (1968): 131-45.

Watt, William Montgomery. TRUTH IN THE RELIGIONS--A SOCIOLOGICAL AND PSYCHOLOGICAL APPROACH. Chicago: Aldine Publishing Co., 1963. 190 p.

Weiss, M.D. "Repression and Monotheism." JUDAISM 10 (Summer 1961): 217-26.

Whitlock, Glenn E. "Structure of Personality in Hebrew Psychology." INTERPRETATION 14 (January 1960): 3-13.

Wilhelm, Hellmut. "The Creative Principle in the BOOK OF CHANGES." SPRING: AN ANNUAL OF ARCHETYPAL PSYCHOLOGY AND JUNGIAN THOUGHT, 1970, pp. 91-110.

E:2 THEOLOGICAL AND BIBLICAL STUDIES

Abel, E.T. "The Psychology of Memory and Rumor Transmission and Their Bearing on Theories of Oral Transmission in Early Christianity." JOURNAL OF RELIGION 51 (1971): 270-81.

> Employs the Allport and Postman studies of rumor transmission. Also see John G. Gager study below.

Alcorn, Douglas E. "New Testament Psychology." BRITISH JOURNAL OF MEDICAL PSYCHOLOGY 16, pts. 3-4 (July 1937): 270-80.

Ansaldi, J. "Discours theologique et avatars de la libido." ETUDES THEOLOGIQUES ET RELIGIEUSES 48, no. 3 (1973): 275-98.

Barker, C. Edward. PSYCHOLOGY'S IMPACT ON THE CHRISTIAN FAITH. London: George Allen and Unwin, 1964. 220 p.

> Contends that Freud's negative evaluation of religion applies to Saint Paul and later Christianity but not to the religion and personality of Jesus.

Bellet, Maurice. FOI ET PSYCHANALYSE. Paris: Desclee de Brouwer, 1972. 142 p.

Bloom, Anthony. "Experience, Doubt and Faith." LUMEN VITAE 26 (1971): 193-214.

Boisen, Anton T. "The Development and Validation of Religious Faith." PSYCHIATRY 14 (1951): 455-62.

Brooke, O. "Psychological Aspect of the Trinitarian Indwelling." DOWNSIDE REVIEW 90 (July 1972): 155-68.

Browning, Don S. "Psychological and Ontological Perspectives on Faith and Reason." JOURNAL OF RELIGION 45 (1965): 296-308.

_____. "Reason and Ecstasy: Psychological and Philosophical Notes on the Emerging Counterculture." ZYGON 7 (June 1972): 80-97.

Butler, J.D. "Theology and Psychology: Some Points of Convergence." EN-COUNTER 19 (Autumn 1958): 391-406.

Cantril, Hadley. "The Nature of Faith." JOURNAL OF INDIVIDUAL PSY-CHOLOGY 13 (1957): 24-37.

Carter, Gerald Emmett. PSYCHOLOGY AND THE CROSS. Milwaukee: Bruce, 1959. xvi, 135 p.

Emphasis on Catholic view of atonement.

Cox, David. JUNG AND ST. PAUL: A STUDY OF THE DOCTRINE OF JUS-TIFICATION BY FAITH AND ITS RELATION TO THE CONCEPT OF INDIVI-DUATION. New York: Association Press, 1959. 358 p.

Crespy, G. "Psychanalyse et foi." ETUDES THEOLOGIQUES ET RELIGIEUSES 41, no. 4 (1966): 241-51.

Curatorium of the C.G. Jung Institute, Zurich, eds. EVIL. Translated by R. Manheim and H. Nagel. Evanston, Ill.: Northwestern University Press, 1967. xiv, 265 p.

Historians of religion, philosophers, psychologists, a literary critic, and a film critic contribute to this stimulating collection of essays.

Daim, Wilfried. DEPTH PSYCHOLOGY AND SALVATION. New York: Frederick Ungar, 1963. 315 p.

Combines the phenomenological method of Husserl and Heidegger; the "understanding" approach of Dilthey, Spranger, and Jaspers; and the depth psychology of Freud in a study of the doctrine of salvation.

Davies, J.W. "Investigation of the History of Agape and Eros from the Per-spective of the Psychoanalytic Phenomenon of Transference." ENCOUNTER 28 (Spring 1967): 151-60.

Diel, Paul. LA DIVINITE: ETUDE PSYCHANALYTIQUE. Paris: Presses Uni-versitaires de France, 1950. 218 p.

Emery, P.Y. "Le Pardon de Dieu comme liberation: Une Sortie de soi spiritu-elle et psychologique." COMMUNION 25, no. 1 (1971): 59-72.

Feinstein, H.M. "Prepared Heart: Puritan Theology and Psychoanalysis." AMERICAN QUARTERLY 22 (Summer 1970): 166-76.

Finch, John. "Toward a Christian Psychology." INSIGHT: INTERDISCIPLIN-ARY STUDIES OF MAN 6 (1967): 42-48.

Fisher, Alden L. "The Human Sciences, Religion and Regression: The Problem of God." INSIGHT: QUARTERLY REVIEW OF RELIGION AND MENTAL HEALTH 4, no. 3 (1966): 42-44.

Fromm, Erich. "Faith as a Character Trait." PSYCHIATRY 5, no. 3 (1942): 307-20.

_____. THE DOGMA OF CHRIST AND OTHER ESSAYS ON RELIGION, PSY-CHOLOGY AND CULTURE. New York: Holt, Rinehart and Winston, 1963. 212 p.

> The title essay, which was originally published in 1930, is a psy-choanalytic interpretation of the views of Christ held by the early Christian community.

Fulcher, J. Rodney. "Puritans and the Passions: The Faculty Psychology in American Puritanism." JOURNAL OF THE HISTORY OF THE BEHAVIORAL SCIENCES 9 (April 1973): 123-39.

Gager, John G. "The Gospels and Jesus: Some Doubts about Method." JOUR-NAL OF RELIGION 54 (July 1974): 244-72.

> Contains further discussion of the use of rumor transmission theory in Biblical scholarship. See E.T. Abel above.

Hiltner, Seward. "The Death of God: A Psychological Perspective." PASTO-RAL PSYCHOLOGY 17 (October 1966): 5-9.

_____. THEOLOGICAL DYNAMICS. Nashville: Abingdon Press, 1972. 224 p.

> Focuses on theological doctrines and correlated areas of human experience, including sin and sickness, grace and gratitude, pro-vidence and trust. Stresses the importance of the behavioral sci-ences for "fleshing out the meaning of the context of the God-man relationship."

Homans, Peter. "Transcendence, Distance, Fantasy: The Protestant Era in Psy-chological Perspective." JOURNAL OF RELIGION 49 (July 1969): 205-27.

_____. "Psychology and Hermeneutics: Jung's Contribution." ZYGON 4 (December 1969): 333-55.

_____. THEOLOGY AFTER FREUD; AN INTERPRETIVE INQUIRY. Indianapolis: The Bobbs-Merrill Co., 1970. xvii, 254 p.

> On the basis of interpretations of theological responses to Freud (Niebuhr, Tillich) and post-Protestant responses to depth psychology (Bakan, Rieff, Brown), this study develops a constructive view of

transcendence, fantasy, and mass society.

_____, ed. THE DIALOGUE BETWEEN THEOLOGY AND PSYCHOLOGY. Chicago: University of Chicago Press, 1968. 295 p.

A collection of original essays on pastoral theology and psychology of religion in commemoration of the one hundredth anniversary of the University of Chicago Divinity School.

Hughes, Thomas Hywel. PSYCHOLOGY AND RELIGIOUS TRUTH. London: George Allen and Unwin, 1942. 160 p.

Views psychology as a valuable resource to understand religion. Focuses on religious truth, Christology, Trinity, atonement, and immortality.

Hunter, David R. "Theology and the Behavioral Sciences." RELIGIOUS EDU-CATION 55 (1960): 248-52.

Jackson, Gordon E. "The Problem of Hostility Psychologically and Theologi-cally Considered." JOURNAL OF RELIGION AND HEALTH 11 (1972): 73-93.

Jordan, R. "Christianity and Psychology." ANGLICAN THEOLOGICAL RE-VIEW 36 (January 1954): 52-67.

Koteskey, Ronald. "A Basis for the Development of Christian Psychology with a Few Initial Ideas." JOURNAL OF PSYCHOLOGY AND THEOLOGY 1 (April 1973): 31-42.

McCutchen, Leighton. "The Father Figure in Psychology and Religion." JOUR-NAL OF THE AMERICAN ACADEMY OF RELIGION 40 (1972): 176-90.

MaGuire, John David. "The Theological Uses of Psychoanalysis: Patterns, Problems, and Proposals." RELIGION IN LIFE 31 (1962): 185-95.

Mauger, Paul A. "Psychology, Theology, and Sin." PASTORAL PSYCHOLOGY 23 (October 1972): 5-11.

Meissner, W [illiam] W. "Prolegomena to a Psychology of Grace." JOURNAL OF RELIGION AND HEALTH 3 (1964): 209-40.

_____. FOUNDATIONS FOR A PSYCHOLOGY OF GRACE. Glen Rock, N.J.: Paulist Press, 1966. 246 p.

A selection of readings from significant figures in religion and psy-chology with supplementary analysis and critique in light of a psychology of grace. Includes James, Allport, Erikson, Fromm, and others.

_____. "Notes on the Psychology of Faith." JOURNAL OF RELIGION AND HEALTH 8 (1969): 47-75.

_____. "Toward a Theology of Human Aggression." JOURNAL OF RELIGION AND HEALTH 10 (October 1971): 324-32.

_____. "Notes on the Psychology of Hope: Part I." JOURNAL OF RELIGION AND HEALTH 12 (January 1973): 7-29.

_____. "Notes on the Psychology of Hope: Part II." JOURNAL OF RELIGION AND HEALTH 12 (April 1973): 120-39.

Menninger, Karl. "Hope." PASTORAL PSYCHOLOGY 11 (April 1960): 11-24.

Miller, David L. GODS AND GAMES: TOWARD A THEOLOGY OF PLAY. New York: Harper & Row, Publishers, 1970. xxx, 209 p.

While oriented primarily toward theology and philosophy, Miller touches on points of view of Freud, Jung, Erikson, and G.H. Mead.

_____. THE NEW POLYTHEISM: REBIRTH OF THE GODS AND GODDESSES. New York: Harper & Row, Publishers, 1974. 86 p.

In advocating a polytheistic theology, the author discusses such psychologists as N.O. Brown, R.D. Laing, and James Hillman.

Moxon, Cavendish. "A Psycho-Analytic Study of the Christian Creed." INTERNATIONAL JOURNAL OF PSYCHOANALYSIS 2 (1921): 59-64.

Narramore, S. Bruce. "Perspectives on the Integration of Psychology and Theology." JOURNAL OF PSYCHOLOGY AND THEOLOGY 1 (January 1973): 3-18.

Niederwimmer, Kurt. "Kerygmatisches Symbol und Analyse: Zur Kritik der Tiefenpsychologischen Bibel-Interpretation." ARCHIV FUR RELIGIONPSYCHOLOGIE 7 (1962): 203-23.

Oates, Wayne [Edward]. "Gospel and Modern Psychology." REVIEW AND EXPOSITOR 46 (April 1949): 181-98.

Philp, Howard Littleton. JUNG AND THE PROBLEM OF EVIL. New York: Robert M. McBride, 1959. xiv, 271 p.

Pohier, Jacques M. PSYCHOLOGIE ET THEOLOGIE. Paris: Editions du Cerf, 1967. 387 p.

A collection of two types of essays by a scholar trained both in theology and psychology: 1) comparisons of religious thought and belief with the thought processes and cosmologies of children, as understood by Piaget; and 2) psychoanalytically-oriented discussions of religious affectivity--knowledge of God, guilt and penitence, and celibacy.

_____. "La Primaute du pere comme attribut du fils dans la foi chretienne." INTERPRETATION 3 (1969): 49-90.

Pruyser, Paul W. "Phenomenology and Dynamics of Hoping." JOURNAL FOR THE SCIENTIFIC STUDY OF RELIGION 3 (1963-64): 86-96.

_____. "Anxiety, Guilt and Shame in the Atonement." THEOLOGY TODAY 21 (April 1964): 15-33.

See additional entries on anxiety in section G:3.

Rachels, James. "God and Human Attitudes." RELIGIOUS STUDIES 7 (1971): 325-38.

Reuter, A.C. "Psychology and Theology: A Return to Dialogue." CONCORD-IA THEOLOGICAL MONTHLY 44 (May 1973): 199-212.

Revers, Wilhelm J. "Uber die Hoffnung die Anthropologische Bedeutung der Zukunft." JAHRBUCH FUR PSYCHOLOGIE, PSYCHOTHERAPIE UND MEDI-ZINISCHE ANTHROPOLOGIE 14, nos. 2-4 (1966): 175-85.

A study on identity and belief in afterlife.

Ricoeur, Paul. "La Paternite." INTERPRETATION 3 (1969): 173-214.

Rogers, William F. "Creation, Redemption, Sanctification, and Mental Health." PASTORAL PSYCHOLOGY 12 (November 1961): 10-15.

Sargant, William. "The Physiology of Faith." BRITISH JOURNAL OF PSYCHI-ATRY 115 (1969): 505-18.

Schindler, Walter. "Depth Psychology and Dream Interpretation in the Bible." INTERNATIONAL JOURNAL OF SEXOLOGY 8 (1954): 77-82.

Stern, E. Mark, and Marino, Bert G. PSYCHOTHEOLOGY. New York: Newman Press, 1970. 146 p.

A series of essays based on Biblical stories chosen to illustrate the convergence of Christian insights and the findings of modern psychology.

Stinnette, Charles R., Jr. "Psychoanalysis and Scientific Method: A Theological Query." JOURNAL OF RELIGION AND HEALTH 7 (April 1968): 131-40.

_____. "Existence and Faith: A Theological Method as Focused in Psychosocial Perspectives." JOURNAL OF PASTORAL CARE 24 (September 1970): 165-77.

Stotland, Ezra. THE PSYCHOLOGY OF HOPE. San Francisco: Jossey-Bass, 1969. xiv, 284 p.

An impressive proposal of a conceptual framework to account for the determinants and effects of hope, and for the cognitive processes which mediate its functioning.

Strasser, Stephen. THE SOUL IN METAPHYSICAL AND EMPIRICAL PSYCHOLOGY. Pittsburgh: Duquesne University Press, 1957. 275 p.

Strommen, Merton P. "The Relation of Christian Theology to Psychological Research." RELIGIOUS EDUCATION 60, no. 3 (1965): 199-208.

Taylor, W.S. "Perfectionism in Psychology and in Theology." CANADIAN JOURNAL OF THEOLOGY 5 (July 1959): 170-79.

Tillich, Paul. "The Significance of Kurt Goldstein for the Philosophy of Religion." JOURNAL OF INDIVIDUAL PSYCHOLOGY 15 (1959): 20-23.

[Ulanov] Belford, Ann. "Where Depth Psychology and Theology Meet." UNION SEMINARY QUARTERLY REVIEW 23 (1967-68): 159-68.

Underwood, Richard A. "Hermes and Hermeneutics: A Viewing from the Perspective of the Death of God and Depth Psychology." HARTFORD QUARTERLY 6 (Fall 1965): 34-53.

Walters, Orville S. "Theology and Changing Concepts of the Unconscious." RELIGION IN LIFE 37 (1968): 112-28.

_____. "Psychodynamics and the Holy Spirit." JOURNAL OF RELIGION AND HEALTH 10 (July 1971): 246-55.

_____. "The Concept of Attainment in John Wesley's Christian Perfection." METHODIST HISTORY 10 (April 1972): 12-29.

_____. "John Wesley's Footnotes to Christian Perfection." METHODIST HIS-

TORY 12 (October 1973): 19-36.

_____. "Psychodynamics in Tillich's Theology." JOURNAL OF RELIGION AND HEALTH 12 (October 1973): 19-36.

Will, James E. "The Psychological Method of Personalistic Theology." RELIGION IN LIFE 35 (1966): 732-50.

Williams, Arthur Hyatt. "Guilt and Atonement: A Post-Freudian View." CHURCH QUARTERLY 1, no. 4 (1969): 279-90.

E:3   ETHICS AND MORAL EXPERIENCE

Aden, LeRoy. "Distortions of a Sense of Guilt." PASTORAL PSYCHOLOGY 15 (February 1964): 16-26.

Anderson, George [Christian]. "The Moral Nature of Man." JOURNAL OF RELIGION AND HEALTH 5, no. 2 (1966): 130-36.

Argyle, Michael. "Psychological Research into the Origins of the Conscience." MODERN CHURCHMAN 5 (October 1961): 50-58.

Aronfreed, Justin. CONDUCT AND CONSCIENCE: THE SOCIALIZATION OF INTERNALIZED CONTROL OVER BEHAVIOR. New York: Academic Press, 1968. 405 p.

   A study of the internalization of moral prohibitions, with particular emphasis on resistance to temptations, self-criticism, guilt, and shame.

Bachmeyer, T.J. "Ethics and the Psychology of Moral Judgment." ZYGON 8 (June 1973): 82-95.

Belgum, David. GUILT: WHERE PSYCHOLOGY AND RELIGION MEET. Englewood Cliffs, N.J.: Prentice-Hall, 1963. 148 p.

   Prompted by the author's work with O. Hobart Mowrer, this book is a study and critique of the way seven religious denominations minister to sin and guilt. Includes historical documentation and contemporary questionnaire survey.

Benda, Clemens E. "Motivation and Conscience." HUMANITAS 3 (1968): 241-58.

Beres, David. "Psychoanalytic Notes on the History of Morality." JOURNAL OF THE AMERICAN PSYCHOANALYTIC ASSOCIATION 13, no. 1 (1965): 3-

37.

Bertocci, Peter A. FREE WILL, RESPONSIBILITY, AND GRACE. Nashville: Abingdon Press, 1957. 110 p.

A Goldstein-Maslow emphasis on self-actualization is brought to bear on a brief discussion of various topics, including agency and guilt as grounded in experience rather than as theoretical constructs.

_____. RELIGION AS CREATIVE INSECURITY. New York: Association Press, 1958. 128 p.

Voices opposition to a view of religion as consolation and security, emphasizing free will and personal initiative.

_____. "Three Visions of Perfection and Human Freedom." PSYCHOLOGIA 5 (1962): 59-67.

Discusses views of Hinduism, Christianity, and Zen Buddhism on perfection and freedom, relating these to the psychological perspectives of Maslow, Rogers, and Fromm.

Bertocci, Peter A., and Millard, Richard M. PERSONALITY AND THE GOOD: PSYCHOLOGICAL AND ETHICAL PERSPECTIVES. New York: David McKay, 1963. 711 p.

Primarily intended as a textbook in ethics, this book nonetheless contains a significant discussion of the "human predicament" as seen by Freud, Jung, Adler, Fromm, Maslow, and Allport.

Bier, William C., ed. CONSCIENCE: ITS FREEDOM AND LIMITATIONS. New York: Fordham University Press, 1971. xii, 397 p.

Bitter, Wilhelm, ed. ANGST UND SCHULD IN THEOLOGISCHER UND PSY-CHOTHERAPEUTISCHER SICHT: EIN TAGUNGSBERICHT. Stuttgart: Ernst Klett, 1959. 186 p.

Fifteen papers from a 1952 congress on anxiety and guilt, most of them presented in English translation.

Black, Michael S., and London, Perry. "The Dimensions of Guilt, Religion, and Personal Ethics." JOURNAL OF SOCIAL PSYCHOLOGY 69 (1966): 39-54.

Brody, Matthew. "Phylogenesis of Sexual Morality: Psychiatric Exegesis of Onan and Samson." NEW YORK STATE JOURNAL OF MEDICINE 68 (1968): 2510-14.

Discusses the evolution of religion from primitive rites to moral codes.

Browning, Don S. GENERATIVE MAN: PSYCHOANALYTIC PERSPECTIVES. Philadelphia: The Westminster Press, 1973. 266 p.

>Viewing psychoanalysis as a modern cultural symbol system, this work compares the moral and ethical visions of man and society implicit in the works of N.O. Brown, Rieff, Fromm, and Erikson, and judges Erikson's to be the most valuable.

Buber, Martin. "Guilt and Guilt-Feelings." In THE KNOWLEDGE OF MAN: SELECTED ESSAYS, pp. 121-48. By Martin Buber. Edited, with an introductory essay, by Maurice Friedman. Translated by Maurice Friedman and Ronald Gregor Smith. New York: Harper & Row, Publishers, 1965.

>An influential essay which isolates levels of guilt and argues that "existential guilt" is not within the province of psychological explanation or treatment.

Carr, Charles. "Kierkegaard: On Guilt." JOURNAL OF PSYCHOLOGY AND THEOLOGY 1 (July 1973): 15-21.

Casey, Robert P. "Oedipus Motivation in Religious Thought and Fantasy." PSYCHIATRY 5, no. 2 (1942): 219-28.

>A psychoanalytic study of the experience of guilt.

Cole, William Graham. SEX IN CHRISTIANITY AND PSYCHOANALYSIS. New York: Oxford University Press, 1955. xiv, 820 p.

>A good historical survey of a single topic in the two bodies of literature, plus a small constructive section.

Eickhoff, Andrew R. "A Psychoanalytical Study of St. Paul's Theology of Sex." PASTORAL PSYCHOLOGY 18 (April 1967): 35-42.

Farber, Leslie H. THE WAYS OF THE WILL. New York: Harper & Row, Publishers, 1966. 226 p.

>A study of the psychology and psychopathology of the will from the perspective of psychoanalysis. Contains a good discussion of Martin Buber.

Feuer, Lewis Samuel. PSYCHOANALYSIS AND ETHICS. Springfield, Ill.: Charles C Thomas, 1955. 134 p.

>Develops a view of psychoanalysis as a basis for testing ethical values.

_____. "God, Guilt and Logic: The Psychological Basis of the Ontological Argument." INQUIRY 11 (1968): 257-81.

Argues that the ontological argument for the existence of God is rooted dynamically in guilt, especially guilt related to the exercise of rational mental processes (e.g., logic).

Fingarette, Herbert. "Psychoanalytic Perspectives on Moral Guilt and Responsibility: A Re-evaluation." PSYCHOANALYSIS 4 (Winter 1955-56): 46-66.

_____. "Real Guilt and Neurotic Guilt." JOURNAL OF EXISTENTIAL PSYCHIATRY 3 (Fall 1962): 145-58.

A critical response to Buber's essay on guilt and guilt feelings cited above.

Fritze, Herbert P. "Displaced Feelings of Guilt and the Grace of God." PASTORAL PSYCHOLOGY 17 (November 1966): 39-44.

Gardner, R.A. "The Use of Guilt as a Defense against Anxiety." PSYCHOANALYTIC REVIEW 57 (July 1970): 124-36.

Gerber, Israel J. IMMORTAL REBELS: FREEDOM FOR THE INDIVIDUAL IN THE BIBLE. New York: Jonathan David, 1963. 267 p.

Ginsberg, Morris. "Psycho-Analysis and Ethics." BRITISH JOURNAL OF SOCIOLOGY 3 (1952): 287-304.

Glaser, J.W. "Conscience and Superego: A Key Distinction." THEOLOGICAL STUDIES 32 (March 1971): 30-47.

Hammes, John A. "Beyond Freedom and Dignity: Behavioral Fixated Delusion?" JOURNAL OF PSYCHOLOGY AND THEOLOGY 1 (July 1973): 8-14.

A pastoral theologian's critical reaction to B.F. Skinner's BEYOND FREEDOM AND DIGNITY.

Henle, Mary. "A Psychological Concept of Freedom: Footnotes to Spinoza." SOCIAL RESEARCH 27 (1960): 359-74.

Hiltner, Seward. "A Religious View of Social Values." AMERICAN JOURNAL OF ORTHOPSYCHIATRY 27 (1957): 475-83.

Hoffman, John C. "Guilt, Aspiration and the Free Self." HUMANITAS 5 (1965): 125-42.

Knight, James A. "Conscience." UNION SEMINARY QUARTERLY REVIEW

19 (1963-64): 131-40. Also published in JOURNAL OF PASTORAL CARE 18 (1964): 132-39.

_____. CONSCIENCE AND GUILT. New York: Appleton-Century-Crofts, 1969. 189 p.

The author is a psychiatrist interested in the relation of psychiatry to religion.

Llewellyn, Russell C. "A Second Look at B.F. Skinner." JOURNAL OF PSYCHOLOGY AND THEOLOGY 1 (July 1973): 3-8.

Loewen, Jacob A. "The Social Context of Guilt and Forgiveness." PRACTICAL ANTHROPOLOGY 17, no. 1 (1970): 80-96.

_____. "Four Kinds of Forgiveness." PRACTICAL ANTHROPOLOGY 17, no. 4 (1970): 153-68.

London, Perry, et al. "Religion, Guilt and Ethical Standards." JOURNAL OF SOCIAL PSYCHOLOGY 63, no. 1 (1964): 145-59.

McCreary, J.K. "Social Character and Psychoanalytic Insight." JOURNAL OF RELIGIOUS THOUGHT 24, no. 2 (1967-68): 68-85.

MacDonald, A.P., Jr. "More on the Protestant Ethic." JOURNAL OF CONSULTING AND CLINICAL PSYCHOLOGY 39 (August 1972): 116-22.

McKenzie, John G [rant]. GUILT: ITS MEANING AND SIGNIFICANCE. London: George Allen and Unwin, 1962. 192 p.

May, Rollo. "The Psychological Bases of Freedom." PASTORAL PSYCHOLOGY 13 (November 1962): 41-46.

_____. LOVE AND WILL. New York: W.W. Norton & Co., 1969. 352 p.

Argues that love and will, which traditionally were viewed as the solution to life's problems, have now become the focus of its problems.

Meissner, W [illiam] W. "Erikson's Truth: The Search for Ethical Identity." THEOLOGICAL STUDIES 31 (June 1970): 310-19.

_____. "Notes Toward a Theory of Values: The Place of Values." JOURNAL OF RELIGION AND HEALTH 9 (1970): 123-37.

_____. "Notes Toward a Theory of Values: Values as Psychological." JOUR-

NAL OF RELIGION AND HEALTH 9 (1970): 233-49.

_____. "Notes Toward a Theory of Values: Value as Cultural." JOURNAL OF RELIGION AND HEALTH 10 (1971): 77-97.

Mirels, Herbert L., and Garrett, James B. "The Protestant Ethic as a Personality Variable." JOURNAL OF CONSULTING AND CLINICAL PSYCHOLOGY 36 (February 1971): 40-44.

Also see A.P. MacDonald entry above.

Morano, Donald V. EXISTENTIAL GUILT: A PHENOMENOLOGICAL STUDY. New York: Humanities Press, 1973. xii, 90 p.

A study of guilt from the perspectives of religion, psychology, and literature.

Morris, Herbert, ed. GUILT AND SHAME. Belmont, Calif.: Wadsworth Publishing Co., 1971. 206 p.

A useful collection of important essays on guilt and shame, including Freud, Erikson, Piers and Singer, Fingarette, Buber, Jaspers, and others.

Narramore, S. Bruce. "Guilt: Where Theology and Psychology Meet." JOURNAL OF PSYCHOLOGY AND THEOLOGY 2 (Winter 1974): 18-25.

_____. "Guilt: Its Universal Hidden Presence." JOURNAL OF PSYCHOLOGY AND THEOLOGY 2 (Spring 1974): 104-15.

_____. "Guilt: Christian Motivation or Neurotic Masochism?" JOURNAL OF PSYCHOLOGY AND THEOLOGY 2 (Summer 1974): 182-89.

Neidhart, Walter. "Terminologische Probleme beim Gesprach von Theologie und Psychologie uber die Schuldenfahrung" [Terminological problems with the dialogue of theology and psychology concerning the experience of guilt]. PRAXIS DER PSYCHOTHERAPIE 13, no. 4 (1968): 157-64.

Neumann, Erich. DEPTH PSYCHOLOGY AND A NEW ETHIC. New York: G.P. Putnam's Sons, 1970. 158.

Nodet, Charles-Henri. "Psychanalyse et sens du peche." REVUE FRANCAISE DE PSYCHANALYSE 21 (1957): 791-805.

Piediscalzi, Nicholas. "Erik H. Erikson's Contribution to Ethics." JOURNAL OF RELIGION AND HEALTH 12 (April 1973): 169-80.

Piers, Gerhart, M.D., and Singer, Milton B. SHAME AND GUILT: A PSY-

CHOANALYTIC AND CULTURAL STUDY. New York: W.W. Norton & Co., 1971. 112 p.

> Originally published in 1953, this study argues for a more sophis-
> ticated employment of the distinction between "shame" and "guilt" '
> cultures than that of internal vs. external sanctions. Psychoanaly-
> tic psychology is employed to analyze the structure and dynamics
> of shame and guilt.

Racker, Heinrich. "Ethics and Psychoanalysis and the Psychoanalysis of Ethics."
INTERNATIONAL JOURNAL OF PSYCHOANALYSIS 47 (1966): 63-80.

Rim, Y., and Kurzweil, Z.E. "The Ten Commandments, Instrumental and Terminal Values." SCIENTIA PAEDAGOGICA EXPERIMENTALIS 8 (1971): 62-75.

Salzman, Leon. "Guilt, Responsibility and the Unconscious." PASTORAL PSY-
CHOLOGY 15 (November 1964): 17-26.

Schneiders, Alexander A. THE ANARCHY OF FEELING: MAN'S STRUGGLE
FOR FREEDOM AND MATURITY. New York: Sheed & Ward, 1963. 204 p.

_____. "The Nature and Origins of Guilt." HUMANITAS 5 (1969): 169-82.

Schulz, Walter. "Wandlungen der Begriffe 'Schuld' und 'Verantwortung'"
[Changes in the concepts of guilt and responsibility]. PRAXIS DER PSYCHO-
THERAPIE 13, no. 3 (1968): 110-17.

Stein, Edward V. "Guilt and the NOW Man." HUMANITAS 5 (1969): 205-
18.

Wheelis, Allen. THE QUEST FOR IDENTITY. New York: W.W. Norton &
Co., 1958. 250 p.

> A practicing psychoanalyst probes the demise of systems of moral
> authority in contemporary America.

Zavalloni, Robert. SELF-DETERMINATION: THE PSYCHOLOGY OF PERSON-
AL FREEDOM. Chicago: Forum Books, 1962. xxi, 341 p.

> Argues for a conception of human freedom which locates choice
> not in a faculty called "will" but as the act of the whole person.
> Written by a former postdoctoral student under Carl Rogers.

Zion, W.P. "Anglican Moral Theology and Psychiatric Evidence." CHURCH
QUARTERLY REVIEW 166 (January-March 1965): 88-95.

E:4 THE PSYCHOLOGY OF RELIGIOUS BELIEF

Baer, Daniel J., and Mosele, Victor F. "Political and Religious Beliefs of Catholics and Attitude toward Involvement in the Vietnam War." JOURNAL OF PSYCHOLOGY 78 (July 1971): 161-64.

Brown, Constance M., and Ferguson, Leonard W. "Self-Concept and Religious Belief." PSYCHOLOGICAL REPORTS 22 (1967): 266.

Brown, D.G., and Lowe, W.I. "Religious Beliefs and Personality Characteristics of College Students." JOURNAL OF SOCIAL PSYCHOLOGY 33 (1951): 103-29.

Brown, L.B. "Religious Belief and Reports of Childhood Experience." PSYCHOLOGICAL REPORTS 108, no. 1 (1962): 269-70.

_____. "A Study of Religious Belief." BRITISH JOURNAL OF PSYCHOLOGY 53, no. 3 (1962): 259-72.

_____. "The Structure of Religious Belief." JOURNAL FOR THE SCIENTIFIC STUDY OF RELIGION 5 (1965-66): 259-72.

_____. "Religious Belief and Skin Conductance." PERCEPTUAL AND MOTOR SKILLS 23, no. 2 (1966): 477-78.

Brown, L.B., and Pallant, D.J. "Religious Belief and Social Pressure." PSYCHOLOGICAL REPORTS 10 (1962): 813-14.

Clark, Walter Houston. "Religion as a Response to the Search for Meaning: Its Relation to Skepticism and Creativity." JOURNAL OF SOCIAL PSYCHOLOGY 60, no. 1 (1963): 127-37.

Cline, Victor B., and Richards, James M., Jr. "A Factor-Analytic Study of Religious Belief and Behavior." JOURNAL OF PERSONALITY AND SOCIAL PSYCHOLOGY 1, no. 6 (1965): 569-78.

Comstock, W. Richard. "William James and the Logic of Religious Belief." JOURNAL OF RELIGION 47 (July 1967): 187-209.

Davidson, James D. "Religious Belief as an Independent Variable." JOURNAL FOR THE SCIENTIFIC STUDY OF RELIGION 11 (March 1972): 65-75.

de Bont, Walter. "La Secularisation de la pensee." VIE SPIRITUELLE SUPPLEMENT 22, no. 88 (1969): 5-28.

De Leeuwe, Jules. "On the Development of Religious Conceptions." INTER-NATIONALE ZEITSCHRIFT FUR PSYCHANALYSE UND IMAGO 25, pts. 3 and 4 (1940): 430-43.

Demerath, Nicholas J. III, and Levinson, Richard M. "Baiting the Dissident Hook: Some Effects of Bias on Measuring Religious Belief." SOCIOMETRY 34 (September 1971): 346-59.

Dittes, James E. "Impulsive Closure as Reaction to Failure-Induced Threat." JOURNAL OF ABNORMAL AND SOCIAL PSYCHOLOGY 63 (1961): 562-69.

> Subjects were Divinity School students. A study of the effect of the reduction of self-esteem on the need to achieve immediate cognitive closure. Subjects not so threatened were more able to recognize and accept cognitive ambiguity.

Farrell, B.A. "Psychological Theory and the Belief in God." INTERNATIONAL JOURNAL OF PSYCHOANALYSIS 36 (1955): 187-204.

Festinger, Leon, et al. WHEN PROPHECY FAILS. New York: Harper Torchbooks, 1964. 256 p.

> An extended case study of a religious sect which predicted the end of the world. Illustrates the authors' theory of cognitive dissonance.

Feuer, Lewis S [amuel]. "Lawless Sensations and Categorical Defenses: The Unconscious Sources of Kant's Philosophy." In PSYCHOANALYSIS AND PHILOSOPHY, pp. 76-125. Edited by Morris Lazerowitz and Charles Hanly. New York: International Universities Press, 1970.

> A study of the emotional determinants of Kant's philosophy, with particular emphasis on the psychological bases for his mistrust of sense perceptions.

Ford, Thomas R. "Religious Thought and Beliefs in the Southern Appalachians as Revealed by an Attitude Survey." REVIEW OF RELIGIOUS RESEARCH 3 (1961): 2-20.

Fukuyama, Yoshio. "Functional Analysis of Religious Beliefs." RELIGIOUS EDUCATION 56 (1961): 446-51.

Gorsuch, Richard L. "The Conceptualization of God as Seen in Adjective Ratings." JOURNAL FOR THE SCIENTIFIC STUDY OF RELIGION 7, no. 1 (1968): 56-64.

Gorsuch, Richard L., and McFarland, Sam G. "Single versus Multiple-Item Scales for Measuring Religious Values." JOURNAL FOR THE SCIENTIFIC STUDY OF RELIGION 11 (1972): 53-64.

> Employs Christological statements.

Grafton, Thomas H. "God in the Personality Paradigm." REVIEW OF RELI-GIOUS RESEARCH 5 (1963): 21-30.

Gutherie, George M., and Marshall, John F. "Cognitive Dissonance among Protestant Fundamentalists." PENNSYLVANIA PSYCHIATRIC QUARTERLY 6, no. 2 (1966): 11-25.

Hanawalt, Nelson G. "Feelings of Security and of Self-Esteem in Relation to Religious Belief." JOURNAL OF SOCIAL PSYCHOLOGY 59 (1963): 347-53.

Heath, Douglas H. "Secularization and Maturity of Religious Beliefs." JOUR-NAL OF RELIGION AND HEALTH 8 (1969): 335-58.

Helfaer, Philip M. THE PSYCHOLOGY OF DOUBT. Boston: Beacon Press, 1972. xiv, 345 p.

> Employs projective techniques and theory to analyze the religious doubts of twelve Protestant seminarians.

Hogge, James H., and Friedman, S. Thomas. "The Scriptural Literalism Scale: A Preliminary Report." JOURNAL OF PSYCHOLOGY 66, no. 2 (1967): 275-79.

Hoppe, Ronald. "Religious Belief and the Learning of Paired Associates." JOURNAL OF SOCIAL PSYCHOLOGY 78 (1969): 275-79.

Jackson, Allen K. "Religious Beliefs and Expressions of the Southern Highland-er." REVIEW OF RELIGIOUS RESEARCH 3 (1961): 21-39.

Jahoda, Gustav. "Supernatural Beliefs and Changing Cognitive Structures among Ghanaian University Students." JOURNAL OF CROSS-CULTURAL PSYCHOLO-GY 1 (June 1970): 115-30.

Jastrow, Joseph. ERROR AND ECCENTRICITY IN HUMAN BELIEF. New York: Dover Publications, 1962. xiv, 394 p.

Jennings, Floyd L. "Religious Beliefs and Self-Disclosure. PSYCHOLOGICAL REPORTS 28 (February 1971): 193-94.

_____. "A Note on the Reliability of Several Belief Scales." JOURNAL FOR THE SCIENTIFIC STUDY OF RELIGION 11 (June 1972): 157-64.

Johnson, Wayne G. "Religion, Racism, and Self-Image: The Significance of Beliefs." RELIGIOUS EDUCATION 68 (September 1973): 620-30.

> Also listed in section F:2.

Ludwig, David J., and Blank, Thomas. "Measurement of Religion as a Perceptual Set." JOURNAL FOR THE SCIENTIFIC STUDY OF RELIGION 8 (1969):
319-21.

McConahay, John B., and Hough, Joseph C., Jr. "Love and Guilt-Oriented
Dimensions of Christian Belief." JOURNAL FOR THE SCIENTIFIC STUDY OF
RELIGION 12 (March 1973): 53-64.

McFadden, William C. "Psychology and Unbelief." RELIGIOUS EDUCATION
64 (1969): 491-98.

Martin, Carol, and Nicholas, Robert C. "Personality and Religious Belief."
JOURNAL OF SOCIAL PSYCHOLOGY 56 (1962): 3-8.

Meredith, Gerald M. "Personality Correlates to Religious Belief Systems."
PSYCHOLOGICAL REPORTS 23, no. 3, pt. 2 (1968): 1039-42.

Nelson, Marven O., and Jones, E.M. "An Application of the Q-Technique to
the Study of Religious Concepts." PSYCHOLOGICAL REPORTS 3 (1957): 293-97.

Parker, Clyde A. "Changes in Religious Beliefs of College Students." In RE-
SEARCH ON RELIGIOUS DEVELOPMENT: A COMPREHENSIVE HANDBOOK,
pp. 724-76. Edited by Merton P. Strommen. New York: Hawthorn Books, 1971.

Parsons, Howard L. "Religious Beliefs of Students at Six Colleges and Universities." RELIGIOUS EDUCATION 58 (1963): 538-44.

Philpott, S.J.F. "Unconscious Mechanisms in Religion." BRITISH JOURNAL
OF MEDICAL PSYCHOLOGY 19 (1942): 292-312.

Piker, Stephen. "The Problem of Consistency in Thai Religion." JOURNAL
FOR THE SCIENTIFIC STUDY OF RELIGION 11 (September 1972): 211-29.

> Addresses the fact that the Thai belief system incorporates conflict-
> ing, even mutually exclusive, beliefs, and shows how various sub-
> groups of the society deal with or ignore the cognitive dissonance
> this situation entails.

Pruyser, Paul W. "Problems of Definition and Conception in the Psychology of
Unbelief." In CHANGING PERSPECTIVES IN THE SCIENTIFIC STUDY OF
RELIGION, pp. 185-200. Edited by Allan W. Eister. New York: John Wiley
& Sons, 1974.

Rogers, David P. "Some Religious Beliefs of Scientists and the Effect of the
Scientific Method." REVIEW OF RELIGIOUS RESEARCH 7, no. 2 (1966): 70-
77.

Rokeach, Milton. THE OPEN AND CLOSED MIND: INVESTIGATIONS INTO THE NATURE OF BELIEF SYSTEMS AND PERSONALITY SYSTEMS. New York: Basic Books, 1960. 447 p.

> A seminal work in the psychological study of belief systems. Includes essays and reports of research findings on such topics as the theory and measurement of belief systems, the nature of authoritarianism and intolerance, the relation between belief and cognitive processes, the study of disbelief systems, and the dynamics of belief systems.

_____. THE THREE CHRISTS OF YPSILANTI: A NARRATIVE STUDY OF THREE LOST MEN. New York: Alfred A. Knopf, 1964. 336 p.

> A study of the belief systems of three mental patients who considered themselves to be Christ.

_____. BELIEFS, ATTITUDES AND VALUES: A THEORY OF ORGANIZATION AND CHANGE. San Francisco: Jossey-Bass, 1968. xvi, 214 p.

> A collection of papers which address the problem of the importance of beliefs to the believer and its consequence for ease in changing beliefs. Develops a central-to-peripheral dimension of beliefs and proposes five steps on this dimension.

_____. "The Paradox of Religious Belief." PROCEEDINGS OF THE CHRISTIAN ASSOCIATION FOR PSYCHOLOGICAL STUDIES, April 1968, pp. 51-58.

Roscoe, John T. "Religious Beliefs of American College Students." COLLEGE STUDENT SURVEY 2, no. 3 (1968): 49-55.

Scheibe, Karl E. BELIEFS AND VALUES. New York: Holt, Rinehart and Winston, 1970. 159 p.

> The role of values and beliefs as determinants of behavior. Contains useful bibliography of related psychological studies.

Scheidt, Rick J. "Belief in Supernatural Phenomena and Locus of Control." PSYCHOLOGICAL REPORTS 32 (June 1973): 1159-62.

Schweiker, William F. "Religion as a Superordinate Meaning System and Socio-Psychological Integration." JOURNAL FOR THE SCIENTIFIC STUDY OF RELIGION 8 (1969): 300-7.

Spilka, Bernard. "Images of Man and Dimensions of Personal Religion: Values for an Empirical Psychology of Religion." REVIEW OF RELIGIOUS RESEARCH 11 (Spring 1970): 171-82.

_____. "Research on Religious Beliefs: A Critical Review." In RESEARCH

ON RELIGIOUS DEVELOPMENT: A COMPREHENSIVE HANDBOOK, pp. 485-520. Edited by Merton P. Strommen. New York: Hawthorn Books, 1971.

Spilka, Bernard, et al. "The Concept of God: A Factor Analytic Approach." REVIEW OF RELIGIOUS RESEARCH 6 (1964): 28-36.

Stanley, Gordon. "God in the Rorschach." PERCEPTUAL AND MOTOR SKILLS 26 (1968): 463-66.

Stark, Stanley. "Toward a Psychology of Knowledge: The Sublime, the Mystical, and the Inner Creative." PERCEPTUAL AND MOTOR SKILLS 27, no. 3, pt. 1 (1968): 767-86.

Strunk, Orlo, Jr. "Time-Cross Examination: A Methodological Innovation in the Study of Religious Beliefs and Attitudes." REVIEW OF RELIGIOUS RESEARCH 7, no. 2 (1966): 121-24.

Thompson, L., and Hostetler, J.A. "The Hutterian Confession of Faith: A Documentary Analysis." ALBERTA JOURNAL OF EDUCATIONAL RESEARCH 16 (1970): 29-45.

> An elucidation of the belief system implicit in a sixteenth-century confession of faith.

Thouless, Robert H. "The Tendency to Certainty in Religious Belief." BRITISH JOURNAL OF PSYCHOLOGY 26 (1935): 16-31.

Van Aerde, Mark. "The Attitude of Adults towards God." SOCIAL COMPASS 19 (1972-73): 407-14.

Vercruysse, Godelieve. "The Meaning of God: A Factor Analytic Study." SOCIAL COMPASS 19 (1972-73): 347-64.

Walberg, Herbert J. "Religious Differences in Cognitive Associations and Self-Concept in Prospective Teachers." JOURNAL OF SOCIAL PSYCHOLOGY 73 (1967): 89-96.

Walker, C. Eugene. "The Effect of a First Encounter with Mental Patients on Religious Beliefs." JOURNAL OF SOCIAL PSYCHOLOGY 78 (1969): 255-61.

E:5   THE PSYCHOLOGY OF RELIGIOUS ATTITUDES

Adinarayan, S.P., and Rajamanickam, M. "A Study of Student Attitude toward Religion, the Spiritual and the Supernatural." JOURNAL OF SOCIAL PSYCHOLOGY 57, no. 1 (1962): 105-11.

Allport, Gordon W., et al. "The Religion of the Post-War College Student." JOURNAL OF PSYCHOLOGY 25 (1948): 3-33.

_____. BECOMING: BASIC CONSIDERATIONS FOR A PSYCHOLOGY OF PERSONALITY. New Haven, Conn.: Yale University Press, 1955. 106 p.

Includes a chapter on the religious sentiment.

Amon, Jesus, and Yela, Mariano. "Dimensiones de la Religiosidad." REVISTA DE PSICOLOGIA GENERAL Y APLICADA 23 (1968): 689-93.

A study of Allport's intrinsic-extrinsic distinction.

Anant, Santokh S. "Caste Hindu Attitudes toward Harijans: A Study of Inter-Caste and Urban-Rural Differences." PSYCHOLOGIA: AN INTERNATIONAL JOURNAL OF PSYCHOLOGY IN THE ORIENT 13 (March 1970): 42-56.

Appleby, Peter C. "On Religious Attitudes." RELIGIOUS STUDIES 6 (1970): 359-68.

Baer, Daniel J., and Mosele, Victor F. "Political and Religious Beliefs of Catholics and Attitudes toward Lay Dress of Sisters." JOURNAL OF PSYCHOLOGY 74 (1970): 77-83.

Broen, William E., Jr. "Personality Correlates of Certain Religious Attitudes." JOURNAL OF CONSULTING PSYCHOLOGY 19 (1955): 64.

Bronson, Louise, and Meadow, Arnold. "The Need Achievement Orientation of Catholic and Protestant Mexican-Americans." REVISTA INTERAMERICANA DE PSICOLOGICA 2 (1968): 159-68.

Brown, L.B. "Classifications of Religious Orientation." JOURNAL FOR THE SCIENTIFIC STUDY OF RELIGION 4 (1964-65): 91-99.

Cameron, Paul. "Valued Aspects of Religion to Negroes and Whites." PROCEEDINGS OF THE 77TH ANNUAL CONVENTION OF THE AMERICAN PSYCHOLOGICAL ASSOCIATION 4 (1969): 741-42.

Coates, Thomas J. "Personality Correlates of Religious Commitment; A Further Verification." JOURNAL OF SOCIAL PSYCHOLOGY 89 (February 1973): 159-60.

Coursey, Robert D. "Liberal and Conservative Roman Catholics." PROCEEDINGS OF THE ANNUAL CONVENTION OF THE AMERICAN PSYCHOLOGICAL ASSOCIATION 6, pt. 1 (1971): 133-34.

Croog, Sydney H., et al. "Value Orientations, Religious Identity, and Career

Decisions of Nursing Students in Japan." NURSING RESEARCH 17 (1968): 161-66.

Danesino, Angelo, and Layman, William A. "Catholic Attitudes and Beliefs in Transition: A Decade Study of a Jesuit College." PSYCHOLOGICAL REPORTS 28 (February 1971): 247-50.

DeFronzo, James. "Religion and Humanitarianism in Eysenck's T Dimension and Left-Right Political Orientation." JOURNAL OF PERSONALITY AND SOCIAL PSYCHOLOGY 21 (1972): 265-69.

Dittes, James E. "Two Issues in Measuring Religion." In RESEARCH ON RELIGIOUS DEVELOPMENT: A COMPREHENSIVE HANDBOOK, pp. 78-108. Edited by Merton P. Strommen. New York: Hawthorn Books, 1971.

_____. "Typing the Typologies: Some Parallels in the Career of Church-Sect and Extrinsic-Intrinsic." JOURNAL FOR THE SCIENTIFIC STUDY OF RELIGION 10 (Winter 1971): 375-83.

Dixit, Ramesh C., and Sharma, Deo D. "Transformation of Social and Religious Values of Different Castes." PSYCHOLOGIA: AN INTERNATIONAL JOURNAL OF PSYCHOLOGY IN THE ORIENT 13 (September 1970): 117-19.

Dodrill, Carl, et al. "The Assessment of Religiosity in Evangelical College Students and Its Relationship to Prior Family Religious Involvement." JOURNAL OF PSYCHOLOGY AND THEOLOGY 1 (January 1973): 52-57.

Dreger, Ralph Mason. "Some Personality Correlates of Religious Attitudes as Determined by Projective Techniques." PSYCHOLOGICAL MONOGRAPHS 66, no. 3 (1952): 18.

_____. "Expressed Attitudes and Needs of Religious Persons Compared with Those Determined by Projective Techniques." JOURNAL OF GENERAL PSYCHOLOGY 58 (1958): 217-24.

Dutt, N.K. "Attitudes of the University Students toward Religion." JOURNAL OF PSYCHOLOGICAL RESEARCHES 9, no. 3 (1965): 127-30.

Eisenman, Russell, and Cole, Spurgeon N. "Prejudice and Conservatism in Denominational College Students." PSYCHOLOGICAL REPORTS 14, no. 2 (1964): 644.

Fagan, Joen, and Breed, George. "A Good Short Measure of Religious Dogmatism." PSYCHOLOGICAL REPORTS 26 (1970): 533-34.

Feather, N.T. "Evaluation of Religious and Neutral Arguments in Religious and

Atheist Student Groups." AUSTRALIAN PSYCHOLOGIST 1 (1966): 85.

Feldman, Kenneth A. "Change and Stability of Religious Orientations during College. Part I: Freshman-Senior Comparisons." REVIEW OF RELIGIOUS RESEARCH 11 (1969): 40-60.

_____. "Change and Stability of Religious Orientations during College. Part II: Social-Structural Correlates." REVIEW OF RELIGIOUS RESEARCH 11 (1970): 103-27.

Ferguson, L.W. "Socio-Psychological Correlates of the Primary Attitude Scales: I. Religionism. II. Humanitarianism." JOURNAL OF SOCIAL PSYCHOLOGY 19 (1944): 81-98.

Fetter, George C. "A Comparative Study of Attitudes of Christian and Moslem Lebanese Villagers." JOURNAL FOR THE SCIENTIFIC STUDY OF RELIGION 4, no. 1 (1964): 48-59.

Francesco, E. "A Pervasive Value: Conventional Religiosity." JOURNAL OF SOCIAL PSYCHOLOGY 57, no. 2 (1962): 467-70.

Garrison, Karl C. "Worldminded Attitudes of College Students in a Southern University." JOURNAL OF SOCIAL PSYCHOLOGY 54 (1961): 147-53.

Gilmore, Susan K. "Personality Differences between High and Low Dogmatism Groups of Pentecostal Believers." JOURNAL FOR THE SCIENTIFIC STUDY OF RELIGION 8 (1969): 161-64.

Glass, Kenneth D. "Denominational Differences in Religious Belief, Practice, Anxiety, and Dogmatism." RELIGIOUS EDUCATION 66 (1971): 204-6.

Godin, Andre, ed. FROM RELIGIOUS EXPERIENCE TO A RELIGIOUS ATTITUDE. Chicago: Loyola University Press, 1965. 210 p.

Graff, Robert W., and Ladd, Clayton E. "POI Correlates of a Religious Commitment Inventory." JOURNAL OF CLINICAL PSYCHOLOGY 27 (1971): 502-4.

Hartnett, Rodney, and Peterson, Richard E. "Religious Preference as a Factor in Attitudinal and Background Differences among College Freshmen." SOCIOLOGY OF EDUCATION 41 (1968): 227-37.

Havens, Joseph. "A Study of Religious Conflict in College Students." JOURNAL OF SOCIAL PSYCHOLOGY 64, no. 1 (1964): 77-87.

147

Hepburn, Lawrence R. "Religion in the Social Studies: The Question of Religious Attitudes." RELIGIOUS EDUCATION 66 (1971): 172-79.

Hites, Robert W. "Change in Religious Attitudes during Four Years of College." JOURNAL OF SOCIAL PSYCHOLOGY 66, no. 1 (1965): 51-63.

Hoge, Dean R. "A Validated Intrinsic Religious Motivation Scale." JOURNAL FOR THE SCIENTIFIC STUDY OF RELIGION 11 (December 1972): 369-76.

Hood, Ralph W., Jr. "A Comparison of the Allport and Feagin Scoring Procedures for Intrinsic-Extrinsic Religious Orientation." JOURNAL FOR THE SCIENTIFIC STUDY OF RELIGION 10 (Winter 1971): 370-74.

Hunt, Richard A. "The Interpretation of the Religious Scale of the Allport-Vernon-Lindzey Study of Values." JOURNAL FOR THE SCIENTIFIC STUDY OF RELIGION 7, no. 1 (1968): 65-77.

_____. "Mythological-Symbolic Religious Commitment: The LAM Scales." JOURNAL FOR THE SCIENTIFIC STUDY FO RELIGION 11 (March 1972): 42-52.

Hunt, Richard A., and King, Morton. "The Intrinsic-Extrinsic Concept: A Review and Evaluation." JOURNAL FOR THE SCIENTIFIC STUDY OF RELIGION 10 (Winter 1971): 339-56.

Jacks, Irving. "Attitudes of College Freshmen and Sophmores toward Interfaith Marriage." ADOLESCENCE 2 (1967): 183-209.

Jones, F. Nowell, et al. "A Direct Scale of Attitude toward the Church." PERCEPTUAL AND MOTOR SKILLS 20, no. 1 (1965): 319-24.

Jones, Marshall B. "Religious Values and Authoritarian Tendency." JOURNAL OF SOCIAL PSYCHOLOGY 48 (August 1958): 83-89.

Kiesler, Charles A. THE PSYCHOLOGY OF COMMITMENT. New York: Academic Press, 1971. xii, 190 p.

Kilpatrick, Dean G., et al. "Dogmatism, Religion, and Religiosity: A Review and Re-Evaluation." PSYCHOLOGICAL REPORTS 26 (February 1970): 15-22.

Kottman, John E. "A Semantic Study of Religious Attitude." JOURNAL OF RELIGION AND HEALTH 5, no. 2 (1966): 119-29.

Kriger, Sara F., and Kroes, William H. "Child-Rearing Attitudes of Chinese, Jewish and Protestant Mothers." JOURNAL OF SOCIAL PSYCHOLOGY 86 (1972): 205-10.

Lechat, Fernand. "Neurotic and Religious Attitudes." REVUE FRANCAISE DE PSYCHANALYSE 14 (1950): 90-105.

Levinson, Boris M. "Some Research Findings with Jewish Subjects of Traditional Background." MENTAL HYGIENE 47 (1963): 129-34.

Lowe, C. Marshall, and Braaten, Roger O. "Differences in Religious Attitudes in Mental Illness." JOURNAL FOR THE SCIENTIFIC STUDY OF RELIGION 5, no. 3 (1965-66): 435-45.

McClelland, David C. THE ACHIEVING SOCIETY. Princeton, N.J.: D. Van Nostrand, 1961. 512 p.

   A classic study which argues that economic growth in a society is dependent on the society's need for achievement and that this need in turn depends on patterns of childhood training which value inde- pendence. Includes a variety of historical demonstrations of this hypothesis, including comparisons of Protestant and Catholic cultures.

Maddock, Richard, and Kenny, Charles T. "Philosophies of Human Nature and Personal Religious Orientation." JOURNAL FOR THE SCIENTIFIC STUDY OF RELIGION 11 (September 1972): 277-81.

Maier, Joseph, and Spinrad, William. "Religiose Uberzeugungen und Religiose Verhaltensweisen." KOLNER ZEITSCHRIFT FUR SOZIALOGIE UND SOZIAL- PSYCHOLOGIE 10 (1958): 439-45.

   A study of religious convictions.

Maranell, Gary M. "A Factor Analytic Study of Some Selected Dimensions of Religious Attitudes." SOCIOLOGY AND SOCIAL RESEARCH 52, no. 4 (1968): 430-37.

Mayo, Clyde C., et al. "MMPI Correlates of Religiousness in Late Adolescent College Students." JOURNAL OF NERVOUS AND MENTAL DISEASE 149 (1969): 381-85.

Mirels, Herbert L., and Garrett, James B. "The Protestant Ethic as a Personal- ity Variable." JOURNAL OF CONSULTING AND CLINICAL PSYCHOLOGY 36 (February 1971): 40-44.

   Also listed in section E:3.

Moberg, David O. "Theological Self-Classification and Ascetic Moral Views of Students." REVIEW OF RELIGIOUS RESEARCH 10 (1969): 100-107.

Murray, Henry A., and Morgan, Christiana D. "A Clinical Study of Senti- ments." GENETIC PSYCHOLOGY MONOGRAPHS 32 (1945): 3-311.

Contains a major discussion of religious sentiments in which the researchers develop a "broader conception of religion" designed to top the religiosity of subjects who were avowed agnostics or indifferent to orthodox religion.

Nelson, Erland. "Patterns of Religious Attitude Shifts from College to Fourteen Years Later." Washington, D.C.: PSYCHOLOGICAL MONOGRAPHS 70, no. 17 (1956): entire booklet, pp. 1-15.

Ostow, Mortimer. "The Nature of Religious Controls." AMERICAN PSYCHOLOGIST 14 (1959): 687-93.

Pang, Henry. "Religious Attitudes of Students." PSYCHOLOGICAL REPORTS 22 (1968): 344.

Pilkington, G.W., et al. "Changes in Religious Attitude and Practices among Students during University Degree Courses." BRITISH JOURNAL OF EDUCATIONAL PSYCHOLOGY 35, no. 2 (1965): 150-57.

Pirojnikoff, Leo A., et al. "Dogmatism and Social Distance: A Cross-Cultural Study." PROCEEDINGS OF THE AMERICAN PSYCHOLOGICAL ASSOCIATION 5, pt. 1 (1970): 323-24.
Study of kibbutz members and non-members.

Poppleton, Pamela K., and Pilkington, G.W. "The Measurement of Religious Attitudes in a University Population." BRITISH JOURNAL OF SOCIAL AND CLINICAL PSYCHOLOGY 2, no. 1 (1963): 20-36.

Pruyser, Paul W. "Assessment of the Patient's Religious Attitudes in the Psychiatric Case Study." BULLETIN OF THE MENNINGER CLINIC 35 (1971): 272-91.

Pyron, Bernard. "Belief Q-sort, Allport-Vernon Study of Values, and Religion." PSYCHOLOGICAL REPORTS 8 (1961): 399-400.

Raschke, Vernon. "Dogmatism and Committed and Consensual Religiosity." JOURNAL FOR THE SCIENTIFIC STUDY OF RELIGION 12 (September 1973): 339-45.

Richek, Herbert G., and Reid, Braxton. "Religious Authoritarianism and Psychopathology in College Students." PSYCHIATRIC QUARTERLY 45 (1971): 363-71.

Rokeach, Milton. "The Nature and Meaning of Dogmatism." PSYCHOLOGICAL REVIEW 61 (1954): 194-204.

_____. "The Similarity Continua for Catholics, Episcopalians, Presbyterians, Lutherans, Methodists and Baptists." In THE OPEN AND CLOSED MIND: INVESTIGATIONS INTO THE NATURE OF BELIEF SYSTEMS AND PERSON-ALITY SYSTEMS, pp. 295-99. By Milton Rokeach. New York: Basic Books, 1960.

_____. "A Theory of Organization and Change within Value-Attitude Systems." JOURNAL OF SOCIAL ISSUES 1, no. 24 (1968): 13-33.

See also his BELIEFS, ATTITUDES AND VALUES in section E:4.

_____. "Value Systems and Religion." REVIEW OF RELIGIOUS RESEARCH 11 (1969): 2-23.

_____. "Religious Values and Social Compassion." REVIEW OF RELIGIOUS RESEARCH 11 (1969): 24-39.

Rosenbloom, Joseph R., and Dobinsky, Paul S. "Student Attitudes in a Reform Jewish Religious School." RELIGIOUS EDUCATION 63 (1968): 323-27.

Rubins, Jack L. "Neurotic Attitudes toward Religion." AMERICAN JOURNAL OF PSYCHOANALYSIS 15 (1955): 71-81.

Rudin, Josef. FANATICISM: A PSYCHOLOGICAL ANALYSIS. Translated by Elizabeth Reineike. Notre Dame, Ind.: University of Notre Dame Press, 1970. 206 p.

Rushby, W.F., and Thrush, J.C. "Mennonites and Social Compassion: The Rokeach Hypothesis Reconsidered." REVIEW OF RELIGIOUS RESEARCH 15 (Fall 1973): 16-28.

Schludermann, Shirin, and Schludermann, Eduard. "Maternal Child-Raising At-titudes in Hutterite Communal Society." JOURNAL OF PSYCHOLOGY 74 (1971): 169-77.

Stanley, Gordon. "Personality and Attitude Characteristics of Fundamentalist University Students." AUSTRALIAN JOURNAL OF PSYCHOLOGY 15, no. 3 (1963): 199-200.

Stellway, Richard J. "The Correspondence between Religious Orientation and Sociopolitical Liberalism and Conservatism." SOCIOLOGICAL QUARTERLY 14 (Summer 1973): 430-39.

Stewart, Robert A., and Webster, Alan C. "Scale for Theological Conservatism, and Its Personality Correlates." PERCEPTUAL AND MOTOR SKILLS 30 (1970): 867-70.

Sutker, Patricia B., et al. "Religious Preference, Practice, and Personal Sexual Attitudes and Behavior." PSYCHOLOGICAL REPORTS 26 (June 1970): 835-41.

Tate, Eugene D., and Miller, Gerald R. "Differences in Value Systems of Persons with Varying Religious Orientations." JOURNAL FOR THE SCIENTIFIC STUDY OF RELIGION 10 (Winter 1971): 357-65.

Tennison, James C., and Snyder, William U. "Some Relationships between Attitudes toward the Church and Certain Personality Characteristics." JOURNAL OF COUNSELING PSYCHOLOGY 15 (1968): 187-89.

Tisdale, John R. "Selected Correlates of Extrinsic Religious Values." REVIEW OF RELIGIOUS RESEARCH 7, no. 2 (1966): 78-84.

Vergote, Antoine. "Psychological Conditions of Adult Faith." LUMEN VITAE 15 (1960): 623-34.

See other items on faith as a theological concept in section E:2.

_____. THE RELIGIOUS MAN: A PSYCHOLOGICAL STUDY OF RELIGIOUS ATTITUDES. Translated by Marie-Bernard Said. Dayton, Ohio: Pflaum Press, 1969. 306 p.

A French psychologist provides a good summary of American and continental theory and research on religious attitudes.

Veroff, J., et al. "Achievement Motivation and Religious Background." AMERICAN SOCIOLOGICAL REVIEW 27, no. 2 (1962): 205-17.

Ward, Charles D., and Barrett, James E. "The Ecumenical Council and Attitude Change among Catholic, Protestant and Jewish College Students." JOURNAL OF SOCIAL PSYCHOLOGY 74 (1968): 91-96.

Wearing, A.J., and Brown, L.B. "The Dimensionality of Religion." BRITISH JOURNAL OF SOCIAL AND CLINICAL PSYCHOLOGY 11 (June 1972): 143-48.

Webb, Sam C. "Convergent-Discriminant Validity of a Role Oriented Interest Inventory." EDUCATIONAL AND PSYCHOLOGICAL MEASUREMENT 33 (Summer 1973): 441-51.

Study of the Inventory of Religious Activities and Interest test.

Webster, Alan C., and Stewart, Robert A. "Theological Conservatism." In THE PSYCHOLOGY OF CONSERVATISM, pp. 129-47. Edited by G.D. Wilson. London: Academic Press, 1973. xv, 277 p.

Weima, J. "Authoritarianism, Religious Conservatism, and Sociocentric Attitudes in Roman Catholic Groups." HUMAN RELATIONS 18 (1965): 231-39.

Wells, Harry K. "Religious Attitudes at a Small Denominational College as

Compared with Harvard and Radcliffe." JOURNAL OF PSYCHOLOGY 53, no. 2 (1962): 349-82.

Willis, Jerry, et al. "Religious Orientations of Three Samples of Graduate Students in Clinical Psychology, Social Work, and Counseling and Guidance." PSYCHOLOGICAL REPORTS 26 (1970): 623-30.

Wilson, Glenn D., ed. THE PSYCHOLOGY OF CONSERVATISM. New York and London: Academic Press, 1972. xv, 277 p.

Wilson, Glenn D., and Lillie, Francis J. "Social Attitudes of Salvationists and Humanists." BRITISH JOURNAL OF SOCIAL AND CLINICAL PSYCHOLOGY 11 (September 1972): 220-24.

Wilson, W. Cody. "Extrinsic Religious Values and Prejudice." JOURNAL OF ABNORMAL AND SOCIAL PSYCHOLOGY 60 (March 1960): 286-88.

    Also listed in section F:2.

Wilson, Warner, and Kawamura, Wallace. "Rigidity, Adjustment, and Social Responsibility as Possible Correlates of Religiousness: A Test of Three Points of View." JOURNAL FOR THE SCIENTIFIC STUDY OF RELIGION 6 (1967): 279-80.

Woodburne, Angus Stewart. THE RELIGIOUS ATTITUDE: A PSYCHOLOGICAL STUDY OF ITS DIFFERENTIATION. New York: Macmillan, 1927. 353 p.

Young, Robert K., et al. "Change in Attitude toward Religion in a Southern University." PSYCHOLOGICAL REPORTS 18 (1966): 39-46.

E:6 THE PSYCHOLOGY OF RELIGIOUS BEHAVIOR

Ancona, Leonardo. "Interpretazione Clinica del Comportamento Religioso." CONTRIBUTI DELL'ISTITUTO DI PSICOLOGIA, no. 24, 1962, pp. 7-25.

Anderson, D.S., and Western, J.S. "Denominational Schooling and Religious Behavior." AUSTRALIAN AND NEW ZEALAND JOURNAL OF SOCIOLOGY 8 (1972): 19-31.

Argyle, Michael. RELIGIOUS BEHAVIOR. London: Routledge and Kegan Paul, 1958; Glencoe, Ill.: Free Press, 1959. 196 p.

    A review of British and American studies in the social psychology of religion from 1900 through 1958, using church attendance as its primary criterion of religious behavior.

Beit-Hallahmi, Benjamin, ed. RESEARCH IN RELIGIOUS BEHAVIOR: SELECT-

ED READINGS. Monterey, Calif.: Brooks/Cole Publishing Co., 1973. 404 p.

A well-selected collection of studies, previously published, which are organized according to the following headings: religious sociali-zation, religious beliefs, values and attitudes, religious beliefs and personal adjustment, intense religious experience, and religion and political behavior.

Bennett, George F. "Religious Activity and the Suspicious Person." JOURNAL OF PASTORAL CARE 18 (1964): 140-47.

Fisher, Seymour. "Acquiescence and Religiosity." PSYCHOLOGICAL REPORTS 15, no. 3 (1964): 784.

Gladstone, Roy, and Gupta, G.C. "A Cross-Cultural Study of the Behavioral Aspects of the Concept of Religion." JOURNAL OF SOCIAL PSYCHOLOGY 60, no. 2 (1963): 203-11.

Greeley, Andrew M. "The Religious Behavior of Graduate Students." JOUR-NAL FOR THE SCIENTIFIC STUDY OF RELIGION 5 (1965): 34-40.

Keene, James J. "Religious Behavior and Neuroticism, Spontaneity, and World-mindedness." SOCIOMETRY 30, no. 2 (1967): 137-57.

Lindenthal, Jacob J., et al. "Mental Status and Religious Behavior." JOUR-NAL FOR THE SCIENTIFIC STUDY OF RELIGION 9 (Summer 1970): 143-50.

McPhail, Clark. "Religious Self-Designating Behaviors." JOURNAL FOR THE SCIENTIFIC STUDY OF RELIGION 11 (September 1972): 262-70.

Marty, Martin E. "Religious Behavior: Its Social Dimension in American His-tory." SOCIAL RESEARCH 41 (Summer 1974): 241-64.

Mayhew, Bruce H., Jr. "Behavioral Observability and Compliance with Reli-gious Proscriptions on Birth Control." SOCIAL FORCES 47 (1968): 60-70.

Middleton, Russell, and Putney, S. "Religion, Normative Standards and Be-havior." SOCIOMETRY 25, no. 2 (1962): 141-52.

Salisbury, W. Seward. "Religious Identity and Religious Behavior of the Sons and Daughters of Religious Inter-Marriage." REVIEW OF RELIGIOUS RESEARCH 11 (1970): 128-35.

Shaw, Blair W. "Religion and Conceptual Models of Behavior." BRITISH JOURNAL OF SOCIAL AND CLINICAL PSYCHOLOGY 9 (December 1970): 320-27.

Siegman, Aron Wolfe. "An Empirical Investigation of the Psychoanalytic Theory of Religious Behavior." JOURNAL FOR THE SCIENTIFIC STUDY OF RELIGION 1 (1961): 74-78.

Walters, Annette, and Bradley, Ritamary. "Motivation and Religious Behavior." In RESEARCH ON RELIGIOUS DEVELOPMENT: A COMPREHENSIVE HANDBOOK, pp. 599-654. Edited by Merton P. Strommen. New York: Hawthorn Books, 1971.

Webb, Sam C. "An Exploratory Investigation of Some Needs Met through Religious Behavior." JOURNAL FOR THE SCIENTIFIC STUDY OF RELIGION 5 (1965): 51-58.

Welford, A.T. "Is Religious Behavior Dependent upon Affect or Frustration?" JOURNAL OF ABNORMAL AND SOCIAL PSYCHOLOGY 42 (1947): 310-19.

Wicker, Allen W. "Overt Behaviors toward the Church by Volunteers, Follow-up Volunteers, and Non-Volunteers in a Church Survey." PSYCHOLOGICAL REPORTS 22 (1968): 917-20.

For studies on affiliative behavior, see section F:1.

E:7 STUDIES OF COGNITIVE AND MORAL DEVELOPMENT

Allen, Edmund E., and Hites, Robert W. "Factors in Religious Attitudes of Older Adolescents." JOURNAL OF SOCIAL PSYCHOLOGY 55 (1961): 265-73.

Amatora, Mary. "Needed Research on Religious Development during Adolescence." CATHOLIC PSYCHOLOGICAL RECORD 1, no. 2 (1963): 1-9.

Ash, Roberta T. "Jewish Adolescents' Attitudes toward Religion and Ethnicity." ADOLESCENCE 4 (1969): 245-82.

Attkisson, C. Clifford, et al. "The Use of Figure Drawings to Assess Religious Values." JOURNAL OF PSYCHOLOGY 71, no. 1 (1969): 27-31.

Bailey, Frances E. "Youth's Response to the Bible." RELIGIOUS EDUCATION 59, no. 3 (1964): 214-49.

Barber, Lucie W., and Atherton, Virginia H. "Religious Convictions as Catalyzers for Youth's Decisions." CHARACTER POTENTIAL: A RECORD OF RESEARCH 4, no. 3 (1968): 54-58.

Beck, C.M., et al. MORAL EDUCATION: INTERDISCIPLINARY APPROACHES. Toronto: University of Toronto Press, 1971. 402 p.
A collection of essays and studies on the psychological, sociologi-

cal, and philosophical nature of moral development.

Benson, Peter, and Spilka, Bernard. "God Image as a Function of Self-Esteem and Locus of Control." JOURNAL FOR THE SCIENTIFIC STUDY OF RELIGION 12 (September 1973): 297-310.

Subjects were Catholic high school boys.

Bier, William C., ed. THE ADOLESCENT: HIS SEARCH FOR UNDERSTAND-ING. New York: Fordham University Press, 1963. 246 p.

Blanchard, W.H. "Medieval Morality and Juvenile Delinquency." AMERICAN IMAGO 13 (1956): 383-98.

Bovet, Pierre. THE CHILD'S RELIGION: A STUDY OF THE DEVELOPMENT OF THE RELIGIOUS SENTIMENT. Translated by George H. Green. New York: E.P. Dutton, 1928. xiii, 202 p.

A classic study which focuses on such topics as children's religious crises, attitudes toward God, and religious aspects of love and re-spect for parents.

Bull, Norman J. MORAL JUDGMENT FROM CHILDHOOD TO ADOLES-CENCE. Beverly Hills, Calif.: Sage Publications, 1970. xiii, 303 p.

Based on testing of the moral judgments of 360 English school children, the book employs a theory of stages of moral development consisting of four overlapping stages: anomy, heteronomy, socionomy, and autonomy.

Burton, William. "Behavioral Morality: A Critique of William Kay's MORAL DEVELOPMENT." RELIGIOUS EDUCATION 67 (1972): 298-304.

Colm, Hanna. "Religious Symbolism in Child Analysis." PSYCHOANALYSIS 2 (Summer 1953): 39-56.

Cook, Stuart W. REVIEW OF RECENT RESEARCH BEARING ON RELIGIOUS AND CHARACTER FORMATION. New York: The Religious Education Associa-tion, 1962. 174 p.

_____, ed. RESEARCH PLANS IN THE FIELDS OF RELIGION, VALUES AND MORALITY AND THEIR BEARING ON RELIGIOUS AND CHARACTER FORMA-TION. New York: The Religious Education Association, 1962. 310 p.

Cooley, C. Ewing, and Hutton, Jerry B. "Adolescent Response to Religious Appeal as Related to IPAT Anxiety." JOURNAL OF SOCIAL PSYCHOLOGY 67 (1965): 325-27.

Crandall, Virginia C., and Gozali, Joaz. "The Social Desirability Responses of Children of Four Religious-Cultural Groups." CHILD DEVELOPMENT 40 (1969): 751-62.

De Blauwe-Plomteux, Magda. "L'Attitude des adolescents et des jeunes adultes envers le-Christ." SOCIAL COMPASS 19 (1972-73): 415-30.

Deconchy, Jean-Pierre. "The Idea of God: Its Emergence between 7 and 16 Years." LUMEN VITAE 19 (1964): 285-96.

_____. STRUCTURE GENETIQUE DE L'IDEE DE DIEU CHEZ LES CATHO-LIQUES FRANCAIS, GARCONS ET FILLES DE 8 A 16 ANS. Brussels: Lumen Vitae, 1967. 373 p.

> A study of the content of the structure of children's ideas of God. Using a sample of 4600 subjects, three phases of conceptual development were discerned.

Decrop, N. "Opinions sur les buts generaux de la vie chez les etudiants de 17 a 18 ans." BULLETIN D'ORIENTATION SCOLAIRE ET PROFESSIONNELLE 10 (1961): 62-65.

> A study of the religious ideas and ideals of Belgian students.

Delay, Jean. THE YOUTH OF ANDRE GIDE. Translated by June Guichanaud. Chicago: University of Chicago Press, 1963. 498 p.

> Develops the thesis that the homosexuality of the French author was part of a larger self-perception as anti-Christ.

Dumoulin, Anne. "The Priest's Occupations as Perceived by 6 to 12-Year-Old Children." LUMEN VITAE 26 (1971): 316-32.

Edward, Fran. EXPLORING CHRISTIAN POTENTIAL. Schenectady, N.Y.: Union College, Character Research Project, 1961.

> A brief report of the Character Research Project's research in religious development and education.

Elkin, Henry. "On the Origin of the Self." PSYCHOANALYSIS AND THE PSYCHOANALYTIC REVIEW 45 (Winter 1958-59): 57-76.

> The author is a psychoanalyst interested in religious ideas and behavior.

_____. "Freudian and Phenomenological Approaches to the Emergence of Individual Consciousness." HUMANITAS 5 (1970): 287-306.

Elkind, David. "The Child's Conception of His Religious Denomination: I.

The Jewish Child." JOURNAL OF GENETIC PSYCHOLOGY 99 (1961): 209-25.

_____. "The Child's Conception of his Religious Denomination: II. The Catholic Child." JOURNAL OF GENETIC PSYCHOLOGY 101 (1962): 185-93.

_____. "Age Changes in the Meaning of Religious Identity." REVIEW OF RELIGIOUS RESEARCH 6 (1964): 36-40.

_____. "The Child's Conception of his Religious Identity." LUMEN VITAE 19 (1964): 635-46.

_____. "Piaget's Semi-Clinical Interview and the Study of Spontaneous Religion." JOURNAL FOR THE SCIENTIFIC STUDY OF RELIGION 4, no. 1 (1964): 40-47.

_____. "The Development of Religious Understanding in Children and Adolescents." In RESEARCH ON RELIGIOUS DEVELOPMENT: A COMPREHENSIVE HANDBOOK, pp. 655-85. Edited by Merton P. Strommen. New York: Hawthorn Books, 1971.

Erikson, Erik H. CHILDHOOD AND SOCIETY. 2nd rev. ed. New York: W.W. Norton & Co., 1963. 445 p.

Explication and application of the author's theory of psychosocial development. Part I focuses on childhood and the modalities of social life; Part II concerns childhood in two American Indian tribes; Part III is about the growth of the ego and contains the author's theory of the life cycle; Part IV centers on youth and the evolution of identity with chapters on the American identity, Adolf Hitler, and Maxim Gorky.

_____. IDENTITY: YOUTH AND CRISIS. New York: W.W. Norton & Co., 1968. 336 p.

Provides a useful restatement of the author's theory of life stages and applies these concepts to the early lives of George Bernard Shaw and William James.

Fichter, Joseph H. "Religion and Socialization among Children." REVIEW OF RELIGIOUS RESEARCH 4 (1962): 24-33.

Fukuyama, Yoshio. "Wonder Letters: An Experimental Study of the Religious Sensitivities of Children." RELIGIOUS EDUCATION 58 (1963): 377-83.

Gillibert, Jean. "L'Eros du pere." INTERPRETATION 5, no. 2-3 (1971): 105-36.

Concerns God as father-figure.

Glass, J. Conrad. "Premarital Sexual Standards among Church Youth Leaders: An Exploratory Study." JOURNAL FOR THE SCIENTIFIC STUDY OF RELIGION 11 (December 1972): 361-67.

Subjects were church youth leaders of high school age.

Godin, Andre. "Application d'un Q-sorting a la psychologie religieuse: Resultats et reflexions critiques." PSYCHOLOGICA BELGICA 5 (1965): 19-26.

On the relation of parental images to concepts of God through the use of Q-sort technique.

_____. "Genetic Development of the Symbolic Function: Meaning and Limits of the Work of R. Goldman." RELIGIOUS EDUCATION 63, no. 6 (1968): 439-45.

See Ronald J. Goldman's study below.

_____. "Genetic Development of the Symbolic and Hermeneutic Function: Meaning and Limits of the Work of R. Goldman." LUMEN VITAE 24 (1969): 95-106.

See Ronald J. Goldman's study below.

_____, ed. CHILD AND ADULT BEFORE GOD. Chicago: Loyola University Press, 1965. 160 p.

Papers by Catholic psychologists on Piaget, mental illness, meditation, catechetical instruction, religious attitudes, and other topics.

Godin, Andre, and Hallez, Monique. "Parental Images and Divine Paternity." LUMEN VITAE 19 (1964): 253-84.

Godin, Andre, and Marthe, S. "Magic Mentality and Sacramental Life in Children of 8 to 14 Years." LUMEN VITAE 15 (1960): 277-96.

Goldman, Ronald J. "Who Wrote the Bible? A Psychological Study of Religious Thinking between 6 and 17 Years." LUMEN VITAE 19 (1964): 311-26.

_____. "The Application of Piaget's Schema of Operational Thinking to Religious Story Data by Means of the Guttman Scalogram." BRITISH JOURNAL OF EDUCATIONAL PSYCHOLOGY 35, no. 2 (1965): 158-70.

Graebner, Oliver E. "Children's Concepts of God." RELIGIOUS EDUCATION 59, no. 3 (1964): 234-41.

Gustafson, James M., et al. MORAL EDUCATION: FIVE LECTURES. Cambridge: Harvard University Press, 1970. 136 p.

A collection of essays on moral development by James Gustafson, Richard Peters, Lawrence Kohlberg, Bruno Bettelheim, and Kenneth Keniston.

Gutauskas, Jonas. "Child's God and Religion." LUMEN VITAE 15 (1960): 7-22.

Havens, Joseph. "College Religion as Personal Experience and as Pilgrimage." PASTORAL PSYCHOLOGY 15 (October 1964): 31-41.

Havighurst, Robert J. "How the Moral Life is Formed." RELIGIOUS EDUCA-TION 57 (1962): 432-38.

_____. "The Religion of Youth." In RESEARCH ON RELIGIOUS DEVELOP-MENT: A COMPREHENSIVE HANDBOOK, pp. 686-723. Edited by Merton P. Strommen. New York: Hawthorn Books, 1971.

Heltsley, Mary E., and Broderick, Carlfred B. "Religiosity and Premarital Sexual Permissiveness: Reexamination of Reiss's Traditionalism Proposition." JOURNAL OF MARRIAGE AND THE FAMILY 31 (1969): 441-43.

Herman, Simon N. ISRAELIS AND JEWS: THE CONTINUITY OF AN IDENTI-TY. New York: Random House, 1970. 331 p.

A study of the self-perception and identity of Israeli teenagers with special reference to their religiousness.

Hilliard, F.H. "The Influence of Religious Education upon the Development of Children's Moral Ideas." BRITISH JOURNAL OF EDUCATIONAL PSYCHOLOGY 29 (1959): 50-59.

Hoffman, Martin L. "Development of Internal Moral Standards in Children." In RESEARCH ON RELIGIOUS DEVELOPMENT: A COMPREHENSIVE HAND-BOOK, pp. 211-63. Edited by Merton P. Strommen. New York: Hawthorn Books, 1971.

Hyde, Kenneth E. "Critique of Goldman's Research." RELIGIOUS EDUCATION 63, no. 6 (1968): 429-35.

See Ronald J. Goldman's study above.

Jaspard, Jean M. "The 6 to 12-year-old Child's Representation of the Eucha-ristic Presence." LUMEN VITAE 26 (1971): 237-62.

_____. "Loi rituelle et structuration de l'attitude religieuse chez l'enfant." SOCIAL COMPASS 19 (1972-73): 459-72.

Johnson, Ronald C., et al., eds. CONSCIENCE, CONTRACT, AND SOCIAL REALITY: THEORY AND RESEARCH IN BEHAVIORAL SCIENCE. New York: Holt, Rinehart and Winston, 1972. xiv, 460 p.

An excellent collection of readings on the study of conscience. Selections from Freud, Piaget, Mead, Lewin, and others.

Kahana, Boaz. "Stages of the Dream Concept among Hasidic Children." JOURNAL OF GENETIC PSYCHOLOGY 116 (1970): 3-9.

Kay, A. William. MORAL DEVELOPMENT: A PSYCHOLOGICAL STUDY OF MORAL GROWTH FROM CHILDHOOD TO ADOLESCENCE. New York: Schocken Books, 1969. 270 p.

Analyzes various moral development theories in terms of stages of development, moral sanctions, moral judgments, and psychosocial development.

Keary, Dermot M. "Adolescent Spirituality." RELIGIOUS EDUCATION 63 (1968): 376-83.

Keniston, Kenneth. THE UNCOMMITTED: ALIENATED YOUTH IN AMERICAN SOCIETY. New York: Harcourt, Brace and World, 1966. 500 p.

Based on in-depth study of twelve Harvard undergraduates, with a full treatment of one student under the heading, "Inburn, an American Ismael," this influential study characterizes alienation as a futile quest for positive values, possession of a pessimistic existentialist orientation, a distrust of commitment, private goals, and a lack of interest in adulthood.

Khandekar, Mandakini, and Barah, B.C. "Adolescents' Image of Ghosts." INDIAN JOURNAL OF SOCIAL WORK 32 (1971): 278-94.

Klingberg, Gote. "Perceptionlike Images in the Religious Experience of the Child." LUMEN VITAE 16 (1961): 289-300.

Knight, James A. "Adolescent Development and Religious Values." PASTORAL PSYCHOLOGY 20 (February 1969): 39-43.

Kohlberg, Lawrence. "Development of Children's Orientations toward a Moral Order." VITA HUMANA 6 (1963): 11-33.

_____. "Moral Development and Identification." In CHILD PSYCHOLOGY, THE SIXTY-SECOND YEARBOOK OF THE NATIONAL SOCIETY FOR THE STUDY OF EDUCATION, part I, pp. 277-332. Edited by Harold W. Stevenson. Chicago: University of Chicago Press, 1963.

An extension and refinement of Jean Piaget's psychology of moral development, Kohlberg's work on stages of moral development has attracted considerable interest among researchers in religion.

_____. "Moral Education, Religious Education, and the Public Schools: A Developmental View." In RELIGION AND PUBLIC EDUCATION, pp. 164-83. Edited by Theodore R. Sizer. Boston: Houghton Mifflin Co., 1967. xix, 361 p.

_____. "Continuities and Discontinuities in Childhood and Adult Moral Development." HUMAN DEVELOPMENT 12 (1969): 93-120.

Koppe, W.A., and Wright, H.D. "Children's Potential Religious Concepts." CHARACTER POTENTIAL 2, no. 2 (1964): 83-90.

Lawrence, P.J. "Children's Thinking about Religion: A Study of Concrete Operational Thinking." RELIGIOUS EDUCATION 60, no. 2 (1965): 111-16.

Lederer, Wolfgang. DRAGONS, DELINQUENTS AND DESTINY: AN ESSAY ON POSITIVE SUPEREGO FUNCTIONS. New York: International Universities Press, 1964. 83 p.

A discussion of the positive nature of the superego in personality development. Also contains interesting discussions of religious symbolism as it relates to strong, protective father figures.

Lee, Roy Stuart. YOUR GROWING CHILD AND RELIGION: A PSYCHOLOGICAL ACCOUNT. New York: Macmillan, 1963. 224 p.

The author is an Anglican clergyman with a Freudian orientation.

Lesser, Gerald S. "Religion and the Defensive Responses in Children's Fantasy." JOURNAL OF PROJECTIVE TECHNIQUES 23 (1959): 64-68.

Levinson, Boris M. "The Problems of Jewish Religious Youth." GENETIC PSYCHOLOGY MONOGRAPHS 60 (November 1959): 309-48.

Ligon, Ernest M., and Penrod, William T. "Religious and Character Education as a Catalyzing Force in Personality." CHARACTER POTENTIAL 2, no. 1 (1963): 3-18.

Long, Diane, et al. "The Child's Conception of Prayer." JOURNAL FOR THE SCIENTIFIC STUDY OF RELIGION 6 (1967): 101-9.

Loomba, Ram M. "Moral and Religious Development in Childhood and Youth." PSYCHOLOGIA: AN INTERNATIONAL JOURNAL OF PSYCHOLOGY IN THE ORIENT 10, no. 1 (1967): 25-32.

Lubin, Albert J. "A Boy's View of Jesus." PSYCHOANALYTIC STUDY OF THE CHILD 14 (1959): 155–68.

_____. "The Influence of the Russian Orthodox Church on Freud's Wolf-Man: An Hypothesis." PSYCHOANALYTIC FORUM 2 (1967): 145–74.

On the elaboration of a primal scene fantasy in terms of religious symbolism.

McLaughlin, Barry. NATURE, GRACE, AND RELIGIOUS DEVELOPMENT. Westminster, Md.: Newman Press, 1964. 164 p.

Martyn, D. "The Idea of God among Roman Catholic Children Aged Seven and Eight." BRITISH JOURNAL OF EDUCATIONAL PSYCHOLOGY 37 (1967): 399–400.

Maves, Paul B. "Religious Development in Adulthood." In RESEARCH ON RELIGIOUS DEVELOPMENT: A COMPREHENSIVE HANDBOOK, pp. 777–800. Edited by Merton P. Strommen. New York: Hawthorn Books, 1971.

Neidhart, Walter. "What the Bible Means to Children and Adolescents." RELIGIOUS EDUCATION 63, no. 2 (1968): 112–19.

Nelson, Marven O. "The Concept of God and Feelings towards Parents." JOURNAL OF INDIVIDUAL PSYCHOLOGY 27 (May 1971): 46–49.

Nunn, Clyde Z. "Child-Control through a 'Coalition with God'." CHILD DEVELOPMENT 35, no. 2 (1964): 417–32.

Pattison, E. Mansell. "The Development of Moral Values in Children." PASTORAL PSYCHOLOGY 20, no. 191 (1969): 14–30.

Peretti, Peter O. "Guilt in Moral Development: A Comparative Study." PSYCHOLOGICAL REPORTS 25 (1969): 739–45.

Piaget, Jean. PLAY, DREAMS, AND IMITATION IN CHILDHOOD. New York: W.W. Norton & Co., 1962. 296 p.

This study, originally published in 1951, concerns the origins of symbolic thought in childhood.

_____. THE MORAL JUDGMENT OF THE CHILD. New York: Macmillan, 1965. 410 p.

Develops a stage theory of moral development by analyzing the ways children of varying ages fashion and interpret game rules.

Pohlman, Edward W. "Infant Experience and Human Beliefs about Ultimate

Causes." JOURNAL OF PASTORAL CARE 19 (1965): 28-32.

Ranwez, Pierre. "Forming a Moral Conscience in the Very Young Child." LUMEN VITAE 15 (1960): 69-78.

_____. "The Awakening of the Child's Moral Conscience and Sense of Sin." LUMEN VITAE 22 (1967): 124-34.

Richard, W.C., and Stubblefield, H.W. "The Concept of God in the Mentally Retarded." RELIGIOUS EDUCATION 60, no. 3 (1965): 184-88.

Rizzuto, Ana-Maria. "Object Relations and the Formation of the Image of God." BRITISH JOURNAL OF MEDICAL PSYCHOLOGY 47 (1974): 83-99.

Rosen, Bernard C. ADOLESCENCE AND RELIGION: THE JEWISH TEENAGER IN AMERICA. Cambridge, Mass.: Schenkman Publishing Co., 1965. xviii, 218 p.

Sanua, Victor D. "The Jewish Adolescent: A Review of Empirical Research." JEWISH EDUCATION 38, no. 3 (1968): 36-52.

Sharma, Satya N., and Chatterjee, Bishwa B. "Application of the Mosaic Test upon Hindus and Muslims." MANAS 13, no. 1 (1966): 41-48.

Subjects were high school boys.

Shoben, Edward Joseph, Jr. "Moral Behavior and Moral Learning." RELIGIOUS EDUCATION 58 (1963): 137-45.

Sholl, Douglas. "The Contributions of Lawrence Kohlberg to Religious and Moral Education." RELIGIOUS EDUCATION 66 (1971): 364-72.

Stauffer, S. Anita. "Identification Theory and Christian Moral Education." RELIGIOUS EDUCATION 67, no. 1 (1967): 60-67.

Stephenson, Geoffrey M., and Barker, John. "Personality and the Pursuit of Distributive Justice: An Experimental Study of Children's Moral Behavior." BRITISH JOURNAL OF SOCIAL AND CLINICAL PSYCHOLOGY 11 (1972): 207-19.

Stinnette, Charles R., Jr. "Communication and Communion in Some Early Modes of Becoming." JOURNAL OF PASTORAL CARE 14 (1960): 129-37.

_____. "The Origin of the Symbolic Process." JOURNAL OF PASTORAL CARE 16 (1962): 14-24.

Strommen, Merton P. PROFILES OF YOUTH. St. Louis: Concordia Publishing House, 1963. xxiv, 356 p.

An extensive report on a study of 3,000 Lutheran high school youth.

_____, ed. RESEARCH ON RELIGIOUS DEVELOPMENT: A COMPREHENSIVE HANDBOOK. New York: Hawthorn Books, 1971. 904 p.

See annotation in section A:2.

Strommen, Merton P., et al. A STUDY OF GENERATIONS. Minneapolis: Augsburg Publishing House, 1972. 411 p.

This book is a report of a two year study of 5,000 Lutherans between the ages of fifteen and sixty-five which seeks to discover their beliefs, values, attitudes, and behaviors.

Strunk, Orlo, Jr. "Relationship between Self-Reports and Adolescent Religiosity." PSYCHOLOGICAL REPORTS 4 (1958): 683-86.

Tewari, J.G., and Singh, R.P. "Conformity in Youths to Parental Religious Beliefs." JOURNAL OF PSYCHOLOGICAL RESEARCHES 11, no. 2 (1967): 49-53.

Turner, Ralph H. "Moral Judgment: A Study in Roles." AMERICAN SOCIOLOGICAL REVIEW 17 (1952): 70-78.

van Dyke, Paul II, and Pierce-Jones, John. "The Psychology of Religion of Middle and Late Adolescence: A Review of Empirical Research, 1950-1960." RELIGIOUS EDUCATION 58 (1973): 529-37.

Vergote, Antoine, and Aubert, Catherine. "Parental Images and Representations of God." SOCIAL COMPASS 19 (1972-73): 431-43.

Vergote, Antoine, et al. "Concept of God and Parental Images." JOURNAL FOR THE SCIENTIFIC STUDY OF RELIGION 8 (1969): 78-87.

Williams, Robert. "A Theory of God-Concept Readiness: From the Piagetian Theories of Child Artificialism and the Origin of Religious Feeling in Children." RELIGIOUS EDUCATION 66 (January 1971): 62-66.

Winand, Paul. "Le Symbole du feu dans la vie des adolescents et dans leur univers religieux." SOCIAL COMPASS 19 (1972-73): 445-58.

Winthrop, Henry. "Social Complexity and Moral Inconsistency." RELIGIOUS EDUCATION 64, no. 3 (1969): 200-203.

Wright, Derek, and Cox, Edwin. "A Study of the Relationship between Moral Judgment and Religious Belief in a Sample of English Adolescents." JOURNAL OF SOCIAL PSYCHOLOGY 72, no. 1 (1967): 135-44.

Section F

THE SOCIAL DIMENSION OF RELIGION

Section F

THE SOCIAL DIMENSION OF RELIGION

F:1   AFFILIATION AND GROUP PARTICIPATION

Abramowitz, Stephen I., and Abramowitz, Christine V.   "Parents' Religious Affiliation and Family Support for Student Activism."   PSYCHOLOGICAL REPORTS 29 (1971):   1078.

Anderson, Charles H.   "Religious Communality among Academics."   JOURNAL FOR THE SCIENTIFIC STUDY OF RELIGION 7, no. 1 (1968):   87-96.

Barocas, Ralph, and Gorlow, Leon.   "Religious Affiliation, Religious Activities, and Conformity."   PSYCHOLOGICAL REPORTS 20, no. 2 (1967):   366.

Bateman, Mildred M., and Jensen, Joseph S.   "The Effect of Religious Background on Modes of Handling Anger."   JOURNAL OF SOCIAL PSYCHOLOGY 47 (1958):   133-41.

Bieri, J., and Lobeck, R.   "Self-Concept Differences in Relation to Identification, Religion, and Social Class."   JOURNAL OF ABNORMAL AND SOCIAL PSYCHOLOGY 62 (1961):   94-98.

Bohrnstedt, George W., et al.   "Religious Affiliation, Religiosity, and MMPI Scores."   JOURNAL FOR THE SCIENTIFIC STUDY OF RELIGION 7 (Fall 1968):   255-58.

Booth, Alan, and Babchuk, Nicholas.   "Personal Influence Inventories and Voluntary Association Affiliation."   SOCIOLOGICAL INQUIRY 39 (1969):   179-88.

Brown, L.B.   "Aggression and Denominational Membership."   BRITISH JOURNAL OF SOCIAL AND CLINICAL PSYCHOLOGY 4 (1965):   175-78.

Capps, Donald.   "Orestes Brownson: The Psychology of Religious Affiliation."

JOURNAL FOR THE SCIENTIFIC STUDY OF RELIGION 7 (Fall 1968): 197-209.

Carrier, Herve. THE SOCIOLOGY OF RELIGIOUS BELONGING. New York: Herder and Herder, 1965. 335 p.

> An interesting social psychological study of religious affiliation by a priest-sociologist. Studies of conversion, sense of belonging, church, sect, and religious training. Originally published in French in Rome in 1960.

Carroll, Jackson W., and Jenkins, Gerald P. "The Development of Religious Commitment--Some Exploratory Research." JOURNAL OF PASTORAL CARE 27 (December 1973): 236-52.

Chambers, Jay L., et al. "Need Differences between Students with and without Religious Affiliation." JOURNAL OF COUNSELING PSYCHOLOGY 15 (1968): 208-10.

Clark, Edward T., and Propper, Martin M. "Alienation Syndrome among Catholic Male Undergraduates." PSYCHOLOGICAL REPORTS 25 (1969): 167-72.

Croog, Sydney H., and Teele, James E. "Religious Identity and Church Attendance of Sons of Religious Intermarriage." AMERICAN SOCIOLOGICAL REVIEW 32 (1967): 93-104.

Dean, Dwight G. "Anomie, Powerlessness, and Religious Participation." JOURNAL FOR THE SCIENTIFIC STUDY OF RELIGION 7, no. 2 (1968): 252-54.

Demerath, Nicholas J. III. "Social Stratification and Church Involvement: The Church-Sect Distinction Applied to Individual Participation." REVIEW OF RELIGIOUS RESEARCH 2 (1961): 146-53.

Dittes, James E. THE CHURCH IN THE WAY. New York: Charles Scribner's Sons, 1967. xvii, 358 p.

> Utilizes the insights of psychotherapy, especially the phenomenon of resistance, to demonstrate the positive uses of ambivalence in church participation.

_____. "Secular Religion: Dilemma of Churches and Researchers." REVIEW OF RELIGIOUS RESEARCH 10 (1969): 65-80.

_____. "Typing the Typologies: Some Parallels in the Career of Church-Sect and Extrinsic-Intrinsic." JOURNAL FOR THE SCIENTIFIC STUDY OF RELIGION 10 (Winter 1971): 375-83.

Forbes, Gordon B., et al. "Willingness to Help Strangers as a Function of

Liberal, Conservative or Catholic Church Membership." PSYCHOLOGICAL RE-
PORTS 28 (June 1971): 947-49.

Glass, Kenneth D. "Denominational Differences in Religious Belief, Practice,
Anxiety, and Dogmatism." RELIGIOUS EDUCATION 66 (1971): 204-6.

Godin, Andre. "Belonging to a Church: What Does It Mean Psychologically?"
JOURNAL FOR THE SCIENTIFIC STUDY OF RELIGION 3, no. 2 (1964): 204-
15.

Goldscheider, Calvin, and Simpson, Jon E. "Religious Affiliation and Juvenile
Delinquency." SOCIOLOGICAL INQUIRY 37 (1967): 297-310.

Greer, J.E. "Religious Belief and Church Attendance of Sixth Form Pupils and
Their Parents." IRISH JOURNAL OF EDUCATION 5 (Winter 1971): 98-106.

Havens, Joseph. "Psychology and Religious Retreats." PASTORAL PSYCHOLO-
GY 20 (April 1969): 45-52.

Hertel, Bradley, et al. "Religion and Attitudes toward Abortion: A Study of
Nurses and Social Workers." JOURNAL FOR THE SCIENTIFIC STUDY OF RELI-
GION 13 (March 1974): 23-34.

    Finds that frequent church attenders are less likely to approve of
    abortion.

Hofman, John E., and Debbiny, Sami. "Religious Affiliation and Ethnic Identity." PSYCHOLOGICAL REPORTS 26 (June 1970): 1014.

Holl, Adolf, and Fischer, Gerhard H. KIRCHE AUF DISTANZ: EINE RELI-
GION-PSYCHOLOGISCHE UNTERSUCHUNG UBER DIE EINSTELLING OSTER-
REICHISCHER SOLDATEN: ZU KIRCHE UND RELIGION. Stuttgart: Wilhelm
Braumuller, Universitats-Verlags-buchhandlung, 1968. 114 p.

    A questionnaire and factor analytic investigation of attitudes toward
    church and religion in Austria. Notes little relation between per-
    sonality traits and the desire to attend church.

Jacks, Irving. "Religious Affiliation and Educational, Political, and Religious
Values of College Freshmen and Sophomores." ADOLESCENCE 6 (1972): 95-
120.

Jourard, Sidney M. "Religious Denomination and Self-Disclosure." PSYCHO-
LOGICAL REPORTS 8 (1961): 446.

Kotre, John Nicholas. THE VIEW FROM THE BORDER: A SOCIAL-PSYCHO-
LOGICAL STUDY OF CURRENT CATHOLICISM. Chicago: Aldine Publishing Co.,

1971. 268 p.

> Concludes that self-definition in relation to church affiliation is
> largely a function of early childhood experiences.

Langston, Robert D. "The MMPI and Perseverence of the Convert." PSYCHO-
LOGICAL REPORTS 27 (December 1970): 811-14.

Lasker, Arnold A. "Motivations for Attending High Holy Day Services." JOUR-
NAL FOR THE SCIENTIFIC STUDY OF RELIGION 10 (1971): 241-48.

Lenski, Gerhard. THE RELIGIOUS FACTOR: A SOCIOLOGICAL STUDY OF
RELIGION'S IMPACT ON POLITICS, ECONOMICS AND FAMILY LIFE. Garden City, N.Y.: Doubleday & Co., 1961. xviii, 381 p.

> A major contribution to the sociology and psychology of religion.
> Lenski distinguishes religious community (friend and mate selection)
> from religious association (attendance at services). He also mea-
> sures personal factors such as doctrinal orthodoxy and devotional-
> ism. Based on an extensive research program in Detroit.

Levinson, Boris M. "The Intelligence of Applicants for Admission to Jewish Day
Schools." JEWISH SOCIAL STUDIES 19 (1957): 129-40.

Loewen, Jacob A. "Socialization and Conversion in the Ongoing Church."
PRACTICAL ANTHROPOLOGY 16 (January-February 1969): 1-17.

Lo Sciuto, Leonard A., and Hartley, Eugene E. "Religious Affiliation and
Open-Mindedness in Binocular Resolution." PERCEPTUAL AND MOTOR SKILLS
17, no. 2 (1963): 427-30.

McClain, Edwin W. "Personality Correlates of Church Attendance." JOURNAL
OF COLLEGE STUDENT PERSONNEL 11 (September 1970): 360-65.

MacDonald, A.P., Jr. "Birth Order and Religious Affiliation." DEVELOP-
MENTAL PSYCHOLOGY 1, no. 5 (1969): 628.

Matras, Judah. "Religious Observance and Family Formation in Israel: Some
Intergenerational Changes." AMERICAN JOURNAL OF SOCIOLOGY 69 (1963-
64): 464-75.

Meadow, Arnold, and Bronson, Louise. "Religious Affiliation and Psychopathology in a Mexican-American Population." JOURNAL OF ABNORMAL PSYCHOL-
OGY 74, no. 2 (1969): 177-80.

Meissner, W[illiam] W. "Alienation: Context and Complications." JOURNAL
OF RELIGION AND HEALTH 13 (January 1974): 23-39.

Meredith, Gerald M. "Religious Affiliation and Self-Conception among Japanese-American College Women." PSYCHOLOGICAL REPORTS 5 (1959): 543.

Monaghan, Robert R. "Three Faces of the True Believer: Motivations for Attending a Fundamentalist Church." JOURNAL FOR THE SCIENTIFIC STUDY OF RELIGION 6 (1967): 236-45.

Mueller, Samuel A. "Rokeach and the Church: A Theory of Organizational Reaction Formation." REVIEW OF RELIGIOUS RESEARCH 8 (1967): 131-39.

Nelson, Hart M., and Allen, H. David. "Ethnicity, Americanization, and Religious Attendance." AMERICAN JOURNAL OF SOCIOLOGY 79 (January 1974): 906-22.

Panchbhai, S.C. "Group-Image, Identification and Preference: A Study in Stereotypes of an Indian Tribe." INDIAN JOURNAL OF PSYCHOLOGY 39, no. 4 (1964): 167-72.

    A study involving Christian and non-Christian students.

Parker, James H. "The Interaction of Negroes and Whites in an Integrated Church Setting." SOCIAL FORCES 46 (1968): 359-66.

Photiadis, John D. "The American Business Creed and Denominational Identification." SOCIAL FORCES 44 (1965): 92-100.

Photiadis, John D., and Johnson, Arthur L. "Orthodoxy, Church Participation, and Authoritarianism." AMERICAN JOURNAL OF SOCIOLOGY 69 (1963-64): 244-48.

Photiadis, John D., and Schweiker, William F. "Attitudes toward Joining Authoritarian Organizations and Sectarian Churches." JOURNAL FOR THE SCIENTIFIC STUDY OF RELIGION 9 (Fall 1970): 227-34.

Propper, Martin M., et al. "Alienation Syndrome among Male Adolescents in Prestige Catholic and Public High Schools." PSYCHOLOGICAL REPORTS 27 (August 1970): 311-15.

Rosenberg, Morris. "The Dissonant Religious Context and Emotional Disturbance." AMERICAN JOURNAL OF SOCIOLOGY 68, no. 1 (1962): 1-10.

St. Clair, Robert James. NEUROTICS IN THE CHURCH. Westwood, N.J.: Fleming H. Revell Co., 1963. 251 p.

Sales, Stephen. "Economic Threat as a Determinant of Conversion Rates in Authoritarian and Nonauthoritarian Churches." JOURNAL OF PERSONALITY

AND SOCIAL PSYCHOLOGY 23 (September 1972): 420-28.

Schachter, Stanley. THE PSYCHOLOGY OF AFFILIATION: EXPERIMENTAL STUDIES OF THE SOURCES OF GREGARIOUSNESS. Stanford, Calif.: Stanford University Press, 1959. 141 p.

Shrauger, J. Sidney, and Silverman, Ronald E. "The Relationship of Religious Background and Participation to Locus of Control." JOURNAL FOR THE SCIENTIFIC STUDY OF RELIGION 10 (Spring 1971): 11-16.

Sunden, Hjalmar. DIE RELIGION UND DIE ROLLEN: EINE PSYCHOLOGISCHE UNTERSUCHUNG DER FROMMIGKEIT. Berlin: Walter de Gruyter, 1966. 451 p.

An application of role theory to the study of religious piety.

Tageson, Carroll F. "The Problem of Religious Commitment among the Aging." CATHOLIC PSYCHOLOGICAL RECORD 3, no. 1 (1965): 23-31.

Tanaka, Hiroko, and Kosukegawa, Tsugio. "A Comparative Research on the 'Ways-to-Live' by Morris' Value Scale of the College Students with Different Affiliation of Religion." TOHOKU PSYCHOLOGICA FOLIA 26, no. 3-4 (1968): 77-86.

Vangerud, Richard D. "Psychology and the Church: The Parish as Encounter Point." DIALOG 13 (Spring 1974): 91-96.

Vaughan, R [ichard] P [atrick]. "The Influence of Religious Affiliation on the MMPI Scales." JOURNAL OF CLINICAL PSYCHOLOGY 21 (1965): 416-17.

Wicker, Allen W. "Size of Church Membership and Members' Support of Church Behavior Settings." JOURNAL OF PERSONALITY AND SOCIAL PSYCHOLOGY 13 (1969): 278-88.

Wicker, Allen W., and Mehler, Anne. "Assimilation of New Members in a Large and a Small Church." JOURNAL OF APPLIED PSYCHOLOGY 55 (April 1971): 151-56.

Williamson, Donald S. "A Study of Selective Inhibition of Aggression by Church Members." JOURNAL OF PASTORAL CARE 21 (1967): 193-208.

Zelan, Joseph. "Religious Apostasy, Higher Education and Occupational Choice." SOCIOLOGY OF EDUCATION 41 (1968): 370-79.

F:2 PSYCHOLOGICAL STUDIES OF PREJUDICE

Adorno, T.W., et al. THE AUTHORITARIAN PERSONALITY. New York:

Harper & Brothers, 1950. xxxiii, 990 p.

> A massive study, composed of individual essays and research reports by a team of psychologists, social psychologists, and social philosophers interested in personality correlations with racial, anti-Semitic, and political prejudice. Of particular interest to psychologists of religion are the chapters on anti-Semitic ideology, on the relation of ethnocentrism to religious attitudes and practices, and on some of the functions of religious ideology.

Allport, Gordon W. THE NATURE OF PREJUDICE. Garden City, N.Y.: Doubleday & Co., 1958. xxii, 496 p.

> A comprehensive study of the origins and nature of prejudice. Develops the extrinsic-intrinsic distinction and its relation to prejudice.

_____. "Religion and Prejudice." CRANE REVIEW 2 (1959): 1-10.

_____. PERSONALITY AND SOCIAL ENCOUNTER. Boston: Beacon Press, 1964. 388 p.

> A collection of essays originally published from the late twenties to early sixties. Includes some of the author's celebrated work on prejudice.

_____. "Prejudice: Is It Societal or Personal?" RELIGIOUS EDUCATION 59 (1964): 20-29.

_____. "The Religious Context of Prejudice." JOURNAL FOR THE SCIENTIFIC STUDY OF RELIGION 5, no. 3 (1966): 448-51.

Allport, Gordon W., and Ross, J. Michael. "Personal Religious Orientation and Prejudice." JOURNAL OF PERSONALITY AND SOCIAL PSYCHOLOGY 5, no. 4 (1967): 432-43.

Bagley, Christopher. "Relation of Religion and Racial Prejudice in Europe." JOURNAL FOR THE SCIENTIFIC STUDY OF RELIGION 9 (Fall 1970): 219-26.

Berkowitz, Leonard. "Anti-Semitism and the Displacement of Aggression." JOURNAL OF ABNORMAL AND SOCIAL PSYCHOLOGY 59 (1959): 182-87.

Brenner, Arthur B. "Some Psychoanalytic Speculations on Anti-Semitism." PSYCHOANALYTIC REVIEW 35 (1948): 20-32.

Chatterjee, Bishwa B., et al. RIOTS IN ROURKELA: A PSYCHOLOGICAL STUDY. New Delhi: Popular Book Services, 1967. 144 p.

> An effort to discover the psychological dynamics behind a massacre

of Muslims by Hindus in India in 1964.

Cheson, Bruce D., et al. "The Repression-Sensitization Scale and Measures of Prejudice." JOURNAL OF SOCIAL PSYCHOLOGY 80 (1970): 197-200.

Studies anti-Semitism.

De Vos, George, and Wagatsuma, Hiroshi, eds. JAPAN'S INVISIBLE RACE: CASTE IN CULTURE AND PERSONALITY. Berkeley and Los Angeles: University of California Press, 1966. xvii, 415 p.

A study of the Burakumin caste in Japan, a group indistinguishable in appearance from other Japanese, but nonetheless segregated and discriminated against. Develops psychological views of the majority group's attitudes and beliefs regarding outcastes.

Dittes, James E. "Religion, Prejudice, and Personality." In RESEARCH ON RELIGIOUS DEVELOPMENT: A COMPREHENSIVE HANDBOOK, pp. 355-90. Edited by Merton P. Strommen. New York: Hawthorn Books, 1971.

_____. BIAS AND THE PIOUS: THE RELATIONSHIP BETWEEN PREJUDICE AND RELIGION. Minneapolis: Augsburg Publishing House, 1973. 102 p.

Draws on research literature on prejudice and develops theological insights into the Christian response to prejudice.

Dreifuss, Gustav. "The Analyst and the Damaged Victim of Nazi Persecution." JOURNAL OF ANALYTICAL PSYCHOLOGY 14 (1969): 163-75.

Ehrlich, Howard J. THE SOCIAL PSYCHOLOGY OF PREJUDICE: A SYSTEMATIC THEORETICAL REVIEW AND PROPOSITIONAL INVENTORY OF THE AMERICAN SOCIAL PSYCHOLOGICAL STUDY OF PREJUDICE. New York: Wiley-Interscience Books, 1973. xii, 208 p.

Engel, Gerald. "Some College Students' Responses Concerning Negroes of Differing Religious Background." JOURNAL OF SOCIAL PSYCHOLOGY 74 (1968): 275-83.

Engel, Gerald, et al. "An Investigation of Anti-Semitic Feelings in Two Groups of College Students: Jewish and Non-Jewish." JOURNAL OF SOCIAL PSYCHOLOGY 48 (August 1958): 75-82.

Feagin, Joe R. "Prejudice and Religious Types: A Focused Study of Southern Fundamentalists." JOURNAL FOR THE SCIENTIFIC STUDY OF RELIGION 4, no. 1 (1964): 3-13.

Fenichel, Otto. "Psychoanalysis of Anti-Semitism." AMERICAN IMAGO 1 (1939-40): 24-39.

Glenn, Jules. "Circumcision and Anti-Semitism." PSYCHOANALYTIC QUARTERLY 29 (1960): 395-99.

Glock, Charles Y., and Siegelman, Ellen, eds. PREJUDICE U.S.A. New York: Praeger Publishers, 1969. xxii, 194 p.

A collection of essays which gives considerable attention to the individual determinants and consequences of prejudice.

Glock, Charles Y., and Stark, Rodney. CHRISTIAN BELIEFS AND ANTI-SEMITISM. New York: Harper & Row, Publishers, 1966. xxi, 266 p.

This book proposes that Christian beliefs cause anti-Semitism. Psychological and sociological methods and concepts are used to examine large amounts of research data on the relationship of religion and prejudice.

Grunberger, Bela. "The Anti-Semite and Oedipal Conflict." INTERNATIONAL JOURNAL OF PSYCHOANALYSIS 45 (1964): 380-85.

Heinz, Walter R., and Geiser, Steven R. "Eine Kognitive Theorie des Antisemitismus im Kontext der Religiosen Ideologie." KOLNER ZEITSCHRIFT FUR SOZIOLOGIE UND SOZIALPSYCHOLOGIE 23 (1971): 519-43.

Discusses the personality and social factors related to the perception of dissimilarity between Judaism and one's own beliefs.

Himmelfarb, Samuel, and Fishbein, Martin. "Studies in the Perception of Ethnic Group Members: Attractiveness, Response Bias, and Anti-Semitism." JOURNAL OF SOCIAL PSYCHOLOGY 83 (April 1971): 289-98.

Hoge, Dean R., and Carroll, Jackson W. "Religiosity and Prejudice in Northern and Southern Churches." JOURNAL FOR THE SCIENTIFIC STUDY OF RELIGION 12 (June 1973): 181-97.

Holtzman, Wayne E., and Young, Robert K. "Scales for Measuring Attitudes toward the Negro and toward Organized Religion." PSYCHOLOGICAL REPORTS 18 (1966): 31-34.

Johnson, Wayne G. "Religion, Racism, and Self-Image: The Significance of Beliefs." RELIGIOUS EDUCATION 68 (September 1973): 620-30.

Kanter, Isaac. "Extermination Camp Syndrome: The Delayed Type of Double-Bind: A Trans-Culture Study." INTERNATIONAL JOURNAL OF SOCIAL PSYCHIATRY 16 (1970): 275-82.

Kovel, Joel. WHITE RACISM: A PSYCHOHISTORY. New York: Pantheon Books, 1970. 300 p.

A study of racism which draws heavily on Norman O. Brown, Herbert Marcuse, and the literary critic, Leslie Fiedler.

Loeblowitz-Lennard, Henry. "A Psychoanalytic Contribution to the Problem of Antisemitism." PSYCHOANALYTIC REVIEW 32 (1945): 259-61.

_____. "The Jew as Symbol." PSYCHOANALYTIC QUARTERLY 16 (1947): 33-38.

Loewenstein, Rudolf M. "The Historical and Cultural Roots of Anti-Semitism." PSYCHOANALYSIS AND THE SOCIAL SCIENCES 1 (1947): 313-56.

_____. CHRISTIANS AND JEWS: A PSYCHOANALYTIC STUDY. New York: International Universities Press, 1951. 224 p.

A careful discussion of some of the factors in anti-Semitism, some character traits of Jews, and the cultural bond between Christians and Jews.

Loomba, Ram M. "A Psychogenetic Approach to Religion, Atheism and Bigotry." RELIGIOUS EDUCATION 61 (1966): 449-52.

Lourie, Anton. "The Jew as a Psychological Type." AMERICAN IMAGO 6 (1949): 119-55.

Maranell, Gary M. "An Examination of Some Religious and Political Attitude Correlates of Bigotry." SOCIAL FORCES 45, no. 3 (1967): 356-62.

Marx, Gary T. PROTEST AND PREJUDICE: A STUDY OF BELIEF IN THE BLACK COMMUNITY. New York: Harper & Row, Publishers, 1967. xxviii, 228 p.

Meserve, Harry C. "Racism and Prejudice." JOURNAL OF RELIGION AND HEALTH 9 (October 1970): 331-70.

Middleton, Russell. "Do Christian Beliefs Cause Anti-Semitism?" AMERICAN SOCIOLOGICAL REVIEW 38 (February 1973): 33-52.

Morrow, Alfred J. CHANGING PATTERNS OF PREJUDICE: A NEW LOOK AT TODAY'S RACIAL, RELIGIOUS, AND CULTURAL TENSIONS. Philadelphia: Chilton Books, 1962. 271 p.

Written by the chairman of the New York City Commission on Intergroup Relations from 1955 to 1960, the book stresses personality determinants of prejudice, especially authoritarianism and childhood deprivation.

Olson, Bernard E. FAITH AND PREJUDICE. New Haven, Conn.: Yale University Press, 1962. 451 p.

This book is based on a seven year study of the prejudice potential of the teaching materials of Protestant churches. Content analysis of the way Roman Catholics and other non-Protestant religious groups are viewed by liberal, neo-orthodox, and fundamentalist denominations. Also gives considerable attention to Protestant attitudes toward Jews and Negroes.

Panchbhai, S.C. "Religion and Race as Determinants of Reference Group: A Study in Stereotype of Three Indian Tribes." INDIAN JOURNAL OF PSYCHOLOGY 41, no. 1 (1966): 1-6.

Parkes, James. ANTISEMITISM. Chicago: Quadrangle Books, 1969. xiii, 192 p.

A revised edition of a book originally published in 1945, this study discusses anti-Semitism in terms of individual defense mechanisms (projection and displacement). Only slightly informed by more recent studies in social psychology.

Roselli, Humberto. "Aspects Medico-Psiquiatricos de la Inquisicion en Cartagena de Indias." ACTA PSIQUIATRICA Y PSICOLOGICA DE AMERICA LATINA 14 (1968): 252-61.

Rudin, Josef. FANATICISM: A PSYCHOLOGICAL ANALYSIS. Translated by Elizabeth Reineike. Notre Dame, Ind.: University of Notre Dame Press, 1970. 206 p.

Rudin, a professor at the University of Innsbruck and a lecturer at the C.G. Jung Institute, studies the subjective life of the fanatic. Focusses on religious zealots and includes discussions of abstainers from various forms of meat and drink.

Rule, Brendan G., et al. "Anti-Semitism, Distraction and Physical Agression." CANADIAN JOURNAL OF BEHAVIORAL SCIENCE 3 (April 1971): 174-82.

Saenger, Gerhart. THE SOCIAL PSYCHOLOGY OF PREJUDICE. New York: Harper & Brothers, 1953. xv, 304 p.

Schick, Alfred. "The Jew as Sacrificial Victim." PSYCHOANALYTIC REVIEW 58 (1971): 75-89.

Selznick, Gertrude J., and Steinberg, Stephen. THE TENACITY OF PREJUDICE: ANTI-SEMITISM IN CONTEMPORARY AMERICA. New York: Harper & Row, Publishers, 1969. xxi, 248 p.

A study based on interviews with 2000 persons which sought to discern the nature, extent, cause, and reasons for the persistence of anti-Semitism.

Siegman, Aron Wolfe. "A Cross-Cultural Investigation of the Relationship between Religiosity, Ethnic Prejudice and Authoritarianism." PSYCHOLOGICAL REPORTS 11, no. 2 (1962): 419-24.

Spilka, Bernard, and Reynolds, James F. "Religion and Prejudice: A Factor Analytic Study." REVIEW OF RELIGIOUS RESEARCH 6 (1965): 163-67.

Stark, Rodney, et al. "Sounds of Silence." PSYCHOLOGY TODAY 3 (April 1970): 38-41, 60-61.

A discussion of prejudice and the church.

Steel, Burton B. "Unconscious Factors in Anti-Semitism." JOURNAL OF THE HILLSIDE HOSPITAL 5 (1956): 328-32.

Stokvis, Berthold von. KULTUR-PSYCHOLOGIE AND PSYCHOHYGIENE. Stuttgart: Hippokrates Verlag, 1965. 169 p.

Written by a Dutch-Jewish psychiatrist who experienced the Nazi occupation of Amsterdam, this book includes a few clinical articles, but is devoted primarily to essays on anti-Semitism.

Strickland, Bonnie R., and Weddell, Sallie Cone. "Religious Orientation, Racial Prejudice and Dogmatism: A Study of Baptists and Unitarians." JOURNAL FOR THE SCIENTIFIC STUDY OF RELIGION 11 (December 1972): 395-400.

Taylor, F. Kraupl. "The Scapegoat Motif in Society." INTERNATIONAL JOURNAL OF PSYCHOANALYSIS 34 (1953): 252-64.

Vanecko, James J. "Religious Behavior and Prejudice: Some Dimensions and Specifications of the Relationship." REVIEW OF RELIGIOUS RESEARCH 8 (1966): 27-36.

Wangh, Martin. "National Socialism and the Genocide of the Jews: A Psycho-analytic Study of a Historical Event." INTERNATIONAL JOURNAL OF PSYCHOANALYSIS 45 (1964): 386-95.

Whitam, Frederick L. "Subdimensions of Religiosity and Race Prejudice." REVIEW OF RELIGIOUS RESEARCH 3 (1962): 166-74.

Wilson, W. Cody. "Extrinsic Religious Values and Prejudice." JOURNAL OF ABNORMAL AND SOCIAL PSYCHOLOGY 60 (March 1960): 286-88.

F:3 THE PERSONALITY FACTOR IN RELIGIOUS GROUPS

Adler, Nathan. THE UNDERGROUND STREAM: NEW LIFE STYLES AND THE

ANTINOMIAN PERSONALITY. New York: Harper & Row, Publishers, 1972. xxiv, 135 p.

A psychohistorical study of the counterculture and its personality types. Sketches the historical precedents of contemporary enthusiastic movements and relates attempts to manipulate self- and body-image to disruptions in the fabric of society.

Anwar, Mah P., and Child, Irwin L. "Personality and Esthetic Sensitivity in an Islamic Culture." JOURNAL OF SOCIAL PSYCHOLOGY 87 (1972): 21-28.

Arasteh, A. Reza. RUMI THE PERSIAN: REBIRTH IN CREATIVITY AND LOVE. Lahore, Pakistan: Shah Muhammed Ashraf, 1965. 196 p.

Aslam, Q.M. "Muhammed: A Psychological Essay." CONFINIA PSYCHIATRICA 11, no. 3-4 (1968): 225-35.

Bainton, Roland H. "Psychiatry and History: An Examination of Erikson's YOUNG MAN LUTHER." RELIGION IN LIFE 40 (1971): 450-78.

A largely negative assessment of Erik H. Erikson's psychoanalytic study of Martin Luther, cited below, by an historian of the Reformation.

Bakan, David. "Some Thoughts on Reading Augustine's Confessions." JOURNAL FOR THE SCIENTIFIC STUDY OF RELIGION 5 (1965-66): 149-52.

Barbu, Zevedei. PROBLEMS OF HISTORICAL PSYCHOLOGY. New York: Grove Press, 1960. 222 p.

A study of the relationship of historical events and the development of personality structure. Views English Puritanism of the sixteenth century as the beginning of a new and relatively permanent personality structure and attempts to identify its major characteristics.

Baudouin, Charles. "Notes pour une psychanalyse de Pascal." REVUE FRANCAISE DE PSYCHANALYSE 23 (1959): 757-74.

Bender, L., and Yarrell, Z. "Psychoses among Followers of Father Divine." JOURNAL OF NERVOUS MENTAL DISORDERS 87 (1938): 418-49.

Berguer, Georges. "Quelques Traits de la vie de Jesus, au point de vue psychologique et psychanalytique." Geneva: Edition Atar, 1920. cviii, 267 p.

Berkeley-Hill, Owen. "A Short Study of the Life and Character of Mohammed." INTERNATIONAL JOURNAL OF PSYCHOANALYSIS 2 (1921): 31-53.

Bonaparte, Marie. "Eros, Saul de Tarse et Freud." REVUE FRANCAISE DE

PSYCHANALYSE 21 (1957): 23-34.

Burrell, David. "Reading THE CONFESSIONS of Augustine: An Exercise in Theological Understanding." JOURNAL OF RELIGION 50 (October 1970): 327-51.

Devotes considerable attention to psychological interpretations of Augustine's conversion.

Bushman, Richard L. "Jonathan Edwards and Puritan Consciousness." JOURNAL FOR THE SCIENTIFIC STUDY OF RELIGION 5, no. 3 (1966): 383-96.

_____. "Jonathan Edwards as Great Man: Identity, Conversion, and Leadership in the Great Awakening." SOUNDINGS 52 (Spring 1969): 15-46.

Bychowski, Gustave. "Oliver Cromwell and the Puritan Revolution." JOURNAL OF CLINICAL PSYCHOPATHOLOGY 7, no. 2 (1945): 281-309.

Capps, Donald. "Orestes Brownson: The Psychology of Religious Affiliation." JOURNAL FOR THE SCIENTIFIC STUDY OF RELIGION 7 (Fall 1968): 197-209.

_____. "John Henry Newman: A Study of Vocational Identity." JOURNAL FOR THE SCIENTIFIC STUDY OF RELIGION 9 (Spring 1970): 33-52.

Capps, Donald, and Capps, Walter H., eds. THE RELIGIOUS PERSONALITY. Belmont, Calif.: Wadsworth Publishing Co., 1970. 281 p.

See annotation in section A:2.

Capps, Walter H. "Ideology, Ego, and Ethos: A Comment on Erikson." HUMANITAS 5 (1970): 255-63.

Clark, Walter Houston. THE OXFORD GROUP: ITS HISTORY AND SIGNIFICANCE. New York: Bookman Associates, 1951. 268 p.

A study of the psychological origins and effects of the Oxford Group (or Moral Re-Armament) and its leader, Frank Buchman.

Cohen, Sheldon. "The Ontogenesis of Prophetic Behavior: A Study in Creative Conscience Formation." PSYCHOANALYSIS AND THE PSYCHOANALYTIC REVIEW 49, no. 1 (1962): 100-22.

Cohn, Norman. "The Cult of the Free Spirit: A Medieval Heresy Reconstructed." PSYCHOANALYSIS AND THE PSYCHOANALYTIC REVIEW 48, no. 1 (1961): 51-68.

Cole, David L. "The Perception of Lincoln: A Psychological Approach to the Public's Conception of Historical Figures." JOURNAL OF SOCIAL PSYCHOL-

OGY 55 (1961): 23-26.

A comparison of college students' perceptions of Lincoln, George Washington, and Christ in terms of fatherliness, military leadership, and statesmanship.

Curle, Adam. MYSTICS AND MILITANTS: A STUDY OF AWARENESS, IDENTITY, AND SOCIAL ACTION. London: Tavistock, 1972. 121 p.

Darroch, Jane. "An Interpretation of the Personality of Jesus." BRITISH JOURNAL OF MEDICAL PSYCHOLOGY 21 (1947): 75-79.

Demos, John. A LITTLE COMMONWEALTH: FAMILY LIFE IN PLYMOUTH COLONY. New York: Oxford University Press, 1970. 201 p.

An historical study of family life and personality dynamics in Puritan New England. Employs personality theory developed by Erik H. Erikson and attempts to correct for the heavy emphasis of much historical scholarship on Puritanism on its "guilt" orientation by stressing the pervasiveness of shame in Puritan culture.

Dittes, James E. "Continuities between the Life and Thought of Augustine." JOURNAL FOR THE SCIENTIFIC STUDY OF RELIGION 5 (1965-66): 130-40.

Dodd, C.H. "The Mind of Paul: A Psychological Approach." BULLETIN OF THE JOHN RYLANDS LIBRARY (Manchester, England) 17 (1933): 91-105.

An attempt by a Biblical scholar to characterize Paul's pre- and post-conversion psychological states on the basis of his letters.

Dodds, E.R. "Augustine's Confessions: A Study of Spiritual Maladjustment." HIBBERT JOURNAL 26 (1927-28): 459-73.

A Jamesian study of Augustine's conversion which focuses on the psychic price he paid in resolving his religious conflicts through conversion.

Domhoff, G. William. "Two Luthers: The Traditional and the Heretical in Freudian Psychology." PSYCHOANALYTIC REVIEW 57 (1970): 5-17.

A discussion of the interpretations of Luther by Erik Erikson and Norman O. Brown.

Eaton, Joseph W., and Weil, Robert J. CULTURE AND MENTAL DISORDERS: A COMPARATIVE STUDY OF THE HUTTERITES AND OTHER POPULATIONS. Glencoe, Ill.: Free Press, 1955. 254 p.

Erikson, Erik H. YOUNG MAN LUTHER: A STUDY IN PSYCHOANALYSIS AND HISTORY. New York: W.W. Norton & Co., 1958. 288 p.

Ground-breaking work in the psychohistorical study of religious figures. Relates Luther's personal development and experiences to his career as a religious leader. Lays particular stress on the period of Luther's "identity crisis."

_____. "Gandhi's Autobiography: The Leader as a Child." AMERICAN SCHOLAR 35 (1966): 732-36.

_____. "On the Nature of Psycho-Historical Evidence: In Search of Gandhi." DAEDALUS 97 (1968): 695-730.

_____. GANDHI'S TRUTH: ON THE ORIGINS OF MILITANT NONVIO-LENCE. New York: W.W. Norton & Co., 1969. 475 p.

Continuing to develop the psychohistorical approach begun with YOUNG MAN LUTHER, cited above, Erikson here takes on more contemporary history. In addition to locating the internal dimensions of Gandhi's career in the context of Indian religion, politics, and history, he exposes more of the working methods of the psycho-historian, describes some of the similarity between psychoanalysis and Satyagraha, and discusses the "religious actualist" as a modern homo religiosus.

Evans, W.N. "Notes on the Conversion of John Bunyan: A Study in English Puritanism." INTERNATIONAL JOURNAL OF PSYCHOANALYSIS 24 (1943): 176-85.

Feldman, A. Bronson. "Animal Magnetism and the Mother of Christian Science." PSYCHOANALYTIC REVIEW 50, no. 2 (1973): 154-60.

Ferm, Vergilius. CROSS CURRENTS IN THE PERSONALITY OF MARTIN LU-THER: A STUDY IN THE PSYCHOLOGY OF RELIGIOUS GENIUS. North Quincy, Mass.: The Christopher Publishing House, 1972. 186 p.

Goodrich, Michael. "Childhood and Adolescence among the Thirteenth-Century Saints." HISTORY OF CHILDHOOD QUARTERLY 1 (1973-74): 285-309.

Hitschmann, Edward. GREAT MEN: PSYCHOANALYTIC STUDIES. New York: International Universities Press, 1956. 278 p.

Contains psychobiographical treatments of such religious figures as Schweitzer, Swedenborg, and Gandhi.

Hopkins, Pryns. WORLD INVISIBLE: A STUDY IN SAGES, SAINTS AND SAVIORS. Penobscot, Maine: Traversity Press, 1973. 205 p.

Klapp, Orrin E. SYMBOLIC LEADERS: PUBLIC DRAMAS AND PUBLIC MEN. Chicago: Aldine Publishing Co., 1964. 272 p.

A social psychologist studies the dramatic interaction of leaders and their audiences and attempts to lay down the structural similarities in large numbers of such interactions.

Klein, Hillel. "Holocaust Survivors in Kibbutzim: Readaptation and Reintegration." ISRAEL ANNALS OF PSYCHIATRY AND RELATED DISCIPLINES 10, no. 1 (1972): 78-91.

Kligerman, Charles. "A Psychoanalytic Study of the CONFESSIONS of St. Augustine." JOURNAL OF THE AMERICAN PSYCHOANALYTIC ASSOCIATION 5 (1957): 469-84.

Kunzli, Arnold. DIE ANGST ALS ABENLANDISCHE KRANKHEIT: DARGESTELLT AM LEBEN UND DENKEN SOREN KIERGAARDS. Zurich: Rascher Verlag, 1948.

A theological-ethical interpretation of Kierkegaard's life as well as his work; employs psychological concepts, particularly those of Jung, to support this task.

Kuo, Zing-Yang, and Lam, Yut-Hang. "Chinese Religious Behavior and the Deification of Mao Tse-tung." PSYCHOLOGICAL RECORD 18 (1968): 455-68.

Kurokawa, Minako. "Acculturation and Mental Health of Mennonite Children." CHILD DEVELOPMENT 40 (1969): 689-705.

La Barre, Weston. THEY SHALL TAKE UP SERPENTS: PSYCHOLOGY OF THE SOUTHERN SNAKE-HANDLING CULT. Minneapolis: University of Minnesota Press, 1962; New York: Schocken Books, 1969. 208 p.

La Barre uses psychoanalytic concepts in analyzing the snakehandling cults of the southeastern United States. In stressing their psychopathological character, he provides a quite thorough and persuasive analysis of the personality of one of the cult leaders.

_____. THE GHOST DANCE: ORIGINS OF RELIGION. Garden City, NY.: Doubleday & Co., 1970. xvi, 677 p.

La Barre, an anthropologist who has done extensive field work with American Indians and is trained in dynamic psychology as well, suggests as a paradigm for the origin and function of religions the Ghost Dance of 1890. A culture in crisis appropriates the dream of the charismatic hero.

Lefevre, Perry. "Erikson's YOUNG MAN LUTHER: A Contribution to the Scientific Study of Religion." JOURNAL FOR THE SCIENTIFIC STUDY OF RELIGION 2 (1962-63): 248-52.

Levy, Robert I. "Tahiti, Sin, and the Question of Integration between Personality and Sociocultural Systems." PSYCHOANALYTIC STUDY OF SOCIETY 5 (1972): 83-108.

Lindbeck, George A. "Erikson's YOUNG MAN LUTHER: A Historical and Theological Reappraisal." SOUNDINGS 56 (Summer 1973): 210-27.

Lipman, Matthew, and Pizzurro, Salvatore. "Charismatic Participation as a Sociopathic Process." PSYCHIATRY 19 (1956): 11-30.

Loewenberg, Peter. "Theodore Herzl: A Psychoanalytic Study in Charismatic Political Leadership." In THE PSYCHOANALYTIC INTERPRETATION OF HIS-TORY, pp. 150-91. Edited by Benjamin B. Wolman. New York: Basic Books, 1971.

Meng, Heinrich. "War Buddha Schizophren?" [Was Buddha Schizophrenic?]. PSYCHE 16, no. 6 (1962): 374-77.

Mitzman, Arthur. THE IRON CAGE: AN HISTORICAL INTERPRETATION OF MAX WEBER. New York: Alfred A. Knopf, 1970. xii, 328 p.

    A psychohistorical study of Max Weber which argues that Weber's relations with this parents, and especially his break with his father, influenced his attempt to relate the Protestant Ethic to capitalism.

Moretti, Girolamo. THE SAINTS THROUGH THEIR HANDWRITING. New York: Macmillan, 1964. xviii, 269 p.

Peacock, James L. "Mystics and Merchants in Fourteenth Century Germany: A Speculative Reconstruction of Their Psychological Bond and Its Implications for Social Change." JOURNAL FOR THE SCIENTIFIC STUDY OF RELIGION 8 (1969): 47-59.

Pfautz, Harold W. "Christian Science: A Case Study of the Social Psycholog-ical Aspect of Secularization." SOCIAL FORCES 34 (1956): 246-51.

Pfister, Oskar [Robert]. "Die Entwicklung des Apostels Paulus: Eine Religions-geschichtliche und Psychologische Skizze." IMAGO 6 (1920): 243-90.

    . DIE LEGENDE SUNDAR SINGHS: EINE AUF ENTHULLUNGEN PRO-TESTANTISCHER AUGENZEUGEN IN INDIAN GEGUNDETE RELIGIONSPSY-CHOLOGISCHE UNTERSUCHUNG. Bern: P. Haupt, 1926. 327 p.

    . CALVINS EINGREIFER IN DIE HEXEN- UND HEXENPROZESSE VON PENEY, 1545, NACH SEINER BEDEUTUNG FUR GESCHICHTE UND GEGEN-WART: EINE KRITISCHER BEITRAG ZUR CHARAKTERISTIK CALVINS UND ZUR GEGENWARTIGEN CALVIN-RENAISSANCE. Zurich: Artemis, 1947. 209 p.

    A classic psychoanalytic attempt to depict the personality structure of John Calvin on the basis of researches into his activities as a religious leader, with special reference to his involvement in witch burning.

Pruyser, Paul W. "Erikson's YOUNG MAN LUTHER: A New Chapter in the Psychology of Religion." JOURNAL FOR THE SCIENTIFIC STUDY OF RELIGION 2 (1962-63): 238-42.

_____. "Psychological Examination: Augustine." JOURNAL FOR THE SCIENTIFIC STUDY OF RELIGION 5 (1966): 284-89.

Raychaunhuri, Arum Kumar. "Jesus Christ and Sri Krishna--a Psychoanalytic Study." AMERICAN IMAGO 14 (1957): 389-405.

Rubenstein, Richard L. MY BROTHER PAUL. New York: Harper & Row, Publishers, 1972. 209 p.

> Rubenstein avers that Paul resolved his conflict between the law and his own failure to achive perfection in becoming a follower of Christ, and states that psychoanalysis continues to play a role similar to that of Christ for modern Jews.

Rudolph, Susanne Hoeber. "Self-Control and Political Potency: Gandhi's Asceticism." AMERICAN SCHOLAR 35 (Winter 1965-66): 79-97.

Schneiderman, Leo. "Ramakrishna: Personality and Social Factors in the Growth of a Religious Movement." JOURNAL FOR THE SCIENTIFIC STUDY OF RELIGION 8 (1969): 60-71.

Schweitzer, Albert. THE PSYCHIATRIC STUDY OF JESUS. Translated by Charles R. Joy. Boston: Beacon Press, 1948. 81 p.

> Published originally in 1913, Schweitzer wrote this study as his doctoral thesis for his medical degree. Describes and rejects various medical studies which asserted that Jesus was suffering from paranoia or other pathologies. Contends that the evidence for such theories is inadequate and that the personality of Jesus remains elusive.

Spitz, Lewis W. "Psychohistory and History: The Case of YOUNG MAN LUTHER." SOUNDINGS 56 (Summer 1973): 182-209.

Sunden, Hjalmar. "Die Personlichkeit der heilgen Birgitta: Versuch einer "rollenpsychologischen" Untersuchung." ARCHIV FUR RELIGIONSPSYCHOLOGIE 10 (1971): 249-59.

> The use of role theory in analyzing the life and legends of St. Bridget.

Tarachow, Sidney. "St. Paul and Early Christianity: A Psychoanalytic and Historical Study." PSYCHOANALYSIS AND THE SOCIAL SCIENCES 4 (1955):

223-81.

Thiessen, Irmgard, et al. "A Comparison of Personality Characteristics of Men-nonites with Non-Mennonites." CANADIAN PSYCHOLOGIST 10, no. 2 (1969): 129-37.

Tsanoff, Radoslav A. AUTOBIOGRAPHIES OF TEN RELIGIOUS LEADERS: ALTERNATIVES IN CHRISTIAN EXPERIENCE. San Antonio, Tex.: Trinity University Press, 1969. xvi, 304 p.

> Essays on ten important Christian leaders who left autobiographical writings. Includes discussion of Augustine, Teresa of Avila, George Fox, John Bunyan, John Henry Newman, Ernest Renan, Leo Tol-stoy, Albert Schweitzer, and Pope John XXIII. The book recog-nizes the importance of alternative styles of religious life, and proposes these ten as potential paradigms for contemporary men.

Weigert [-Vowinkel], Edith. "Soren Kierkegaard's Mood Swings." INTER-NATIONAL JOURNAL OF PSYCHOANALYSIS 41 (1960): 521-25.

Wittmer, Joe. "Homogeneity of Personality Characteristics: Comparison between Old Order Amish and Non-Amish." AMERICAN ANTHROPOLOGIST 72 (1970): 1063-67.

_____. "Old Order Amish and Non-Amish Youth: A Personality Comparison Using the 16 PF." PERSONALITY 2 (1971): 305-13.

_____. "Perceived Parent-Child Relationships: A Comparison between Amish and Non-Amish Young Adults." JOURNAL OF CROSS-CULTURAL PSYCHOLO-GY 2 (March 1971): 87-94.

_____. "Amish Homogeneity of Parental Behavior Characteristics." HUMAN RELATIONS 26 (April 1973): 143-54.

Wood, William W. CULTURE AND PERSONALITY ASPECTS OF THE PENTE-COSTAL HOLINESS RELIGION. The Hague: Mouton and Co., 1965. 125 p.

> Based on the general hypothesis that "personality types participating in highly emotional religions will vary in some regular way from types participating in more sedate religions." Makes extensive use of the Rorschach technique.

Woolcott, Philip. "Erikson's Luther: A Psychiatrist's View." JOURNAL FOR THE SCIENTIFIC STUDY OF RELIGION 2 (1962-63): 243-48.

_____. "Some Considerations of Creativity and Religious Experience in St. Augustine of Hippo." JOURNAL FOR THE SCIENTIFIC STUDY OF RELIGION 5 (1966): 272-83.

F:4   THE CLERGY—PERSONALITY AND ROLE PERFORMANCE

a'Brook, M.F., et al. "Psychiatric Illness in the Clergy." BRITISH JOURNAL OF PSYCHIATRY 115 (1969): 457–63.

Alberts, W.E. "Personality and Attitudes toward Juvenile Delinquency: A Study of Protestant Ministers." JOURNAL OF SOCIAL PSYCHOLOGY 60 (1963): 71–83.

Allen, P.J. "Childhood Backgrounds of Success in a Profession." AMERICAN SOCIOLOGICAL REVIEW 20 (1955): 186–90.

   Study of Methodist bishops and clergy.

Ashbrook, James B., and Guthrie, H. "When Ministers Face Themselves: A Candid Study of the Personal Life of the Minister." PULPIT 31 (1960): 168–72.

Ball, Richard. "A Father is Being Beaten." JOURNAL OF RELIGION AND HEALTH 8 (1969): 255–67.

Bamberger, B.J. "The American Rabbi--His Changing Role." JUDAISM 3 (1954): 488–97.

Bartlett, Willie E., ed. EVOLVING RELIGIOUS CAREERS. Washington, D.C.: Center for Applied Research in the Apostolate, 1970. xii, 207 p.

   Interdisciplinary study of religious professionals, primarily priests.

Becker, Anthony J. "A Study of the Personality Traits of Successful Religious Women of Teaching Orders." THE 20TH YEARBOOK OF THE NATIONAL COUNCIL OF MEASUREMENT IN EDUCATION 20 (1963): 124–25.

Bennett, Thomas R. "Can the Minister Risk Role Change?" MINISTRY STUDIES 2, no. 1 (1968): 27–29.

Bentz, Kenneth W. "Consensus between Role Expectations and Role Behavior among Ministers." COMMUNITY MENTAL HEALTH JOURNAL 4 (1968): 301–6.

Bier, William C. "The Guidance Counselor and the Spiritual Director: The Distinct Role of Each." NATIONAL CATHOLIC EDUCATIONAL ASSOCIATION BULLETIN 61 (1964): 112–21.

Bissonier, H. "Some Conflicts and Psychological Motivations in the Life of the Active Religious." In APOSTOLIC LIFE, pp. 178–91. Religious Life Series, vol. 10. London: Blackfriars, 1958.

Blain, D. "Fostering the Mental Health of Ministers." PASTORAL PSYCHOLOGY 9, no. 84 (1958): 9–18.

Blizzard, Samuel W. "Role Conflicts of the Urban Minister." CITY CHURCH 7, no. 4 (1956): 13-15.

_____. "The Parish Minister's Self-image of His Master Role." PASTORAL PSYCHOLOGY 9, no. 89 (1958): 25-32.

_____. "The Protestant Parish Minister's Integrating Roles." RELIGIOUS EDUCATION 53 (1958): 374-80.

_____. "The Parish Minister's Self-Image and Variability in Community Culture." PASTORAL PSYCHOLOGY 10, no. 97 (1959): 27-36.

_____. "The Clergyman Views Himself." CHRISTIAN ADVOCATE 4, no. 25 (1960): 10-11

Bloom, Jack H. "Who Become Clergymen?" JOURNAL OF RELIGION AND HEALTH 10 (January 1971): 50-76.

Blount, Louise F., and Boyles, J.H. "The Theological Seminary and the Pastor's Wife." PASTORAL PSYCHOLOGY 12, no. 119 (1961): 40-45, 66.

Booth, G. "Unconscious Motivation in the Choice of the Ministry as Vocation." PASTORAL PSYCHOLOGY 9, no. 89 (1958): 18-24.

Bowers, Margaretta K. CONFLICTS OF THE CLERGY. New York: Thomas Nelson and Sons, 1963. xvi, 252 p.
   Based on fifteen years' experience of treating in psychotherapy people in religious vocations.

_____. "Psychotherapy of Religious Personnel: Some Observations and Recommendations." JOURNAL OF PASTORAL CARE 71 (1963): 11-16.

Bowers, Margaretta, K., et al. "Therapeutic Implications of Analytic Group Psychotherapy of Religious Personnel." INTERNATIONAL JOURNAL OF GROUP PSYCHOTHERAPY 8 (1958): 243-56.

Braude, Lee. "The Rabbi: Some Notes on Identity Clash." JEWISH SOCIAL STUDIES 22 (1960): 43-52.

Brooks, R.M. "The Ex-Seminarian." AVE MARIA 92 (1960): 5-10.

Burchard, W.W. "Role Conflicts of Military Chaplains." AMERICAN SOCIOLOGICAL REVIEW 19 (1954): 528-35.

Callahan, Luke J., and Wauck, LeRoy A. "Characteristics of a Minor Seminary

Population on the Edwards Personal Preference Schedule." NATIONAL CATHO-LIC GUIDANCE CONFERENCE JOURNAL 13, no. 3 (1969): 30-37.

Cardwell, Sue W. "The MMPI as a Predictor of Success among Seminary Students." MINISTRY STUDIES 1 (1967): 3-28.

Carlin, J.E., and Mendlovitz, S.H. "The American Rabbi: A Religious Specialist Responds to Loss of Authority." In THE JEWS: SOCIAL PATTERNS OF AN AMERICAN GROUP, pp. 377-414. Edited by M. Sklare. Glencoe, Ill.: Free Press, 1958.

Christensen, Carl W. "The Occurrences of Mental Illness in the Ministry: Introduction." JOURNAL OF PASTORAL CARE 13 (1959): 79-87.

_____. "The Occurrence of Mental Illness in the Ministry: Family Origins." JOURNAL OF PASTORAL CARE 14 (1960): 13-20.

_____. "The Occurrence of Mental Illness in the Ministry: Psychotic Disorders." JOURNAL OF PASTORAL CARE 15 (1961): 153-59.

_____. "The Occurrence of Mental Illness in the Ministry: Psychoneurotic Disorders." JOURNAL OF PASTORAL CARE 17 (1963): 1-10.

_____. "The Occurrence of Mental Illness in the Ministry: Personality Disorders." JOURNAL OF PASTORAL CARE 17 (1963): 125-35.

Cockrum, L.V. "Personality Traits and Interests of Theological Students." RELIGIOUS EDUCATION 47 (1952): 28-32.

_____. "Predicting Success in Training for the Ministry." RELIGIOUS EDUCATION 47 (1952): 198-202.

Crumbaugh, James C., et al. "Frankl's Will to Meaning in a Religious Order." JOURNAL OF CLINICAL PSYCHOLOGY 26 (1970): 206-7.

Curran, Charles A. PSYCHOLOGICAL DYNAMICS IN RELIGIOUS LIVING. New York: Herder and Herder, 1971. 228 p.

   A Catholic perspective, bringing a model of authentic communication and giving to discussions of celibacy, community, prayer, and belief.

D'Arcy, P.F. "Underachieving and Vocation." NATIONAL CATHOLIC EDUCATIONAL ASSOCIATION BULLETIN 60 (1963): 512-14.

D'Arcy, P.F., and Kennedy, Eugene C. THE GENIUS OF THE APOSTOLATE:

PERSONAL GROWTH IN THE CANDIDATE, THE SEMINARIAN, AND THE PRIEST. New York: Sheed & Ward, 1965. 273 p.

Dauw, Dean C. "Research on Religious Who Wish to Change Careers." IN-SIGHT: QUARTERLY REVIEW OF RELIGION AND MENTAL HEALTH 4, no. 3 (1966): 24-30.

de Bont, Walter. "Identity Crisis and the Male Novice." REVIEW FOR RELI-GIONS 21 (1962): 104-28.

Deegan, A.X. "Significant Factors in the Choice of Pastors." AMERICAN EC-CLESIASTICAL REVIEW 61 (1964): 97-111.

Del Arroyo, T. "An Experiment in the Discernment of Vocations." SUPPLE-MENT DE LA VIE SPIRITUELLE 12 (1959): 183-202.

DeMilan, Jean. "Personality Changes in Religious Life." CATHOLIC EDUCA-TOR 27 (1956): 133-34, 173-74.

Dennis, Wayne, and Uras, Alev. "The Religious Content of Human Figure Drawings Made by Nuns." JOURNAL OF PSYCHOLOGY 61 (1965): 263-66.

Denton, G.W. "Role Attitudes of the Minister's Wife." PASTORAL PSYCHOL-OGY 12, no. 119 (1961): 17-23.

_____. THE ROLE OF THE MINISTER'S WIFE. Philadelphia: The Westminister Press, 1962. 175 p.

Dittes, James E. "Facts and Fantasy in (the Minister's) Mental Health." PAS-TORAL PSYCHOLOGY 10 (March 1959): 15-24.

_____. "Research on Clergymen: Factors Influencing Decisions for Religious Service and Effectiveness in the Vocation." RELIGIOUS EDUCATION (research supplement) 57, no. 4 (1962): 141-65.

_____. "Breakdown of Society, Opinion Pollster, and Ministry." THEOLOG-ICAL EDUCATION 7 (Winter 1971): 146.

_____. "Psychological Characteristics of Religious Professionals." In RESEARCH ON RELIGIOUS DEVELOPMENT: A COMPREHENSIVE HANDBOOK, pp. 422-60. Edited by Merton P. Strommen. New York: Hawthorn Books, 1971.

Douglas, William G.T. "Ministers' Wives: A Tentative Typology." PASTORAL PSYCHOLOGY 12, no. 119 (1961): 11-16.

_____. "Role Orientation of Future Ministers' Wives." In RESEARCH PLANS, pp. 189-95. Edited by S.W. Cook. New York: The Religious Education Association, 1962.

_____. MINISTERS' WIVES. New York: Harper & Row, Publishers, 1965. xv, 265 p.

> A major empirical study of the role of ministers' wives in their husbands' professional careers. Develops a typology, including the teamworker, the background supporter, and the detached, and discusses wives' responses to popular stereotypes of the Clergyman's wife.

Dunn, Ralph H. "Personality Patterns among Religious Personnel: A Review." CATHOLIC PSYCHOLOGICAL RECORD 3 (1965): 125-37.

Eggleston, Donald, and Snyder, Robert T. "The Priest's Role as Seen by Seminarians and Faculty." CATHOLIC EDUCATIONAL REVIEW 66 (1969): 617-31.

Erikson, Erik H. "The Nature of Clinical Evidence." DAEDALUS 87 (1958): 65-87. Also published in INSIGHT AND RESPONSIBILITY, pp. 49-80. Edited by Erik H. Erikson. New York: W.W. Norton & Co., 1964.

> Discusses the author's psychotherapeutic treatment of a young man who had recently left the seminary.

Evans, Theodore Q. "The Brethren Pastor: Differential Conceptions of an Emerging Role." JOURNAL FOR THE SCIENTIFIC STUDY OF RELIGION 3 (1963): 43-51.

Evoy, John J., and Christoph, Van F. PERSONALITY DEVELOPMENT IN THE RELIGIOUS LIFE. New York: Sheed & Ward, 1963. 247 p.

> A study of the life of nuns.

_____. MATURITY IN THE RELIGIOUS LIFE. New York: Sheed & Ward, 1965. vii, 310 p.

Falk, L.L. "The Minister's Response to Role Conflict." DISCOURSE 6 (1963): 216-28.

Fecher, C.J. "Mortality and Morbidity Studies of Religious." LINACRE QUARTERLY 27 (1960): 157-65.

_____. "Health of Religious Clergy." REVIEW FOR RELIGIOUS 23 (1964): 316-28.

> Also a study of mortality among clergy.

Fichter, Joseph H. SOCIAL RELATIONS IN THE URBAN PARISH. Chicago: University of Chicago Press, 1954. 263 p.

_____. "The Religious Professional: Part I." REVIEW OF RELIGIOUS RE-SEARCH 1 (1960): 89-101.

_____. "The Religious Professional: Part II." REVIEW OF RELIGIOUS RE-SEARCH 1 (1960): 150-70.

_____. RELIGION AS AN OCCUPATION: A STUDY IN THE SOCIOLOGY OF PROFESSIONS. Notre Dame, Ind.: University of Notre Dame Press, 1961. 295 p.

_____. PRIEST AND PEOPLE. New York: Sheed & Ward, 1965. xiv, 203 p.

Foley, A.S. "United States Colored Priests: Hundred Year Survey." AMERICA 89 (1953): 295-97.

_____. "The Status and Role of the Negro Priest in the American Catholic Clergy." AMERICAN CATHOLIC SOCIOLOGICAL REVIEW 16 (1955): 83-93.

Ford, John Cuthbut. RELIGIOUS SUPERIORS, SUBJECTS, AND PSYCHIATRISTS. Westminster, Md.: Newman Press, 1963. 101 p.

Fulton, R.L. "The Clergyman and the Funeral Director: A Study in Role Conflict." SOCIAL FORCES 39 (1961): 317-23.

Glock, Charles Y., and Ringer, B.B. "Church Policy and the Attitudes of Ministers and Parishioners on Social Issues." AMERICAN SOCIOLOGICAL REVIEW 21 (1956): 148-56.

Glock, Charles Y., and Roos, P. "Parishioners' View of How Ministers Spend Their Time." REVIEW OF RELIGIOUS RESEARCH 2 (1961): 170-75.

Godin, Andre. "Problems of Mental Health before and after Entering Religious Life." SISTER FORMATION BULLETIN 6, no. 2 (1959-60): 1-5.

Goldstein, S.E. "The Roles of an American Rabbi." SOCIOLOGY AND SOCIAL RESEARCH 38 (1953): 32-37.

Goodling, R.A., and Webb, Sam C. "An Analysis of Faculty Ratings of Theology Students." RELIGIOUS EDUCATION 54 (1959): 228-33.

Greenfield, Murray. "Typologies of Persisting and Non-Persisting Jewish Clergymen." JOURNAL OF COUNSELING PSYCHOLOGY 16, no. 4 (1969): 368-72.

Guinan, St. Michael. "Aging and Religious Life." GERONTOLOGIST 12 (1972): 21.

Gustafson, James M. "Theological Students: Varieties of Types and Experience." In THE ADVANCEMENT OF THEOLOGICAL EDUCATION, pp. 145-73. By H. Richard Niebuhr, et al. New York: Harper & Brothers, 1957.

_____. "The Clergy in the U.S." DAEDALUS 92 (1963): 722-44.

Analyzes the sociological conditions under which ministers in the United States perform their tasks.

Hadden, Jeffrey K. "A Study of the Protestant Ministry of America." JOURNAL FOR THE SCIENTIFIC STUDY OF RELIGION 5 (1965): 10-23.

Hagmaier, George. "Today's Religious Candidate: Psychological and Emotional Considerations." NATIONAL CATHOLIC EDUCATIONAL ASSOCIATION BULLETIN 59 (1962): 110-18.

Hall, Douglas T., and Schneider, Benjamin. ORGANIZATIONAL CLIMATES AND CAREERS: THE WORK LIVES OF PRIESTS. New York: Seminar Press, 1973. xix, 291 p.

Presents a theory of career development and analyzes the work and self-image of the Roman Catholic priest. Particular attention to adaptation to failure.

Hall, J.O. "Note on Relationships between Attitudes toward the Scientific Method and the Background of Seminarians." SOCIAL FORCES 39 (1960): 49-52.

Ham, H.M. "Personality Correlates of Ministerial Success." ILIFF REVIEW 17 (1960): 3-9.

Harrower, Molly. "Mental-Health Potential and Success in the Ministry." JOURNAL OF RELIGION AND HEALTH 4 (1964): 30-58.

Hertzberg, A. "Conservative Rabbinate--A Sociological Study." In ESSAYS ON JEWISH LIFE AND THOUGHT, pp. 309-32. Edited by J.L. Blau. New York: Columbia University Press, 1959.

Heusher, Julius S. "Vocational Celibacy and Authenticity." COMPREHENSIVE PSYCHIATRY 10 (September 1972): 445-57.

Hibbard, D.L., and Lee, J.P. "Presbyterian Ministers and Their Widows in Retirement." JOURNAL OF GERONTOLOGY 9 (1954): 46-55.

Hickey, Tom. "Catholic Religious Orders and the Aging Process: Research, Training, and Service Program." GERONTOLOGIST 12 (1972): 16-17.

Hickey, Tom, and Kalish, Richard A. "American Catholic Sisters and the Aging Process." PROCEEDINGS OF THE 77TH ANNUAL CONVENTION OF THE AMERICAN PSYCHOLOGICAL ASSOCIATION 4 (1969): 739-40.

Higgins, Paul S., and Dittes, James E. "Changes in Laymen's Expectations of the Minister's Roles." MINISTRY STUDIES 2, no. 1 (1968): 5-23.

Hostie, Raymond. THE DISCERNMENT OF VOCATIONS. Translated by Michael Barry. New York: Sheed & Ward, 1963. 160 p.

    Distinguishes internal and external types of religious vocations.

Hudson, R.L. "The Emotions of the Minister." PASTORAL PSYCHOLOGY 2, no. 14 (1951): 32-37.

Jamison, W.G. "Predicting Academic Achievement of Seminary Students." REVIEW OF RELIGIOUS RESEARCH 6 (1965): 90-96.

Jansen, David G., et al. "Personality Characteristics of Clergymen Entering a Clinical Training Program at a State Hospital." PSYCHOLOGICAL REPORTS 31 (December 1972): 878.

Johensen, Roger B. "The Dynamics of Role Leaving: A Role Theoretical Approach to the Leaving of Religious Organizations." JOURNAL OF APPLIED BEHAVIORAL SCIENCE 5 (1969): 287-308.

Johnson, Paul E. "The Emotional Health of the Clergy." JOURNAL OF RELIGION AND HEALTH 9 (1970): 50-59.

Judy, M.T. "The Christian Clergy: Their Vocational Concepts and Performance Observed in a Theological Dimension." In RESEARCH PLANS IN THE FIELDS OF RELIGION, VALUES AND MORALITY AND THEIR BEARING ON RELIGIOUS AND CHARACTER FORMATION, pp. 200-205. Edited by S.W. Cook. New York: The Religious Education Association, 1962.

Kaam, Adrian van. THE VOWED LIFE: DYNAMICS OF PERSONAL AND SPIRITUAL UNFOLDING. Denville, N.J.: Dimension Books, 1968. 363 p.

    Discusses the place of religious life in Western culture, avowing
    and being called, and the healing power of vows.

Kalthoff, R.J., and Gunter, F.L. "Collaboration of Psychiatrist and Supervised Psychotherapist in the Treatment of People in Religious Life." BULLETIN OF THE GUILD OF CATHOLIC PSYCHIATRISTS 10 (1963): 18-28.

Kania, Walter. "Healthy Defensiveness in Theological Students." MINISTRY

STUDIES 1, no. 4 (1967): 3-20.

Keefe, Jeffrey. "Maturity in the High School Seminarian: An Empirical Approach." CATHOLIC PSYCHOLOGICAL RECORD 6, no. 1 (1968): 15-29.

Kelley, Sister Mary W. "The Incidence of Hospitalized Mental Illness among Religious Sisters in the United States." AMERICAN JOURNAL OF PSYCHIATRY 115 (1958): 72-75.

_____. "Depression in the Psychoses of Members of Religious Communities of Women." AMERICAN JOURNAL OF PSYCHIATRY 118 (1961): 423-25.

Kelly, Henry E. "Role Satisfaction of the Catholic Priest." SOCIAL FORCES 50 (1971): 75-84.

Kling, F.R. "Value Structures and the Minister's Purpose." PASTORAL PSYCHOLOGY 12, no. 112 (1961): 13-23.

Kniepf, Lotus M. "The Personality of Pre-Theological Majors." JOURNAL OF EXPERIMENTAL EDUCATION 34, no. 4 (1966): 62-68.

Lenzeder, Freiderike. "Autonomie, Integration und Intimitat als Probleme der Selbstverwirklichung bei Ordensfrauen." ZEITSCHRIFT FUR KLINISCHE PSYCHOLOGIE UND PSYCHOTHERAPIE 19 (1971): 254-68.

Lonsway, Francis A. "Background Characteristics and Goals of Catholic Theological Students." NATIONAL CATHOLIC GUIDANCE CONFERENCE JOURNAL 12 (1968): 101-18.

Lubin, Albert J. STRANGER ON THE EARTH: A PSYCHOLOGICAL BIOGRAPHY OF VINCENT VAN GOGH. New York: Holt, Rinehart and Winston, 1972. xxii, 265 p.

> A psychobiography which traces the forces at play in Van Gogh's life as he abandoned plans for the Protestant ministry and became an artist, transferring his religious concerns to the medium of painting.

McAllister, R.J., and Vanderveldt, A. "Factors in Mental Illness among Hospitalized Clergy." JOURNAL OF NERVOUS AND MENTAL DISEASE 132 (1961): 80-88.

_____. CONFLICTS IN COMMUNITY. Collegeville, Minn.: St. John's University Press, 1969. xv, 110 p.

> A study of stress and conflict in a convent.

McCarthy, Thomas N., and Dondero, E. Austin. "Predictor Variables and Criteria of Success in Religious Life: Needed Research." CATHOLIC PSYCHO-LOGICAL RECORD 1, no. 1 (1963): 71-80.

MacGuigan, J. Elliot. "The Aging Religious Priest." GERONTOLOGIST 12 (1972): 19-21.

McMahon, Sister Miriam D. "Religious Vocational Concepts Revealed by Survey." LUMEN VITAE 12 (1957): 326-41.

Attitudes toward the religious life of high school Catholic girls.

Maddi, Salvatore, and Rulla, Luigi M. "Personality and the Catholic Religious Vocation: Self and Conflict in Female Entrants." JOURNAL OF PERSONALITY 40 (March 1972): 104-22.

Also see Rulla entry below.

Maehr, M.L., and Stake, R.E. "The Value Patterns of Men Who Voluntarily Quit Seminary Training." PERSONNEL AND GUIDANCE JOURNAL 40 (1962): 537-40.

Mason, Robert, et al. "Human Nature and Authoritarianism in Seminary Students and Counselor Trainees." PERSONNEL AND GUIDANCE JOURNAL 47, no. 7 (1969): 689-92.

Masson, J. "Vocations to the Priesthood and Environment: An Enquiry in the Belgian Congo, Ruanda and Urundi." LUMEN VITAE 13 (1958): 120-45.

Studies family and socioeconomic background of seminarians in these areas.

Meiburg, Albert L., and Young, Richard K. "The Hospitalized Minister: A Preliminary Study." PASTORAL PSYCHOLOGY 9, no. 84 (1958): 37-42.

Meissner, W [illiam] W. "Affective Response to Psychoanalytic Death Symbols." JOURNAL OF ABNORMAL AND SOCIAL PSYCHOLOGY 56 (1958): 295-99.

Employs sample of forty Catholic seminarians.

Moberg, David O. THE CHURCH AS A SOCIAL INSTITUTION. Prentice-Hall Sociology Series. Englewood Cliffs, N.J.: Prentice-Hall, 1962. 569 p.

Morentz, P.E. "The Image of the Seminary Wife." PASTORAL PSYCHOLOGY 12, no. 119 (1961): 46-52.

Morgan, L. "Mental Illness Among the Clergy: A Survey of State Mental Hospitals in America." PASTORAL PSYCHOLOGY 9, no. 84 (1958): 29-36.

Muntz, E.E., Jr. "Opinions of Divinity and Law Students on Social Class." JOURNAL OF EDUCATIONAL SOCIOLOGY 34 (1961): 221-29.

Murphy, G.M. "Our Experience with Delayed Vocations." NATIONAL CATH-OLIC EDUCATIONAL ASSOCIATION BULLETIN 47 (1950): 133-39.

Murphy, Owen. "Psychological Suitability of Candidates to Priesthood and Religious Life." CATHOLIC EDUCATOR 49, no. 8 (1969): 40-46.

Nauss, Allen. "The Ministerial Personality: On Avoiding a Stereotype Trap." JOURNAL OF COUNSELING PSYCHOLOGY 15, no. 6 (1968): 581-82.

_____. "Personality Changes among Students in a Conservative Seminary." JOURNAL FOR THE SCIENTIFIC STUDY OF RELIGION 11 (December 1972): 377-88.

_____. "The Ministerial Personality: Myth or Reality?" JOURNAL OF RE-LIGION AND HEALTH 12 (January 1973): 77-96.

Oates, Wayne Edward, ed. THE MINISTER'S OWN MENTAL HEALTH. Great Neck, N.Y.: Channel Press, 1961. 335 p.

   A collection of twenty-nine articles, most of which appeared earlier
   in PASTORAL PSYCHOLOGY.

O'Donovan, Thomas R., and Deegan, Arthur X. "Some Career Determinants of Church Executives." SOCIOLOGY AND SOCIAL RESEARCH 48, no. 1 (1963): 58-68.

Pallone, Nathaniel J. "Religious Authority and Social Perception: A Labora-tory Exploration in Social Influence." JOURNAL OF SOCIAL PSYCHOLOGY 68 (1966): 229-41.

Pallone, Nathaniel J., and Branks, R. Richard. "Vocational Satisfaction among Ministerial Students." PERSONNEL AND GUIDANCE JOURNAL 46 (1968): 870-75.

Pallone, Nathaniel J., and Yeandel, Francis A. "Religious Influence and So-cial Perception: The Clear Triumph of Religious over Military Authority." JOURNAL OF SOCIAL PSYCHOLOGY 75 (1968): 147-54.

Pallone, Nathaniel J., et al. "Correlates of Vocational Satisfaction among Nuns and Brothers." NATIONAL CATHOLIC GUIDANCE CONFERENCE JOUR-NAL 14, no. 1 (1969): 5-20.

Palomo, Francisco, and Wauck, Leroy A. "Personality Adjustment of Minor Semi-

narians and of Catholic High School Seniors." NATIONAL CATHOLIC GUID-
ANCE CONFERENCE JOURNAL 12 (1968): 253-56.

Pruyser, Paul W. "Impact of the Psychological Disciplines on the Training of
Clergy." PASTORAL PSYCHOLOGY 19 (October 1968): 21-32.

Rabinowitz, Seymour. "Developmental Problems in Catholic Seminarians." PSY-
CHIATRY 32 (1969): 107-17.

Rankin, R.P. "The Ministerial Calling and the Minister's Wife." PASTORAL
PSYCHOLOGY 11, no. 106 (1960): 16-22.

Rodehaver, M.W., and Smith, L.M. "Migration and Occupational Structure:
The Clergy." SOCIAL FORCES 29 (1951): 416-21.

Roman, Mary. "Negro Vocations and Religious Communities." REVIEW FOR
RELIGIOUS 23 (1964): 129-34.

Rooney, John J. "Problems of Interpretation: A Commentary." MINISTRY
STUDIES 1, no. 4 (1967): 21-24.

    A criticism of standard use of MMPI in clergy studies.

Rosilda, Sister M. "Religious Vocations Among Women--A Comparative Study
of Schools and Places They Come From." CATHOLIC EDUCATIONAL REVIEW
53 (1955): 296-305.

Rossman, P. "The Morale of the Campus Pastor." RELIGIOUS EDUCATION
57 (1962): 110-13.

Rulla, Luigi M., and Maddi, Salvatore R. "Personality and the Catholic Religious Vocation: Self and Conflict in Male Entrants." JOURNAL OF PERSON-
ALITY 40 (December 1972): 564-87.

    Also see Maddi entry above.

Ryan, E.J. "Some Psychological Implications of the Vocational Survey: Natural
Factors Affecting Vocations to the Priesthood." NATIONAL CATHOLIC EDU-
CATIONAL ASSOCIATION BULLETIN 53 (1956): 57-63.

Salisbury, W. Seward. RELIGION IN AMERICAN CULTURE: A SOCIOLOGI-
CAL INTERPRETATION. The Dorsey Series in Anthropology and Sociology.
Homewood, Ill.: Dorsey Press, 1964. ix, 538 p.

    The chapter, "The Clergy," summarizes sociological research on
    recruitment, training, and role definitions of ministers, rabbis, and
    priests.

Scanzoni, J. "Resolution of Occupational-Conjugal Role Conflict in Clergy Marriages." JOURNAL OF MARRIAGE AND THE FAMILY 27 (August 1965): 397-402.

Scherer, Ross P. "The Lutheran Ministry: Origins, Careers, Self-Appraisal." CRESSET 26, no. 3 (1963): 9-17.

Schroeder, W.W. "Lay Expectations of the Ministerial Role: An Exploration of Protestant-Catholic Differentials." JOURNAL FOR THE SCIENTIFIC STUDY OF RELIGION 2 (1963): 217-27.

Schuldt, David L., and Stahmann, Robert F. "Interest Profiles of Clergymen as Indicated by the Vocational Preference Inventory." EDUCATIONAL AND PSYCHOLOGICAL MEASUREMENT 31 (1971): 1025-28.

Schultz, K.V. "The Psychologically Healthy Person: A Study in Identification and Prediction." JOURNAL OF CLINICAL PSYCHOLOGY 14 (1958): 112-17.

A study based on forty graduates of a school of religion.

Shanas, Ethel, and Havighurst, Robert J. "Retirement in Four Professions." JOURNAL OF GERONTOLOGY 8 (1953): 212-21.

Sheridan, Edward P., and Kobler, Frank J. "The Loyola Seminarian Sentence Completion Test." JOURNAL OF PROJECTIVE TECHNIQUES AND PERSONALITY ASSESSMENT 33 (1969): 507-12.

Shimada, K. "Social Role and Role Conflicts of the Protestant Parish Minister: Focused on S.W. Blizzard's Study." JAPANESE SOCIOLOGICAL REVIEW 10, no. 2 (1960): 29-50.

Siegelman, M., and Peck, R.F. "Personality Patterns Related to Occupational Roles." GENETIC PSYCHOLOGY MONOGRAPHS 61 (1960): 291-349.

Comparative study of ministers, chemists, and military officers.

Simmons, Milton D., and Parker, Harry J. "Attitude and Personality Traits of Ministerial Students: The Influence and Control of Reference Group Phenomena." RELIGIOUS EDUCATION 63 (1968): 309-14.

Sklare, M. "The Conservative Rabbi." In CONSERVATIVE JUDAISM: AN AMERICAN RELIGIOUS MOVEMENT, pp. 159-98. By M. Sklare. Glencoe, Ill.: Free Press, 1955.

Smith, J.O., and Sjoberg, G. "Origins and Career Patterns of Leading Protestant Clergymen." SOCIAL FORCES 39 (1961): 290-96.

Smith, L.M. "The Clergy: Authority Structure, Ideology, Migration." AMERI-CAN SOCIOLOGICAL REVIEW 18 (1953): 242–48.

Southard, Samuel. "The Mental Health of Ministers." PASTORAL PSYCHOLO-GY 9, no. 84 (1958): 43–48.

_____. "Faithful Commitment to the Ministry." PASTORAL PSYCHOLOGY 14, no. 139 (1963): 31–36.

_____. "The Personal Life of the Frontier Minister: 1760–1860." JOURNAL FOR THE SCIENTIFIC STUDY OF RELIGION 5 (1966): 213–23.

Stanley, Gordon. "Personality and Attitude Characteristics of Fundamentalist Theological Students." AUSTRALIAN JOURNAL OF PSYCHOLOGY 15, no. 2 (1963): 121–23.

Stern, George G. "Personality Assessment and the Prediction of Academic Suc-cess." AMERICAN PSYCHOLOGIST 7 (1952): 324.

_____. "Assessing Theological Student Personality Structure." JOURNAL OF PASTORAL CARE 8 (1954): 76–83.

Stern, George G., et al. METHODS IN PERSONALITY ASSESSMENT. Glen-coe, Ill.: Free Press, 1956. 271 p.
   Contains chapter devoted to analysis of personalities of theological students and another chapter which compares theology, education, and physics students.

Stogdill, R.M., et al. "New Leader Behavior Description Subscales." JOUR-NAL OF PSYCHOLOGY 54 (1962): 259–69.
   Sample includes 150 clergymen and 150 community leaders.

Strunk, Orlo, Jr. "Theological Students: A Study in Perceived Motives." PERSONNEL AND GUIDANCE JOURNAL 36 (1958): 320–22.

_____. "Interest and Personality Patterns of Preministerial Students." PSY-CHOLOGICAL REPORTS 5 (1959): 740.

_____. "Man, Emotions, and the Ministry." RELIGIOUS EDUCATION 54 (1959): 425–34.
   Analysis of the motivations of ministry students through the examina-tion of one hundred autobiographies.

Vaughan, Richard Patrick. "The Neurotic Religious." REVIEW FOR RELIGIOUS 17 (1958): 271–78.

_____. "Severe Mental Illness Among Religious." REVIEW FOR RELIGIOUS 18 (1959): 25-36.

_____. MENTAL ILLNESS AND THE RELIGIOUS LIFE. Milwaukee: Bruce Publishers, 1962. 198 p.

Expanding on his earlier articles in REVIEW FOR RELIGIOUS, the author describes the mental illness of clergy and its effects on their religious lives. Favorably views psychoanalysis as a means for understanding and treating emotional disturbances among the clergy.

_____. "Seminary Training and Personality Change." RELIGIOUS EDUCATION 65 (1970): 56-59.

Very, Philip S., et al. "Birth Order, Personality Development, and Vocational Choice of Becoming a Carmelite Nun." JOURNAL OF PSYCHOLOGY 85 (September 1973): 75-80.

Webster, Alan C., and Stewart, Robert A. "Psychological Attitudes and Beliefs of Ministers." ANVIL QUARTERLY 1, no. 3 (1969): 11-16.

Weisgerber, Charles. "The THEOLOGICAL SCHOOL INVENTORY and Some Roman Catholic and Protestant Differences." COUNSELING AND VALUES 16 (Fall 1971): 54-65.

Whitcomb, J.C. "The Relationship of Personality Characteristics to the Problems of Ministers." RELIGIOUS EDUCATION 52 (1957): 371-74.

Whitlock, Glenn E. "The Choice of the Ministry as an Active or Passive Decision." PASTORAL PSYCHOLOGY 12, no. 112 (1961): 47-53.

_____. "Role and Self Concepts in the Choice of the Ministry as a Vocation." JOURNAL OF PASTORAL CARE 17 (1963): 208-12.

Wilson, B.R. "The Pentecostalist Minister: Role Conflicts and Status Contradictions." AMERICAN JOURNAL OF SOCIOLOGY 64 (1959): 494-504.

Based on study of Pentecostal movement in Great Britain.

Zax, M., et al. "A Comparative Study of Novice Nuns and College Females Using the Response Set Approach." JOURNAL OF ABNORMAL AND SOCIAL PSYCHOLOGY 66 (1963): 369-75.

Comparison based Rorschach inkblots and social desirability ratings.

Section G

THE DIRECTIONAL DIMENSION OF RELIGION

Section G

THE DIRECTIONAL DIMENSION OF RELIGION

G:1   RELIGIOUS PSYCHOTHERAPY AND COUNSELING

Aldrich, C. Knight, and Nighswonger, Carl. A PASTORAL COUNSELING CASEBOOK. Philadelphia: The Westminster Press, 1968. 224 p.

> A collection of synopses of specific cases of emotional problems (guilt, anxiety, depression, marital difficulty, suicide), each followed by informal conversations between the authors, one a psychiatrist and the other a clergyman.

Anderson, Herbert. "Alfred Adler's Individual Psychology and Pastoral Care." PASTORAL PSYCHOLOGY 21 (October 1970): 15-26.

_____. "Individual Psychology and Pastoral Psychology." JOURNAL OF INDIVIDUAL PSYCHOLOGY 27 (1971): 25-35.

Ashbrook, James B. "A Preface to Pastoral Care Research." MINISTRY STUDIES 3, no. 2 (1969): 3-9.

_____. "Characteristics of Parish Counseling." PASTORAL PSYCHOLOGY 21 (May 1970): 27-38.

_____. "Paul Tillich Converses with Psychotherapists." JOURNAL OF RELIGION AND HEALTH 11 (January 1972): 40-72.

Assagiolo, Roberto. PSYCHOSYNTHESIS: A MANUAL OF PRINCIPLES AND TECHNIQUES. New York: Hobbs, Dorman, 1965. 323 p.

> A collection of essays by an Italian therapist who combines psychoanalytic and religious concepts.

Baute, Paschal. "The Place of Counseling in the Church: The Work of the Pastoral Counselor." RELIGIOUS EDUCATION 61 (1966): 120-27.

Bier, William C., ed. PERSONALITY AND SEXUAL PROBLEMS IN PASTORAL PSYCHOLOGY. New York: Fordham University Press, 1964. xiii, 256 p.

Bonnell, George C. "Salvation and Psychotherapy." JOURNAL OF RELIGION AND HEALTH 8 (1969): 382-98.

Cavanagh, J.R. FUNDAMENTAL PASTORAL COUNSELING: TECHNIQUE AND PSYCHOLOGY. Milwaukee: Bruce Publishers, 1962. 326 p.

Clinebell, Howard J., [Jr.]. "Pastoral Psychology: The Next 20 Years in Pastoral Counseling." PASTORAL PSYCHOLOGY 21 (February 1970): 28-35.

Coyle, F.A., Jr., and Erdberg, Philip. "A Liberalizing Approach to Maladaptive Fundamentalist Hyperreligiosity." PSYCHOTHERAPY: THEORY, RESEARCH AND PRACTICE 6, no. 2 (1969): 140-42.

Crumbaugh, James C. "Frankl's Logotherapy: A New Orientation in Counseling." JOURNAL OF RELIGION AND HEALTH 10 (October 1971): 373-86.

Cumming, Elaine, and Harrington, C. "Clergyman as Counselor." AMERICAN JOURNAL OF SOCIOLOGY 69 (1963): 234-43.

Curran, Charles A. "A Catholic Psychologist Looks at Pastoral Counseling." PASTORAL PSYCHOLOGIST 10, no. 91 (1959): 21-28.

_____. "The Counseling Relationship and Some Religious Factors." JOURNAL OF COUNSELING PSYCHOLOGY 6 (1959): 266-70.

_____. COUNSELING AND PSYCHOTHERAPY: THE PURSUIT OF VALUES. New York: Sheed & Ward, 1968. 403 p.

The author, a priest and trained psychotherapist, advocates "value counseling psychotherapy," a form of therapy which aids clients in their search for meaning through the reorganization of their personal value investments.

_____. RELIGIOUS VALUES IN COUNSELING AND PSYCHOTHERAPY. New York: Sheed & Ward, 1969. 398 p.

Also listed in section G:4.

de Bont, Walter. "Chronicle of General, Pastoral, and Religious Psychology." SOCIAL COMPASS 14 (1967): 310-28.

Devlin, William J. "Catholicism and Its Therapeutic Applications." ANNALS OF PSYCHOTHERAPY 1, no. 2 (1959): 20-26.

Dittes, James E. "Pastoral Psychology: The Next 20 Years in Relation to All Psychology." PASTORAL PSYCHOLOGY 21 (February 1970): 43-49.

Doniger, Simon, ed. HEALING: HUMAN AND DIVINE. New York: Association Press, 1957. 254 p.

Ducker, E.N. A CHRISTIAN THERAPY FOR A NEUROTIC WORLD. London: George Allen and Unwin, 1961. 225 p.

An introduction to the possibilities of a psychotherapeutic ministry.

_____. PSYCHOTHERAPY: A CHRISTIAN APPROACH. London: George Allen and Unwin, 1964. 126 p.

A minister-therapist advocates a rapprochement between psychology and the church in serving people in need of help.

Faber, H. PRAKTIKUM DES SEELSORGERLICHEN GESPRACHES. Gottingen: Vandenhoeck and Ruprecht, 1969. 225 p.

A practicum for pastoral counseling.

Farnsworth, Dana L., and Braceland, Francis J., eds. PSYCHIATRY, THE CLERGY, AND PASTORAL COUNSELING: THE ST. JOHN'S STORY. Collegeville, Minn.: St. John's University Press, 1969. xviii, 356 p.

Ferm, Vergilius. A DICTIONARY OF PASTORAL PSYCHOLOGY. New York: Philosophical Library, 1955. 336 p.

A basic guide to the field of pastoral psychology.

Ford, Peter S. THE HEALING TRINITY: PRESCRIPTIONS FOR BODY, MIND, AND SPIRIT. New York: Harper & Row, Publishers, 1971. xii, 133 p.

A study by a psychiatrist of the potential unification of the perspectives of medicine, psychiatry, and theology for a theory and therapy capable of dealing with the "whole" man.

Fox, Douglas A. "Logotherapy and Religion." RELIGION IN LIFE 34 (1965): 235-44.

Frankl, Viktor E. "Logotherapy and the Challenge of Suffering." PASTORAL PSYCHOLOGY 13 (June 1962): 25-28.

_____. MAN'S SEARCH FOR MEANING: AN INTRODUCTION TO LOGO-THERAPY. Translated by Ilse Lasch. New York: Washington Square Press, 1963. xv, 222 p.

The first part of the book provides a dramatic account of the author's experience in Nazi concentration camps. The second is devoted to a theory of psychotherapy derived from this experience. Argues that

meaning is the core need of man and that he can transcend any
condition if he has a vital sense of the meaningfulness of his life.

_____. THE DOCTOR AND THE SOUL: FROM PSYCHOTHERAPY TO LOGO-
THERAPY. Translated by Richard Winston and Clara Winston. New York: Ban-
tam Books, 1967. xix, 236 p.

Contending that the major cause of neurosis in the modern world
is the absence of meaning, the author articulates a theory for the
treatment of a meaningless life.

_____. THE WILL TO MEANING: FOUNDATIONS AND APPLICATIONS OF
LOGOTHERAPY. New York: World Publishing Co., 1969. 180 p.

Gerber, Israel J. MAN ON A PENDULUM: A CASE HISTORY OF AN INVERT
PRESENTED BY A RELIGIOUS COUNSELOR. New York: American Press, 1956.
320 p.

Gilbreath, Stuart, and Hoenig, Martin. "Rabbis and Pastoral Counseling."
JOURNAL OF PASTORAL CARE 22, no. 1 (1968): 28-33.

Glasner, Samuel. "Judaism and Its Therapeutic Applications." ANNALS OF
PSYCHOTHERAPY 1, no. 2 (1959): 40-46.

Grollman, E [arl] A. "Logotherapy of Viktor E. Frankl: A Search for the
Authentic Self." JUDAISM 14 (Winter 1965): 22-38.

See Victor E. Frankl's MAN'S SEARCH FOR MEANING: AN
INTRODUCTION TO LOGOTHERAPY cited above.

_____. RABBINICAL COUNSELING. New York: Bloch Publishing Co.,
1966. 190 p.

A collection of papers on the role of the rabbi as teacher and
counselor. Discusses problems relating to religious beliefs, inter-
marriage, aging, mental illness, suicide, and other topics.

Guntrip, Henry. PSYCHOTHERAPY AND RELIGION. New York: Harper &
Brothers, 1957. 206 p.

Expanded from a 1951 presentation at a theological conference, and
published originally in England as MENTAL PAIN AND THE CURE OF
SOULS. A well-written work in non-technical language by a former
minister who is now a psychotherapist and advocate of the object-
relational point of view in psychology.

Haas, Harold I. PASTORAL COUNSELING WITH PEOPLE IN DISTRESS. St.
Louis: Concordia Publishing House, 1970. 193 p.

Hagmaier, George, and Gleason, Robert W. COUNSELING THE CATHOLIC: MODERN TECHNIQUES AND EMOTIONAL CONFLICTS. New York: Sheed & Ward, 1959. xiv, 301 p.

> Two priests, using both Freudian and Rogerian perspectives on issues of moral and psychological conflict, attempt to sort out the roles of priest and confessor in their religious functions, and in their referring cases to other agencies.

Havens, Joseph. "Psychotherapy and Salvation." PASTORAL PSYCHOLOGY 12 (February 1961): 10-18.

Hiltner, Seward. "The Contribution of the Behavioral Sciences to Pastoral Care and Counseling." MINISTRY STUDIES 3, no. 2 (1969): 10-17.

Hiltner, Seward, and Colston, Lowell G. THE CONTEXT OF PASTORAL COUNSELING. New York: Abingdon Press, 1961. 272 p.

Hora, Thomas. "Psychotherapy, Existence and Religion." PSYCHOANALYSIS AND THE PSYCHOANALYTIC REVIEW 46 (Summer 1959): 91-98.

Johnson, Paul E. PERSON AND COUNSELOR: RESPONSIVE COUNSELING IN THE CHRISTIAN CONTEXT. Nashville: Abingdon Press, 1962. 208 p.

Knowles, Joseph W. "Awareness and Taking Responsibility as Two Significant Goals of Pastoral Counseling." PASTORAL PSYCHOLOGY 23 (1972): 7-14.

Lee, Roy Stuart. PRINCIPLES OF PASTORAL COUNSELING. London: Society for the Propagation of Christian Knowledge, 1968. 135 p.

Leslie, Robert C. JESUS AND LOGOTHERAPY. Nashville: Abingdon Press, 1965. 144 p.

> A survey of Viktor Frankl's logotherapy in light of the teachings of Jesus. Important passages from the four gospels illustrate the relevance of logotherapy to Christian belief. See Victor E. Frankl's MAN'S SEARCH FOR MEANING: AN INTRODUCTION TO LOGOTHERAPY cited above.

McClelland, David C. THE ROOTS OF CONSCIOUSNESS. Princeton, N.J.: D. Van Nostrand, 1964. 219 p.

> A collection of eight essays which probe the motivational and psychodynamic factors underlying conscious behavior and cognitive processes. Contains an interesting psychoanalytic treatment of Andre Gide in light of French Puritan family tradition and an essay on the emergence of pastoral psychology.

Mace, David R. "The Sexual Revolution: Its Impact on Pastoral Care and Counseling." JOURNAL OF PASTORAL CARE 25 (1971): 220-32.

May, Rollo. THE ART OF COUNSELING. Nashville: Cokesbury Press, 1939. 247 p.

Meany, J.O. "Psychological Struggle with Dependency in Current Catholicism." JOURNAL OF PASTORAL COUNSELING 7, no. 2 (1972-73): 17-23.

Moser, Leslie E. COUNSELING: A MODERN EMPHASIS IN RELIGION. Englewood Cliffs, N.J.: Prentice-Hall, 1962. 354 p.

Murray, James A. Cameron. AN INTRODUCTION TO A CHRISTIAN PSYCHO-THERAPY. New York: Charles Scribner's Sons, 1938. xii, 279 p.

Nameche, J.F. "The Minister and His Counselee." In THE MINISTRY AND MENTAL HEALTH, pp. 221-51. Edited by Hans Hofmann. New York: Association Press, 1960.

Nouwen, Henri J.M. INTIMACY: PASTORAL PSYCHOLOGICAL ESSAYS. Notre Dame, Ind.: Fides Publishers, 1969. 164 p.

   A priest-psychologist contrasts religion as protective magic with a
   mature internalized religious attitude.

Oates, Wayne E [dward]. "Religious Attitudes and Pastoral Counseling." In SEXUAL BEHAVIORS: SOCIAL, CLINICAL, AND LEGAL ASPECTS, pp. 227-38. Edited by H.L. Resnik and M.E. Wolfgang. Boston: Little, Brown and Co., 1972.

O'Connell, Walter E. "Frankl, Adler and Spirituality." JOURNAL OF RELIGION AND HEALTH 11 (April 1972): 134-38.

O'Flaherty, Vincent, S.J. HOW TO CURE SCRUPLES. Milwaukee: Bruce Publishers, 1966. 108 p.

Olsen, Peder. PASTORAL CARE AND PSYCHOTHERAPY: A STUDY IN CO-OPERATION BETWEEN PHYSICIAN AND PASTOR. Translated by H.E. Jorgensen. Minneapolis: Augsburg Publishing House, 1961. xii, 144 p.

Pacella, Bernard L. "A Critical Appraisal of Pastoral Counseling." AMERICAN JOURNAL OF PSYCHIATRY 123, no. 6 (1966): 646-51.

Pattison, E. Mansell. "Systems Pastoral Care." JOURNAL OF PASTORAL CARE 26 (March 1972): 2-14.

Rader, Blaine B. "Pastoral Care Functioning." MINISTRY STUDIES 3, no. 2

(1969): 18-21.

Redding, David A. THE COUCH AND THE ALTAR. Philadelphia: J.B. Lippincott Co., 1968. 125 p.

Reissner, Albert. "Religion and Psychotherapy." JOURNAL OF INDIVIDUAL PSYCHOLOGY 13 (1957): 165-70.

Schnitzer, Jeshaia. "Rabbis and Counseling." JEWISH SOCIAL STUDIES 20 (1958): 131-52.

Scholefield, H.B. "Psychoanalysis and the Parish Ministry." JOURNAL OF RELIGION AND HEALTH 2 (1963): 112-18.

> A graduate of the Philadelphia Psychoanalytic Institute describes how his educative analysis relates to his own parish ministry. Particular reference to preaching and pastoral counseling.

Smith, Mader S. "Parish Clergymen's Role Images as Pastoral Counselors." JOURNAL OF PASTORAL CARE 14 (1960): 21-28.

Stein, Calvert. PRACTICAL PASTORAL COUNSELING. Springfield, Ill.: Charles C Thomas, 1970. xiii, 283 p.

Stem, E. Mark. "Psychotherapy as an Approach to Religious Concern." JOURNAL OF CONTEMPORARY PSYCHOTHERAPY 4 (Spring 1972): 115-20.

Strunk, Orlo, Jr., and Reed, K.E. "The Learning of Empathy: A Pilot Study." JOURNAL OF PASTORAL CARE 14 (1960): 44-48.

Turner, F. Bernadette. GOD-CENTERED THERAPY: HOW TO LIVE ABUNDANTLY. New York: Speller, 1968. xvii, 277 p.

Tweedie, Donald F., Jr. THE CHRISTIAN AND THE COUCH: AN INTRODUCTION TO CHRISTIAN LOGOTHERAPY. Grand Rapids, Mich.: Baker Book House, 1963. 240 p.

Ungersma, A.J. THE SEARCH FOR MEANING. Philadelphia: The Westminster Press, 1961. 188 p.

> A discussion of Frankl's logotherapy. See Victor E. Frankl's MAN'S SEARCH FOR MEANING: AN INTRODUCTION TO LOGOTHERAPY cited above.

Vaughan, R [ichard] P [atrick]. "Counseling the Former Seminarian." CATHOLIC COUNSELOR 2 (1957): 3-5.

_____. AN INTRODUCTION TO RELIGIOUS COUNSELING: A CHRISTIAN HUMANISTIC APPROACH. Englewood Cliffs, N.J.: Prentice-Hall, 1969. 164 p.

Weigert [-Vowinkel], Edith. "The Contribution of Pastoral Counseling and Psychotherapy to Mental Health." BRITISH JOURNAL OF MEDICAL PSYCHOLOGY 33 (1960): 269-73.

West, F.E., and Kew, Clifton E. "Clergyman's Resistances to Training in Pastoral Counseling." PASTORAL COUNSELOR 1 (1963): 11-24.

Wheelis, Allen. HOW PEOPLE CHANGE. New York: Harper & Row, Publishers, 1973. 117 p.

> Considers the processes of human transformation with special notice of suffering, freedom, and modes of therapy.

Wise, Carroll A. PSYCHIATRY AND THE BIBLE. New York: Harper & Brothers, 1956. 169 p.

_____. "Pastoral Counseling and Human Values." PASTORAL COUNSELOR 6, no. 2 (1968): 1-8.

Ziegler, J.H. "Christian Vocation in Psychotherapy." BRETHREN LIFE 4 (Summer 1959): 23-30.

G:2   PSYCHOTHERAPY AND THEOLOGY

Akahoshi, S. "Unity and Union in Psychotherapy and Salvation." INTERNATIONAL REVIEW OF MISSIONS 57 (April 1968): 175-84.

Anant, Santokh S. "Integrity Therapy and the Sikh Religion." INSIGHT: QUARTERLY REVIEW OF RELIGION AND MENTAL HEALTH 5, no. 1 (1966): 22-29.

Anderson, George Christian. MAN'S RIGHT TO BE HUMAN: TO HAVE EMOTIONS WITHOUT FEAR. New York: Morrow, 1959. 191 p.

_____. YOUR RELIGION: NEUROTIC OR HEALTHY? Garden City, N.Y.: Doubleday & Co., 1970. 191 p.

Ashbrook, James B. "Paul Tillich Converses with Psychotherapists." JOURNAL OF RELIGION AND HEALTH 11 (January 1972): 40-72.

_____. "Paul Tillich in Conversation on Psychology and Theology." JOUR-

NAL OF PASTORAL CARE 26 (1972): 176-89.

Baum, Gregory. MAN BECOMING: GOD IN SECULAR LANGUAGE. New York: Herder and Herder, 1970. xiv, 285 p.

Deals with the value of psychotherapy for illuminating and clarifying religious language. Emphasizes the highly dramatic nature of everyday life, characterizing it as "a field of conflict between forces of self-destruction and powers--unexpected powers--of creativity and new life."

Beniskos, Jean M. "Theotherapy: A First Outline." REVUE DE L'UNIVERSITE D'OTTAWA 4, no. 36 (1966): 625-42.

Bonnell, George C. "Salvation and Psychotherapy." JOURNAL OF RELIGION AND HEALTH 8 (1969): 382-98.

Bonthius, Robert Harold. CHRISTIAN PATHS TO SELF-ACCEPTANCE. New York: King's Crown Press, 1948. 254 p.

An informed study in the mode of David Roberts and Albert Outler.

Bowers, Margaretta K. "Protestantism and Its Therapeutic Implications." ANNALS OF PSYCHOTHERAPY 1, no. 2 (1959): 6-14.

Braaten, Leif J. "Psychology: Twentieth Century Religion? A Psychologist's View." PASTORAL PSYCHOLOGY 13 (December 1962): 27-34.

Braceland, Francis J., ed. FAITH, REASON, AND MODERN PSYCHIATRY. New York: P.J. Kenedy & Sons, 1955. xv, 310 p.

See annotation in section G:6.

Browning, Don S. "A Doctrine of the Atonement Informed by the Psychotherapeutic Process." JOURNAL OF PASTORAL CARE 17 (1963): 136-47.

_____. ATONEMENT AND PSYCHOTHERAPY. Philadelphia: The Westminster Press, 1966. 288 p.

A study of the values of utilizing insights derived from psychotherapy to evaluate and enrich theology. Explores the theories of atonement represented by Irenaeus, Anselm, and Bushnell in light of Rogers' notion of unconditional positive regard.

_____. "Analogy, Symbol, and Pastoral Theology in Tillich's Thought." PASTORAL PSYCHOLOGY 19 (February 1968): 41-54.

_____. "Rogers, Perls, and Schutz in Theological and Philosophical Perspective." DIALOGUE 13 (Spring 1974): 104-9.

Bryant, C. "Psychosynthesis and the Christian Spiritual Tradition." JOURNAL OF PASTORAL COUNSELING 7, no. 2 (1972-73): 48-55.

Burhoe, R.W. "Bridging the Gap between Psychiatry and Theology." JOURNAL OF RELIGION AND HEALTH 7 (July 1968): 215-26.

Collins, Gary R. SEARCH FOR REALITY: PSYCHOLOGY AND THE CHRISTIAN. Wheaton, Ill.: Key Press, 1969. 207 p.

_____. THE CHRISTIAN PSYCHOLOGY OF PAUL TOURNIER. Grand Rapids, Mich.: Baker Book House, 1973. 222 p.

Curran, Charles A. "What Can Man Believe In?" JOURNAL OF RELIGION AND HEALTH 11 (1972): 7-39.

Dewart, J. "Some Theological Aspects in the Writings of R.D. Laing." STUDIES IN RELIGION, SCIENCES RELIGIEUSES 3 (Summer 1973): 63-70.

Duncombe, David C. THE SHAPE OF THE CHRISTIAN LIFE. New York: Abingdon Press, 1969. 208 p.

　　Advocates a "behavioral theology" which combines theological perspectives and experimental psychology. Certain behaviors are considered most compatible with Christian doctrine which encourages accurate self-knowledge, accurate perceptions of the outside world, honest expression, and adequate response to situations.

Ebeling, G. "Lebensangst und Glaubensanfectung: Erwagungen zum Verhaltnis von Psychotherapie und Theologie." ZEITSCHRIFT FUR THEOLOGIE UND KIRCHE 70, no. 1 (1973): 77-100.

Glen, S. "Psychological Therapy and Christian Salvation." THEOLOGY TODAY 14 (January 1958): 491-505.

Greene, Thayer A. "The Dream: Clinical Aid and Theological Catalyst." UNION SEMINARY QUARTERLY REVIEW 24, no. 2 (1969): 171-80.

Healer, Carl T. FREUD AND SAINT PAUL. Philadelphia: Dorrance and Co., 1972. xii, 55 p.

　　A short, simplistic attempt to develop a "theology of persons" for pastoral counselors.

Kaam, Adrian van. "Religious Anthropology--Religious Counseling." INSIGHT: QUARTERLY REVIEW OF RELIGION AND MENTAL HEALTH 4, no. 3 (1966): 1-7.

Lapsley, James N. SALVATION AND HEALTH: THE INTERLOCKING PRO-
CESSES OF LIFE. Philadelphia: The Westminster Press, 1972. 174 p.

> Compares notions of salvation and health from theological and psy-
> chological points of view. Utilizes process theology derived from
> A.N. Whitehead and C. Hartshorne and theories of psychotherapy
> to construct a philosophical anthropology.

Lynch, William F. IMAGES OF HOPE: IMAGINATION AS HEALER OF THE
HOPELESS. Baltimore: Helicon Press, 1965. 278 p.

> A Catholic theologian relates theology and psychotherapy by dis-
> tinguishing the privatized and absolutized wish from the public and
> mutual imagination. Points to an "incarnational drive to know and
> encounter reality."

> See other entries on hope in section E:2.

Meany, J.O. "Reflections on Thomism and Client-Centered Psychotherapy."
JOURNAL OF RELIGION AND HEALTH 9 (July 1970): 203-17.

Nouwen, Henri J.M. "Anton T. Boisen and Theology through Living Human
Documents." PASTORAL PSYCHOLOGY 19 (September 1968): 49-63.

Oden, Thomas C. "A Theologian's View of the Process of Psychotherapy."
JOURNAL OF INDIVIDUAL PSYCHOLOGY 20, no. 1 (1965): 69-78.

_____. KERYGMA AND COUNSELING. Philadelphia: The Westminster
Press, 1966. 186 p.

> Explicates the parallels between psychotherapy and the Christian
> gospel with specific reference to self-disclosure and God's revela-
> tion. Argues that the hidden assumptions of psychotherapy are
> made explicit in the Christian message.

_____. "Theology and Therapy: A New Look at Bonhoeffer." DIALOG 5
(Spring 1966): 98-111.

_____. CONTEMPORARY THEOLOGY AND PSYCHOTHERAPY. Philadelphia:
The Westminster Press, 1967. 158 p.

_____. THE STRUCTURES OF AWARENESS. Nashville: Abingdon Press,
1969. 283 p.

> An analysis of the nature of man's awareness of reality, this study
> combines psychological and theological perspectives to elucidate
> the search for salvation.

_____. GAME FREE: THE MEANING OF INTIMACY. New York: Harper

& Row, Publishers, 1974. 163 p.

> A theological critique of transactional-analysis therapy and a psychological-theological explication of the nature of intimacy.

Oglesby, William B., Jr., ed. THE NEW SHAPE OF PASTORAL THEOLOGY. Nashville: Abingdon Press, 1969. 383 p.

> A collection of papers on pastoral theology, pastoral psychology, and pastoral care by students and onetime associates of Seward Hiltner.

Outler, Albert Cook. PSYCHOTHERAPY AND THE CHRISTIAN MESSAGE. New York: Harper & Brothers, 1954. 254 p.

> A pioneer study in the relation of psychotherapy and Christian doctrine. See David E. Roberts' PSYCHOTHERAPY AND A CHRISTIAN VIEW OF MAN cited below.

Paddock, F. "A Philosophical Investigation of the Relation between Psychoanalysis and Theology." JOURNAL OF PASTORAL CARE 13 (1959): 38-41.

Powell, L. Mack. "Religious Views before and after Psychotherapy." PASTORAL COUNSELOR 1, no. 2 (1963): 31-38.

Rader, Blaine B. "Koinonia and the Therapeutic Relationship." PASTORAL PSYCHOLOGY 21 (October 1970): 39-44.

Reeves, Robert B., Jr. "Healing and Salvation: Some Research and Its Implications." UNION SEMINARY QUARTERLY REVIEW 24 (1969-70): 187-98.

Roberts, David E. PSYCHOTHERAPY AND A CHRISTIAN VIEW OF MAN. New York: Charles Scribner's Sons, 1950. xiv, 161 p.

> With Albert C. Outler's PSYCHOTHERAPY AND THE CHRISTIAN MESSAGE, this is one of the pioneer efforts to reconcile theology and psychotherapeutic ideas. See above.

Rudin, Josef. PSYCHOTHERAPY AND RELIGION. Translated by Elisabeth Reinecke and Paul C. Bailey. Notre Dame, Ind.: University of Notre Dame Press, 1958. xiii, 244 p.

> Originally published in German in 1960, a Catholic thinker discusses theological perspectives on religious and psychotherapeutic experiences and thought, drawing particularly on Jung.

Spiegelman, J. Marvin. "Notes from the Underground: A View of Love and Religion from a Psychotherapist's Cave." SPRING: AN ANNUAL OF ARCHETYPAL PSYCHOLOGY AND JUNGIAN THOUGHT, 1970, pp. 196-211.

Stein, Edward V. "Psychiatric Elements in Theological Formulations." PAS-
TORAL COUNSELOR 3, no. 1 (1965): 9-19.

_____. GUILT: THEORY AND THERAPY. Philadelphia: The Westminster
Press, 1968. 238 p.

> A study of the psychoanalytic view of the nature and function of
> guilt. Summarizes the views of Freud, Hartmann, Fromm, and
> others, and stresses the positive contribution of the Christian gos-
> pel to the relief of guilt.

Stern, E. Mark, and Marino, Bert G. PSYCHOTHEOLOGY. New York:
Newman Press, 1970. 146 p.

> See annotation in section E:2.

Stern, Karl. THE THIRD REVOLUTION: A STUDY OF PSYCHIATRY AND
RELIGION. New York: Harcourt, Brace, 1954. 306 p.

> A thoughtful work by a Catholic psychiatrist and convert from
> Judaism, relating psychoanalysis to other sciences and philosophies,
> and attempting to separate its antireligious bias from those of its
> discoveries that can be valuable to the faithful.

Taylor, W.S. "Theological Models for Therapy." SCOTTISH JOURNAL OF
THEOLOGY 21 (June 1968): 187-98.

Terruwe, A.A.A. PSYCHOPATHIC PERSONALITY AND NEUROSIS. New York:
P.J. Kenedy & Sons, 1958. 178 p.

> A Thomistic critique of psychoanalytic views of pathology.

Tharp, Louis. "Mowrer's 'Integrity Therapy': A Psychological and a Protestant
Theological Critique." INSIGHT: A QUARTERLY REVIEW OF RELIGION AND
MENTAL HEALTH 5, no. 4 (1967): 31-44.

Thilo, Hans-Joachim. "Sin and Psychotherapy." RELIGION IN LIFE 30 (1960-
61): 243-55.

_____. UNFRAGMENTED MAN: A STUDY IN PASTORAL PSYCHOLOGY.
Translated by Arthur J. Seegers. Minneapolis: Augsburg Publishing House,
1964. 208 p.

Thurneysen, Eduard. A THEOLOGY OF PASTORAL CARE. Translated by Jack
A. Worthington and Thomas Wieser. Richmond, Va.: John Knox Press, 1962.
343 p.

> A Swiss pastor emphasizes the theological side of the religion-psy-
> chology dialogue. He cautions against enthusiasm in counseling,
> which he characterizes as a conversation that makes possible the
> forgiveness of sins under the mystery of grace.

Tournier, Paul. GUILT AND GRACE; A PSYCHOLOGICAL STUDY. New York: Harper & Brothers, 1962. 224 p.

   A Swiss physician discusses neurotic and constitutional guilt, and nonjudgmental psychotherapy and grace as the solutions respectively to each. Stresses phenomenological questions and theological answers.

Tournier, Paul, et al. ARE YOU NOBODY? Richmond, Va.: John Knox Press, 1966. 77 p.

   Brief essays by Tournier, Victor Frankl, the theologian Helmut Thielicke, and others.

Tweedie, Donald F., Jr. LOGOTHERAPY AND THE CHRISTIAN FAITH; AN EVALUATION OF FRANKL'S EXISTENTIAL APPROACH TO PSYCHOTHERAPY. Grand Rapids, Mich.: Baker Book House, 1961. 183 p.

Wall, Ernest A. "The Kerygma's Psychology and Human Distress." JOURNAL OF PSYCHOLOGY AND THEOLOGY 1 (October 1973): 48-56.

Walters, Orville S. "Metaphysics, Religion, and Psychotherapy." JOURNAL OF PASTORAL CARE 14 (Summer 1960): 78-91. Previously published in JOURNAL OF COUNSELING PSYCHOLOGY 5 (1958): 243-52.

_____. "Psychodynamics and the Holy Spirit." JOURNAL OF RELIGION AND HEALTH 10 (July 1971): 246-55.

Weatherhead, Leslie Dixon. PSYCHOLOGY, RELIGION, AND HEALING. London: Hodder and Stoughton, 1951. 544 p.

   See annotation in section G:8.

Weatherhead, Leslie Dixon, et al. "Christian Faith and Psychotherapy." RELIGION IN LIFE 21 (1952): 483-512.

White, Victor. SOUL AND PSYCHE: AN ENQUIRY INTO THE RELATIONSHIP OF PSYCHOTHERAPY AND RELIGION. London: Collins and Harvill Press, 1958. 312 p.

   White, a Catholic priest, draws attention to the common ground of religion and psychotherapy. He uses the analytic psychology of Jung as the basis for creative interaction of therapy and theology.

Whitlock, Glenn E. "Personality, Psychotherapy, and Christian Salvation." JOURNAL OF RELIGION AND HEALTH 7 (1958): 175-81.

Wilson, Thomas J. "Theological Assimilation of Rogerian Therapy." INSIGHT:

QUARTERLY REVIEW OF RELIGION AND MENTAL HEALTH 5, no. 4 (1967): 18-30.

G:3 CONCEPTS OF SELF AND PERSONAL GROWTH

Academy of Religion and Mental Health. RELIGION IN THE DEVELOPING PERSONALITY. Proceedings of the Second Academy Symposium, 1958. New York: New York University Press, 1960. 110 p.

> Synopses of discussions on the role of religion in various stages of the development of the personality, including childhood, adolescence, adulthood, and the aging.

Adkins, Leslie John. "The Independent Self: Link between Science and Religion." PASTORAL PSYCHOLOGY 11 (April 1960): 44-52.

Adler, Alfred. SUPERIORITY AND SOCIAL INTEREST: A COLLECTION OF LATER WRITINGS. Evanston, III.: Northwestern University Press, 1964. xix, 432 p.

> A collection of Adler's papers with particular emphasis on man's "striving for completion" and self-created "goals of perfection."

Allport, Gordon W. THE INDIVIDUAL AND HIS RELIGION, A PSYCHOLOGICAL INTERPRETATION. New York: Macmillan, 1950. xi, 147 p.

> A study of the nature and function of religion in the development of a normal and productive personality. Religion is viewed as a positive contribution to the development of a healthy maturity and conscience. Also explores the nature of faith and doubt. Also listed in section A:2.

_____. THE PERSON IN PSYCHOLOGY: SELECTED ESSAYS. Boston: Beacon Press, 1968. 440 p.

> A collection of essays originally published in the 1960s, includes items of interest to the psychologist of religion, e.g., a short piece on William James, a section on prejudice and religion, and a new formulation of the author's distinction between idiographic and nomothetic types of research.

Arasteh, A. Reza. FINAL INTEGRATION IN THE ADULT PERSONALITY. Leiden: E.J. Brill, 1965. xvii, 404 p.

> A psychologist who is also a devotee of Sufism points out and attempts to fill a gap in most Western forms of psychology. Criticizing Erikson and Sullivan, while admiring Maslow, Rogers, and Jung, he discusses mystical experience and wisdom as a transcultural but human goal beyond social-psychological maturity.

Arnold, Magda D. "Psychology and the Image of Man." RELIGION EDUCA-

TION 54 (1959): 30-36.

Babin, P. CRISIS OF FAITH: THE RELIGIOUS PSYCHOLOGY OF ADOLES-CENCE. New York: Herder and Herder, 1963. 251 p.

Baker, Oren Huling. HUMAN NATURE UNDER GOD: OR, ADVENTURE OF PERSONALITY. New York: Association Press, 1958. 316 p.

Barkman, Paul Friesen. MAN IN CONFLICT. Grand Rapids: Zondervan Publishing House, 1965. 189 p.

Bartemeier, Leo H. "Healthy and Unhealthy Patterns of Religious Behavior." JOURNAL OF RELIGION AND HEALTH 4 (1965): 309-14.

Berthold, Fred, Jr. THE FEAR OF GOD: THE ROLE OF ANXIETY IN CONTEM-PORARY THOUGHT. New York: Harper & Brothers, 1959. 158 p.

> A study of anxiety as a religious category in the thought of Teresa of Avila, Luther, Freud, Kierkegaard, Heidegger, and Barth. De-lineates the constructive aspects of anxiety and demonstrates the importance of anxiety for personal growth as well as theological considerations of the nature of man.

Bertocci, Peter H. SEX, LOVE AND THE PERSON. New York: Sheed & Ward, 1967. xvi, 173 p.

Blake, John A. "Faith as a Basic Personality Need." PASTORAL PSYCHOLO-GY 13 (June 1962): 43-47.

Brown, William [Adams]. PERSONALITY AND RELIGION. London: University of London Press, 1946. 295 p.

Buss, Martin J. "Self-Theory and Theology." JOURNAL OF RELIGION 45 (1965): 46-53.

Chauchard, Paul. LA MAITRISE DE SOI. Brussels: Charles Dessart, 1963. 226 p.

Chein, Isador. SCIENCE OF BEHAVIOR AND THE IMAGE OF MAN. New York: Basic Books, 1972. 347 p.

Chiang, Hung-Min, and Maslow, Abraham H., eds. THE HEALTHY PERSON-ALITY. New York: Van Nostrand Reinhold, 1969.

> A collection of articles from a humanistic psychology perspective, dealing with such topics as man's intrinsic nature, the phenomenol-

ogy of experience, and the concept of normality.

Clark, Walter Houston. "The Psychology of Religion and the Understanding of Man in Religious Education." RELIGIOUS EDUCATION 54 (1959): 18-23.

_____. "A Religious Approach to the Concept of the Self." ANNALS OF THE NEW YORK ACADEMY OF SCIENCES 96, no. 3 (1962): 831-42.

Clippinger, J.A. "Toward a Human Psychology of Personality." JOURNAL OF RELIGION AND HEALTH 12 (July 1973): 241-58.

Cole, J. Preston. THE PROBLEMATIC SELF IN KIERKEGAARD AND FREUD. New Haven, Conn.: Yale University Press, 1971. 244 p.

Colston, Lowell G., and Johnson, Paul E. PERSONALITY AND CHRISTIAN FAITH. New York: Abingdon Press, 1973. 240 p.
> Argues that alienation is the central problem of modern man and that the Christian gospel is the most powerful means by which alienation can be overcome and a healthy personality developed.

Counts, William M. "The Nature of Man and the Christian's Self-Esteem." JOURNAL OF PSYCHOLOGY AND THEOLOGY 1 (January 1973): 38-44.

Cousins, Ewert. "Psychotherapy and Spiritual Growth." PASTORAL COUN-SELOR 7 (1969): 3-9.

Dare, Christopher. "An Aspect of the Ego Psychology of Religion." BRITISH JOURNAL OF MEDICAL PSYCHOLOGY 42 (1969): 335-40.

Drapela, V.J. "Personality Adjustment and Religious Growth." JOURNAL OF RELIGION AND HEALTH 8 (January 1969): 87-97.

Droege, T.A. "Developmental View of Faith." JOURNAL OF RELIGION AND HEALTH 11 (October 1972): 313-28.

Edinger, Edward F. EGO AND ARCHETYPE: INDIVIDUATION AND THE RELIGIOUS FUNCTION OF THE PSYCHE. New York: G.P. Putnam's Sons, 1972. xv, 304 p.

Ellenberger, Henri F. "The Concept of Creative Illness." PSYCHOANALYTIC REVIEW 55 (1968): 442-56.

Erb, Everett D., and Hooker, Douglas. THE PSYCHOLOGY OF THE EMERG-
ING SELF. Philadelphia: F.A. Davis Co., 1967. xiii, 289 p.

Adresses the problem of growth vs. deficit models of man, with
particular reliance on the work of Rogers, Maslow, Kelly, and
Allport.

Erickson, Richard D. "The Vulnerable Hero: Theology and the Goals of Therapy." JOURNAL OF RELIGION AND HEALTH 12 (October 1973): 328-36.

Felix, Robert H. "Religion and the Healthy Personality." PASTORAL PSYCHOL-
OGY 15 (November 1964): 9-16.

Fingarette, Herbert. THE SELF IN TRANSFORMATION: PSYCHOANALYSIS,
PHILOSOPHY, AND THE LIFE OF THE SPIRIT. New York: Basic Books, 1963.
356 p.

Written by a philosopher trained in linguistic philosophy who is
also conversant with Freudian psychology and Eastern religious systems. Through reformulations of the notions of the unconscious
and anxiety, the author traces the pilgrimage of the self to an
ultimate "selflessness" as advocated in Eastern mysticism.

Foley, Daniel Patrick. "The Psychology of a Personal Ideal, Part I." JOUR-
NAL OF RELIGION AND HEALTH 3 (1964): 309-26.

_____. "The Psychology of a Personal Ideal, Part II." JOURNAL OF RELI-
GION AND HEALTH 6 (1967): 33-45.

France, M. "Learning to Think of Oneself as a Self." JOURNAL OF PAS-
TORAL CARE 27 (June 1973): 83-93.

Frankenstein, Carl. THE ROOTS OF THE EGO: A PHENOMENOLOGY OF
DYNAMICS AND OF STRUCTURE. Baltimore: The Williams & Wilkens
Co., 1966. 286 p.

An essentially Jungian study of the ego which nonetheless draws on
a wide range of theories, including Piaget, Erikson, and Buber,
and containing a chapter on transpersonal consciousness entitled
"The Reality of the Soul."

Goldbrunner, Josef. HOLINESS IS WHOLENESS. New York: Pantheon Books,
1955. 63 p.

A Catholic Jungian deals with the issues of health and illness,
body and psyche.

_____. INDIVIDUATION: A STUDY OF THE DEPTH PSYCHOLOGY OF CARL GUSTAV JUNG. Notre Dame, Ind.: University of Notre Dame Press, 1964. xii, 204 p.

A study of continuities between Jung's interpretation of personality development and theological conceptions of the healthy personality. Stresses the role of therapy in enabling the individual to achieve the necessary clarity of perception to understand the relation of the self and God.

_____. THE DIMENSION OF FUTURE IN OUR FAITH. Translated by M. Veronica Riedl. Notre Dame, Ind.: University of Notre Dame Press, 1966. 137 p.

_____. REALIZATION: ANTHROPOLOGY OF PASTORAL CARE. Translated by P.C. Bailey and E. Reinecke. Notre Dame, Ind.: University of Notre Dame Press, 1966. 221 p.

Gordon, Chad. "Systemic Senses of Self." SOCIOLOGICAL INQUIRY 38 (1968): 161-78.

Gordon, Rosemary. "Gods and the Deintegrates." JOURNAL OF ANALYTICAL PSYCHOLOGY 8 (1963): 25-44.

Griesl, G. "On the Psychology of the Expectation of Holiness." JAHRBUCH FUR PSYCHOLOGIE, PSYCHOTHERAPIE, AND MEDIZINISCHE ANTHROPOLO-GIE 8 (1961): 47-67.

Grounds, Vernon C. "Holiness and Healthymindedness." JOURNAL OF PSY-CHOLOGY AND THEOLOGY 2 (Winter 1974): 3-11.

Guntrip, Henry. "Religion in Relation to Personal Integration." BRITISH JOUR-NAL OF MEDICAL PSYCHOLOGY 42 (1969): 323-35.

Hammond, Guyton B. MAN IN ESTRANGEMENT: PAUL TILLICH AND ERICH FROMM COMPARED. Nashville: Vanderbilt University Press, 1965. xii, 194 p.

A rigorous and detailed discussion of a theologian's and a psychologist's views on human alienation.

Hendrix, Harville. "The Power of Transformation." JOURNAL OF RELIGION AND HEALTH 10 (1971): 160-79.

Hillman, James. INSEARCH: PSYCHOLOGY AND RELIGION. New York: Charles Scribner's Sons, 1967. 126 p.

Written by a Jungian therapist and theorist, this book seeks to draw a distinction between the psyche and the soul. Hillman rejects the common tendency among psychologists and pastors to see no contrast between the psyche and soul, and thus he recognizes and explores the boundary between religion and psychology. Also listed in section A:2.

Hiltner, Seward. SELF UNDERSTANDING THROUGH PSYCHOLOGY AND RE-LIGION. New York and Nashville: Abingdon Press, 1962. xiii, 224 p.

A nontechnical work on normal human development; discusses tension, conscience, insight, socialization, and other topics.

Hiltner, Seward, and Rogers, William R. "Research on Religion and Personality Dynamics." RELIGIOUS EDUCATION 57, no. 4 (research supplement), 1962, p. 128-40.

Holt, Herbert, and Winick, Charles. "Psychiatry, Religion, and Self." PAS-TORAL PSYCHOLOGY 19 (April 1968): 35-38.

Hosinski, Thomas E. "Science, Religion, and the Self-Understanding of Man." RELIGION IN LIFE 42 (1973): 179-93.

Jacobson, N.P. "Religion and the Fragmentation of Man." JOURNAL OF RELIGION 32 (1952): 18-30.

Johnson, Paul E. "The Trend toward Dynamic Interpersonalism." RELIGION IN LIFE 35 (1966): 751-59.

Jourard, Sidney M. PERSONAL ADJUSTMENT: AN APPROACH THROUGH THE STUDY OF HEALTHY PERSONALITY. 2nd ed. New York: Macmillan, 1963. xiii, 477 p.

Discusses healthy personality symptoms and the means for achieving personal adjustment. Considers the healthy personality in light of Freud, Adler, Jung, Rank, Fromm, Sullivan, Maslow, Rogers, and other psychologists as well as existential philosophers and Zen Buddhists.

Jung, Carl G., and Hisamatsu, Shin-ichi. "On the Unconscious, the Self and the Therapy: A Dialogue." PSYCHOLOGIA: AN INTERNATIONAL JOUR-NAL OF PSYCHOLOGY IN THE ORIENT 11, nos. 1-2 (1968): 25-32.

Jung, C.G. Institute. DIE ANGST. Zurich: Rascher, 1959. 253 p.

A collection of essays on the nature of anxiety from Jungian perspectives.

Kaam, Adrian van. RELIGION AND PERSONALITY. New York: Prentice-Hall, 1964. 195 p.

A Catholic existential psychologist's reflection on modes of presence, perfection, will, and memories in character development. Emphasizes the concepts "mode of existence" and "existential project."

_____, ed. "Personality and Play." HUMANITAS 5 (1969): 5-98.

A special issue of HUMANITAS on play.

Kaam, Adrian van, and Healy, Kathleen. THE DEMON AND THE DOVE: PERSONALITY GROWTH THROUGH LITERATURE. Pittsburgh: Duquesne University Press, 1967. 308 p.

Kaplan, Abraham. "Maturity in Religion." BULLETIN OF THE PHILADELPHIA ASSOCIATION FOR PSYCHOANALYSIS 13 (1963): 101-19.

Kuenzli, Alfred E., ed. RECONSTRUCTION IN RELIGION: A SYMPOSIUM. Boston: Beacon Press, 1961. xiii, 253 p.

Essays appraising the beliefs, values, and practices that may support greater rationality, creativity, and humanism in personal conduct and social order. Articles relevant to psychology by Dreikurs, Fromm, Cantril, Snygg, and Rogers.

Kunkel, Fritz. IN SEARCH OF MATURITY: AN INQUIRY INTO PSYCHOLOGY, RELIGION, AND SELF-EDUCATION. New York: Charles Scribner's Sons, 1943. xii, 292 p.

An early attempt to construct a religious psychology through particular attention to the ego.

Laing, R.D. THE DIVIDED SELF. New York: Pantheon Books, 1969. 237 p.

This, together with the author's SELF AND OTHERS, is a significant study of the "ontological insecurity" of individuals. Employs concepts developed by existential theologians as well as psychoanalytic psychologists. (See below.)

_____. SELF AND OTHERS. New York: Random House, 1969. xiii, 169 p.

Focuses on the subjective experience of self-being, with particular stress on the concept of fantasy understood as a primordial level of experiencing of the world and the self. (See above.)

Lambourne, R.A. "Personal Reformation and Political Transformation in Pastoral Care." JOURNAL OF PASTORAL CARE 25 (1971): 182-87.

Ligon, Ernest M. THE PSYCHOLOGY OF CHRISTIAN PERSONALITY. New York: Macmillan, 1961. 393 p.

The teachings of Jesus interpreted in terms of modern psycholorical research in order to illuminate the nature of the Christian personality.

Loomis, Earl A., Jr. THE SELF IN PILGRIMAGE. New York: Harper & Brothers, 1960. 109 p.

A small but stimulating work by a psychoanalyst who was formerly on the staff of Union Theological Seminary in New York.

Lubin, Albert J. "A Feminine Moses: A Bridge between Childhood Identifications and Adult Identity." INTERNATIONAL JOURNAL OF PSYCHOANALYSIS 39 (1958): 535-46.

McClendon, James William. "Biography as Theology." CROSS CURRENTS 21 (1971): 415-31.

Recommends the use of life-stories, especially those of extraordinary religious individuals, in developing and refining theological perspectives.

McConnell, Theodore A. "Gordon Allport and the Quest for Selfhood." JOURNAL OF RELIGION AND HEALTH 8 (1969): 375-81.

_____. THE SHATTERED SELF: THE PSYCHOLOGICAL AND RELIGIOUS SEARCH FOR SELFHOOD. Philadelphia: Pilgrim Press, 1971. xiii, 109 p.

A psychological and religious discussion of major psychological thinkers, with chapters on Erikson, Allport, Fromm, Frankl, May, and Maslow. A concluding chapter notes similarities and differences in the six points of view on selfhood.

McCurdy, Harold G. PERSONALITY AND SCIENCE: A SEARCH FOR SELF-AWARENESS. Princeton, N.J.: Van Nostrand, 1965. 151 p.

The author is a psychologist with interests in humanistic psychology and the role of religion in concepts of self.

Maher, Trafford P., S.J. SELF: A MEASURELESS SEA. St. Louis: Catholic Hospital Association, 1966. 196 p.

Marchesan, Marco. "Il Cosiddetto Comportamento Religioso Immaturo e la Perversione della Religiosita." REVISTA DE PSICOLOGIA NORMAL E PATOLOGICA 12 (1966): 416-18.

Masserman, Jules H. "The Conceptual Dynamics of Person, Religion and Self." PSYCHOANALYTIC REVIEW 41 (1954): 303-29.

May, Gerald G. "The Psychodynamics of Spirituality." JOURNAL OF PASTORAL CARE 28 (June 1974): 84-91.

May, Rollo. THE SPRINGS OF CREATIVE LIVING. Nashville: Abingdon-Cokesbury, 1940. 271 p.

An early work by May which focuses on human nature and God.

_____. THE MEANING OF ANXIETY. New York: The Ronald Press Co., 1950. xv, 376 p.

An existentialist study of the nature of anxiety and its role in the formation of the self-image. Assesses theories of anxiety enunciated by Spinoza, Pascal, Kierkegaard, Freud, Jung, Adler, Mowrer, and others. Includes useful case studies.

_____. MAN'S SEARCH FOR HIMSELF. New York: W.W. Norton & Co., 1953. 239 p.

A major study of the dilemmas and possibilities of the self in the modern world. Includes chapters on anxiety and loneliness, becoming a person, freedom and inner strength, the creative conscience, courage as the virtue of maturity, and man as the transcender of time.

Meland, Bernard E. "The Self and Its Communal Good." RELIGIOUS EDUCATION 59 (1964): 363-70.

The author is a theologian with particular interests in problems of faith and culture.

Menninger, Karl, et al. THE VITAL BALANCE: THE LIFE PROCESS IN MENTAL HEALTH AND ILLNESS. New York: The Viking Press, 1963. 531 p.

A major work which addresses the view that the human organism is self-regulating, striving for a state of balance through the reconciliation of all the demands operating on and within the organism. Paul Pruyser, one of the co-authors, is prominent in the psychology of religion.

Moore, Thomas Verner. HEROIC SANCTITY AND INSANITY: AN INTRODUCTION TO THE SPIRITUAL LIFE AND MENTAL HYGIENE. New York: Grune & Stratton, 1959. 243 p.

Identifies heroic sanctity as the Christian goal of life. Extensive discussion of St. Therese of Lisieux.

Morris, Robert R. "Anxiety: Freud and Theology." JOURNAL OF RELIGION AND THEOLOGY 12 (April 1973): 189-201.

Mounier, Emmanuel. THE CHARACTER OF MAN. Translated by Cynthia Rowland. London: Rocklift, 1956. 341 p.

Written by a French psychologist, this is a study of the nature of human character with emphasis on personality and the self. Concludes with discussion of the "spiritual life within the limits of character."

Nuttin, Joseph. PSYCHOANALYSIS AND PERSONALITY: A DYNAMIC THEORY OF NORMAL PERSONALITY. New York: New American Library, 1962. 332 p.

Originally published in 1953 and written by a Belgian priest and psychologist. Concerns the integration of psychoanalysis and Christianity.

_____. LA STRUCTURE DE LA PERSONNALITIE. Paris: Presses Universitaires de France, 1965. 270 p.

Oates, Wayne E[dward]. RELIGIOUS DIMENSIONS OF PERSONALITY. New York: Association Press, 1957. 320 p.

An anthology of writings on personality, from Augustine to twentieth-century writers, in an attempt to correct psychology through Christian insights.

_____. CHRIST AND SELFHOOD. New York: Association Press, 1961. 252 p.

Meditations on encounter with Christ in worship and daily living and the resulting enrichment of the self. Discusses such topics as incarnation, sin, vocation, resurrection, and Holy Spirit.

Oden, Thomas C. "Human Potential and Evangelical Hope." DREW GATEWAY 43 (Fall 1972): 2-15. Also published in DIALOG 13 (Spring 1974): 121-28.

O'Doherty, E.F. RELIGION AND PERSONALITY PROBLEMS. London: Burns and Oates; Dublin: Clonmore and Reynolds, 1965. 240 p.

A Catholic scholar's essays on psychological approaches to such topics as adolescence, mental health, mysticism, and immortality.

Pattison, E. Mansell. "Ego Morality: An Emerging Psychotherapeutic Concept." PSYCHOANALYTIC REVIEW 55 (Summer 1968): 187-222.

Pfuetze, Paul E. THE SOCIAL SELF. Library of Current Philosophy and Religion. New York: Bookman Associates, 1954. 392 p.

A systematization and comparison of the thought of George Herbert Mead and Martin Buber, a criticism of the former through the latter, and a constructive critique of both.

Progoff, Ira. DEPTH PSYCHOLOGY AND MODERN MAN. New York: Mc-

Graw-Hill, 1959. xii, 277 p.

> Views depth psychology's contribution to a wholistic understanding
> of man. Particular emphasis on similarities between depth psychol-
> ogy and religious concepts and practices of self-transformation.

_____. THE SYMBOLIC AND THE REAL: A NEW PSYCHOLOGICAL AP-
PROACH TO THE FULLER EXPERIENCE OF PERSONAL EXISTENCE. New York:
McGraw-Hill, 1963. xv, 234 p.

> A book whose subtitle accurately describes its contents. Includes
> chapters on psyche-evoking, ways of directing the growth of the
> psyche, ways of personal growth, and the description of a program
> for the achievement of personal growth.

_____. THE DEATH AND REBIRTH OF PSYCHOLOGY. New York: Dell
Publishing Co., 1964. xii, 275 p.

> Chapters on Freud, Adler, Jung, and Rank with attention to their
> basic images of man.

Rank, Otto. PSYCHOLOGY AND THE SOUL. Translated by William D. Turner. Philadelphia: University of Pennsylvania Press, 1950. 195 p.

> Originally published in German in 1932 and written by a one-time
> disciple of Freud. Views will and immortality as central to indi-
> vidual development and cultural evolution.

Ritey, Hector J. THE HUMAN KINGDOM: A STUDY OF THE NATURE AND
DESTINY OF MAN IN THE LIGHT OF TODAY'S KNOWLEDGE. New York:
University Publishers, 1962. 498 p.

> Argues for the integration of psychiatry and religion.

Rogers, Carl R. ON BECOMING A PERSON: A THERAPIST'S VIEW OF PSY-
CHOTHERAPY. Boston: Houghton Mifflin Co., 1961. xii, 420 p.

> Contains Carl Rogers' statement on self-actualization. This book
> has been used by many students of religion as the bridge between
> psychological and religious understandings of the self.

Rolan, Alejandro. PERSONALITY TYPES AND HOLINESS. Staten Island, N.Y.:
Alba House, 1968. 384 p.

> Uses Sheldon's physiological types and develops correlary types of
> religious personality. Illustrations of the typology drawn from the
> lives of Christian saints.

Ronaldson, Agnes Sutherland. THE SPIRITUAL DIMENSION OF PERSONALITY.
Philadelphia: The Westminster Press, 1965. 156 p.

Rotenberg, Mordecai, and Diamond, Bernard L. "The Biblical Conception of

Psychopathy: The Law of the Stubborn and Rebellious Son." JOURNAL OF THE HISTORY OF THE BEHAVIORAL SCIENCES 7 (January 1971): 29-38.

Schlein, John M. "The Self-Concept in Relation to Behavior: Theoretical and Empirical Research." RELIGIOUS EDUCATION 57 (1962): 111-27.

A discussion by a Rogerian theorist and counselor.

Seifert, Harvey, and Clinebell, Howard J., Jr. PERSONAL GROWTH AND SOCIAL CHANGE: A GUIDE FOR MINISTERS AND LAYMEN AS CHANGE AGENTS. Philadelphia: The Westminster Press, 1969. 240 p.

Sevigny, Robert. L'EXPERIENCE RELIGIEUSE CHEZ LES JEUNES: UNE ETUDE PSYCHO-SOCIOLOGIQUE DE L'ACTUALIZATION DE SOI. Montreal: Les Presses de l'Universite de Montreal, 1971. xxii, 323 p.

A study of the religious experience of adolescents from the perspective of Carl Rogers' psychology of self-actualization. See Carl R. Rogers' ON BECOMING A PERSON: A THERAPIST'S VIEW OF PSYCHOTHERAPY cited above. Also listed in section D:1.

Shostrom, Everett L. MAN THE MANIPULATOR: THE INNER JOURNEY FROM MANIPULATION TO ACTUALIZATION. Nashville: Abingdon Press, 1967. 256 p.

A study in the self-actualization tradition drawing on the work of Binswanger, Fromm, Heidegger, Frankl, Tillich, Maslow, and others.

Stinnette, Charles R., Jr. FAITH, FREEDOM, AND SELFHOOD: A STUDY IN PERSONAL DYNAMICS. Greenwich, Conn.: The Seabury Press, 1959. 239 p.

A study in the pastoral theological tradition which focuses on the psychological and motivational conditions necessary for the experience of freedom and selfhood.

Strunk, Orlo, Jr. "Religion, the Id, and the Superego." JOURNAL OF BIBLE AND RELIGION 28 (July 1960): 317-28.

_____. RELIGION: A PSYCHOLOGICAL INTERPRETATION. New York: Abingdon Press, 1962. 128 p.

See section A:2 for annotation.

_____. "Insights on Human Personality Gained within Psychology in the Past Seventy-Five Years." RELIGIOUS EDUCATION 59 (1964): 283-94.

_____. "Self-Anchoring Scaling for Study of Perceptions of Religious Maturity." PERCEPTUAL AND MOTOR SKILLS 5 (1967): 471-72.

_____. "The Religious Maturities of the Adult Person." PROCEEDINGS OF THE CHRISTIAN ASSOCIATION FOR PSYCHOLOGICAL STUDIES, April 1968, pp. 4-18.

Sugerman, Shirley. "Sin and Madness: The Flight from the Self." CROSS CURRENTS 21 (1971): 129-54.

Thomas, Owen C. "Psychology and Theology on the Nature of Man." PASTORAL PSYCHOLOGY 13 (February 1962): 41-46.

Tillich, Paul. THE COURAGE TO BE. New Haven and London: Yale University Press, 1952. 197 p.

> First presented as the Yale University Terry Lectures, this study has played an influential role in the development of an existential approach to the psychology of religion. After developing a typology of anxiety, the author proceeds to discuss the conquest of anxiety by means of courage. The modes of courage are analyzed as participation, individualization, and transcendence.

_____. "What is Basic in Human Nature." AMERICAN JOURNAL OF PSYCHOANALYSIS 22 (1962): 115-21.

Tournier, Paul. THE MEANING OF PERSONS. Translated by Edwin Hudson. New York: Harper & Brothers, 1957. 238 p.

> Tournier, a physician in Switzerland, makes the case for an intimate interrelationship between a person's health and his psychological and moral well-being.

Tracy, James J. "Faith and Growth: A Psychology of Faith." INSIGHT: QUARTERLY REVIEW OF RELIGION AND MENTAL HEALTH 5, no. 3 (1967): 15-22.

Ulanov, Ann 'B [elford]. "The Self as Other." JOURNAL OF RELIGION AND HEALTH 12 (April 1973): 140-68.

Vilakazi, Absolom. "Changing Concepts of the Self and the Supernatural in Africa." ANNALS OF THE NEW YORK ACADEMY OF SCIENCE 96 (1962): 670-75.

> Discusses the effects of colonialization and missions on the self-concepts of native Africans.

White, Robert W. "The Concept of Healthy Personality: What Do We Really Mean?" COUNSELING PSYCHOLOGIST 4, no. 2 (1973): 3-12.

> A useful discussion by a psychologist often identified with psychoanalytic ego psychology.

Williams, C.G. "Selflessness in the Pattern of Salvation." RELIGIOUS
STUDIES 7 (1971): 153-68.

G:4 VALUES IN PSYCHOTHERAPY

Academy of Religion and Mental Health. MORAL VALUES IN PSYCHOANALY-
SIS. Proceedings of the Sixth Academy Symposium. New York: 1965. 131 p.

Arbuckle, Dugald S. "Values, Ethics, and Religion in Counseling." NATION-
AL CATHOLIC GUIDANCE CONFERENCE JOURNAL 13 (1968): 5-16.

Baruk, Henri. "Les Fondements de la psychologie medicale." ANNALES MED-
ICO-PSYCHOLOGIQUES 2 (1969): 244-47.

> Advocates biblical values for rejuvenating the practice of the medi-
> cal psychologist.

Buhler, Charlotte, ed. VALUES IN PSYCHOTHERAPY. New York: Free Press
of Glencoe, 1962. 251 p.

> Arguing that the absence of valuing in psychotherapy is unnatural,
> the authors advocate explicit openness about the values employed
> in treatment, with particular stress on those values which contribute
> to creative self-expansion and the establishment of internal order.

Chung, Chang Y. "Differences of the Ego, As Demanded in Psychotherapy, in
the East and West." PSYCHOLOGIA: AN INTERNATIONAL JOURNAL OF
PSYCHOLOGY IN THE ORIENT 12 (1969): 55-58.

Curran, Charles A. RELIGIOUS VALUES IN COUNSELING AND PSYCHO-
THERAPY. New York: Sheed & Ward, 1969. 398 p.

Deed, Martha. "Attitutdes of Four Religiously-Oriented Psychotherapists." PAS-
TORAL PSYCHOLOGY 20 (1969): 39-44.

> Compares C. Jung, F. Kunkel, C. Rogers, and R. Murphy.

Ellis, Albert, REASON AND EMOTION IN PSYCHOTHERAPY. New York:
Lyle Stuart, 1962. 442 p.

> Argues for rational therapy on the grounds that individuals want to
> replace irrational thoughts, emotions, and behaviors with rational
> and logical responses. Ellis contends that this form of therapy is
> rooted in principles developed by early Greek and Roman Stoic
> philosophers as well as by various Taoist and Buddhist thinkers.

Halmos, Paul. THE FAITH OF THE COUNSELLORS: A STUDY IN THE THEO-

RY AND PRACTICE OF SOCIAL CASE WORK AND PSYCHOTHERAPY. New York: Schocken Books, 1966. 220 p.

> A British sociologist emphasizes the importance of the counsellor's own faith in making him an effective healer.

Hora, Thomas. "Psychotherapy, Existence, and Religion." PSYCHOANALYSIS AND THE PSYCHOANALYTIC REVIEW 46 (Summer 1959): 91-98.

Johnson, Paul E. "The Faith of a Psychologist." PASTORAL PSYCHOLOGY 21 (October 1970): 33-38.

_____, ed. HEALER OF THE MIND: A PSYCHIATRIST'S SEARCH FOR FAITH. Nashville: Abingdon Press, 1972. 270 p.

> Brief spiritual autobiographies of ten psychotherapists, some of whom have had theological training in addition to medical and psychiatric educations.

Kagan, Henry E. "Psychotherapy as a Religious Value." JOURNAL OF COUNSELING PSYCHOLOGY 6 (1959): 263-66.

Kanoti, George A. "Ethical Implications in Psychotherapy." JOURNAL OF RELIGION AND HEALTH 10 (1971): 180-91.

Knight, James A. "Calvinism and Psychoanalysis: A Comparative Study." PASTORAL PSYCHOLOGY 14 (December 1963): 10-17.

Levy-Suhl, Max. "The Role of Ethics and Religion in Psycho-Analytic Theory and Therapy." INTERNATIONAL JOURNAL OF PSYCHOANALYSIS 27 (1946): 110-19.

London, Perry. THE MODES AND MORALS OF PSYCHOTHERAPY. New York: Holt, Rinehart and Winston, 1964. 278 p.

> Argues that "insight" therapy avoids the moral implications of the behavior of its patients, and recommends "action" therapy as a corrective.

Lorand, Sandor. "Psychoanalytic Therapy of Religious Devotees." INTERNATIONAL JOURNAL OF PSYCHOANALYSIS 43 (1962): 50-58.

McClelland, David C. "Religious Overtones in Psychoanalysis." PRINCETON SEMINARY BULLETIN 52 (January 1959): 15-32. Also published in THEOLOGY TODAY 16 (April 1959): 40-64.

Mann, Kenneth W. "Religious Factors and Values in Counseling: Their Relationship to Ego Organization." JOURNAL OF COUNSELING PSYCHOLOGY 6 (1959): 259-62.

Marx, John H., and Spray, S. Lee. "Religious Biographies and Professional Characteristics of Psychotherapists." JOURNAL OF HEALTH AND SOCIAL BE-HAVIOR 10 (1969): 275-88.

May, Rollo. "The Healing Power of Symbols." PASTORAL PSYCHOLOGY 11 (November 1960): 37-49.

_____. "Humanism and Psychotherapy." PASTORAL PSYCHOLOGY 19 (April 1968): 11-17.

Meehl, Paul E. "Some Technical and Axiological Problems in the Therapeutic Handling of Religious and Valuational Material." JOURNAL OF COUNSELING PSYCHOLOGY 6 (1959): 255-59.

Meng, Heinrich. "Psychoanalysis, Ethics and Worldly Care of the Soul." AMERICAN IMAGO 13 (1956): 335-46.

Miller, William Robert. "Dynamics of Reconciliation." PASTORAL PSYCHOL-OGY 18 (October 1967): 25-32.

Murphy, Carol. "Conscience and Psychotherapy." JOURNAL OF PASTORAL CARE 16 (1962): 81-94.

Nishijima, Y. "On the Problems of Theories of Psychotherapy and Counseling." PSYCHOLOGIA 7 (1964): 55-59.

Olsen, LeRoy C. "Religious Values and Counselor Fantasies." JOURNAL OF GENERAL PSYCHOLOGY 74 (1966): 81-88.

Pattison, E. Mansell. "Social and Psychological Aspects of Religion in Psycho-therapy." JOURNAL OF NERVOUS AND MENTAL DISEASE 141, no. 5 (1965): 586-97. Also published in INSIGHT: QUARTERLY REVIEW OF RELI-GION AND MENTAL HEALTH 5, no. 2 (1966): 27-35.

Perls, Frederick, et al. GESTALT THERAPY. New York: Delta Books, 1965. 470 p.

> Originally published in 1951, this book develops a theory of thera-py based on Gestalt psychology stressing the notion of personal wholeness.

Salzman, Leon. "Morality of Psychoanalysis." PASTORAL PSYCHOLOGY 13 (March 1962): 24-29.

Segal, Stanley J. "The Role of the Counselor's Religious Values in Counseling." JOURNAL OF COUNSELING PSYCHOLOGY 6 (1959): 270-74.

Sequin, Carlos Albertos. LOVE AND PSYCHOTHERAPY: THE PSYCHOTHERA-PEUTIC EROS. New York: Libra, 1965. xvi, 138 p.

Stahlin, R. "Psychotherapie und Religion." PRAXIS DER KINDERPSYCHOLO-GIE UND KINDERPSYCHIATRIE 15, no. 6 (1966): 225-32.

Steinzor, Bernard. THE HEALING PARTNERSHIP: THE PATIENT AS COL-LEAGUE IN PSYCHOTHERAPY. New York: Harper & Row, Publishers, 1967. 264 p.

A clinical psychologist and occasional lecturer in psychiatry and religion at Union Theological Seminary in New York, the author views the patient as equal partner with the therapist in psychotherapy.

Szasz, Thomas E. THE ETHICS OF PSYCHOANALYSIS: THE THEORY AND METHOD OF AUTONOMOUS PSYCHOTHERAPY. New York: Basic Books, 1965. xii, 226 p.

Twerski, Abraham J. "Psychotherapy and Religion." PENNSYLVANIA PSY-CHIATRIC QUARTERLY 4, no. 1 (1964): 31-34.

Vaughan, Richard P[atrick]. "Religious Belief, Values, and Psychotherapy." JOURNAL OF RELIGION AND HEALTH 2 (1963): 198-209.

Walters, Orville S. "Metaphysics, Religion and Psychotherapy." JOURNAL OF PASTORAL CARE 14 (Summer 1960): 78-91. Previously published in JOUR-NAL OF COUNSELING PSYCHOLOGY 5 (1958): 243-52.

Weisman, Avery D. THE EXISTENTIAL CORE OF PSYCHOANALYSIS: REALITY SENSE AND RESPONSIBILITY. Boston: Litte, Brown and Co., 1965. xii, 268 p.

A psychoanalyst attempts to incorporate into Freudian theory an existential concern for concrete human experiencing. Distinguishes the "sense of reality" of concrete experiencing from "reality testing."

G:5 RELIGION AND GROUP DYNAMICS

Ashbrook, James B. "The Small Group as an Instrument in Personal Growth and Organizational Change." JOURNAL OF PASTORAL CARE 24 (September 1970): 178-92.

Back, Kurt W. BEYOND WORDS: THE STORY OF SENSITIVITY TRAINING

AND THE ENCOUNTER MOVEMENT. New York: Russell Sage Foundation, 1972. xii, 266 p.

An interpretation of the small group movement as basically religious. The author is a sociologist.

Bobroff, Alvin J. "Religious Psychodrama." GROUP PSYCHOTHERAPY 16, nos. 1-2 (1963): 36-38.

Burns, George W. "Religious Influences on Behavior of the Group Therapist." PSYCHOLOGICAL REPORTS 31 (October 1972): 638.

Chase, P., and Farnham, B. "A Report on Religious Psychodrama." GROUP PSYCHOTHERAPY 18 (1965): 177-90.

Christopher, James A., and Willits, Robin D. "Using the Behavioral Sciences in Church Committees." PASTORAL PSYCHOLOGY 23 (1972): 41-46.

Clayton, G. Maxwell. "Sociodrama in a Chruch Group." GROUP PSYCHO-THERAPY AND PSYCHODRAMA 24, no. 3-4 (1971): 97-100.

Clinebell, Howard J., Jr. THE PEOPLE DYNAMIC: CHANGING SELF AND SOCIETY THROUGH GROWTH GROUPS. New York: Harper & Row, Publishers, 1972. 176 p.

A consideration of the contribution of various groups (youth, singles, other school and church organizations) to personal growth.

Goffman, Erving. ENCOUNTERS: TWO STUDIES IN THE SOCIOLOGY OF INTERACTION. Indianapolis: The Bobbs-Merrill Co., 1961. 152 p.

Two long essays concerned with encounters or "focussed gatherings." Particular emphasis on those considerations (status, sex, physical handicaps, anxieties) which may interfere with the stated goals of the group.

Hill, Wayne. "Some Aspects of Group Psychotherapy and Psychodrama Used in a Modern Religious Cult." GROUP PSYCHOTHERAPY 21 (December 1968): 214-18.

Holt, Herbert, and Winick, Charles. "Group Psychotherapeutic Experiences with Clergymen." JOURNAL OF RELIGION AND HEALTH 1 (1962): 113-26.

Howe, Reuel L. MAN'S NEED AND GOD'S ACTION. Greenwich, Conn.: The Seabury Press, 1953. xiii, 159 p.

Emphasizes the need for relationships and the Christian affirmation of same.

_____. THE MIRACLE OF DIALOGUE. Greenwich, Conn.: The Seabury Press, 1963. 154 p.

Kidorf, Irwin W. "The Shiva: A Form of Group Psychotherapy." JOURNAL OF RELIGION AND HEALTH 5, no. 1 (1966): 43-46.

Lyon, W.H., and Riggs, M.D. "An Experience of Group Psychotherapy for the Parish Minister: I. A Process of Selection and Motivation." JOURNAL OF PASTORAL CARE 15 (1961): 172-73.

> This, and the study which follows, concerns the group psychotherapeutic situation in which ministers are a part of the group.

_____. "An Experience of Group Psychotherapy for the Parish Minister: II. The Experience Itself--and a Look to the Future." JOURNAL OF PASTORAL CARE 18 (1964): 166-69.

Meissner, William W. GROUP DYNAMICS IN THE RELIGIOUS LIFE. Notre Dame, Ind.: University of Notre Dame Press, 1965. xii, 188 p.

> Using findings of research on group dynamics, this study provides insights into the problems and possibilities of group life in various religious settings, especially in Roman Catholic orders.

Mowrer, O. Hobart. THE NEW GROUP THERAPY. Princeton, N.J.: D. Van Nostrand, 1964. 262 p.

> Noting that the church and its ministers have abandoned their roles as upholders of morality, Mowrer points to the usefulness of group therapy in reinforcing moral sanctions.

_____. "Is the Small-Groups Movement a Religious Revolution?" PASTORAL PSYCHOLOGY 23 (March 1972): 19-22.

Oden, Thomas C. THE INTENSIVE GROUP EXPERIENCE: THE NEW PIETISM. Philadelphia: The Westminster Press, 1972. 189 p.

> Contends that the contemporary small group movement is the secular equivalent of the early Christian and Jewish pietism which encouraged intimacy, trust, and confession.

_____. "The New Pietism." JOURNAL OF HUMANISTIC PSYCHOLOGY 12 (1972): 24-41.

> Compares contemporary encounter groups with antecedent Protestant and Jewish pietistic movements.

Pasework, R.A., et al. "Patients' Perceptions of Clergy as Group Psychotherapists." PASTORAL COUNSELOR 7, no. 2 (1969): 18-19.

Peterson, N.L. "Group Dynamics Found in Scriptures." GROUP PSYCHO-THERAPY 15, no. 2 (1962): 126-28.

Pompilo, Peter T., and Krebs, Richard. "A Time-Limited Group Experience with a Religious Teaching Order." JOURNAL OF RELIGION AND HEALTH 11 (1972): 139-52.

Reid, Clyde. GROUPS ALIVE--CHURCH ALIVE. New York: Harper & Row, Publishers, 1969. 126 p.

> Essentially a guidebook for ministers in the effective use of intensive small groups in the church.

Seda, Eduardo. "Spiritualism and Psychodrama." REVISTA INTERAMERICANA DE PSICOLOGIA 2 (1968): 189-96.

Shulman, Bernard H. "The Ten Commandments and Insights from Group Psycho-therapy." JOURNAL OF RELIGION AND HEALTH 12 (October 1973): 354-66.

Slater, Philip E. MICROCOSM: STRUCTURAL, PSYCHOLOGICAL AND RELI-GIOUS EVOLUTION IN GROUPS. New York: John Wiley & Sons, 1966. xii, 276 p.

> Describes the emergence and function of fundamental religious sym-bolism in small training groups; extends this, via Freud and socio-logical role theory, to individuals and groups of all sizes. An important study in the relation of religion and group processes.

Southard, Samuel. "How Sensible is Sensitivity Training?" RELIGION IN LIFE 42 (1973): 224-34.

Spehn, Mel R. "The Small Group Religion." PASTORAL PSYCHOLOGY 23 (January 1972): 50-58.

Stinnette, Charles R. ANXIETY AND FAITH: TOWARD RESOLVING ANXIETY IN CHRISTIAN COMMUNITY. Greenwich, Conn.: The Seabury Press, 1955. 209 p.

> Contends that anxiety can be overcome not by the solitary individ-ual but by a community of people who are recipients of the grace of God.

Willeford, W. "Group Psychotherapy and Symbol Formation." JOURNAL OF ANALYTIC PSYCHOLOGY 12 (1967): 137-60.

G:6   RELIGION AND MENTAL HEALTH

Academy of Religion and Mental Health. RELIGION, SCIENCE AND MENTAL HEALTH. (Proceedings of the First Academy Symposium, 1957.) New York:

New York University Press, 1959. 107 p.

> Synopses of discussions on the contributions and responsibilities of
> the various behavioral sciences (psychology, sociology, cultural
> anthropology, and psychiatry) in the study of the relation of reli-
> gion and mental health.

_____. RELIGION, CULTURE, AND MENTAL HEALTH. (Proceedings of the
Third Academy Symposium, 1959.) New York: New York University Press,
1961. 157 p.

> Includes synopses of presentations and discussions on religion and
> mental health from the perspectives of sociology, anthropology,
> and social psychiatry.

_____. THE PLACE OF VALUE SYSTEMS IN MEDICAL EDUCATION. (Pro-
ceedings of the Fourth Academy Symposium, 1960.) New York: 1961. 218 p.

> Includes synopses of presentations and discussions on the importance
> of ethical values and their communication in medical education.

_____. RESEARCH IN RELIGION AND HEALTH. (Proceedings of the Fifth
Academy Symposium, 1961.) New York: Fordham University Press, 1963. 165 p.

> Includes synopses of presentations and discussions on the following
> topics: methods of data collection in studies of religion, religion
> and social attitudes, selection of personnel for the clergy, psycho-
> pathology in religious experience, and methodology.

Allport, Gordon W. "Behavioral Science, Religion, and Mental Health."
JOURNAL OF RELIGION AND HEALTH 2 (1963): 187-97.

Anderson, George C[hristian]. "Pastoral Psychology: The Next Twenty Years in
Relation to Mental Health." PASTORAL PSYCHOLOGY 21 (February 1970): 63-68.

Andreasen, N.J. "The Role of Religion in Depression." JOURNAL OF RELI-
GION AND HEALTH 11 (1972): 153-66.

Armstrong, Renate G., et al. "Religious Attitudes and Emotional Adjustment."
JOURNAL OF PSYCHOLOGICAL STUDIES 13, no. 1 (1962): 35-47.

Barron, Frank. CREATIVITY AND PSYCHOLOGICAL HEALTH. Princeton,
N.J.: Van Nostrand, 1963. 292 p.

> A research psychologist's collection of interrelated empirical studies
> of religious belief, psychotherapy, originality, and psychedelic
> drugs.

Becker, Russell J. "Religion and Psychological Health: In RESEARCH ON
RELIGIOUS DEVELOPMENT: A COMPREHENSIVE HANDBOOK, pp. 391-421.

Edited by Merton P. Strommen. New York: Hawthorn Books, 1971.

Belgum, David, ed. RELIGION AND MEDICINE: ESSAYS ON MEANING, VALUES AND HEALTH. Ames: Iowa State University Press, 1967. xxiii, 345 p.

A collection of twenty-two articles focusing on interprofessional concerns of clergymen, physicians, psychologists, and professors of health education. Majority of articles by clergymen with strong theological interests.

Bentz, Kenneth W. "The Clergyman's Role in Community Mental Health." JOURNAL OF RELIGION AND HEALTH 9 (1970): 7-15.

Bergman, Robert L. "Navajo Peyote Use: Its Apparent Safety." AMERICAN JOURNAL OF PSYCHIATRY 128 (1971): 695-99.

The low incidence of mental disturbances following use of peyote in religious ceremonies is attributed to the ego-strengthening context of church-beliefs and practices.

Biddle, W. Earl. INTEGRATION OF RELIGION AND PSYCHIATRY. New York: Macmillan, 1955. 171 p.

Argues that the role of the clergyman and psychiatrist are intimately related and that the insights of each should be utilized to enhance their respective practices. Includes discussion of motivation, symbolism, ethics, authority, and interpersonal relations.

Billinski, John Milton, ed. PSYCHOLOGY, PSYCHIATRY AND RELIGION. ANDOVER NEWTON BULLETIN 44 (February 1952): 1-55.

Entire issue devoted to psychology and religion. Includes essays by Gordon W. Allport on "The Individual and His Religion," Jay Hoffman on "Guilt Feelings and Psychiatry," and A.P. Guiles on "Guilt Feelings and Religion."

Birmingham, William, and Cunneen, Joseph E., eds. CROSS CURRENTS OF PSYCHIATRY AND CATHOLIC MORALITY. New York: Pantheon Books, 1964. xvi, 396 p.

A collection of eighteen essays originally published in CROSS CURRENTS and all written by Roman Catholics. Most of the essayists concern themselves with Freudian psychology.

Boisen, Anton T. "Religion and Personality Adjustment." PSYCHIATRY 5, no. 2 (1942): 209-18.

_____. THE EXPLORATION OF THE INNER WORLD. New York: Harper & Brothers, 1952. 322 p.

Originally published in 1936, this book was an early and formative contribution to religion and psychiatry dialogue. Stresses the role of religion in mental illness but emphasizes the importance of taking the religious contents and dynamics of the illness seriously.

_____. RELIGION IN CRISIS AND CUSTOM. New York: Harper & Brothers, 1955. xv, 271 p.

An application to American Protestantism of the author's theory of the potential religious growth that can follow psychosis.

_____. "Religious Experience and Psychological Conflict." AMERICAN PSYCHOLOGIST 13 (1958): 568-70.

_____. "Inspiration in the Light of Psychopathology." PASTORAL PSYCHOLOGY 11 (October 1960): 10-18.

_____. OUT OF THE DEPTHS. New York: Harper & Brothers, 1960. 216 p.

An autobiography by a pioneer minister-psychologist who, on the basis of his personal experience, developed the theory that extreme mental disorder can be religiously fruitful if adequately understood. The book devotes considerable attention to the author's psychotic episodes in his young manhood and, somewhat more obliquely, recounts his continuing struggles in areas of sexuality and marital commitment.

Bonacker, Ralph D. "Clinical Pastoral Training for the Pastoral Ministry: Purposes and Methods." JOURNAL OF PASTORAL CARE 14 (1960): 1-12.

A useful discussion of the intentions and goals behind the movement to train ministers through exposure to hospital and mental hospital settings.

Bonstedt, Theodore. "Religion as an Asset in a Psychiatric Patient: An Historical and Clinical Comment." JOURNAL OF PASTORAL CARE 22, no. 2 (1968): 82-92.

Bowers, Margaretta K. "Friend or Traitor? Hypnosis in the Service of Religion." INTERNATIONAL JOURNAL OF CLINICAL AND EXPERIMENTAL HYPNOSIS 7 (1959): 205-15.

Braceland, Francis J. "Psychiatry and the Science of Man." PASTORAL PSYCHOLOGY 13 (May 1962): 18-28.

_____, ed. FAITH, REASON, AND MODERN PSYCHIATRY. New York: P.J. Kenedy & Sons, 1955. xv, 310 p.

A collection of essays dealing with the interaction of religion and psychiatry. Contributors include Gregory Zilboorg, Edward Smith, Jordan Aumann, and others.

Braceland, Francis J., and Stock, Michael. MODERN PSYCHIATRY: A HANDBOOK FOR BELIEVERS. New York: Doubleday & Co., 1963. 346 p.

An introduction to psychiatry for the religious public.

Brodsky, Carroll M. "Clergymen as Psychotherapists: Problems in Interrole Communication." COMMUNITY MENTAL HEALTH JOURNAL 4 (1968): 482-91. Also published in PASTORAL PSYCHOLOGY 23 (October 1972): 42-50.

Carrington, William L. PSYCHOLOGY, RELIGION, AND HUMAN NEED: A GUIDE FOR MINISTERS, DOCTORS, TEACHERS, AND SOCIAL WORKERS. Great Neck, N.Y.: Channel Press, 1957. 315 p.

A presentation of the contributions of psychiatry and the church to personal, educational, and healing ministry.

Chesen, Eli S. RELIGION MAY BE HAZARDOUS TO YOUR HEALTH. New York: Peter H. Wyden/Publisher, 1972. 145 p.

A psychiatrist who has since written a psychiatric study of Richard Nixon, former President of the United States, here discusses the ways in which religion can be psychologically damaging.

Clark, Robert A. "Theosophical Occultism and Mental Hygiene." PSYCHIATRY 7, no. 3 (1944): 237-43.

Clinebell, Howard J., Jr. MENTAL HEALTH THROUGH CHRISTIAN COMMUNITY. New York: Abingdon Press, 1965. 300 p.

A discussion of the role of the Christian church and Christian faith in the maintenance of mental health among its members. Various aspects of church participation are examined with respect to their contributions to mental health: worship, preaching, small groups, counseling, and others.

_____. "Mental Health through the Religious Community." PASTORAL PSYCHOLOGY 20, no. 194 (1969): 33-42.

Cole, W. Edward. "The Social Worker and the Chaplain: Institutional Teammates." PASTORAL PSYCHOLOGY 23 (1972): 31-38.

Committee on Psychiatry and Religion. "The Psychic Function of Religion in Mental Illness and Health." GROUP FOR THE ADVANCEMENT OF PSYCHIATRY REPORTS 6, no. 67 (1968): 653-727.

Condrau, Gion, et al. NEUROSE UND RELIGION: KRANKHEITSBILDER UND IHRE PROBLEMATIK. Olten and Freiburg: Walter Verlag, 1964. 166 p.

A collection of four essays, first presented at a symposium of Catholic psychotherapists in Zurich in 1962, representing a variety of psychotherapeutic schools. Essays by Condrau, Josef Rudin, Armin Beeli, and Jolande Jacobi.

Cortes, Juan B. "Religious Aspects of Mental Illness." JOURNAL OF RELIGION AND HEALTH 4 (1965): 315-21.

Cushing, Richard. A LOOK AT PSYCHIATRY. Boston: Daughters of St. Paul, 1959. 14 p.

A famous cardinal argues that a view of the imitation of Christ as part of man's ego-ideal renders psychiatry and religion complementary.

Demogeot, C., et al. "Reflexions sur les racines religieuses de l'alcoolisme." ANNALES MEDICO-PSYCHOLOGIQUES 2 (1969): 337-48.

Desilets, Raymond. "Alcoolisme et approaches pastorales actuelles." TOXICOMANIES 1 (1968): 51-60.

Dominian, Jacob. PSYCHIATRY AND THE CHRISTIAN. London: Burns and Oates, 1962. 141 p.

A Catholic psychiatrist's brief summary of mental disorders and their treatment, with some incidental reflections from a Christian point of view.

Draper, Edgar, et al. "On the Diagnostic Value of Religious Ideation." ARCHIVES OF GENERAL PSYCHIATRY 13, no. 3 (1965): 202-7.

A psychiatric team discuss the use of religious ideas of patients (e.g., "Who is your favorite Biblical figure and why?") in order to elicit material useful for a psychiatric diagnosis. The authors suggest that this method is especially useful with people less capable of articulating their mental difficulties due to educational deficiencies.

Duke, Robert W. "Religion and Mental Health: A Theological Point of View." PASTORAL PSYCHOLOGY 21 (May 1970): 14-18.

El-Islam, M [ohamed] Fakhr. "Depression and Guilt: A Study at an Arab Psychiatric Clinic." SOCIAL PSYCHIATRY 4, no. 2 (1969): 56-58.

Farber, Leslie H. "Martin Buber and Psychiatry." PSYCHIATRY 19 (1956): 109-20.

Farnsworth, Dana L., and Braceland, Francis J., eds. PSYCHIATRY, THE CLERGY, AND PASTORAL COUNSELING; THE ST. JOHN'S STORY. Collegeville, Minn.: St. John's University Press, 1969. xviii, 356 p.

A collection of essays based on lectures by seventeen psychiatrists at psychiatric–pastoral workshops conducted by the Institute for Mental Health at St. John's Abbey, Collegeville, Minnesota.

Farr, C.B., and Howe, Reuel L. "The Influence of Religious Ideas on the Etiology, Symptomatology, and Prognosis of the Psychoses: With Special Reference to Social Factors." AMERICAN JOURNAL OF PSYCHIATRY 11 (1932): 845–65.

Feifel, Herman. "Symposium on Relationships between Religion and Mental Health: Introductory Remarks." AMERICAN PSYCHOLOGIST 13 (1958): 565–66.

Fodor, Nandor. "People Who Are Christ." PSYCHOANALYSIS AND THE PSY-CHOANALYTIC REVIEW 45 (Spring–Summer 1958): 100–19.

Frankl, Viktor E. "Psychiatry and Man's Quest for Meaning." JOURNAL OF RELIGION AND HEALTH 1 (1962): 93–103.

Galdston, Iago. "Are Psychiatry and Religion Reconcilable?" PASTORAL PSY-CHOLOGY 11 (May 1960): 39–48.

Gallemore, J.L., et al. "The Religious Life of Patients with Affective Disorders." DISEASES OF THE NERVOUS SYSTEM 30 (1969): 483–87.

Gittelsohn, R.B. "Judaism and Mental Health." JUDAISM 8 (Fall 1959): 323–28.

Group for the Advancement of Psychiatry (GAP). See Committee on Psychiatry and Religion above.

Guttmacher, Sally, and Elinson, Jack. "Ethno–Religious Variation in Percep-tions of Illness: The Use of Illness as an Explanation for Deviant Behavior." SOCIAL SCIENCE AND MEDICINE 5 (1971): 117–25.

Gynther, Malcolm D., and Kempson, J. Obert. "Seminarians and Clinical Pas-toral Training: A Follow-up Study." JOURNAL OF SOCIAL PSYCHOLOGY 56 (1962): 9–14.

Haas, H.I. "Relations between Clergymen and Psychiatrists." PSYCHIATRIC QUARTERLY SUPPLEMENT 41 (1967): 40–56.

Hacker, Frederick J. "Psychiatry and Religion." JOURNAL OF RELIGION 35 (1955): 74–84.

Hall, Charles E., Jr. "Some Contributions of Anton T. Boisen (1876–1965) to Understanding Psychiatry and Religion." BULLETIN OF THE MENNINGER CLINIC 31 (1967): 42–52. Also published in PASTORAL PSYCHOLOGY 19

(1968): 40-48.

Heath, Sheldon. "The Minister as a Mental Health Worker." CANADIAN PSY-
CHIATRIC ASSOCIATION JOURNAL 12 (1967): 607-10.

Helweg, Hjalmar. SOUL SORROW: THE PSYCHIATRIST SPEAKS TO THE MIN-
ISTER. Translated by Jens Grano. New York: Pageant Press, 1955. 151 p.

A Danish psychiatrist here attributes mental problems, marital in-
compatibility, and the various religious views of Luther, Calvin,
and Loyola to inherited constitution.

Herr, Vincent V. "Mental-Health Training in Catholic Seminaries." JOURNAL
OF RELIGION AND HEALTH 5, no. 1 (1966): 27-34.

Hiemstra, William L. "Self Perceptions and Perceptions of Selected Bible Char-
acters: A Study of Depressed Psychiatric Patients." RELIGIOUS EDUCATION
61, no. 1 (1966): 42-48, 80.

Hiltner, Seward. RELIGION AND HEALTH. New York: Macmillan, 1943.
xiii, 292 p.

Explores the relationship between religion and mental health. Of
particular value are the portions of the book devoted to the history
of healing in Christianity as this bears on the role of the minister
in the cure of souls.

_____. "Appraisal of Religion and Psychiatry since 1954." JOURNAL OF
RELIGION AND HEALTH 4 (April 1965): 217-26.

_____. "Theological Consultants in Hospitals and Mental Health Centers."
AMERICAN JOURNAL OF PSYCHIATRY 128 (1972): 965-69.

Hiltner, Seward, and Menninger, Karl, eds. CONSTRUCTIVE ASPECTS OF
ANXIETY. New York and Nashville: Abingdon Press, 1963. 173 p.

An interesting collection of papers which draws on the resources
of religion and psychiatry. Includes contributions by Hiltner, Fred
Berthold, Albert Outler, Paul Pruyser, and others.

Hofmann, Hans. RELIGION AND MENTAL HEALTH. New York: Harper &
Brothers, 1961. 333 p.

_____. "Religion and Mental Health." JOURNAL OF RELIGION AND MEN-
TAL HEALTH 1 (1962): 319-36.

_____, ed. THE MINISTRY AND MENTAL HEALTH. New York: Association
Press, 1960. xi, 251 p.

A collection of essays by major figures in the psychology of religion, pastoral psychology, and related fields.

Hollander, Fred I. "The Specific Nature of the Clergy's Role in Mental Health." PASTORAL PSYCHOLOGY 10 (November 1959): 11-21.

Howard, James S. "Schizophrenia and the Balinese." CONDITIONAL REFLEX 7 (October 1972): 232-43.

Discusses trance states, mental illness, hypnosis, and religion in Bali.

Howland, Elihu S. SPEAK THROUGH THE EARTHQUAKE: RELIGIOUS FAITH AND EMOTIONAL CRISIS. Philadelphia: Pilgrim Press, 1972. 125 p.

Ikin, A. Graham. NEW CONCEPTS OF HEALING: MEDICAL, PSYCHOLOGICAL, RELIGIOUS. New York: Association Press, 1956. xxiii, 262 p.

Johnson, Paul E. "Symposium on Relationships between Religion and Mental Health: Discussion." AMERICAN PSYCHOLOGIST 13 (1958): 576-77.

_____. "The Clinical Approach to Religion." JOURNAL OF PASTORAL CARE 15 (1961): 7-12.

_____. "New Religions and Mental Health." JOURNAL OF RELIGION AND HEALTH 3 (1964): 327-34.

_____. "The Church's Mission to Mental Health." JOURNAL OF RELIGION AND HEALTH 12 (January 1973): 30-40.

Kagan, Henry E., and Zucker, Arnold H. "Treatment of a 'Corrupted' Family by Rabbi and Psychiatrist." JOURNAL OF RELIGION AND HEALTH 9 (1970): 22-34.

Kaufman, M. Ralph. "Religious Delusions in Schizophrenia." INTERNATIONAL JOURNAL OF PSYCHOANALYSIS 20 (1939): 363-76.

Kearney, Michael. "Drunkenness and Religious Conversion in a Mexican Village." QUARTERLY JOURNAL OF STUDIES ON ALCOHOL 31 (March 1970): 132-52.

Kiev, Ari. TRANSCULTURAL PSYCHIATRY. New York: The Free Press, 1972. xii, 223 p.

A discussion of cultural stress, of cultural influence on views of normality and abnormality, of culture-bound disorders, and of problems in the providing of mental health care in developing countries. See other entries by the author in section G:8.

Kirkpatrick, W.J. "Psychiatry and Religion: Conflict or Cooperation." MODERN CHURCHMAN 10 (July 1967): 296-301.

Klausner, Samuel Z. PSYCHIATRY AND RELIGION: A SOCIOLOGICAL STUDY OF THE NEW ALLIANCE OF MINISTERS AND PSYCHIATRISTS. New York: The Free Press, 1964. xvi, 299 p.

> A study whose purpose is to evaluate ministers' and psychiatrists' encounters with the mentally ill. Employs a typology, drawn from Robert Merton's famous study of anomie, in which ministers and psychiatrists involved in mental health work are labelled conformists, ritualists, innovators, or rebels with respect to their own professional groups.

_____. "The Religio-Psychiatric Movement: Participation by Protestant, Catholic and Jew." REVIEW OF RELIGIOUS RESEARCH 5 (1964): 63-74.

_____. "Role Adaptation of Pastors and Psychiatrists." JOURNAL FOR THE SCIENTIFIC STUDY OF RELIGION 4 (1964-65): 14-39.

Klink, Thomas W. "How the Minister Can Recognize Serious Mental Illness." PASTORAL PSYCHOLOGY 10, no. 94 (1959): 43-48.

_____. "The Ministry and Medicine: A New Examination." PASTORAL PSYCHOLOGY 10, no. 95 (1959): 39-49.

Knight, James A. A PSYCHIATRIST LOOKS AT RELIGION AND HEALTH. New York: Abingdon Press, 1964. 207 p.

> Written by a psychiatrist who was then affiliated with Union Theological Seminary in its Religion and Psychiatry program.

Knupfer, G., and Room, R. "Drinking Patterns and Attitudes of Irish, Jewish and White Protestant American Men." QUARTERLY JOURNAL OF STUDIES ON ALCOHOL 28 (1967): 676-99.

Kushner, A.W. "Two Cases of Auto-Castration Due to Religious Delusions." BRITISH JOURNAL OF MEDICAL PSYCHOLOGY 40 (1967): 293-98.

Kysar, John E. "Mental-Health Implications of Aggiornamento." JOURNAL OF RELIGION AND HEALTH 5, no. 1 (1966): 35-42.

Lapsley, James N. "The Devotional Life and Mental Health." JOURNAL OF PASTORAL CARE 20 (1966): 138-48.

Larson, Richard F. "The Clergyman's Role in the Therapeutic Process: Disagreement between Clergymen and Psychiatrists." PSYCHIATRY 31 (1968): 250-63.

Lawson, D.W. "Religious Programs for the Mentally Retarded Residing in Institutions." AMERICAN JOURNAL OF MENTAL DEFICIENCY 66 (1961): 459-63.

Levison, Peritz. "Religious Delusions in Counter-Culture Patients." AMERICAN JOURNAL OF PSYCHIATRY 130 (November 1973): 1265-69.

Levy, Alan M., et al. "A Meeting of Minds: How Psychiatry, Psychology and Religion Work Together." PASTORAL COUNSELOR 2, no. 1 (1964): 21-28.

Liebman, Joshua, ed. PSYCHIATRY AND RELIGION. Boston: Beacon Press, 1948. xix, 202 p.

> A symposium in which clergymen and psychiatrists discuss their practical and theoretical areas of difference and common concern. An early contribution to the religion and psychiatry movement.

Linn, Louis, and Schwarz, Leo W. PSYCHIATRY AND RELIGIOUS EXPERIENCE. New York: Random House, 1958. 307 p.

Linsky, Arnold S. "Religious Differences in Lay Attitudes and Knowledge on Alcoholism and Its Treatment." JOURNAL FOR THE SCIENTIFIC STUDY OF RELIGION 5 (1965): 41-50.

Loschen, E.L. "Psychiatry and Religion: A Variable History." JOURNAL OF RELIGION AND HEALTH 13, no. 2 (1974): 137-41.

Lowe, C. Marshall, and Braaten, Roger O. "Differences in Religious Attitudes in Mental Illness." JOURNAL FOR THE SCIENTIFIC STUDY OF RELIGION 5, no. 3 (1965-66): 435-45.

_____. "The Relationship between Self-Report of Religious and Personality Needs among Psychiatric Patients." JOURNAL OF SOCIAL PSYCHOLOGY 75 (1968): 261-68.

Lubchansky, Isaac, et al. "Puerto Rican Spiritualists View Mental Illness: The Faith Healer as a Para-Professional." AMERICAN JOURNAL OF PSYCHIATRY 127 (September 1970): 312-21.

McCann, Richard V. THE CHURCHES AND MENTAL HEALTH. Joint Commission on Mental Illness and Health Monograph Series, no. 8. New York: Basic Books, 1962. 278 p.

> Addresses the problems posed by the facts that high formal religiosity prevails in this country and personality dislocation and disorder is mounting. Is there some relationship between these two facts? If so, what is it?

McDowell, Frank K. "The Pastor's Natural Ally against Alcoholism." JOUR-

NAL OF PASTORAL CARE 26 (1972): 26-32.

Malzberg, Benjamin. "Mental Disease among Jews in New York State, 1960-61." ACTA PSYCHIATRICA SCANDINAVICA 49, no. 4 (1973): 479-518.

Mann, Kenneth W. "The Mission of the Church in a Drugs Culture." JOURNAL OF RELIGION AND HEALTH 11 (October 1972): 329-48.

Mason, Randall C., Jr., et al. "Acceptance and Healing." JOURNAL OF RELIGION AND HEALTH 8 (1969): 123-42.

> On the attitudes toward others and philosophy of evil of eye-surgery patients.

Masserman, Jules H. THE PRACTICE OF DYNAMIC PSYCHIATRY. Philadelphia: W.B. Saunders, 1955. 790 p.

Maves, Paul B. "The Church and Mental Illness." CHRISTIAN ACTION 21, no. 7 (1966): 14-20.

Meyer, George G., et al. "The Chaplain's Role in Milieu Therapy." DISEASES OF THE NERVOUS SYSTEM 28 (1967): 749-53.

Midgley, J. "Drinking and Attitudes toward Drinking in a Muslim Community." QUARTERLY JOURNAL OF STUDIES ON ALCOHOL 32 (March 1971): 148-58.

Moore, Thomas Verner. "Religion, Psychiatry and Mental Hygiene." PSYCHIATRY 7, no. 4 (1944): 321-25.

Morrow, William R. "Role-Definitions of Mental Hospital Chaplains." JOURNAL FOR THE SCIENTIFIC STUDY OF RELIGION 5, no. 3 (1966): 421-34.

Mowrer, O. Hobart. "Symposium on Relationships between Religion and Mental Health: Discussion." AMERICAN PSYCHOLOGIST 13 (1958): 577-79.

_____. THE CRISIS IN PSYCHIATRY AND RELIGION. Princeton, N.J.: D. Van Nostrand Co., 1961. 264 p.

> In the course of reformulating the essential task of psychotherapy, Mowrer attacks Freudianism and Calvanism as inadequate for understanding psychopathology and guilt, sin and confession.

_____, ed. MORALITY AND MENTAL HEALTH. Chicago: Rand McNally & Co., 1967. xvii, 669 p.

> A collection of seventy-five previously published articles which support the editor's view that emotional disturbance is rooted in

the violation of moral precepts.

Nelson, Scott H., and Torrey, E. Fuller. "The Religious Functions of Psychiatry." AMERICAN JOURNAL OF ORTHOPSYCHIATRY 43 (April 1973): 362-67.

Noveck, Simon, ed. JUDAISM AND PSYCHIATRY: TWO APPRAOCHES TO THE PERSONAL PROBLEMS AND NEEDS OF MODERN MAN. New York: Basic Books, 1956. 197 p.

Novey, Samuel. "Considerations on Religion in Relation to Psychoanalysis and Psychotherapy." JOURNAL OF NERVOUS AND MENTAL DISEASE 130 (1960): 315-24.

Oates, Wayne E[dward]. RELIGIOUS FACTORS IN MENTAL ILLNESS. New York: Association Press, 1955. xv, 239 p.

_____. "Religious Factors in Mental Illness." INTERNATIONAL YEARBOOK FOR THE SOCIOLOGY OF RELIGION 2 (1966): 217-30.

O'Connell, Daniel C. "Is Mental Illness a Result of Sin?" LUMEN VITAE 16 (1961): 233-42.

O'Doherty, E.F., and McGrath, S. Desmond, eds. THE PRIEST AND MENTAL HEALTH. Dublin: Clonmore and Reynolds, 1962. 249 p.

This collection of essays stresses the distinctive role of the priest as a minister of the church and rejects the view that his primary role is mental therapy. The book is especially critical of psychoanalysis, but accepts psychiatry when appropriately limited.

Opler, Marvin K. CULTURE, PSYCHIATRY AND HUMAN VALUES: THE METHODS AND VALUES OF A SOCIAL PSYCHIATRY. Springfield, Ill.: Charles C Thomas, 1956. xiii, 242 p.

_____, ed. CULTURE AND MENTAL HEALTH: CROSS-CULTURAL STUDIES. New York: Macmillan, 1959. xxii, 533 p.

A good collection of essays by anthropologists, including Hallowell, Spiro, DeVos, Wallace, Caudill, and others, on concepts of disease, means of treatment, and cultural tension and variability among "primitive" and "high" cultures.

Parsons, Talcott. "Mental Illness and 'Spiritual Malaise': The Role of the Psychiatrist and of the Minister of Religion." In SOCIAL STRUCTURE AND PERSONALITY, pp. 292-324. By Talcott Parsons. New York: The Free Press, 1964.

Pattison, E. Mansell, ed. CLINICAL PSYCHIATRY AND RELIGION. Boston:

Little, Brown and Co., 1969. xv, 327 p.

A collection of essays on clinical aspects of primitive religions, rites, glossolalia, psychedelic drugs, moral problems, and the mental health problems of clergymen and their families.

Pond, Desmond. COUNSELLING IN RELIGION AND PSYCHIATRY. New York: Oxford University Press, 1973. 81 p.

Powell, L. Mack. "Efforts by the Mentally III to Solve Problems through Religion." PASTORAL COUNSELOR 3, no. 2 (1965): 29-32.

Pruyser, Paul W. "Religion and Psychiatry: A Polygon of Relationships." JOURNAL OF AMERICAN MEDICAL ASSOCIATION 15, no. 3 (1966): 197-202.

_____. "Assessment of the Patient's Religious Attitudes in the Psychiatric Case Study." BULLETIN OF THE MENNINGER CLINIC 35, no. 4 (1971): 272-91.

_____. "The Minister as Diagnostician." PERKINS SCHOOL OF THEOLOGY JOURNAL 27, no. 2 (1973): 1-10.

Ranck, J.G. "Religious Conservatism, Liberalism and Mental Health." PASTORAL PSYCHOLOGY 12, no. 112 (1961): 34-40.

Ratanakern, Prasop. "Schizophrenia in Thailand." INTERNATIONAL JOURNAL OF SOCIAL PSYCHIATRY 5 (1959): 47-49.

The relation of Buddhism to the incidence of mental illness in general and schizophrenia in particular.

Reider, Norman. "The Demonology of Modern Psychiatry." AMERICAN JOURNAL OF PSYCHIATRY 111 (1955): 851-56.

Rosenberg, Morris. "The Dissonant Religious Context and Emotional Disturbance." AMERICAN JOURNAL OF SOCIOLOGY 68, no. 1 (1962): 1-10.

Rosenbloom, Joseph R. "Notes on Jewish Drug Addicts." PSYCHOLOGICAL REPORTS 5 (1959): 769-72.

Royce, James E., S.J. PERSONALITY AND MENTAL HEALTH. Milwaukee: Bruce Publishers, 1964. xiv, 353 p.

A revision of a book originally published in 1955, this study places strong emphasis on the continuities between ancient and medieval thought and modern psychology and psychiatry. Somewhat behaviorist in outlook.

Rubins, Jack L. "Religion, Mental Health and the Psychoanalyst." AMERI-
CAN JOURNAL OF PSYCHOANALYSIS 30, no. 2 (1970): 127-34.

Sandler, Nat H. "Attitudes of Ministers toward Psychiatry." JOURNAL OF
RELIGION AND HEALTH 5, no. 1 (1966): 47-60.

Sanua, Victor D. "Religion, Mental Health, and Personality: A Review of
Empirical Studies." AMERICAN JOURNAL OF PSYCHIATRY 125, no. 9 (1969):
1203-13.

Schneiders, Alexander A. "Religion and Psychological Health: A New Approach."
JOURNAL OF EXISTENTIAL PSYCHIATRY 2 (Summer 1961): 93-104.

_____. "Catholics and Psychology." CATHOLIC PSYCHOLOGICAL RECORD
5, no. 2 (1967): 102-10.

Shapiro, David S., et al. THE MENTAL HEALTH COUNSELOR IN THE COM-
MUNITY: TRAINING OF PHYSICIANS AND MINISTERS. Springfield, Ill.:
Charles C Thomas, 1968. xii, 207 p.

> Concerned with the difficulty of bringing mental health resources to
> the average person, the authors have developed methods and pro-
> cedures to enable physicians and ministers to use their limited time
> to best advantage in diagnosing mental problems.

Siirala, Aarne. THE VOICE OF ILLNESS: A STUDY OF THERAPY AND PRO-
PHECY. Philadelphia: Fortress Press, 1964. 214 p.

> A study of the relationship between prophetic religion and schizo-
> phrenia.

Silverstone, Harry. RELIGION AND PSYCHIATRY. New York: Twayne, 1956.
214 p.

> A personal effort to demonstrate the partnership of religion and psy-
> chiatry in dealing with mental problems.

Snyder, C.R. ALCOHOL AND THE JEWS. Monographs of the Yale Center
of Alcohol Studies, no. 1. Glencoe, Ill.: The Free Press, 1958. 226 p.

> See annotation in section C:3.

Sobosan, Jeffrey G. "Existential Psychiatry and Religion." PASTORAL PSY-
CHOLOGY 23 (October 1972): 24-28.

Southard, Samuel. CHRISTIANS AND MENTAL HEALTH. Nashville: Broadman Press, 1972. 128 p.

> Discusses the contributions of Christian theology and pastoral minis-
> try to mental health objectives.

Spilka, Bernard, and Werme, Paul H. "Religion and Mental Disorder: A Research Perspective." In RESEARCH ON RELIGIOUS DEVELOPMENT: A COMPREHENSIVE HANDBOOK, pp. 461-84. Edited by Merton P. Strommen. New York: Hawthorn Books, 1971.

Steere, David A. "Anton Boisen: Figure of the Future." JOURNAL OF RELIGION AND HEALTH 8 (1969): 359-74.

Stein, Leonard I., and Thomas, John R. "The Chaplain as a Member of the Psychiatric Team." HOSPITAL AND COMMUNITY PSYCHIATRY 18 (1967): 197-200.

Stern, Karl. THE THIRD REVOLUTION: A STUDY OF PSYCHIATRY AND RELIGION. New York: Harcourt, Brace, 1954. 306 p.

> See annotation in section G:2.

Stern, Paul J. THE ABNORMAL PERSON AND HIS WORLD. Princeton, N.J.: Van Nostrand, 1964. 239 p.

> A book which grew out of a course which has been offered by the author at Harvard Divinity School. Gives particular emphasis to the relationship between psychological and religious issues in abnormal psychology.

Stevenson, Ian. "Assumptions of Religion and Psychiatry." PASTORAL PSYCHOLOGY 20 (June 1969): 41-50.

Stinnette, Charles R., Jr. "Bibliography for Ministers: Psychiatry and Religion." UNION SEMINARY QUARTERLY REVIEW 14 (May 1959): 49-54.

Streenland, Roger. "The Development of a Religious Neuroticism Inventory." PROCEEDINGS OF THE CHRISTIAN ASSOCIATION FOR PSYCHOLOGICAL STUDIES, April 1968, pp. 96-106.

Strunk, Orlo, Jr. "Relationships of Psychology of Religion and Clinical Pastoral Education." PASTORAL PSYCHOLOGY 22 (October 1971): 29-35.

Svenaeus, Gosta. EDVARD MUNCH: DAS UNIVERSUM DER MELANCHOLIE. Lund: Publications of the New Society of Letters at Lund, 1968. 285 p.

> A psychological study concerned with the theme of the inevitability of death as manifest in Edvard Munch's art.

Tellenbach, Hubert. "Die Dekomposition Religioser Grundakte in Wahn und Melancholie." JAHRBUCH FUR PSYCHOLOGIE, PSYCHOTHERAPIE UND MEDIZINISCHE ANTHROPOLOGIE 14, nos. 2-4 (1966): 278-87.

Thorner, Isidor. "Ascetic Protestantism and Alcoholism." PSYCHIATRY 16 (1953): 167-76.

Trew, Alberta. "The Religious Factor in Mental Illness." PASTORAL PSYCHOL-OGY 22 (May 1971): 21-28.

VanderVeldt, J.H., and Odenwald, R.P. PSYCHIATRY AND CATHOLICISM. 2nd ed. New York: McGraw-Hill, 1957. 474 p.

Waldman, Roy D. "The Sin-Neurotic Complex: Perspectives in Religion and Psychiatry." PSYCHOANALYTIC REVIEW 57, no. 1 (1970): 143-52.

Walters, Orville S. "Religion and Psychopathology." COMPREHENSIVE PSY-CHIATRY 5, no. 1 (1964): 24-35.

Waterman, Minnie L. "Pastoral Decision: To Counsel or Refer." JOURNAL OF PASTORAL CARE 14 (1960): 34-38.

Webb, N.J., and Kobler, Frank J. "Clinical-Empirical Techniques for Assessing the Attitudes of Religious toward Psychiatry." JOURNAL OF SOCIAL PSYCHOL-OGY 55 (1961): 245-51.

Wechsler, Henry, et al. "Religious-Ethnic Differences in Alcohol Consumption." JOURNAL OF HEALTH AND SOCIAL BEHAVIOR 11 (1970): 21-29.

Westberg, Granger E., and Draper, Edgar. COMMUNITY PSYCHIATRY AND THE CLERGYMAN. Springfield, Ill.: Charles C Thomas, 1966. xxi, 110 p.

> An account of two projects, administered by the authors (a theolo-gical educator and a psychiatrist) for the training of clergymen in mental health roles.

Williams, Daniel Day. "What Psychiatry Means to Theological Education." JOURNAL OF PASTORAL CARE 18 (1964): 129-31.

Wilson, William P. "Mental Health Benefits of Religious Salvation." DISEASES OF THE NERVOUS SYSTEM 33 (June 1972): 382-86.

Wolff, Kurt. "Religion and Mental Health." JOURNAL OF PASTORAL CARE 14 (1960): 39-43.

Young, Richard K., and Meiburg, Albert L. SPIRITUAL THERAPY: HOW THE PHYSICIAN, PSYCHIATRIST AND MINISTER COLLABORATE IN HEALING. New York: Harper & Brothers, 1960. 184 p.

> Practical advice for those who serve patients suffering from such di-verse diseases as ulcers, heart disease, colitis, asthma, anxiety, recent surgery, and others.

Zentner, Henry. "Durkheim, Mental Health and Religious Socialization."

SOCIOLOGICAL INQUIRY 34 (1964): 92-107.

Zilboorg, Gregory. "Scientific Psychopathology and Religious Issues." JOUR-
NAL OF MENTAL SCIENCE 100 (1954): 402-10.

G:7 AGING, DEATH, AND BEREAVEMENT

Anderson, Douglas A. "A Resurrection Model for Suicide Prevention through
the Church." PASTORAL PSYCHOLOGY 23 (1972): 33-40.

Banks, Sam A. "Dialogue on Death: Freudian and Christian Views." PAS-
TORAL PSYCHOLOGY 14 (June 1963): 41-49.

Becker, Ernest. THE DENIAL OF DEATH. New York: The Free Press, 1973.
xiv, 314 p.

> Argues that the key to the unification of the sciences of man lies
> in the overcoming of death through the creation of cultural systems
> which grant man forms of dignity and even heroism. Contains in-
> teresting interpretations of Freud, Rank, Kierkegaard, and others.

Benson, George. "Death and Dying: A Psychoanalytic Perspective." JOUR-
NAL OF PASTORAL CARE 26 (1972): 77-85.

Berman, Alan L., and Hayes, James E. "Relation between Death Anxiety, Belief in Afterlife, and Locus of Control." JOURNAL OF CONSULTING AND
CLINICAL PSYCHOLOGY 41 (October 1973): 318.

Bonnell, George C. "The Pastor's Role in Counseling the Bereaved." PAS-
TORAL PSYCHOLOGY 22 (1971): 27-36.

Bowers, Margaretta K., et al. COUNSELING THE DYING. New York:
Thomas Nelson and Sons, 1964. 183 p.

> Written by prominent individuals in religion and psychiatry, includ-
> ing Edgar N. Jackson, James A. Knight, and Lawrence LeShan, as
> well as the senior author. Emphasizes the importance of significant
> others in the comforting of the dying, but also wants to carve out
> an additional and distinctive role for the professional counselor.

Cappon, Daniel. "The Psychology of Dying." PASTORAL PSYCHOLOGY 12
(February 1961): 35-44.

Carlozzi, Carl G. DEATH AND CONTEMPORARY MAN: THE CRISIS OF
TERMINAL ILLNESS. Grand Rapids, Mich.: Wm. B. Eerdmans Publishing
Co., 1968. 79 p.

Durkheim, Emile. SUICIDE. Translated by John A. Spaulding and George Simpson. Glencoe, Ill.: Free Press, 1951. 405 p.

> A sociological classic, originally published in 1897. In the course of separating out psychopathological, individual factors in suicide from social factors, uses the differing suicide rates of Catholics and Protestants to point out differences in religious individualism and social integration. Also discusses anomie and the moral poverty of contemporary society.

Feifel, Herman, ed. THE MEANING OF DEATH. New York: McGraw-Hill, 1959. xviii, 351 p.

Fulton, Robert, ed. DEATH AND IDENTITY. New York: John Wiley & Sons, 1965. xv, 415 p.

Glaser, Barney G. "Temporal Aspects of Dying as a Non-Scheduled Status Passage." AMERICAN JOURNAL OF SOCIOLOGY 71 (1965-66): 48-60.

_____. TIME FOR DYING. Chicago: Aldine Publishing Co., 1968. xiv, 270 p.

Glaser, Barney G., and Strauss, Anselm L. AWARENESS OF DYING. Chicago: Aldine Publishing Co., 1965. 305 p.

> A study of the dying patient, with special emphasis on the widsom of informing patients of their terminal conditions.

Godin, Andre. "Has Death Changed?" LUMEN VITAE 26 (1971): 407-30.

Hall, Stanley. "Thanatophobia and Immortality." AMERICAN JOURNAL OF PSYCHOLOGY, October 1915, pp. 550-613.

Herzog, Edgar. PSYCHE AND DEATH: ARCHAIC MYTHS AND MODERN DREAMS IN ANALYTICAL PSYCHOLOGY. Translated by David Cox and Eugene Rolfe. New York: G.P. Putnam's Sons, 1967. 224 p. (For C.G. Jung Foundation for Analytical Psychology.)

> The first part of the book provides mythological material from a variety of cultures on human attitudes toward death. The second part discusses dreams of patients as illuminative of their struggle with the experience and meaning of death.

Hillman, James. SUICIDE AND THE SOUL. New York: Harper & Row, Publishers, 1965. 191 p.

> Discussion of the role of the therapist in dealing with suicidal patients. Includes some consideration of the survival of the soul and the implications of this view for therapeutic intervention with

suicidal patients.

Hole, Gunther. "Some Comparisons among Guilt Feelings, Religion, and Suicidal Tendencies in Depression Patients." LIFE-THREATENING BEHAVIOR 1
(Summer 1971): 138-42.

Irwin, Keith W. "Toward a Phenomenology of Death." DIALOGUE 11 (1972):
177-82.

Kalish, Richard A. "Some Variables in Death Attitudes." JOURNAL OF SO-
CIAL PSYCHOLOGY 59 (1963): 137-45.

Kidorf, Irwin W. "Jewish Tradition and the Freudian Theory of Mourning."
JOURNAL OF RELIGION AND HEALTH 2 (1962-63): 248-52.

Kranitz, Lionel, et al. "Religious Beliefs of Suicidal Patients." PSYCHOLOG-
ICAL REPORTS 22 (1958): 936.

Kubler-Ross, Elisabeth. ON DEATH AND DYING. New York: Macmillan,
1969. xii, 260 p.

     An analysis of the death process in five stages: denial, anger,
     bargaining, depression, and acceptance. Based on an interdisci-
     plinary seminar involving medical and theological students.

Lepp, Ignace. DEATH AND ITS MYSTERIES. Translated by Bernard Murch-
land. New York: Macmillan, 1968. xxv, 194 p.

     Addresses the problem of reconciling Catholic concepts of eternal
     life with modern scientific and psychological interpretations.

Lester, David. "Religious Behavior and the Fear of Death." OMEGA 1, no. 3
(1970): 181-88.

Lifton, Robert J. "Psychological Effects of the Atomic Bomb in Hiroshima: The
Theme of Death." DEADALUS 92 (1963): 462-97.

_____. "On Death and Death Symbolism." AMERICAN SCHOLAR 34 (1965):
257-73.

_____. DEATH IN LIFE: SURVIVORS OF HIROSHIMA. New York: Random
House, 1967. 594 p.

     Based on the author's extensive interviews with suvivors of the
     atomic bomb in Hiroshima. Discusses guilt of survivors, their sense
     of apocalyptic doom, and other themes relating to the experience
     of "death in life."

_____. BOUNDARIES: PSYCHOLOGICAL MAN IN REVOLUTION. New York: Random House, 1969. xii, 113 p.

> Based on five radio speeches for the Canadian Broadcasting Corporation. Summarizes in one speech the basic ideas of his full-length study of Hiroshima survivors.

_____. "On Death and the Continuity of Life: A 'New' Paradigm." AMERICAN JOURNAL OF PSYCHOANALYSIS 33, no. 1 (1973): 3-15.

Loveland, Glenn G. "The Effects of Bereavement on Certain Religious Attitudes and Behavior." SOCIOLOGICAL SYMPOSIUM, no. 1, 1968, pp. 17-27.

Martin, David. "The Relationship between Religious Behavior and Concern about Death." JOURNAL OF SOCIAL PSYCHOLOGY 65, no. 2 (1965): 317-23.

Martin, David, and Wrightsman, Lawrence S. "Religion and Fears about Death: A Critical Review of Research." RELIGIOUS EDUCATION 59 (1964): 174-76.

Meerloo, Joost A.M. SUICIDE AND MASS SUICIDE. New York: Grune & Stratton, 1962. 153 p.

> An analysis of types of motivation of suicide, including those involving magic and religious intentions.

Mitchell, Marjorie Editha. THE CHILD'S ATTITUDE TO DEATH. New York: Schocken Books, 1967. 162 p.

> Emphasizes that children have considerable anxiety about death and shows how ritual, myth, and superstition still play a major role in determining attitudes toward death.

Morphew, J.A. "Religion and Attempted Suicide." INTERNATIONAL JOURNAL OF SOCIAL PSYCHIATRY 14 (1968): 188-92.

Neale, Robert E. "Between the Nipple and the Everlasting Arms." UNION SEMINARY QUARTERLY REVIEW 27 (1971-72): 81-90.

> Psychological and religious reflections on the care for the dying at St. Christopher's Hospice in England.

Parkes, Colin Murray. BEREAVEMENT: STUDIES OF GRIEF IN ADULT LIFE. New York: International Universities Press, 1972. xiii, 233 p.

Rheingold, Joseph C. THE MOTHER, ANXIETY, AND DEATH: THE CATASTROPHIC DEATH COMPLEX. Boston: Little, Brown and Co., 1967. 271 p.

> Argues that fear of catastrophic death is universal in man, and that its origins lie in the actual destructive behavior of mothers toward infants.

Rodin, A., ed. DEATH AND PRESENCE: THE PSYCHOLOGY OF DEATH AND THE AFTER-LIFE. Brussels: Lumen Vitae Press, 1972. 314 p.

A collection of essays on the psychology of death from the perspective of Catholic psychology of religion. Essays concern attitudes toward death, religious behavior in relation to death, and various other topics.

Ross, Richard W. "Towards a Theology of Death." PASTORAL PSYCHOLOGY 23 (January 1972): 15-23.

Ruitenbeck, Hendrik M., ed. DEATH: INTERPRETATIONS. New York: Dell Books, 1969. 286 p.

A collection of essays, all previously published, some of which concern the religious aspects of death.

Strunk, Orlo, Jr., and Jordan, Merle R. "An Experimental Course for Clergymen in Suicidology and Crisis Intervention." JOURNAL OF PASTORAL CARE 26 (1972): 50-54.

Switzer, David K. THE DYNAMICS OF GRIEF. Nashville: Abingdon Press, 1970. 221 p.

Templer, Donald I. "Death Anxiety in Religiously Very Involved Persons." PSYCHOLOGICAL REPORTS 31 (October 1972): 361-62.

Templer, Donald I., and Dotson, Elsie. "Religious Correlates of Death Anxiety." PSYCHOLOGICAL REPORTS 26 (June 1970): 895-97.

Whalley, Elsa A. "Religion and Suicide." REVIEW OF RELIGIOUS RESEARCH 5 (1964): 91-109.

Williams, Mary. "The Fear of Death: Part I. The Avoidance of the Fear of Death." JOURNAL OF ANALYTICAL PSYCHOLOGY 3 (1958): 157-66.

_____. "The Fear of Death: Part II. The Fear of Death in Consciousness." JOURNAL OF ANALYTICAL PSYCHOLOGY 7 (1962): 29-40.

Williams, Robert L., and Spurgeon, Cole. "Religiosity, Generalized Anxiety, and Apprehension concerning Death." JOURNAL OF SOCIAL PSYCHOLOGY 75 (1968): 111-17.

Yamamoto, Joe, et al. "Mourning in Japan." AMERICAN JOURNAL OF PSYCHIATRY 125 (1969): 1660-65.

Zilboorg, Gregory. "The Sense of Immortality." PSYCHOANALYTIC QUARTERLY 7 (1938): 171-99.

G:8   RELIGIONS AS THERAPY SYSTEMS

Akhilananda, Swami. MENTAL HEALTH AND HINDU PSYCHOLOGY. New York: Harper & Brothers, 1951. 231 p.

>   An attempt to translate Hindu thought and practice into Western modes of understanding.

Alexander, Franz. "Buddhistic Training as an Artificial Catatonia." PSYCHO-ANALYTIC REVIEW 18 (1931): 129-45.

Alpert, Richard. "Baba Ram Das Lecture at the Menninger Foundation." JOUR-NAL OF TRANSPERSONAL PSYCHOLOGY 2 (1970): 91-139.

Ando, S. "Zen and Christianity." PSYCHOLOGIA 8 (1965): 123-34.

Antonelli, Feruccio. "Psicoanalisis y Confesion." REVISTA DE PSICOLOGIA GENERAL Y APLICADA 20, nos. 76-77 (1965): 73-78.

Anzai, Jiro. "Two Cases of Zen Awakening (Kensho) Experiences: I. Master Shibayama's Case." PSYCHOLOGIA: AN INTERNATIONAL JOURNAL OF PSYCHOLOGY IN THE ORIENT 13 (September 1970): 140-44.

Arasteh, A. Reza. "Patterns and Processes of Self-Liberation in the Near Eastern Sufism (Art of Rebirth)." PSYCHOLOGIA: AN INTERNATIONAL JOURNAL OF PSYCHOLOGY·IN THE ORIENT 13 (March 1970): 5-11.

Bagchi, B.K. "Mental Hygiene and the Hindu Doctrine of Relaxation." MEN-TAL HYGIENE 20 (1936): 424-40.

Beck, R.J. "Some Proto-Psychotherapeutic Elements in the Practice of the Sha-man." HISTORY OF RELIGIONS 6 (May 1967): 303-27.

>   See other entries on Shamanism in section C:5.

Becker, Ernest. "Psychotherapeutic Observations on the Zen Discipline: One Point of View." PSYCHOLOGIA: AN INTERNATIONAL JOURNAL OF PSY-CHOLOGY IN THE ORIENT 3 (1960): 100-12.

_____. "The Psychotherapeutic Meeting of East and West." AMERICAN IMA-GO 18 (1961): 3-20.

Behanan, K.T. YOGA: A SCIENTIFIC EVALUATION. New York: Dover Books, 1960. xxiv, 270 p.

>   Originally published in 1937.

Belshaw, G.P.M. "Prayer and Personality." SAINT LUKE'S JOURNAL OF THEOLOGY 16 (December 1972): 57-67.

Berger, Emmanuel M. "Zen Buddhism, General Psychology, and Counseling Psychology." JOURNAL OF COUNSELING PSYCHOLOGY 9, no. 2 (1962): 122-27.

Bowman, George W. THE DYNAMICS OF CONFESSION. Richmond, Va.: John Knox Press, 1969. 125 p.

Brar, Harchand Singh. "Yoga and Psychoanalysis." BRITISH JOURNAL OF PSYCHIATRY 116 (1970): 201-206.

Bromberg, Walter. THE MIND OF MAN: A HISTORY OF PSYCHOTHERAPY AND PSYCHOANALYSIS. New York: Harper & Brothers, 1959. 334 p.

A history of mental healing from witchcraft to psycho-surgery.

Brown, L.B. "Egocentric Thought in Petitionary Prayer: A Cross-Cultural Study." JOURNAL OF SOCIAL PSYCHOLOGY 68 (1966): 197-210.

Calestro, Kenneth M. "Psychotherapy, Faith Healing, and Suggestion." INTERNATIONAL JOURNAL OF PSYCHIATRY 10 (June 1972): 83-113.

Clebsch, William A., and Jaekle, Charles R. PASTORAL CARE IN HISTORICAL PERSPECTIVE. Englewood Cliffs, N.J.: Prentice-Hall, 1964. xix, 344 p.

A history of the cure of souls in the Judeo-Christian tradition.

Crapanzano, Vincent. THE HAMADSHA: A STUDY IN MOROCCAN ETHNO-PSYCHIATRY. Berkeley: University of California Press, 1973. xiv, 258 p.

Dean, Stanley R., and Thong, Denny. "Shamanism versus Psychiatry in Bali, 'Isle of the Gods': Some Modern Implications" AMERICAN JOURNAL OF PSYCHIATRY 129 (July 1972): 59-62.

See other entries on Shamanism in section C:5.

Devereux, George. MOHAVE ETHNOPSYCHIATRY AND SUICIDE: THE PSYCHIATRIC KNOWLEDGE AND THE PSYCHIC DISTURBANCES OF AN INDIAN TRIBE. Bureau of American Ethnology Bulletin, no. 175. Washington, D.C.: U.S. Government Printing Office, 1961.

Dobkin, Marlene. "Fortune's Malice: Divination, Psychotherapy, and Folk Medicine in Peru." JOURNAL OF AMERICAN FOLKLORE 82 (1969): 132-41.

Edmunds, Vincent, and Scorer, C. Gordon. SOME THOUGHTS ON FAITH

HEALING. London: The Tyndale Press, 1956. 72 p.

> Two British physicians present the scriptural evidence for miracle-
> cures, discuss the lack of contemporary medical evidence, and re-
> affirm their faith in divine providence.

Ekstein, Rudolf. "A Clinical Note on the Therapeutic Use of a Quasi-Religious Experience." JOURNAL OF THE AMERICAN PSYCHOANALYTIC ASSOCIATION 4 (1956): 304-13.

Ellenberger, Henri F. "The Pathogenic Secret and Its Therapeutics." JOURNAL OF THE HISTORY OF THE BEHAVIORAL SCIENCES 2 (1966): 29-42.

Finucane, Ronald C. "Faith Healing in Medieval England: Miracles at Saints' Shrines." PSYCHIATRY 36 (1973): 341-46.

Frank, Jerome D. PERSUASION AND HEALING: A COMPARATIVE STUDY OF PSYCHOTHERAPY. Baltimore: The Johns Hopkins University Press, 1961. xiv, 282 p.

> Probes the contemporary nature of psychotherapy and its historical
> roots in the religious cure of souls and primitive forms of healing.
> Focuses on such topics as the relationship between the healer and
> patient, group influence on the healing process, and the nature of
> healing itself. Places particular emphasis on the structural similar-
> ities between traditional religious forms of healing and modern psy-
> chotherapy.

Fromm, Erich. "Psychoanalysis and Zen Buddhism." In ZEN BUDDHISM AND PSYCHOANALYSIS, pp. 77-141. Edited by D.T. Suzuki, et al. New York: Grove Press, 1963.

Fujita, K., and Takido, S. "Sermon and Counseling from the Buddhist Point of View." PSYCHOLOGIA: AN INTERNATIONAL JOURNAL OF PSYCHOLOGY IN THE ORIENT 5 (1962): 181-84.

Giel, R. "Freud and the Devil in Ethiopian Psychiatry." PSYCHIATRIA, NEUROLOGIA, NEUROCHIRURGIA: JOURNAL OF THE NETHERLANDS SOCIETY OF PSYCHIATRY AND NEUROLOGY 71 (1968): 177-83.

Godin, Andre. "Psychological Growth and Christian Prayer." LUMEN VITAE 13 (1958): 517-30.

_____, ed. FROM CRY TO WORD: CONTRIBUTIONS TOWARD A PSYCHOLOGY OF PRAYER. Brussels: Lumen Vitae Press, 1968. 270 p.

> Thirteen papers based largely on data derived from questionnaires,
> with interpretations of both a psychological and theological nature.

Goldbrunner, Josef. CURE OF MIND AND CURE OF SOULS. Translated by Stanley Goodman. New York: Pantheon Books, 1958. 127 p.

Harms, Ernest. "Historical Background of Psychotherapy as a New Scientific Field." DISEASES OF THE NERVOUS SYSTEM 31, no. 2 (1970): 116-18.

Develops the religious background of psychotherapy.

Held, F. "Studia zur Psychologie der Meditation am Modell der Indischen Lehren." ZEITSCHRIFT FUR PSYCHOTHERAPIE UND MEDIZINISCHE PSYCHOL-OGIE 5 (1955): 122-33.

Holmes, S.W. "Zen and Transactional Psychology." ETC.: REVIEW OF GEN-ERAL SEMANTICS 14 (1957): 243-49.

Hora, Thomas. "Tao, Zen and Existential Psychotherapy." PSYCHOLOGIA: AN INTERNATIONAL JOURNAL OF PSYCHOLOGY IN THE ORIENT 2 (1959): 236-42.

Jacobs, Hans. WESTERN PSYCHOTHERAPY AND HINDU SADHANA. New York: International Universities Press, 1961. 232 p.

Johansson, Rune E.A. THE PSYCHOLOGY OF NIRVANA: A COMPARATIVE STUDY OF THE NATURAL GOAL OF BUDDHISM AND THE AIMS OF MODERN WESTERN PSYCHOTHERAPY. London: George Allen and Unwin, 1969; New York: Doubleday & Co., 1970. 142 p.

An analysis of the basic mental concepts in some selected Pali texts, with a limited discussion in terms of the psychologies of Os-good and Cattell.

Joyce, C.R.B., and Wellson, R.M.C. "The Objective Efficacy of Prayer: A Double-Bind Clinical Trial." JOURNAL OF CHRONIC DISEASES 18, no. 4 (1965): 367-77.

Kelsey, Morton T. HEALING AND CHRISTIANITY: IN ANCIENT THOUGHT AND MODERN TIMES. New York: Harper & Row, Publishers, 1973. 398 p.

Kew, Clifton E. "Understanding Spiritual Healing." PASTORAL PSYCHOLOGY 12, no. 118 (1961): 29-34.

Kiev, Ari. "Psychotherapeutic Aspects of Pentecostal Sects among West Indian Immigrants to England." BRITISH JOURNAL OF SOCIOLOGY 15 (1964): 129-38.

_____. CURANDERISMO: MEXICAN-AMERICAN FOLK PSYCHIATRY. New York: The Free Press, 1958. xiv, 207 p.

A detailed study of folk-healers in Texas, comparing their understanding and practice with modern psychiatry.

_____, ed. MAGIC, FAITH, AND HEALING: STUDIES IN PRIMITIVE PSY-
CHIATRY TODAY. New York: The Free Press, 1964. xvii, 475 p.

A valuable collection of essays on primitive psychotherapy practices,
systems, concepts, and roles, in sixteen different cultures. See a
related entry by Kiev in section G:6.

Kondo, Akihisa. "Zen in Psychotherapy: The Virtue of Sitting." CHICAGO
REVIEW 12 (1958): 57-64.

Kora, T., and Sato, K. "Morita Therapy: A Psychotherapy in the Way of
Zen." PSYCHOLOGIA: AN INTERNATIONAL JOURNAL OF PSYCHOLOGY
IN THE ORIENT 1 (1957): 219-25.

Kouretas, D. "Aspects modernes des cure psychotherapiques pratiquees dans les
sanctuaires de la Grece antique." REVUE FRANCAISE DE PSYCHANALYSE 26
(1962): 299-309.

Kretschmer, W. "Meditation Techniques in Psychotherapy." PSYCHOLOGIA:
AN INTERNATIONAL JOURNAL OF PSYCHOLOGY IN THE ORIENT 5 (1962):
76-83.

Lederer, Wolfgang. "Primitive Psychotherapy." PSYCHIATRY 22 (1959): 255-
65.

Compares psychotherapy to practices in sixteenth-century France,
the African Gold Coast, and Zen.

Lerner, Marcelo. "Concentracion Yoga y Psicoterapia." ACTA PSIQUIATRICA
Y PSICOLOGICA DE AMERICA LATINA 17 (1971): 410-17.

Lesh, Terry V. "Zen Meditation and the Development of Empathy in Counselors." JOURNAL OF HUMANISTIC PSYCHOLOGY 10 (Spring 1970): 39-74.

_____. "Zen and Psychotherapy: A Partially Annotated Bibliography." JOUR-
NAL OF HUMANISTIC PSYCHOLOGY 10 (Spring 1970): 75-83.

Loehr, Franklin. THE POWER OF PRAYER ON PLANTS. Garden City, N.Y.:
Doubleday & Co., 1959. 144 p.

A thorough empirical study which demonstrates, perhaps not con-
clusively, the positive effect of human prayer on plant growth.

Lorand, Sandor. "Dream Interpretation in the Talmud." INTERNATIONAL
JOURNAL OF PSYCHOANALYSIS 38 (1957): 92-97.

McBroom, P. "Martyrs May Not Feel Pain: Contemplation Practiced in Eastern Religions Akin to Auto-Hypnosis." SCIENCE NEWSLETTER 89 (1966): 505-6.

McConnell, Theodore A. "Confession in Cross-Disciplinary Perspective." JOURNAL OF RELIGION AND HEALTH 8 (1969): 76-86.

McNeill, John T. A HISTORY OF THE CURE OF SOULS. New York: Harper & Row, Publishers, 1965. xii, 371 p.

Malhotra, J.C. "Yoga and Mental Hygiene." AMERICAN JOURNAL OF PSYCHOTHERAPY 17 (July 1963): 436-42.

Maupin, Edward W. "Zen Buddhism: A Psychological Review." JOURNAL OF CONSULTING PSYCHOLOGY 26 (1962): 362-78.

_____. "Individual Differences in Response to a Zen Meditation Exercise." JOURNAL OF CONSULTING PSYCHOLOGY 29 (1965): 139-45.

Meadows, Paul. "The Cure of Souls and the Winds of Change." PSYCHOANALYTIC REVIEW 55 (1968): 491-504.

Meier, C.A. ANCIENT INCUBATION AND MODERN PSYCHOTHERAPY. Translated by Monica Curtis. Evanston, Ill.: Northwestern University Press, 1967. xx, 152 p.

> Greek healing rites and their relation to Christian faith healing are discussed from a Jungian perspective, with some comparison to contemporary therapy.

Meyer, Donald. THE POSITIVE THINKERS: A STUDY OF THE AMERICAN QUEST FOR HEALTH, WEALTH, AND PERSONAL POWER FROM MARY BAKER EDDY TO NORMAN VINCENT PEALE. New York: Doubleday & Co., 1966. xvii, 342 p.

> An historical study of popular psychology and folk therapy in the United States.

Mishra, Rammurti S. THE TEXTBOOK OF YOGA PSYCHOLOGY: A NEW TRANSLATION AND INTERPRETATION OF PATANJALIS YOGA SUTRAS FOR MEANINGFUL APPLICATION IN ALL MODERN PSYCHOLOGIC DISCIPLINES. Edited by Ann Adman. New York: Julian Press, 1963. ix, 401 p.

> This large work is divided into two major sections. The first consists of an introduction to Yoga philosophy; the second, of yogic texts in the original, a translation, and minute commentary. Was republished by Doubleday in 1973.

Naranjo, Claudio, and Ornstein, Robert E. ON THE PSYCHOLOGY OF MED-

ITATION. New York: Viking Press, 1971. 248 p.

> An exploratory study into the nature of meditation and its impli-
> cations for modern psychology.

Neki, J.S. "Yoga and Psychoanalysis." COMPREHENSIVE PSYCHIATRY 8 (1967): 160–67.

Nelson, Benjamin N. "Self-Images and Systems of Spiritual Direction in the History of European Civilization." In THE QUEST FOR SELF-CONTROL, pp. 49–103. Edited by Samuel Z. Klausner. New York: The Free Press, 1965.

> An interesting discussion of mental healing, from Socrates through
> Luther to Freud.

Noyes, Humphrey F. "Meditation: The Doorway to Wholeness." HUMANITAS 3 (1967): 171–84.

Oates, Wayne E[dward]. "The Cult of Reassurance." RELIGION IN LIFE 24 (1954–55): 72–82.

Prince, Raymond H. "Fundamental Differences of Psychoanalysis and Faith Healing." INTERNATIONAL JOURNAL OF PSYCHIATRY 10 (June 1972): 125–28.

Robbins, Thomas, and Anthony, Dick. "Getting Straight with Meher Baba: A Study of Mysticism, Drug Rehabilitation and Postadolescent Role-Conflict." JOURNAL FOR THE SCIENTIFIC STUDY OF RELIGION 11 (June 1972): 122–40.

Rogler, Lloyd H., and Hollingshead, August B. "The Puerto Rican Spiritualist as a Psychiatrist." AMERICAN JOURNAL OF SOCIOLOGY 67 (1961–62): 17–22.

Romano, Octavio Ignacio. "Charismatic Medicine, Folk-Healing, and Folk Sainthood." AMERICAN ANTHROPOLOGIST 67 (1965): 1151–73.

Sargant, William. "Witch Doctoring, Zar, and Voodoo: Their Relation to Modern Psychiatric Treatments." PROCEEDINGS OF THE ROYAL SOCIETY OF MEDICINE 60 (1967): 1055–60.

Sato, K. "Psychotherapeutic Implications of Zen." PSYCHOLOGIA: AN INTERNATIONAL JOURNAL OF PSYCHOLOGY IN THE ORIENT 1 (1957): 213–18.

_____. "Personality Change through Naikan and Zen." PSYCHOLOGIA: AN INTERNATIONAL JOURNAL OF PSYCHOLOGY IN THE ORIENT 8 (1965): 1–2.

Schaer, Hans. RELIGION AND THE CURE OF SOULS IN JUNG'S PSYCHOL-OGY. Translated by R.F.C. Hull. New York: Pantheon Books, 1950. 221 p.

> Translated from the original 1946 German, an account of Jung's psychology of religion and of the constricting role of the church in fostering religious experience.

_____. SEELSORGE UND PSYCHOTHERAPIE. Zurich and Stuttgart: Rascher Verlag, 1961. 270 p.

> A study of common problems in psychotherapy and the cure of souls, with particular emphasis on issues of truth and authority.

Seeman, William, et al. "Influence of Transcendental Meditation on a Measure of Self-Actualization." JOURNAL OF COUNSELING PSYCHOLOGY 19 (1972): 184-87.

Shepard, R.F. "Cranmer's Prayer Books and the Redemptive Process: Introductory Notes to a Psychobiological Approach." ANGLICAN THEOLOGICAL REVIEW 53 (July 1971): 138-58.

Shrut, Samuel D. "Coping with the 'Evil Eye,' or Early Rabbinical Attempts at Psychotherapy." AMERICAN IMAGO 17 (1960): 201-13.

Smiley, Blanton. "Analytic Study of a Cure at Lourdes." PSYCHOANALYTIC QUARTERLY 9 (1940): 348-62.

Snoeck, Andre, S.J. CONFESSION ET PSYCHANALYSE. Paris: Desclee de Brouwer, 1964. 126 p.

Stevenson, Beaumont. "Confession and Psychotherapy." JOURNAL OF PASTORAL CARE 20 (1966): 10-15.

Strunk, Orlo, Jr. "Motivational Factors and Psychotherapeutic Aspects of a Healing Cult." JOURNAL OF PASTORAL CARE 9 (1955): 213-20.

Suzuki, D.T., et al. ZEN BUDDHISM AND PSYCHOANALYSIS. New York: Evergreen, 1963. 180 p.

> Suzuki, aided by Erich Fromm and Richard DeMartino, argues for the similarity in the objectives of Zen meditation and psychoanalysis, basing this argument on the grounds that both concern freeing the individual to perceive reality.

Tenzel, James H. "Shamanism and Concepts of Disease in a Mayan Indian Community." PSYCHIATRY 33, no. 3 (1970): 372-80.

Tomoda, F. "Client-Centered Therapy in Japan." PSYCHOLOGIA: AN IN-

TERNATIONAL JOURNAL OF PSYCHOLOGY IN THE ORIENT 1 (1958): 237-41.

Concerns Carl Rogers, Mencius, and Morita therapy.

Torrey, E. Fuller. "What Western Psychotherapists Can Learn from Witchdoctors." AMERICAN JOURNAL OF ORTHOPSYCHIATRY 42 (1972): 69-76.

Valentine, Alonzo M. "Zen and the Psychology of Education." JOURNAL OF PSYCHOLOGY 79 (1971): 103-10.

Van Dusen, Wilson. "Zen and Western Psychotherapy." PSYCHOLOGIA: AN INTERNATIONAL JOURNAL OF PSYCHOLOGY IN THE ORIENT 1 (1957): 229-30.

_____. "Wu Wei, No-Mind and the Fertile Void in Psychotherapy." PSYCHOLOGIA: AN INTERNATIONAL JOURNAL OF PSYCHOLOGY IN THE ORIENT 1 (1958): 253-56.

Wardwell, Walter I. "Christian Science Healing." JOURNAL FOR THE SCIENTIFIC STUDY OF RELIGION 4 (1964-65): 175-81.

Watts, Alan W. "Asian Psychology and Modern Psychiatry." AMERICAN JOURNAL OF PSYCHOANALYSIS 13 (1953): 25-30.

_____. PSYCHOTHERAPY EAST AND WEST. New York: Ballantine Books, 1961. xiii, 220 p.

Explores parallels between Western psychotherapy and Eastern forms of meditation, giving particular attention to the view that both are concerned with the liberation of man from debilitating forms of consciousness and behavior.

_____. "Psychotherapy and Eastern Religion: Metaphysical Bases of Psychiatry." JOURNAL OF TRANSPERSONAL PSYCHOLOGY 6, no. 1 (1974): 18-31.

Weatherhead, Leslie Dixon. PSYCHOLOGY, RELIGION, AND HEALING. London: Hodder and Stoughton, 1951. 544 p.

Examines all methods of nonphysical healing from the time of the Christian gospels up to modern psychology, and suggests that religious and psychological perspectives complement one another. Also listed in section G:2.

Wendt, I.Y. "Eine Japanische Klinik im Westen." SCHWEIJERISCHE ZEITSCHRIFT FUR PSYCHOLOGIE UNDE IHRE ANWENDUNGEN 24 (1965): 366-70.

Based on Morita therapy.

Westermeyer, Joseph J. "Lao Buddhism, Mental Health, and Contemporary Implications." JOURNAL OF RELIGION AND HEALTH 12 (April 1973): 181-88.

Williams, Daniel Day. THE MINISTER AND THE CARE OF SOULS. New York: Harper & Brothers, 1961. 157 p.

Wirz, Paul. EXORCISM AND THE ART OF HEALING IN CEYLON. New York: W.S. Heinman, 1954. 253 p.

Zempleni, A. "La Dimension therapeutique du cult des Rab." PSYCHOPATHOLOGIE AFRICAINE 2 (1966): 295-439.

Zilboorg, Gregory. THE MEDICAL MAN AND THE WITCH DOCTOR DURING THE RENAISSANCE. Baltimore: The Johns Hopkins University Press, 1935. 215 p.

The psychology and physiology of sixteenth-century witchcraft, and its relation to the medicine and psychiatry of the day.

Also see section C:5 for entries on witchcraft, Shamanism, and spirit possession.

INDEXES

Author Index

Title Index

Subject Index

AUTHOR INDEX

Author Index

Almansi, Renato J.   45

Alpert, Richard   262

Amatora, Mary   155

Ames, Edward Scribner   12

Amon, Jesus   145

Amsel, Abraham   119

Anant, Santokh S.   145, 214

Ancona, Leonardo   153

Anderson, Charles H.   169

Anderson, D.S.   153

Anderson, Douglas A.   257

Anderson, George Christian   132, 214, 241

Anderson, Herbert   207

Anderson, Robert D.   85

Ando, S.   262

Andreasen, N.J.   241

Angers, William P.   5, 28

Angoff, Allan   102

Annett, Edward A.   98

Ansaldi, J.   125

Ansbacher, Heinz L.   29

Anthony, Dick   268

Antonelli, Feruccio   262

Anwar, Mah P.   181

Anzai, Jiro   262

Apolito, Arnaldo   29

Appleby, Peter C.   145

Arapura, J.G.   119

Arasteh, A. Reza   181, 221, 262

Arbuckle, Dugald S.   234

Argyle, Michael   132, 153

Arieti, Silvano   102

Arlow, Jacob A.   45, 65, 76

Armstrong, Renate G.   241

Arnold, Magda D.   221

Aronfreed, Justin   132

Ash, Roberta T.   155

Ashbrook, James B.   189, 207, 214, 237

Aslam, Q.M.   181

Assagioli, Roberto   102, 207

Atherton, Virginia H.   155

Attkisson, C. Clifford   155

Aubert, Catherine   165

B

Babchuk, Nicholas   169

Babin, P.   222

Bachelard, Gaston   45

Bachmeyer, T.J.   132

Bachofen, Johann Jakob   65

Bachrach, Arthur J.   81

Author Index

Dewart, J.   216

Dewey, John   15

Dewhurst, Kenneth   99

Diamond, Bernard L.   231

Diel, Paul   126

Diethelm, Oskar   86

Dimond, Sydney George   15

Dittes, James E.   3, 4, 6, 140, 146, 170, 176, 183, 192, 196, 209

Dixit, Ramesh C.   146

Dobinsky, Paul S.   151

Dobkin, Marlene   263

Dodd, C.H.   15, 183

Dodds, E.R.   16, 120, 183

Dodrill, Carl   146

Domhoff, G. William   183

Dominian, Jacob   245

Dondero, E. Austin   198

Doniger, Simon   209

Dotson, Elsie   261

Douglas, Mary   73

Douglas, William G.T.   101, 192, 193

Douglas-Smith, Basil   105

Drake, Carlos C.   68

Drakeford, John W.   6

Drapela, V.J.   223

Draper, Edgar   245, 256

Dreger, Ralph Mason   146

Dreifuss, Gustav   57, 77, 176

Dresser, Horatio Willis   16

Droege, T.A.   223

du Buy, Jean   16

Ducker, E.N.   209

Duke, Robert W.   245

Dumoulin, Anne   157

Duncombe, David C.   216

Dundes, Alan   68, 82

Dunlap, Knight   16

Dunn, Ralph H.   193

Durand, Gilbert   47

Durkheim, Emile   82, 258

Dutt, N.K.   146

E

Eaton, Joseph W.   183

Ebeling, G.   216

Eberz, Jakob   53

Eckstein, Jerome   82

Edelheit, Henry   47

Eder, M.D.   80

Edie, James M.   39

Edinger, Edward F.   223

Edmunds, Vincent   263

Author Index

Author Index

Kouretas, D.   55, 266

Kovel, Joel   177

Kranitz, Lionel   259

Kraus, Robert F.   87

Krebs, Richard   240

Kretschmer, W.   266

Kriger, Sara F.   148

Krippner, Stanley   108

Krishnamurthy, N.   75

Kroes, William H.   148

Kubler-Ross, Elisabeth   259

Kuenzli, Alfred E.   227

Kunkel, Fritz   227

Kunzli, Arnold   185

Kuo, Zing-Yang   185

Kupky, Oskar   20

Kuppuswamy, B.   122

Kurokawa, Minako   185

Kursh, Charlotte O.   55

Kurty, Paul S.   109

Kurzweil, Z.E.   138

Kushner, A.W.   249

Kysar, John E.   249

L

La Barre, Weston   87, 109, 185

Ladd, Clayton E.   147

La Grasserie, Raoul de   20

Laing, R.D.   227

Lam, Yut-Hang   185

Lambourne, R.A.   227

Langston, Robert D.   172

Lantis, Margaret   122

Lapsley, James N.   114, 217, 249

Larson, Gerald J.   109

Larson, Richard F.   249

Lasker, Arnold A.   172

Laski, Margharita   109

Laufer, Berthold   20

Laughlin, Henry P.   58

Lawrence, P.J.   162

Lawson, D.W.   250

Layard, John   84

Layman, William A.   146

Leary, Timothy   109

Lebra, Takie S.   100

Lechat, Fernand   149

Le Coeur, Charles   75

Lederer, Wolfgang   55, 56, 162, 266

Lee, Harry B.   96

Lee, J.P.   195

Lee, Roy Stuart   33, 75, 162, 211

Leemon, Thomas A.   78

Author Index

Maybaum, Ignaz   34

Mayer-Oakes, F.T.   22

Mayhew, Bruce H., Jr.   154

Mayo, Clyde C.   149

Meadow, Arnold   145, 172

Meadows, Paul   267

Meany, J.O.   212, 217

Meehl, P.E.   236

Meerloo, Joost A.M.   41, 80, 260

Mehler, Anne   174

Mehta, Mohan Lal   122

Meiburg, Albert L.   198, 256

Meier, C.A.   267

Meissner, William W.   4, 122, 128, 129, 136, 137, 172, 198, 239

Meland, Bernard E.   229

Mellone, Sydney Herbert   22

Mendlovitz, S.H.   191

Meng, Heinrich   34, 186, 236

Menges, Robert J.   4

Menninger, Karl   129, 229, 247

Meredith, Gerald M.   142, 173

Merten, Don   78

Meserve, Harry C.   178

Metheny, Eleanor   75

Meyer, Donald   267

Meyer, George G.   251

Meyerson, Bernard G.   80

Micklem, Nathaniel   59

Middlemore, Merell   88

Middleton, John   86

Middleton, Russell   154, 178

Midgley, J.   251

Millard, Richard M.   133

Miller, David L.   129

Miller, Gerald R.   152

Miller, William Robert   236

Mirels, Herbert L.   137, 149

Mischel, Frances   88

Mischel, Walter   88

Mishra, Rammurti S.   267

Mitchell, John D.   80

Mitchell, Marjorie Editha   260

Mitscherlich, Alexander   34

Mitzman, Arthur   186

Moberg, David O.   75, 149, 198

Moller, Herbert   69, 110

Moloney, James Clark   50, 55, 64, 66, 69

Monaghan, Robert R.   173

Moody, Robert   50

Moon, Sheila   50

Moore, Robert L.   100

Moore, Thomas Verner   229, 251

Author Index

Author Index

Author Index

Tyson, Herbert A.   97

U

Ulanov, Ann Belford   63, 67, 131, 233

Underhill, Evelyn   27

Underwood, Richard A.   131

Ungersma, A.J.   213

Upadhyaya, Hari S.   69

Uras, Alev   192

Uren, A. Rudolph   27

V

Valentine, Alonzo M.   270

Van Aerde, Mark   144

Van den Berg, J.H.   42

Vanderveldt, A.   197

VanderVeldt, J.H.   256

Van Dusen, Wilson   270

Van Dyke, Paul II   4, 165

Vanecko, James J.   180

Vangerud, Richard D.   174

van Teslaar, J.S.   27

Vasavada, A.U.   124

Vaughan, Richard Patrick   174, 202, 213, 214, 237

Vercruysse, Godelieve   144

Vergote, Antoine   97, 152, 165

Verlynde, Noelle   81

Vernant, Jean-Piere   56

Vernon, Glenn M.   11

Veroff, J.   152

Very, Philip S.   203

Veszy-Wagner, Lilla   70

Vetter, George B.   85

Vilakazi, Absolom   233

Vivier, L.M.   115

von Grunebaum, G.E.   113

W

Wagatsuma, Hiroshi   176

Wainwright, W.J.   113

Walberg, Herbert J.   144

Waldman, Roy D.   256

Walker, C. Eugene   144

Walker, Eugene C.   39

Walker, Ronald E.   11

Wall, Ernest A.   220

Wallace, Anthony F.C.   76

Wallis, Wilson D.   27, 28

Walsh, Maurice N.   81

Walters, Annette   155

Walters, Orville S.   131, 132, 220, 237, 256

Walther, Gerda   113

Wangh, Martin   180

Wapnick, Kenneth   113

Author Index

TITLE INDEX

Title Index

SUBJECT INDEX

Aspects of religion and psychology are listed as main subject entries within the index.

A

Abraham   56, 57, 59, 61

Adler, Alfred   32, 38, 207, 212, 221

Adolescents' religion: 4; conversion 98, 100; Jewish attitudes 155; nature and development 20, 25, 158, 160, 161; psychological approach 17; religious experience 95, 96; search for understanding 156

Aesthetics.   See Art

Affiliation, religious   169-74.   See also Church; Commitment

African religion: changing self-concepts 233; rituals 67, 75, 78

Aging: 39; clergy 195, 196, 198, 201; death anxiety 257-61; religious commitment 10, 174

Alchemy   48-49

Alcohol consumption: conversion 248; pastoral intervention 245, 250; religious affiliation 249, 254, 255, 256

Allport, Gordon W.   9, 11, 12, 40

American Indian: Ghost Dance 87; initiation rites 77; myths 50, 64, 67, 69; new religions 14; peyote cults 87, 103; shamanism 86

Amish   188

Anglicanism   115, 138

Anti-Semitism: aggression 175, 179; Christian beliefs 177, 178; college students 176; ethnicity 177; historical roots 178; psychoanalytic views 175, 176, 180

Anxiety: adolescents 156; atonement 130; constructive aspects 247; courage 233; death 257, 260, 261; existentialism 229; guilt 133, 135; psychological perspective 7, 226, 229; psychotherapeutic perspective 7; theological perspective 7, 133, 229; within Christian community 240

Archetypes   48, 63, 66, 223

Art: 4; African sculpture 78; assessment of religious attitudes 155, 192; Greek 56; Islamic 181; magic 82; Medieval and Renaissance 63; Michelangelo 31; Edvard Munch 255; religious experience 95, 96; shamanism 88; Vincent Van Gogh 197

Asceticism   22, 149, 195, 255

Subject Index